"Liam Halligan is a one-off – a card-carrying economist, with high-level political access, who can explain complex issues in readable, vivid prose. *Home Truths* nails the how and why of fixing Britain's broken housing market – the most pressing domestic issue of our time. A must-read across Westminster, Whitehall and beyond."
ANDREW NEIL

"Liam Halligan shows – and shows brilliantly – how the vested interests of landowners and big property developers have wrecked the 'British Dream' of home ownership. He argues persuasively that the building of homes was sacrificed to speculation in land originally unleashed by the Conservative governments of the 1950s and 1960s, resulting in windfall gains for landowners but an increasing fraction of wage earners without the prospect of decent homes. Echoing Henry George, Halligan proposes restoring the tax on rising land values created by planning permission, cancelled in 1961 – a radical idea whose second coming is long overdue."
ROBERT SKIDELSKY, WOLFSON HISTORY PRIZE WINNER

"Many people claim to speak truth to power but very few actually do. Liam Halligan is one of the few – a great and fearless truth-teller. Here he takes on that prime driver of inequality in the UK – our warped and unfair housing market. Property monopolists and their tame political allies should be afraid, very afraid, of this book."
BRYAN APPLEYARD, SUNDAY TIMES

"There is no bigger issue facing the UK than the nation's housing crisis, the full extent of which is outlined in Liam Halligan's splendid book. Halligan explains, simply and clearly, exactly what the problem is. Even better, he comes up with a workable solution for tackling it."
LARRY ELLIOTT, THE GUARDIAN

"As this book points out with eloquence and moral clarity, out-of-date land legislation is holding up a genuine revival of social housebuilding and is the only solution to the national emergency our housing crisis has become. *Home Truths* is a call to arms for politicians and campaigners of all parties and none in the fight to defend the basic right to a decent home."
POLLY NEATE, CHIEF EXECUTIVE, SHELTER

"A country where young people cannot hope to save enough to buy their own home is a country facing a social and economic catastrophe. Successive British governments have not just allowed this to happen but have made matters worse – and we need to fix it. Liam Halligan is one of the UK's most thoughtful economic journalists. In his characteristically robust, clear-minded and sensible way, he shows how this can be done."
HAMISH McRAE, THE INDEPENDENT

LIAM HALLIGAN

HOME TRUTHS

THE UK'S CHRONIC HOUSING SHORTAGE

— HOW IT HAPPENED, WHY IT MATTERS AND HOW TO SOLVE IT —

Biteback Publishing

First published in Great Britain in 2019 by
Biteback Publishing Ltd
Westminster Tower
3 Albert Embankment
London SE1 7SP
Copyright © Liam Halligan 2019

ISBN 978-1-78590-469-1

10 9 8 7 6 5 4 3 2 1

A CIP catalogue record for this book is available from the British Library.

Set in Minion Pro and Trade Gothic

Printed and bound in Great Britain by
CPI Group (UK) Ltd, Croydon CR0 4YY

For my daughter, Ailis – and her generation.

CONTENTS

FOREWORD

The housing situation in Britain is a disgrace. We are in the midst of a national crisis, generated by our planning system – and this book is a timely and most welcome response.

Houses are built on land, and the increase in real house prices is not due to any increase in the real cost of building houses. It is due entirely to the real cost of land with planning permission to build. So the shortage of houses, and their increased price, is due entirely to a man-made scarcity of building land.

This is grossly inefficient. All over England you can see land that is worth £2,000,000 per hectare if it has planning permission and next door to it land without planning permission worth £20,000 per hectare – a hundred times less. Thus the increase in social value if one more hectare is developed is nearly £2,000,000 – with one caveat, namely the amenity value of the land if it remains undeveloped. Sometimes this amenity value will be huge, and no one with any sense wants houses on land of outstanding natural beauty. But much of the existing green belt around London, for instance, is scrappy agricultural land, and over half of it has no public access. If we allowed building on all such land within 800 metres of an Underground or train station, we could have one million more homes.

To refuse such permission is inefficient madness. It is also grossly unjust. For the scarcity of building land has produced a country of haves and have nots. Those who are lucky enough to own houses or building land grow rich while those who don't, often the younger generations, pay exorbitant prices or rents. This unfairness is generated solely by the political process.

We must find ways to incentivise local authorities to give more planning permission. The simplest way is to stuff their mouths with gold, by giving them a decent share in the increased value created when planning permission is given. One could for example give local authorities 40 per cent of the sale value of any new development after subtracting from it £100 per square foot of housing (to allow for the cost of building).

In this incisive book, Liam Halligan discusses a whole range of possible approaches. The book is forcefully written, as we expect from Liam, and should be read by supporters of every political party. To date no party has begun to address the fundamentals of this problem, even though it is one of the greatest crises facing our country. Read on.

Lord Richard Layard
Professor of Economics
London School of Economics
August 2019

GLOSSARY

CIH	Chartered Institute of Housing
CIL	Community Infrastructure Levy
CMA	Competition and Markets Authority
ECHR	European Convention on Human Rights
FTB	First Time Buyer
GDP	Gross Domestic Product (National Income)
HBF	Home Builders Federation
HOA	HomeOwners Alliance
HTB	Help to Buy scheme
LDC	Local Development Corporation
LFB	London Fire Brigade
LGA	Local Government Association
LKP	Leasehold Knowledge Partnership
LVC	Land Value Capture
LVT	Land Value Tax
MHCLG	Ministry of Housing, Communities and Local Government
NAEA	National Association of Estate Agents
NHBC	National House Building Council
NHF	National Housing Federation
NIMBY	'Not in my backyard' – a term used to describe implacable opponents of housebuilding close to their home
NPPF	National Planning Policy Framework

NTDC	New Town Development Corporation
OFT	Office of Fair Trading
PDRs	Permitted Development Rights
PIP	Permission in Principle
PPI	Payment Protection Insurance
RTB	Right to Buy
S106	Section 106 agreements made between local authorities granting planning permission and developers to provide social and affordable homes and other social infrastructure
SMEs	Small and medium-sized enterprises
YIMBY	'Yes in my backyard' – a campaign group that wants more homes built, particularly for young adults

INTRODUCTION

There's no place like home. There's no place like home.
There's no place like home.[1]
L. FRANK BAUM, 1900

The big issue facing Britain, as I write these words in the early autumn of 2019, and I suspect for some time to come, is the nature of our relationship with the European Union. For over three years now, ever since the June 2016 referendum, this subject has dominated the news agenda – as we've woken up to EU-related headlines and listened to similar such bulletins while brushing our teeth at night. The entire country, it seems, is suffering from 'Brexit fatigue'. Yet, still, the division, rancour and political and economic uncertainty – deeply damaging, we can surely agree, whichever side you backed – look set to continue.

Amid the wall-to-wall Brexit coverage, other important domestic policy stories have occasionally broken through. The row over the economic case for the London-to-Birmingham High Speed Rail 2 trainline, Europe's biggest single infrastructure project, sometimes commands the headlines. There was a flurry of interest last summer in the managerial and auditing failures behind the demise of Carillion, the UK's second-largest construction firm, which, when it collapsed, boasted hundreds of government contracts. Ordinarily, such policy issues, while perhaps complex and challenging, would generate sustained and forensic news coverage. Brexit, though, has kept such coverage to a minimum.

Another vital area of public policy which has been all but drowned out by our EU withdrawal over recent years is housing. This will surely become the stuff of daily political debate once the Brexit clouds clear. The average UK home now costs eight times average annual earnings, over twice the historic norm. This crippling affordability multiple rises to twelve times across London and the south-east. In many parts of the country – including the north-west, the Midlands, the West Country and parts of Scotland and Wales too – countless young adults, even well-paid professionals, are 'priced out' of the housing market. Often spending half their income on rent, while enduring long commutes, their home ownership dream is slipping away.

Back in the early 1990s, 36 per cent of 16–24-year-olds owned their own home. Now it's just 10 per cent. The share of 25–34-year-old owner-occupiers has plunged from 67 to 38 per cent over the same period – with well over half a generation denied the security of home ownership at this crucial family-forming age. Some 78 per cent of 35–44-year-olds were homeowners in 1991, but now that figure stands at just 56 per cent.

The share of pensioner owner-occupiers has soared, but UK home ownership overall has plunged – from a high of 73 per cent of households in 2007 to just over 60 per cent today, well below the EU average. And, lower down the income scale, high rents, reduced housing benefit payments and a chronic shortage of social housing, available at below-market rents, have all added to a shocking increase in over-crowding, homelessness and the expansion of a marginalised underclass. Again, the sense of public outrage which followed the Grenfell Tower tragedy of June 2017 in which seventy-two people lost their lives, and the clamour for more and better social housing, has been lost under Brexit-related noise.

While the UK needs around 250,000 new homes a year to meet population growth and household formation, housebuilding has failed to reach that level since the mid-1970s. There's a huge backlog shortage of homes, built up under successive governments over decades, which has seen property prices spiral way ahead of earnings. As a result, millions of young adults are stuck in shared, rented accommodation and have put their lives on hold.

No less than four out of every ten thirty-year-olds now lives in private rented accommodation, compared to just one in ten as recently as 1996. Not only is the incidence of renting among young adults so much higher now than in the past, but these would-be homebuyers are spending a much higher share of their total incomes on housing costs. With house prices consistently outpacing earnings, today's generation of young adults are spending more on housing, and are less likely to be owner-occupiers, than any cohort since the 1930s. We are in the midst of a near-nationwide housing affordability crisis.

Fixated on Brexit, our political and media class has forgotten that a major reason Jeremy Corbyn came so close to power in the last general election was the sharp rise in support for Labour among 'generation rent' – the millions of 30–39-year-old voters who, unlike their parents, are unable to buy a home. Growing numbers of voters entering middle age, even high-achieving professionals, now face the locked door of housing unaffordability – and, as a result and quite understandably, feel capitalism isn't working for them. Just as owner-occupiers are more likely to vote Tory, young adults desperately upset they cannot buy a property are prone to vote for 'a shake-up' – an electoral trend which took Corbyn to within a few thousand votes of Downing Street in 2017.

Since 1997, the number of UK households in the private rented sector has risen substantially, from 2.1 million to 4.7 million. Some nine million working-age adults now live in rented homes. As prices spiral way ahead of wages, ever more first-time buyers (FTBs) – including those holding down professional jobs – need financial help from their family if they are to buy their first property. Half of all FTBs now rely to some extent on 'the bank of Mum and Dad', rising to no less than two-thirds in London and the south-east – an option that only exists, of course, for those from relatively wealthy backgrounds.

Rising house prices mean that 'generation rent' will keep expanding; it is set to increase to 7.2 million by the late 2020s, by which time little more than a quarter of 25–34-year-olds will own their own home. The sense of injustice they feel at being denied a fair chance to buy a property is one of the cardinal political developments of our time. These voters are coming of age, voting in greater numbers and, as their chance of buying a home seems to slip away, they are becoming increasingly angry. This growing gulf between Britain's 'property haves' and 'property have-nots', a gulf now increasingly being maintained from one generation to the next, casts serious doubt over the UK's claim to be a progressive society.

Since 2013, the government has responded with Help to Buy (HTB). But this has just further stoked demand, handing huge profits to large developers by channelling first-time buyers into often sub-standard new-build homes. The central argument of *Home Truths* is that we must radically reform the supply side of UK housebuilding instead, particularly the opaque and deeply dysfunctional market for land. At present, landowners and large developers, who increasingly dominate the industry, have every incentive to sit on their land holdings, even if they have planning permission. Relentless housing demand, in the face of slow supply, pushes up land prices and ultimately homebuyer prices and developer profit margins even more. As local councils grant more planning permissions, the big players are engaged in a deliberate building go-slow, making higher profits overall by building fewer homes.

Official 'net additional dwellings' numbers are up – but this increase reflects a spate of often shoddy one-off conversions of office buildings and shops, rather than the sustained rise in housebuilding required. Overmighty builders are producing far fewer homes than before the financial crisis, despite gorging on taxpayer's cash courtesy of the misguided HTB scheme. Only bold action can break this deadlock. There should be stiff fines for firms that unduly delay building once planning permission has been granted. The threat of compulsory purchase should be used, if necessary, to release acreage. When residential planning permission is granted, land values rocket, often more than 100-fold. This vast 'planning gain', which currently accrues entirely to landowners, should be shared with local government instead, ring-fenced to fund the new schools, hospitals and other infrastructure that would make housebuilding more popular with existing communities.

Land values reflect the proximity of existing state-funded infrastructure and local commerce, so the community should benefit from windfall profits related to further development. Planning gain is shared in many countries – including France, Germany, much of the United States and many Asian nations too. It's an idea that goes back to Adam Smith and the Scottish Enlightenment. And it used to happen here. The UK's post-war building boom was driven by legislation allowing land value capture (LVC) by government – which damped down speculative demand for land, keeping the cost of building plots reasonable. This, in turn, allowed millions of affordable homes to be built, mainly by SMEs (small- and medium-sized enterprises) – with developers competing on both price and quality.

The 1946 New Towns Act had LVC at its heart – and led to the creation of thirty-two settlements, funded partly on shared planning gain, that are now home to three million people. Cheaper land also meant that, throughout the 1950s, local authorities were able to build millions of new low-density social homes – that were spacious and with decent gardens, because acreage was available at reasonable cost.

During the 1950s, though, Conservative governments led by Churchill and then Macmillan pandered to big landowners and developers, passing a series of laws stymying the use of LVC. Ultimately, the Tories passed the 1961 Land Compensation Act, which ensures that landowners and land-holding developers are entitled to the full land valuation upside when planning permission is granted, including the 'hope value' of any conceivable future development – this has fuelled speculative investment in land. This single piece of legislation, more than anything else, explains why the prices of land for residential building – and, in turn, the cost of housing – has spiralled over the past half-century, resulting in our current affordability crisis.

A wide range of policy reforms is needed urgently to raise the rate of UK housebuilding, to start to address the huge backlog shortage and, over a significant period, gradually bring prices back more in line with earnings – making homes affordable for would be owner-occupiers, while providing enough decent social housing, too. But this book argues that one rather bold policy shift – reversing the 1961 legislation and introducing a transparent system under which planning gain is shared fifty–fifty between owners and local authorities – is an essential prerequisite, if we are to have any chance of fixing the UK's broken housing market.

HOME TRUTHS

Housing is a particularly complicated and multi-faceted area of public policymaking, ranging from planning and credit availability to architecture, climate change and design. Few aspects of government, though, have a potentially more immediate and direct impact on the lives and livelihoods of millions of people across the UK.

Home Truths does not present a detailed history of UK housing policy – not least as there are several such volumes already.[2] Many important aspects of Britain's housing debate will be barely touched upon in this relatively short book, and some won't be covered at all.

What this book seeks to do, instead, is to explain the current reality of our housing market to as broad an audience as possible, while drawing on the author's countless discussions over many years with ministers, MPs, civil servants, housing industry professionals and priced-out potential homebuyers to highlight some policy options.

Many of the recommendations made, despite resulting from conversations with those at the front line of policymaking, will no doubt be dismissed as unworkable and simplistic by powerful vested interests opposed to change and who benefit handsomely from the status quo. The author would observe, though, that rising numbers of young adults are spending half their incomes on rent and are unable to buy a home – causing immense frustration to themselves and their parents. And as home ownership falls, and successive waves of 'generation rent' emerge, the political geometry is starting to shift – with the previous large majority who wanted less housebuilding soon to be outvoted by the growing ranks of priced-out younger adults who want much more.

Homelessness, meanwhile, is at record levels and rough sleeping has sadly become a common sight in towns and cities across the UK. Senior politicians from all parties are increasingly convinced that major reforms are needed to address the UK's highly dysfunctional housing market, so it delivers homes for rent and purchase, at reasonable prices, to as broad a range of people as possible.

Chapter I – 'The British Dream' – provides a summary of housing policy since the end of the First World War, explaining how the UK became 'a nation of homeowners' and why the rate of owner-occupancy in this country has recently plunged.

Chapter II then outlines the scale of the UK's current housing crisis in twelve graphs, focusing on the long-standing and significant shortfall in the building of new homes compared to the growing number of households. This widening gap between supply and demand has seen house prices increase much faster than wages over several decades, particularly since the mid-1990s, and then again after the 2008 financial crisis, resulting in a sharp fall in owner-occupancy among certain age groups, and particularly young adults.

Chapter III – 'A Place of Our Own' – restates the case for home ownership, countering those who say that, for a large part of the workforce, living in your own property is now an unobtainable dream. Buying a home is generally cheaper than renting each month and gives ordinary working people the opportunity to amass some capital, providing greater financial security. The fall in home owner-ship since 2005, particularly among young families, is now driving wealth inequality and social division, as the gulf grows between the UK's 'property haves' and 'property have-nots'.

Chapter IV – 'A Broken Market' – identifies seven features of our housebuilding industry, and the regulatory system in which it oper-ates, that help explain why successive generations are being 'priced out'. Too few homes are 'completed' each year because the house-building industry has become much too concentrated. Powerful developers are engaged in a deliberate building 'go-slow' – exerting undue control over the pace at which new homes come to market, which keeps prices rising far faster than earnings. Starved of access to land and finance, there are now far too few SMEs involved in housebuilding to challenge the bigger players. Frequent political donations from large developers have coincided with a marked lack of policies to counter their growing dominance, a manifest expres-sion of modern-day 'crony capitalism'.

Chapter V – 'How Ministers Made the Housing Crisis Worse' – assesses UK housing policies since 2010. Rather than supply-side measures to ensure more homes are built, successive Conservative-led governments have instead stoked up the demand side of the market via the flagship HTB scheme, reinforcing the dominance of the largest industry players. Dubbed 'Help to Sell' by housing industry insiders, HTB has pushed up prices and handed massive multibillion-pound windfalls to the UK's leading developers, consolidating their grip on the market.

Far from reversing the policies of David Cameron, his successor Theresa May compounded the error by repeatedly extending what was meant to be a one-off HTB programme, pouring further billions of pounds of taxpayers' money into a scheme that has helped a lucky few but made affordability far worse for the vast majority.

Chapter VI – '"No Shortage" Nonsense' – tackles the notion, increasingly promoted by large developers and their political and media allies, that there is no shortage of homes in the UK. Easily disproved, the promotion of this idea is an insult to the millions of young adults still in their childhood bedroom, the additional millions of 'concealed households' in cramped lodgings and other 'priced-out' young and middle-aged adults across the country unable to buy or rent their own home. This chapter also discusses another highly contentious issue – the link between years of net UK immigration and our current homes shortage.

Chapter VII – 'New-Build Nightmares' – focuses on Persimmon, one of the UK's largest developers. Over recent years, Persimmon has been widely criticised for producing shoddy houses and flats and selling homes with extremely punitive leaseholds. At the same time, senior executives have been awarded disproportionately large multimillion-pound bonus payments. While operating within the law, Persimmon has, for many, become emblematic of a house-building industry that is overmighty and exploitative, providing a sub-standard product to customers who face little choice amid an ongoing shortage of available homes.

Chapter VIII – 'Fat of the Land' – traces the history of LVC in the UK, outlining how the policy was effectively used following the Second World War, a period of mass housebuilding, before it was then abolished. There is growing realisation across the political spectrum – from campaigning housing charities to centre-right thinktanks and Conservative Cabinet ministers – that our housing shortage is now so serious and the affordability crisis so acute that meaningful LVC should be reintroduced.

The focus of Chapter IX – 'Beyond Grenfell' – is the UK's social housing sector in the aftermath of the worst residential fire since the Second World War. Some 17 per cent of the UK population live in social housing, down from a third in the late 1970s. There will always be a need, in any advanced economy, for some subsidised housing that provides affordable yet decent accommodation for low-income households and other vulnerable groups. The UK's current policy, of increasing reliance on private landlords to house social tenants, is causing the housing benefit bill to spiral as rents rise. These costs will escalate, and over-crowding and homelessness will rise, until the UK decisively reverses the long-term decline in social housebuilding. This chapter also asks what lessons can be learnt, both good and bad, from the UK's post-war New Towns programme. While often criticised for shoddy architecture, the New Towns successfully used gains accruing from the granting of planning permission to build local amenities and provide other community development priorities, including social housing.

Home Truths then presents 'A Manifesto for Change' – ten explicit proposals to encourage more housebuilding across the UK, in the right places, at affordable prices. The state needs to make better use of land it already owns. Steps must be taken to address the over-concentration of the UK's housebuilding industry, with particular incentives and assistance for SME builders. Developers granted planning permission must be incentivised to deliver homes promptly – and penalised if they do not.

With no new, substantial settlement built since 1970, the UK needs to launch a modern-day 'New Town' movement. The legal basis of LVC must be finally reinstated so commercially built homes are affordable and social housing can be built more economically, while raising funds to provide local amenities to go alongside new homes – making housebuilding more popular with existing communities.

Housing is the most pressing domestic challenge facing the UK today. Far too few homes have been built over the last thirty years – and relentless demand, in the face of inadequate supply, has seen prices spiral upward. Millions of hard-working people are now being denied the security and stability of home ownership.

Our housing shortage is now so chronic that any failure to grapple with this problem, and bring about meaningful change, could lead to a significant radicalisation of British politics. Legions of priced-out voters will opt for the aggressive taxation of residential property, the easy promises of punitive rent controls and other increasingly extreme and counter-productive solutions.

At the time of writing, of course, Boris Johnson's government is clearly concentrating on Brexit and the fallout from the June 2016 referendum. Yet the lack of focus on housing is long-standing and has been demonstrated by successive governments. When Esther McVey became Housing Minister in July 2019, she was the eighteenth person to hold this vital post in little more than twenty years.

Once Brexit is resolved, this country's chronic housing shortage will surely return to front-line daily politics. So this book has been written to explain how this shortage happened, why it matters and to offer a series of much-needed policy solutions capable of attracting widespread support.

Liam Halligan
September 2019

I

THE BRITISH DREAM

Roses are blooming in Metro-Land, just as they do in the brochures.[1]
JOHN BETJEMAN, 1973

'When we bought this house back in the 1930s, it was brand
new,' Mr Ings told me, as he expertly trimmed the hedge.
'There was a big gate at the end of the road, which led to a field full
of cows,' he said, the tips of his clippers moving busily, at the level
of my eyes.

Harold Ings, and his wife May, lived next door to my childhood
home in Kingsbury, London, NW9. The conversation above –
between a kindly elderly gentleman and his inquisitive infant neighbour – amounts to my earliest memory. It took place sometime in the
early 1970s, when I was four or five years old.

Mr and Mrs Ings lived in the other half of our suburban, semi-
detached house – the kind of unflashy, commonplace two-storey
residence that typifies the UK's mid-1930s residential building
boom. Our respective households lived under a single roof, sepa-
rated by what I learnt later in life was called a party wall.

What I knew as a child was that, having removed a low fence,
the Ings and Halligan families had chosen to share a combined,
but still tiny front garden. That meant shared gardening duties too.
So Mr Ings, a short, rather rotund man, in his V-neck jumper and

worsted trousers with turn-ups, would wield his hedge clippers and prune the roses. My young mother, in what she called her 'scruffy old jeans' and with her hair tied back, would join him, weeding the flowerbeds and using hand shears and a kneeling pad to trim the pocket handkerchief-sized lawn.

Mr Ings had long retired. But I knew, from what he told me and the fascinating paraphernalia I saw in his garage, that he'd worked for London Underground. During the 1940s and 1950s, Mr Ings was, in fact, one of the station masters at Baker Street – the Tube station which links the Metropolitan Line to central London. And it was in Metro-Land where he and I and our adjacently housed families lived. Each in a 'standard three-bedroomed semi'.

Metro-Land was the name given to acres of suburban housing estates built in the north-west of London and out into Middlesex, Hertfordshire and Buckinghamshire in the early and mid-twentieth century. The term was coined in 1915, by the marketing board of the Metropolitan Railway Line – which, prior to the First World War, had bought huge tracts of farmland from Neasden, then a suburb of central London, all the way to the Chiltern Hills.

Metro-Land is where I was born and raised, until I left home to go to university.[2] It's the place, perhaps more than any other, where the 'British Dream' – home ownership for the masses – was nurtured and pursued. My parents are working-class people who, having themselves grown up in sub-standard housing amid financial insecurity, then strove in their young adulthood to put all that behind them by buying their own home.

The fact that they managed to do so, as their children were born, revolutionised their view of themselves and their broader attitude towards the country in which they lived. Home ownership allowed Eve and Martin Halligan to achieve a decent if modest lifestyle and, above all, that vital sense of security, for themselves and their children, which their respective childhoods had sorely lacked.

My parents both left school at the age of sixteen. They have no professional qualifications and didn't go to university. But they were part of that generation born in the 1930s, 1940s and 1950s who, as the UK grew wealthier, through hard work and saving were able to forge for themselves a life demonstrably more prosperous, and with more choice, than that of their parents. My generation, those born in the 1960s and 1970s, were for the most part able to do the same.

The key financial event in our lives, often achieved before the age of thirty, was buying our first home. For many of us, that was the all-important step – contributing to a mortgage each month, rather than paying rent to someone else. That meant we could gradually build equity value, trade upward as we started a family and needed more space and – eventually, after twenty-five years or so of monthly payments – own a substantial asset outright.

'Getting on the property ladder' has, since the Second World War, given tens of millions of people living in Britain, whether they were born here or elsewhere, not just freedom from landlords and physical security but, more than that, a meaningful 'stake' in an increasingly wealthy society.

Today, of course, the situation is very different. If you're a child of the 1980s, 1990s or beyond, the progress that previous generations routinely enjoyed now seems unobtainable. For millions of so-called 'Millennials', and 'Generation Z' who will follow them into adulthood, the 'British Dream' of home ownership has been crushed.[3]

When I left home back in the early 1990s, over 45 per cent of 25–29-year-olds owned their own home. Since then, that figure has plunged to less than 25 per cent.[4] Even professional couples with impressive qualifications and relatively high incomes are increasingly 'locked out' of the property market as prices keep rising faster than earnings – putting even a modest home out of reach. Sky-high house prices are, across much of the UK, lowering the quality of life for millions, stopping people moving to good jobs and creating vast inequities of opportunity, wealth and freedom between young and old.

Owner-occupiers, meanwhile, and those who have amassed large buy-to-let portfolios, effortlessly accumulate ever more unearned wealth and claims on society's resources. Far more than zero-hour contracts, or even galling fat-cat pay, the true driver of UK wealth inequality is our chronically dysfunctional residential property market. High housing costs and the daunting impossibility of buying a home contributes mightily to a sense among many young voters that society is 'rigged' against them, leading many to believe that 'capitalism doesn't work'.

Politicians like to be seen urging privatised energy companies to cut household utility bills. They argue over future increases in the minimum wage. But, when it comes to living standards, what really matters is the cost of housing – and for many young renters and would-be buyers, those costs are simply out of control.

Cripplingly expensive housing is now affecting fertility rates – propelling the UK towards a demographic crisis.[5] Countless young adults have put their lives on hold, and are delaying having a family, because they are stuck in shared, rented accommodation and can't buy a home. Frustration and insecurity abound as, for millions, the instinctive and entirely reasonable ambition of home ownership is thwarted. And, at the sharp end, of course, high rents and a chronic shortage of social housing are adding to a shocking increase in homelessness and the expansion of a marginalised underclass.

Since the end of the Second World War, one of the basic features of the UK's free society – the 'British Dream' – has been that anyone who works hard and saves for a few years should be able to buy a decent home at a reasonable price. As such, the chronic unaffordability of housing, in many areas of the country, is now the major economic and political scandal of our time. It is disgraceful that over recent decades, a combination of cowardice and neglect on the part of successive governments means that, for countless young adults, the dream of home ownership is being cruelly denied.

My parents had the opportunity to buy their own home – for much of their generation, a commonplace yet profoundly positive event. I did too. Subsequent generations, however hard they work and save, for the most part, are not getting that same fair chance – which has huge negative implications, not just for the individuals concerned, but for British politics, society and the country as a whole. That's why I'm writing *Home Truths*.

HOMES FIT FOR HEROES

In 1918, as the First World War came to an end, David Lloyd George's coalition government viewed the provision of good-quality affordable homes as essential for maintaining social harmony and boosting the UK's war-torn economy. There was also the need to stave off the threat of industrial and political unrest, as dramatically illustrated by the ongoing revolution in Russia, which had started the year before.

After surviving the horrors of the First World War, returning British troops expected the world to be a better place, where they could find work and raise a family with dignity, not return to the sub-standard housing they had left, often disease-ridden Victorian-era slums. A programme of state-backed housebuilding was seen as vital, then, to enable a healthy, growing workforce to tackle the challenges of the new post-war world. But British politicians were also eager to avoid the shift towards riot and revolution that had swept Europe in the later stages of the war.

In a speech given the day after the November 1918 Armistice, Lloyd George famously promised there would be 'homes fit for heroes'. Except that he didn't. What he actually said was that the UK should build 'habitations fit for the heroes who have won the war'. It was the nation's newspaper headline writers who contributed the somewhat punchier version of this phrase to the annals of British political folklore.[6]

As a Liberal Prime Minister, Lloyd George presented his post-war housebuilding effort as a mission driven by morality and gratitude, given the need for both slum clearance and to recognise the war-time hardships of returning troops. 'I cannot think what these men have been through,' he said, in a speech in Wolverhampton, two weeks after the Armistice. 'There are millions who will come back – let us make this a land fit for them to live in.'[7]

There can be no doubt, though, that the provision of decent working-class housing was also seen as a strategic necessity – imperative, in fact, if Britain was to retain 'moderate' politics as temperatures rose elsewhere. 'Even if this programme costs one hundred million pounds,' Lloyd George remarked, while discussing his housing plans with the rest of the Cabinet, 'what is that compared to the stability of the state and the threat posed by Bolshevism?'[8]

The resulting Housing and Town Planning Act of 1919 provided government subsidies to finance the construction of social housing – with a target of 500,000 homes within three years. There had been some social housing prior to the First World War, built mainly by philanthropists. But this legislation – also known as the 'Addison Act', after the Minister of Health Christopher Addison, who brought the legislation to Parliament – marked the beginnings of the UK's nationwide system of council housing, designed to provide low-income households with secure, state-owned accommodation, while paying subsidised rents.[9]

Despite huge public expectations, though, once the immediate post-war crisis was over and amid shortages of both building materials and skilled labour, the plan stalled. By the time Lloyd George left office in 1922, around 170,000 new homes had been built under the 'Home Fit for Heroes' scheme – far fewer than the numbers needed and a long way short of the hopes roused by his stirring rhetoric.[10]

Yet the 1919 legislation was still game-changing, as it meant ministers were politically on the hook and subsequent governments could no longer ignore the housing problem. The 1923 Housing Act resurrected Lloyd George's plan but encouraged private developers to build social housing rather than the state. This reflected a change of government, the Conservatives having won an outright majority in the election of 1922.[11]

The first Labour administration introduced the 1924 Housing Act, extending further grants for local authorities to address acute housing shortages among working people. The 1930 Housing Act, also under Labour, provided more subsidies, while facilitating slum clearance. This legislation was radical – empowering local councils to knock down swathes of low-quality, privately owned rented accommodation built during a period of rapid industrialisation in the mid- and late nineteenth century, often with little thought for water supply, ventilation and sunlight.

Despite fierce resistance, the 1930 legislation was implemented across the country, finally sparking the mass construction of decent, low-cost accommodation. By 1939, local councils had built a total of 1.1 million homes since the end of the First World War. Around 10 per cent of UK households were living in social housing, up from 1 per cent prior to 1914.[12]

The inter-war period also saw a sharp rise in home-building for sale by private developers, and the related spread of home ownership. Britain recovered impressively from a double-dip recession during the early 1930s, with growth exceeding 4 per cent a year from 1933 to 1936. This happened before rearmament began in anticipation of another world war and with the government running budget surpluses throughout this period – so there was no major fiscal stimulus either. The economic boost came, instead, from commercial construction, as the number of houses built by developers for private sale rocketed – from 133,000 in 1932 to 293,000 in 1935, remaining steady at 279,000 the year after.

Many of these private dwellings are the archetypal 1930s semi-detached houses still seen on the outskirts of many UK cities – most famously on the outskirts of London, in Metro-Land suburbs such as Barnet, Wembley, Harrow and Kingsbury. Two vital factors drove this residential building boom. The first was 'cheap money' – interest rates were low during the 1930s, just as they have been since the 2007 global financial crisis. The second factor was that land available for housebuilding was cheap and abundant – the direct opposite of the situation today.

In the early 1930s, the Metropolitan Railway was amalgamated into the broader London Underground network. This ushered in Metro-Land's interwar heyday, given the introduction of fast and frequent train services to central London. Private developers such as T. F. Nash, F. & C. Costin and Comben & Wakeling, the company which constructed my childhood home, bought land cheaply and built out at an impressive rate.[13]

They were helped by a near absence of planning laws – existing regulations were barely enforced and the restrictions of the 1947 Town and Country Planning Act were yet to come. Despite this lack of state oversight, these small and medium-sized developers still built attractive, relatively spacious homes, laid out on generous plots – and they did so quickly.

This happened precisely because land was available and relatively inexpensive – so the housebuilding market was competitive, with lots of firms able to enter the industry, develop houses with relatively little capital outlay and vie for customers. The supply of homes, then, was what economists call 'elastic'. There was no incentive for developers to sit on large land banks, or delay building, as they waited for prices to further increase. If they did, other developers would provide homes instead – which kept price rises broadly in check.

The supply of mortgage finance was also expanding, allowing

more potential homebuyers to come forward. This was a time when there was much uncertainty about the security of savings, given the cataclysmic 1929 Wall Street Crash and its impact on share prices everywhere, including the UK. This encouraged ordinary workers to flock towards the rapidly expanding building societies, where they could take out loans which allowed them to buy their own home and 'save in bricks and mortar' instead.

New suburbs sprung up across Britain. The monotony of Victorian terraces was rejected in favour of cottage-style two-storey homes. Rows and rows of semi-detached 'mock-Tudor' units were built, arranged along streets named Drive, Crescent, Avenue and Close. While far from exclusive, they were still wildly popular with ordinary working people who wanted an escape from inner-city congestion and freedom from landlords by buying their own suburban home instead.

Cheap land meant such houses were built in low densities, with generous gardens and green spaces close by. Low land costs, and the resulting competition, also meant homes were affordable, even for those on relatively low incomes. Some 85 per cent of new houses sold during the mid-1930s were priced at less than £750 (equivalent to around £55,000 in 2019).[14] Terraced houses in the London area could be bought for £395 when average wages were about £165 a year – a price–earnings multiple of around 2.4, a fraction of the relative cost faced by homebuyers today.

In sum, around four million homes were built in England between 1919 and 1939 – approximately one million by local authorities and the rest by the private sector. During this period, the slum tenements and exploitative landlords of the Victorian and Edwardian era began to fade, as the 'British Dream' came into view. Owner-occupancy, at 18 per cent of UK households at the end of the First World War, had risen to 32 per cent when hostilities broke out anew.

RADICAL MISSTEPS

During the Second World War, nearly half a million homes were destroyed or made uninhabitable by aerial bombing – not only in Greater London but also other large provincial cities.[15] These losses worsened the pre-war housing shortage which, despite the 1930s building boom, remained chronic. And while some 300,000 slum homes were demolished during the inter-war years, many remained, with millions of families still living in deeply sub-standard housing.

In 1945, Clement Attlee's Labour Party was elected by a landslide on a manifesto – 'Let Us Face the Future' – declaring that 'the nation wants food, work and homes'.[16] The clamour for post-war renewal, and a new left-leaning consensus, was enough to oust Winston Churchill, despite his heroic and steadfast leadership during 'Britain's darkest hour'.[17]

Plans made during the war to relieve acute over-crowding were enacted, although there was a desperate shortage of skilled labour and building materials and the government was virtually bankrupt. Prefabricated houses were used on a massive scale as a way of urgently supplying new homes, playing both a symbolic and practical role in the nation's recovery.

The successful war effort had been driven by the state – and, in that context, Britain's weak and fragmented planning system seemed woefully out-dated and ripe for reform. The patchwork of existing planning law could deal neither with chronically poor housing conditions, nor the growth of private sector development on the outskirts of town and cities, particularly London – already pejoratively known as 'urban sprawl'.[18]

The result was the 1947 Town and Country Planning Act, which took a decisive and radical step. This legislation asserted for the first time that the state had a legitimate role in the development of privately owned land – with almost all building now requiring planning permission, which only the state could grant. Up until that point, decisions over land use were effectively in the hands of the landowner, seeing as existing weak regulations, which many local authorities failed to adopt, were largely unenforced.[19] The new legislation fundamentally changed that, by 'democratising' the use of land.

The intellectual foundations of the 1947 Act were provided by three official war-time studies. The 1940 Barlow Report investigated urban population density and the regeneration of derelict industrial real estate, mainly in the Midlands and the North of England. The Scott Report, published the following year, looked into rural land use. But perhaps the most reformist study was that produced by Australian-born judge Sir Augustus Uthwatt in 1942 – examining the issue of 'betterment', the increase in land value created when planning permission is granted.[20]

While nationalising the right to develop land, the 1947 Act also reflected Uthwatt's central recommendation that 'betterment' should accrue wholly to the state. This amounted to a new and comprehensive system of land taxation. Under the measures, builders would purchase agricultural land for new homes at a relatively low 'existing use' value. But a 'development charge' would become due, payable to a newly created Central Land Board, equivalent to the increase in the value of the land once planning consent was given.

Private sector developers, then, were to make returns on their housebuilding activities, not on trading land – with local authorities raising funds from the development charge to build schools, hospitals and other public amenities which the new housing required. 'The reputable builder does not normally look for his profits to the sale of land,' said Labour's Planning Minister Lewis Silkin from the despatch box, as this historic Bill was passing through the House of Commons. 'This is a practice which I regard as undesirable, and no harm will come to the community if it is no longer possible.'[21]

As such, when it came to encouraging housebuilding, the 1947 legislation struck a balance. On the one hand, developers now needed to deal with the complexities and bureaucracy of a new planning system, potentially slowing down the pace at which homes were built. On the other, 'existing use' prices meant land remained cheap. And that, in turn, was likely to keep new homes relatively affordable and of a decent standard, as a large number of builders could still enter the market, competing on both quality and price, without needing prohibitive amounts of capital. The development charge, meanwhile, would help finance the roads, other transport links and common spaces that make housing developments desirable places to live.

The trouble was, of course, that powerful landowners were strongly opposed to a law which forced them to sell land cheaply – and were determined to change it. Clement Attlee's Labour government floundered – and the Conservatives regained power in 1951, returning Churchill to Downing Street. The Tories' new *cri de coeur* was 'to give housing a priority second only to national defence', promising that 300,000 houses a year would be built, turning the UK into 'a property-owning democracy'.[22]

With the immediate post-war emergency over, though, to the delight of large landowners, the Conservatives were, despite all this communitarian rhetoric, quick to scrap the development charge – doing so in 1953. So the carefully crafted post-war planning system, combining the need for permissions with a development charge that damped down speculative pressure on land prices, while extracting value for what we today call 'place-making' infrastructure, started to unravel within just a few years of its introduction.

It also turned out that compulsory purchase order (CPO) powers contained in the 1947 Act, when applied to land the state was buying to facilitate development by commercial housebuilders, were badly drafted and largely unenforceable.[23] Yet even after the development charge was abolished, the 1947 Act still allowed the state to use

CPOs, at 'existing use' value, when acquiring land to build social housing. This helped drive the construction of 1.8 million local authority homes during the 1950s, almost twice as many as had been built during the two decades ahead of the Second World War.

After 1953, though, landowners forced to sell to the state railed against what had become a 'dual market' – as they watched others offload acreage to private builders at full price, including the development value that planning permission conferred. In 1959, under pressure from landowners, Macmillan's Conservative government passed legislation requiring local authorities to purchase land at its residential value once more, including 'betterment' or 'planning gain', even when acquiring sites for social housing. And there was more capitulation to come.

The New Towns Act, passed in 1946, sought to emulate the success of the garden city movement – which had seen the partial development of Letchworth Garden City, begun in 1903, and Welwyn Garden City, begun in 1919. In both cases, the anti-poverty campaigner Ebenezer Howard, having laid out his vision in a celebrated book, had raised money from philanthropists to build decent homes for working people, allowing them to escape the squalor of London.[24]

At the heart of both of Howard's schemes was the successful purchase of a large agricultural acreage at 'existing use' value, which was then transferred to a new 'co-operative land society'. Monies raised when additional plots within the garden city were sold were then ploughed back into the co-operative, which reinvested in civic infrastructure and other improvements.

The New Towns Act allowed local authorities to set up publicly held 'development corporations' with formal, well-defined powers to CPO land at existing-use value – if the land was contributing to a designated 'New Town'. In practice, the threat of CPO was often sufficient to provoke a voluntary sale. Obtaining land in this way meant the New Town Development Corporations (NTDCs) reaped surpluses, whether the properties it built were rented or sold. These funds, with a nod to Ebenezer Howard, were then channelled into social housing and local infrastructure as the New Town developed.

Between 1946 and 1950, under Attlee's administration, no fewer than ten NTDCs were established by newly designated New Towns – including Stevenage (Hertfordshire) in 1946, Crawley (Sussex) and Harlow (Essex) in 1947, Peterlee (County Durham) and Hatfield (Hertfordshire) in 1948 and Corby (Northamptonshire) in 1950. During the ten years from 1951, though, with the Tories in office throughout, not a single New Town designation took place. The successive governments of Churchill and Macmillan knew the 1946 legislation contained well-defined CPO and existing use powers, and channelled money into existing towns instead.[25]

Then, as a new decade began, the Conservatives capitulated to landowners entirely, passing the 1961 Land Compensation Act. This enshrined the right of landowners to receive full value for all sites, including any prospective 'planning gain', even in the case of future New Towns. With landowners now entitled to so-called 'hope value' under practically all circumstances, whether the acreage to be sold was for social housing, private development or to an NTDC, local authorities were left largely powerless when it came to pressing for community-based housing interests when land was sold.

As a result, almost immediately after the 1961 legislation, land prices soared, with landholders standing to make huge windfalls if they, or a prospective developer, could secure planning permission. The cost of residential sites started to absorb large chunks of the state's housebuilding budget, while feeding through into prices of private homes too, pushing them upward.[26] But given the ongoing need to tackle the housing shortage, and with almost four million people still living in sub-standard housing as the 1960s dawned, local authorities desperately needed to build more social housing. They responded to the soaring land costs unleashed by the semi-dismantling of the 1947 planning regime by building high-density tower blocks. In many cases, these turned out to be economic and social failures, with horizontal slums being replaced by vertical slums instead.[27]

Despite all this legislative upheaval, some 2.8 million houses were built in the UK during the 1950s – almost two-thirds of them by local authorities. The 1960s saw the building – or 'completion' – of 3.6 million homes, but with the social housing share falling to 40 per cent. During the twenty-five years from 1945 until the 1960s ended, 3.1 million council homes were built by local authorities, almost 70 per cent of the 4.5 million such homes ever construct-ed across the UK. Many were built on land secured by the state at 'existing use' cost, between the 1946 New Towns Act and the 1961 legislation guaranteeing landowners full development value.

Over the 1970s and 1980s, housing completions fell to 2.5 million and 1.8 million houses in each respective decade, with the share of local authority new-builds falling sharply to less than 20 per cent. As speculative pressure drove up the price of land, and fewer homes were built, house prices began to surge. Countless academic stud-ies have borne out a relationship that amounts to common sense – when fewer homes are built, in the face of rising demand from a growing population, house prices go up.[28]

During the 1990s, 2000s and from 2010 to 2018, total housing completions have been continually falling, from 1.6 million to 1.5 million and then 1.1 million during the first eight years of the current decade. The share of homes built by local authorities had plunged from less than a fifth in the 1980s, to as little as 2 per cent during the 1990s and then just a fifth of 1 per cent from 2000 to 2010, only slightly increasing since.

It was from the 1980s onwards, when a sharp drop-off in social housebuilding combined with slower commercial completions, that speculative pressure really began to build and house prices spiralled upward. Since then, the average UK house price has increased more than nine-fold, far out-stripping the growth of earnings and generating today's chronic affordability crisis.

In 1980, the average house cost £23,288 and the average annual full-time wage was £5,270. So, the price of a typical home was equivalent to 4.4 times the earnings of a typical worker.[29] By 2018, the cost of an average house had spiralled to £214,162, while the average wage was £28,677 – representing a much higher 7.5 times price–earnings ratio. That's why, with most mortgage companies compelled to limit loans to around four times earnings, affordability has become a major problem for young adults desperate to buy a home.

In February 2017, Theresa May's Conservative government rightly acknowledged that 'the UK's housing market is broken'.[30] This has been true for several decades – although the scale of the dysfunction has become worse over the last ten years, catapulting our housing crisis to the top of the political agenda. Whether it is the unaffordability of homes for young professionals trying to get on the housing ladder, or the unavailability of decent social housing for low-income families and other vulnerable households, the UK's chronic housing shortage is now the most pressing domestic policy issue of our time.

When it comes to the UK's housing market, the normal laws of economics don't apply. As prices rise, instead of supply increasing to match demand, developers build slowly to ensure prices rise further. This is possible because the UK's housebuilding industry is controlled by just a few large, highly influential operators, who are barely exposed to genuine competition. A major reason for that, in turn, is sky-high land prices – with smaller builders often finding it impossible to raise the finance necessary to acquire the land they need to challenge the handful of dominant firms.

The reasons behind spiralling house prices, and our increasingly concentrated housebuilding industry, are complex, multi-faceted and inter-related. *Home Truths* will explore these issues, while offering policy solutions to break the deadlock and, once again, make property ownership a realisable dream for ordinary people on ordinary salaries, as it was in the past.

The very heart of the problem, though, is that the post-war planning system was semi-dismantled – and, to this day, we have one side of it operating, but not the other. The 1947 Town and Country Planning Act introduced the need for planning permission, which is totally right and proper. But the legislation also required that land be sold at 'existing-use' value – ensuring there would be a plentiful supply of acreage so housebuilders could obtain land at reasonable prices, so providing homes that were affordable for a broad range of people, working across a wide range of occupations.

When it comes to planning, the UK, for decades, has been using 'half a system', says Hugh Ellis, head of policy at the Town and Country Planning Association, the lobby group set up over a century ago by Ebenezer Howard himself, to promote the original garden cities and the sharing of land value uplift between the seller, developer, the local community and the broader population.

'People criticise our planning system for being very negative – but we don't use the parts designed to do the positive stuff, to create an income stream to fund the building of new communities,' Ellis says. 'The price differential between agricultural land and land with planning permission is staggering but the value accumulates to landowners and not the community that created it.'[31]

Passing the 1947 Town and Country Planning Act, and the New Towns Act the previous year, were radical steps. But the carefully balanced post-war planning system was then seriously destabilised during the 1950s and early 1960s by subsequent legislation, with successive missteps driven by land-owning vested interests. That resulted in a system that stokes up speculation, providing only a restricted supply of land at enormously inflated prices – a system which remains with us today, contributing significantly to the unaffordable prices faced by millions of homebuyers and the under-provision of decent social housing too.

Reintroducing 'existing use' value rules would remove the incentive for landowners to hoard their acreage and stoke speculative pressure in the hope of larger future windfalls. Smaller developers could then enter the market, injecting much-needed competition and encouraging quicker build-out rates by all housebuilders. With cheaper land, houses sold on the open market would be priced more reasonably, and there would be scope to oblige developers to provide more 'affordable' housing, available to rent and buy at sub-market rates, while still allowing for healthy profits and steady shareholder dividends. Restoring 'existing use' value rules would also make it much easier and cheaper for local authorities to launch a 21st-century generation of New Towns, along with a fresh building wave of quality social housing too.

All this involves the reversal of the 1961 Land Compensation Act. This would be a controversial move – a radical shift that would be vigorously resisted, a return to the original vision of Uthwatt, Barlow and the other founders of the UK's post-war planning system. Yet upending this pivotal 1961 law – little known outside professional legal and property circles, but the ultimate cause of the misery and resentment felt by a generation of priced-out homebuyers – is the central recommendation of this book.

The UK's housing shortage is now so serious and causing such economic and social damage, that it is no longer feasible to hope that the situation will change without radical reform.

LOST ELYSIUM

By the mid-1970s, when I was an inquisitive infant talking to my elderly neighbour as he clipped the hedge, the share of UK households that were owner-occupiers had risen above 50 per cent.[32] My parents were part of that trend – as increasing numbers of ordinary, working people were able to escape generations of sub-standard rented accommodation and buy their own homes, doing much to secure their physical and financial security.

My father, having spent his boyhood in the west of Ireland, emigrated to England in his early teens. He became, along with numerous cousins and childhood friends, part of the civilian army of Irish labourers and sub-contractors which helped power the UK's residential building boom of the 1960s and 1970s. Living in the then predominantly Irish area of Willesden Green, near central London, he met my mother, the youngest of ten siblings raised in a council house. For them, moving out to Kingsbury was an enormous achievement, taking on a mortgage and fulfilling their modest dream of buying their own home, with a garden front and back, where their children could safely play.

The first Metro-Land marketing booklets, produced after the First World War by the Metropolitan Railway company, were filled with pastel drawings of idyllic cottages, telling of 'a land where the wild flowers grow'.[33] A semi-rural arcadia was offered to Londoners sick of congestion, smog and over-crowding. The marketing campaign was hugely successful and waves of aspiring young couples, both blue-collar and white-collar, flocked to the north-western outskirts of London, in search of greenery and space.

During the 1930s, more than 500,000 homes were built in London, almost entirely in the suburbs, many of them in Metro-Land. The open countryside featured in the posters and brochures of the 1920s was gradually covered with acres of semis, pavements and lampposts. Despite the uniformity of the housing and rapid pace of development, John Betjeman in 1954 published a series of poems – 'Middlesex', 'Harrow-on-the-Hill' and 'Baker Street Station Buffet' – lauding the quiet, everyday dignity of Metro-Land's inhabitants and its semi-rural landscape.[34] In 'Middlesex', Betjeman tells of a young woman – 'Elaine' – returning from her central London job and 'daintily alighting' at Ruislip Gardens Tube station. She hurries home: 'Out into the outskirt's edges | Where a few surviving hedges | Keep alive our lost Elysium – rural Middlesex again'.

Betjeman went on to write and present a noted BBC television documentary in 1973 entitled *Metro-Land*, celebrating and even romanticising this suburban patchwork of homes, streets and quiet aspiration, which in his view retained at least some of its original inter-war charm. 'Roses are blooming in Metro-Land,' he told viewers, 'just as they do in the brochures'.

Much of the UK's literary establishment despised Betjeman, not least because his poetry celebrated the suburbs. For much of the period after the Second World War, and certainly when I was a child in the 1970s, 'suburban' was a dirty word.[35] But many of the families living there felt very fortunate, having worked hard to buy their Metro-Land home and often just one generation on from sub-standard housing.

Even in the mid-1970s, a million homes across the UK were still rated as slums, with another 1.8 million deemed 'unfit for habitation' but inhabited anyway, lacking basic amenities such as running water, baths and toilets. At the same time, at least half a million additional families were sharing homes and 30,000 were homeless.[36] Across Metro-Land, though, Betjeman's 1973 documentary found a residential community of quiet contentment, a vast expanse of striving home ownership and hedge trimming.

Today, several decades on, the suburb where I spent my youth has changed markedly. The slow pace of housebuilding in and around London, and soaring prices for those trying either to rent or buy, has led to desperate measures – including chronic over-crowding and the creation of modern-day slums.

Walking around Kingsbury, or nearby Wembley or Ealing, the

residential streets are mostly quiet. The front gardens, where they haven't been paved to provide extra parking, still look reasonably well kept. But peer down the sides of houses and you can often spot newly built, temporary-looking structures at the bottom of gardens – highlighting a problem known as 'beds in sheds'.

In recent years, councils in outlying London boroughs, in what used to be called Metro-Land and elsewhere, have taken to using thermal-imaging planes and drones to fly over suburban streets at night, attempting to detect the extent to which outbuildings are being used as rented accommodation. A recent report found that tens of thousands of people are sleeping in such illegal, sub-standard housing across the outskirts of the capital.[37]

In Kingsbury, in September 2018, one police raid found twenty-six beds crammed into a single three-bedroom house and its out-buildings, with people living in what the local council described as 'slum-like conditions'.[38] Soon after, in November 2018, nearby Ealing council fined one Southall landlord £42,000 for repeatedly ignoring warnings to stop illegally letting an outbuilding at one of his rental properties.[39]

Later that same month, another Southall landlord was fined £450,000 for flagrantly disregarding official requests to pull down outhouses she was renting to five tenants. 'It's a tragedy people are being exploited in this way, forced to live in Dickensian conditions by unscrupulous landlords,' said the councillor who took the case to court. 'The landlord completely ignored our requests to act within the law – indeed, the only reason she stopped letting these sub-standard buildings was because we demolished them'.[40]

'Beds in sheds' isn't only happening in London, though. Councils in cities as diverse as Oxford, Salford and Bristol have been forced to launch crackdowns on this egregious practice – which often involves renting out unsanitary, damp and unsafe accommodation, plus the evasion of council tax.[41]

Alongside an explosion of illegal renting, the UK's chronic housing shortage is also driving what is now an epidemic of outright
homelessness and rough sleeping. In 2017, the highly respected
charity Shelter estimated there were 306,000 homeless people
across the UK, up from 293,000 the year before. That's a ten-fold
increase in my lifetime.[42]

Shelter estimates that around one in every 200 people in England
is currently homeless, with various London boroughs featuring
heavily among the fifty top hotspots – Newham, Haringey, Westminster and Ealing are top of the list. But Luton, Birmingham and
Manchester are also among the worst areas – and, as Shelter says,
the battle to escape homelessness is made much tougher by a lack
of affordable homes to rent and the UK's ongoing social housing
shortage.

Another long-established housing charity, Crisis, highlighted a 21
per cent rise in the number of households in temporary accommodation in England between October and December 2018, compared
with the same period the year before. Crisis drew attention to a harsh
reality – that Local Housing Allowance, and other forms of housing
benefit, 'no longer cover the true cost of renting in large parts of the
country'.[43]

Over decades, then, for my parents' generation and my own, the
UK housing market helped to drive social mobility, progress and
contentment – as countless millions achieved the satisfaction and
security of home ownership. For successive generations of today's
young adults, in stark contrast, the housing market is now a source
of social immobility, resentment and rancour. The 'British Dream'
has become, for them, an ongoing nightmare of endless over-priced
renting, thwarted ambitions and lives put on hold.

The UK's current housing crisis, though, goes way beyond the
crushed aspirations linked to the fall in home ownership, given the
extreme shortage not just of homes available for private ownership

and rent, but social housing too. The next chapter outlines the scale of the UK's housing crisis in twelve graphs, focusing on the long-standing and significant shortfall in the building of new homes of all types – both to buy and rent, whether private or publicly owned – compared to the growing number of households.

This widening gap between housing supply and demand has seen house prices increase much faster than wages over several decades, particularly since the mid-1990s, and then again after the 2008 financial crisis. This has generated a sharp fall in owner-occupancy among certain age groups – particularly young adults. It has also caused private rents to spiral, along with an epidemic of over-crowding and homelessness. The UK's chronic housing shortage really is the most pressing domestic policy issue we face. Solving this complex and urgent problem requires, first, understanding the growing extent of our housing shortage and why it is happening.

II

THE UK HOUSING CRISIS
IN TWELVE GRAPHS

*It is essential to have not only more houses, but more houses of the
required type in the right place. There are technical difficulties that
have to be overcome over land, financing and the organization
of the building industry. But there is also the question of will.
Housing has not yet achieved the place of priority in official
policy justified both by the social suffering involved and
by the public concern that has been aroused.[1]*

TIMES EDITORIAL, 1969

The words above appeared in an editorial in *The Times* on 22
December 1969. That year, 378,320 homes were built across the
UK. Post-war demolition and slum clearances were ongoing – and
continued into the 1970s. But, despite this depletion of the housing stock, the rate at which new homes became available in 1969
was still a very long way ahead of the formation of new households
across Britain, which then averaged around 160,000 per annum.[2]

The current situation could hardly be more different. Official
figures show 178,960 homes were completed across the UK during
2016/17 – less than half the 1969 total.[3] Yet, the number of new homes
required each year is now between 240,000 and 340,000, up to
twice as much as during the late 1960s on some estimates, given the

number of households now being created and the backlog shortage built up over many decades.[4] When *The Times* penned the editorial above, entitled 'Housing Anguish', far more houses and flats were being built each year than the number of new households. Now, the precise opposite applies, with the demand for new housing hugely out-stripping newly available supply – and that has been the case each and every year since the early 1990s.

Successive governments have repeatedly emphasised the importance of making sure more homes are built. Politicians clearly understand that a lack of affordable housing, for both renters and buyers across almost all ranges of income, has been driving social division and deep discontent. 'We've become accustomed to politicians sporting a hard hat and high-vis jacket whilst enthusiastically waving a clay brick,' quipped a recent report from the Building Societies Association, 'as they aim to symbolise their support to get Britain building again.'[5]

Yet policymaking in this vital area has, for too long, been denied the consistency of leadership needed to see through reforms and initiatives that might deliver significantly more homes. Esther McVey, appointed as Housing Minister in July 2019, became the fourth person to take on this crucial role in just over eighteen months – a veritable ministerial merry-go-round.

Housing is increasingly unaffordable in many parts of the UK – going way beyond London and the south-east – with prices and rents rising much faster than earnings. A major reason is because, for decades now, far too few homes have been built. Over the last fifty years, the rate of UK housebuilding has fallen well behind our demographic requirements – determined by natural population growth and net immigration. And, since the 2008 financial crisis, the homes shortage has become even more acute, sending housing affordability to the top of the political agenda.

Professor Paul Cheshire of the London School of Economics, an eminent housing expert who has advised successive governments, says the 'chronic' and 'acute' lack of homes has caused prices to spiral. 'We have not been building nearly enough housing since the 1960s, but over the last twenty years we've built around 2.3 million too few homes,' he says. 'This growing supply gap over recent years has seen prices become more and more unaffordable.'[6]

This, above all, is what explains the UK's housing affordability crisis – a long-standing and endemic lack of housing supply.[7] The shortage, as this book will argue, is primarily caused by policies which have constrained the supply of land upon which houses are allowed to be built.

House prices across the UK have risen substantially over the past half-century and particularly during the past twenty-five years. The average UK house price in 1995 was £56,522, according to Land Registry data. By 2018, that average price had ballooned to £226,703, an increase of more than 300 per cent.[8]

To give a sense of just how large that rise is relative to the cost of living, if the average house price in 1995 had increased each year only by the general rate of inflation across the entire economy, the average 2018 house price would have been just £105,000 – far less than half what it actually was. That's why, in many parts of the country, it is now a real struggle for first-time buyers (FTBs) to step onto the property ladder, even if they receive considerable financial help from their parents – the so-called 'bank of Mum and Dad'. And that widespread reliance on parental backing means that the many millions of young adults who don't come from property-owning families are now being denied the chance of owning their own home, despite saving hard and holding down relatively well-paid jobs.

There are two sides to any market, of course – demand and supply. Over recent decades, housing demand has been supported by relatively fast economic growth, which has driven up wages, and also easy access to mortgages. Average real (inflation-adjusted) UK wages have doubled since the mid-1970s, even allowing for the fall in the aftermath of the 2008 financial crisis.[9] Lenders, meanwhile, have for the most part been keen to extend mortgages to both homebuyers and buy-to-let investors – too eager at times, in fact, with over-indebtedness contributing to the 2008 collapse.

The number of mortgage approvals for house purchases peaked in December 2003 at 132,700 a month. Back then, many buyers were securing 100 per cent mortgages and taking on debts that were six or even seven times annual household income, higher than the three or four times income multiples generally available today. Such irresponsible lending fuelled booming demand for both residential and buy-to-let properties.

Mortgage approvals remain buoyant now, reaching 66,300 for home purchases in April 2019. But demand continues to be boosted by years of ultra-low interest rates and schemes such as Help to Buy. There are also signs that 'monster mortgages' – offering very high lending multiples with little or no deposit – are starting to make a comeback.[10]

The main reason behind high price growth, though, is that this sustained and ever-rising housing demand is set against a severe shortage of supply. This is most acute in London and south-east England, but affects many other parts of the UK as well, particularly urban centres. 'The housing shortage isn't a looming crisis, a distant threat that will become a problem if we fail to act,' said the government's own Housing White Paper, published in February 2017. 'We're already living in it.'[11]

This fundamental demand–supply mismatch has been blindingly obvious for decades. Yet successive governments, each of them declaring they will 'finally get Britain building again', have largely failed. For a long time now, the number of new homes becoming available each year gets nowhere near to the number of households created, let alone starting to address the backlog shortage, the fundamental lack of homes highlighted by Professor Cheshire, which has amassed over several decades. The UK's housing shortage now seems so intractable that senior civil servants grappling with the problem daily, when talking in public, appear to have stopped even trying to put a gloss on reality.

Just days after the White Paper cited above was published, Melanie Dawes, Permanent Secretary at the Ministry for Housing, Communities and Local Government, appeared before the House of Commons Public Accounts Committee.[12] Asked when the gap between housing demand and supply would be eliminated, she replied, to her credit: 'It will continue as it has done for decades … and that will show itself primarily in affordability and in some places in homelessness – I am simply being honest with you.'[13]

This chapter of *Home Truths* outlines the scale of the UK's housing crisis in twelve graphs, focusing on the long-standing and significant shortfall in the building of new homes compared to the growing number of households – and the resulting impact on prices and affordability. Our seeming inability to build enough houses and flats, in the right places, has a starkly uneven impact. Older homeowners benefit as prices keep rising much faster than earnings, while priced-out younger adults, often forced to spend so much on rent that they cannot save, become increasingly less likely to be able to afford a home. Lower-income and other vulnerable households also suffer, of course, from the UK's long-standing shortage of social housing.

NO PLACE LIKE HOME

The seminal Barker Review, written for HM Treasury by the economist Kate Barker and published in 2004, established beyond doubt that there was 'considerable evidence' of a shortage of homes in the UK.[14] Barker pointed to 'significant benefits from a higher rate of housebuilding', arguing that a failure to do so would lead to 'problems of homelessness, affordability and social division, decline in standards of public service delivery and increasing the costs of doing business in the UK – hampering our economic success'. Her report indicated that around 250,000 new homes needed to be built each year across the UK to meet population growth and the formation of new households.

When Barker wrote her report, housebuilding had not reached 250,000 since the early 1980s. A later government study, published in 2011, estimated that the number of households in England alone was growing by 232,000 a year – yet by then, housebuilding had fallen even further away from Barker's implied target.[15] Since the Barker Report appeared, in fact, UK-wide housebuilding has averaged 170,625 annually, remaining well short of 250,000 each and every year.

During the 1970s, some 2.5 million homes were built in total, by private housebuilders, housing associations and local authorities – with social housing built by the latter accounting for around 40 per cent of all new homes. From 1979 to 1990, under Margaret Thatcher's successive Conservative governments, an average of 220,505 new homes were constructed each year – as shown in Figure 2.1.[16] While Thatcher was Prime Minister, over half a million council houses were built, but the share of homes developed by local authorities fell below a fifth of the total, compared to two-fifths the decade before.

FIGURE 2.1: UK HOUSING COMPLETIONS (BY TYPE, 1970–2017)

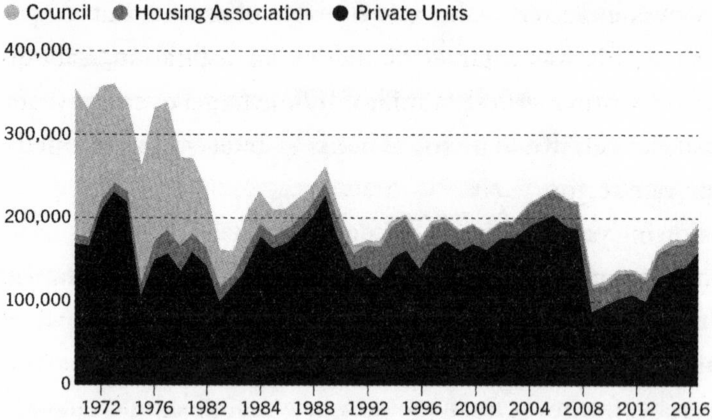

Source: MHCLG

Under John Major, who was Prime Minister from 1990 to 1997, an average of just 190,423 new homes were completed each year, as far fewer council homes were built. Total housebuilding stayed close to that level until 2007, under Tony Blair, as private sector building rose but local authorities developed almost no new social housing at all. From 2008 to 2010, under Gordon Brown, housebuilding fell to 181,883 a year, as SME builders struggled in the aftermath of the credit crunch. And during David Cameron's coalition government of 2010 to 2015, the number of new homes completed annually dropped further to just 141,324 per annum.

In 2013/14, there were just 133,050 homes built by private developers, housing associations and local authorities – the lowest peacetime number since the 1926 general strike. During the year marking the tenth anniversary of the 2004 Barker Report, annual UK housebuilding was, at that time, around 120,000 less than the report recommended. Having averaged some 173,000 a year during the decade after Barker, rather than 250,000 as the study indicated, the UK had added another 750,000 or so to its long-standing and ever-rising shortfall of homes.

Ahead of the 2015 election, Cameron promised that one million new homes would be built by 2020, an average of 200,000 a year over what was expected to be a five-year parliament. But it was never clear if this was a target or merely an 'aspiration'. Labour leader Jeremy Corbyn also set a million-home target over five years – pledging that half would be social housing, built by both councils and the private sector.

The following year, the House of Lords Select Committee on Economic Affairs concluded these targets were 'not based on a robust analysis' and failed to take account of the huge backlog of housing need. This influential Lords report recommended, instead, that 'for the foreseeable future', at least 300,000 new homes should be built annually.[17]

The national homes shortage looks different, of course, in different parts of the country. Official regional data on housing demand and supply in Figure 2.2 suggests a cumulative building shortfall between 2000 and 2017 of 343,000 homes in London and 96,000 across the south-east outside the capital.[18] This is hardly surprising. Some 80,000 homes a year were built across Greater London during the 1930s. Since the early 1980s, though, housebuilding in London has only occasionally reached 20,000 a year.

FIGURE 2.2: CUMULATIVE OVER/UNDER SUPPLY (BY REGION, 2000–18)

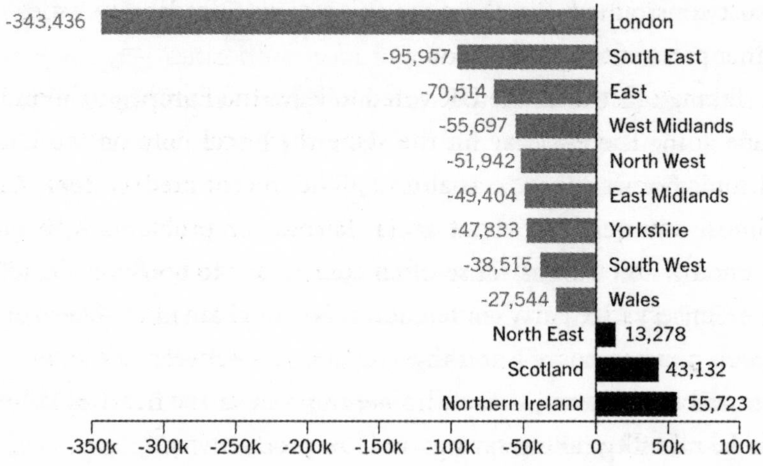

Source: MHCLG

This 'under-build' has also been significant across the Midlands, the east and the north-west – other areas where prices have markedly risen. Over recent years, for instance, twice as many houses have been built in Doncaster and Barnsley, where the housing market is relatively depressed, than in the hotspots of Oxford and Cambridge, where there is a chronic shortage of homes relative to demand. We have not only been building too few homes over the last thirty years, but those we have built have too often been in the wrong place or meeting the wrong type of demand.

In Northern Ireland, the north-east and Scotland, in contrast, a small excess of supply has been built over the last two decades, helping explain weaker price growth in those parts of the UK. At the time of writing, in fact, house prices in Northern Ireland remain below their 2007 peak.

The ratio of UK housebuilding to population growth from 1991 to 2014 was just 0.46 – indicating that, across the country, less than half the required number of new homes were built. This figure ranged from 0.31 in London to 0.66 in the north-west and 0.9 in the north-east.[19] House prices have risen most where supply has been most constrained. But there are still serious affordability issues in other parts of the country too.

Taking office after the UK voted to leave the European Union in June 2016, Theresa May hit the same rhetorical note on the UK's chronic homes shortage as almost all her recent predecessors. 'Ask almost any question about social fairness or problems with our economy, and the answer so often comes back to housing,' she told the Conservative Party conference in Birmingham in October 2016. 'High housing costs – and the growing gap between those on the property ladder and those who are not – lie at the heart of falling social mobility, falling savings and low productivity.'[20]

Initially, the February 2017 Housing White Paper, delayed by Downing Street because May's advisors were determined to remove more radical measures proposed by Communities Secretary Sajid Javid, contained no housebuilding target. Under intense political pressure, though, as Labour leader Jeremy Corbyn repeatedly stressed the housing affordability crisis, the Tory manifesto ahead of the June 2017 election not only restored the promise to 'deliver one million homes by the end of 2020' but upped the ante, pledging 'half a million more by the end of 2022'.[21]

During the autumn of 2018, the government announced that the total housing stock had increased by 222,190 in 2017/18, with residential housebuilding 'returning to levels not seen since before the global financial crisis'. Communities Secretary James Brokenshire spread the news with much fanfare, ignoring the 2020 target in favour of a new one – claiming that housebuilding was on course to reach '300,000 new homes a year by the mid-2020s'.[22]

Yet there are two important caveats to this latest data regarding new homes delivered. The first is that the 2017/18 total – 222,190 – was just 2 per cent higher than the 2016/17 figure of 217,350. That's sharply down on the 15 per cent growth rate achieved the year before. If the housing stock continues to grow by just 2 per cent per annum, it will take until the early 2030s until we reach 300,000 new homes a year.

Secondly, the 222,190 figure is not actually new homes built, but another measure called 'net additional dwellings'.[23] As such, this includes over 25,000 gains from 'change of use between non-domestic and residential' (that is, the conversion of shops and office blocks into homes) plus another 5,000 or so conversions of existing homes into a number of flats.

The genuine total of new homes constructed across the UK in 2017/18 was 192,070 – considerably less than the headlined net additional dwellings number, and still over 10 per cent below total new homes routinely built per annum during the years just before the 2008 financial crisis. While residential conversions from offices and shops, and turning houses into multiple flats, does create new homes, this is by definition a one-off activity – you can only convert the same shop or office block once – and does not point to a sustainable rise in housebuilding. As such, the use of net additional dwellings to measure progress in the underlying rate of housebuilding may be seen as somewhat misleading and controversial.

The same view may be taken of recent changes in the methodology used to estimate the growth in the number of UK households, after responsibility for making such projections was transferred from MHCLG to the Office for National Statistics in 2017. The result is that, from December 2018, household growth numbers have been revised down, both retrospectively and going forward – and, because of this methodological change, the UK's housing shortage now looks less serious, at least on paper, than it previously did.[24]

These are rather technical issues, but there is, at the very least, a risk that ministers and civil servants could be accused of manipulating statistics in order to make the UK's housing crisis – an issue of cardinal economic and political importance – look less pressing than it truly is. *Home Truths* will return to this subject in Chapter VI.

Since 1960, the UK population has risen from 52.3 million to 66.6 million. For the first forty years of that period, annual population growth was just over 150,000. From 2000 onwards, that figure has averaged around 410,000 a year – in part due to rising net immigration. This acceleration in population growth over the last two decades has clearly boosted housing demand.[25] Between 1960 and 2017, the average UK household size also fell from 3.01 people to 2.33, further increasing the latent demand for more homes.

In 2017/18, then, almost fifteen years on from the Barker Review, the UK is still not managing to build 200,000 homes per year. That leaves us way short of Barker's implied recommendation of 250,000 new houses per annum and even further adrift from the 300,000 annual total suggested by the House of Lords Economic Affairs Select Committee in its 2016 report. It is now clear, in fact, that the years 2010 to 2019 will represent the UK's worst decade for house-building since the Second World War.

The average number of annual housing completions rose steadily during the 1950s and 1960s to peak at an average of over 314,000 in the 1970s. That average fell to 217,000 during the 1980s, then dropped again to around 188,000 in both the 1990s and 2000s. Since 2010, though, the UK has built an average of just 156,000 homes a year.

This is barely half the level seen during the 1960s and 1970s, continuing what is now a fifty-year pattern of successive governments failing to create an environment in which enough new homes are built adequately to house our population.

Throughout the 1960s, one new home was delivered each year for every fourteen people in this country. Population growth, and a sharp slow-down in residential building, means that during the years 2010 to 2018, one home was built per annum for every forty-three people living in the UK.[26]

While the rate of housebuilding has risen in recent years – from the low of 133,050 completions in 2013/14 to 192,070 in 2017/18 – this total is still far too low. Bold, radical action is clearly needed to kick-start a consistently higher rate of residential construction. The latest annual completions number is, after all, little more than half the total number of homes built in 1969 when *The Times* wrote its 'Housing Anguish' leading article. And back then, the UK population was 15 per cent smaller and population growth was much slower than it is today.

TOO MUCH OF A STRETCH

From the Second World War until the mid-1990s, buying a home was broadly affordable for most working households. Rapidly rising wages, the sizeable housing stock constructed during the 1930s onwards and a high rate of building in subsequent decades, kept prices manageable for most aspiring homeowners. Since then, though, the combination of slow building, a rising population and, above all, sharply rising land prices has seen house prices increase far faster than wages, making home ownership increasingly unaffordable.

Britain had its first modern experience of a housing bubble during the so-called Barber Boom of 1973. An easing of credit conditions by the Bank of England coupled with the go-for-growth strategy of the

Conservative Chancellor Tony Barber stoked annual house-price inflation of no less than 36 per cent. The average price of a home, which had risen from approximately £2,000 to around £4,500 from the early 1950s to the early 1970s, then doubled again from 1973 to 1976. The boom gradually faded, though, due to both a demand slow-down, as the economy slumped amid industrial unrest and high oil prices, and a supply response – with over a million houses being built during the three years from 1976 to 1978.

There was soon another boom under another Tory Chancellor, Nigel Lawson – this time followed by a bust. A combination of tax cuts, low interest rates and speculative hubris saw house prices rise 16 per cent in 1987 and 25 per cent the year after. The fallout was painful, as prices then fell sharply over four successive years – with interest rates put up to 15 per cent to squeeze out inflation, causing high unemployment. Many who had taken out large mortgages were forced to renege on their loans, then face repossession, or were otherwise left in 'negative equity'.

From the mid-1990s, though, steady economic growth, cheap credit and – above all – slow housebuilding on top of a fundamental shortage of homes inflated the UK's third big post-war housing bubble. The average price rose almost four-fold from £59,199 in 1997 to £214,162 in 2018, despite dropping for two years in the aftermath of the 2008 financial crisis.[27]

This sharp rise in UK house prices stands in stark contrast to most other European countries, particularly when one looks at the increases in real (inflation-adjusted) terms. While the average real house price across Britain has increased 3.5-fold since 1980, according to Organisation for Economic Co-operation and Development (OECD) data, in the US, and the countries which now make up the eurozone, such prices have risen by far less – around 50 per cent in real terms over the same period.[28]

FIGURE 2.3: REAL-TERMS HOUSE PRICES – UK, US, EUROZONE

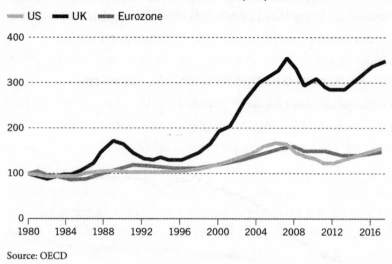

Source: OECD

Consider, also, that from the mid-1940s until the late 1990s, house prices and UK equities grew at broadly the same pace, with both rising three-fold in real terms. Since 1997, though, while equities have been broadly flat (volatile, but ending up roughly where they were), house prices have soared. That has attracted speculative investment flows to housing over the past two decades, bidding up prices further.

This speculative effect has been exacerbated by quantitative easing, emergency measures which rapidly expanded the Bank of England's balance sheet in response to the 2008 financial crisis. Since launching in March 2009, QE has pushed down bond yields and interest rates more generally, flattening returns on savings to such an extent that millions of UK adults have invested in a buy-to-let property rather than a company or personal pension. This has pushed up house prices more.

Official recognition of this side effect of such 'extraordinary monetary measures' has been a long time coming. But a 2018 Bank of England study acknowledged that extensive use of QE, which continued far longer than originally envisaged, explains an estimated 22 per cent of the rise in UK house prices since 2009.[29]

FIGURE 2.4: HOUSING AFFORDABILITY (1998–2017, 1998 = 100)

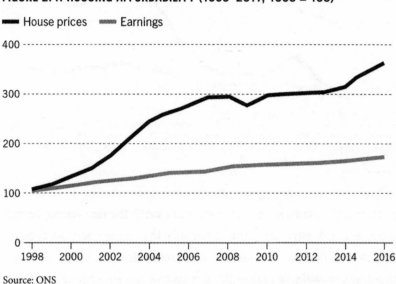

Source: ONS

During this third post-war house prices boom, the average UK house price rose 258 per cent between 1998 and 2017, while average household earnings grew just 68 per cent – as shown in Figure 2.4. This gets to the heart of the current affordability crisis, as expressed by the multiple of median-house-price to median-earnings multiple – in Figure 2.5. This key affordability metric has soared, with the average house costing the equivalent of 3.5 times average earnings in 1997, but almost 8 times today – an all-time high.

This is a UK-wide average ratio, of course. So in many parts of the country, the price–earnings affordability measures are far higher – with even a modest home costing ten times the average annual wage, or even more.

FIGURE 2.5: HOUSE-PRICE-TO-EARNINGS RATIO (1997–2015)

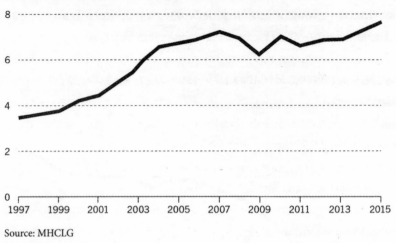

Source: MHCLG

Where the demand–supply mismatch is greatest – London and the south-east – house-price-to-earnings multiples are 12.2 times and 9.1 times respectively, as shown in Figure 2.6. These numbers are well above their 2007 peak. With banks rarely lending over five times salary, even a couple both working full time, with no child-care costs, can struggle to buy an average home in the UK's most populous region, even outside the capital.

But crushing affordability multiples extend way beyond the south-east and across the country – reaching 7.6 times in the south-west and 6.5 times across the Midlands, well over the long-term UK average of 3 to 4 times. In almost all parts of Britain, in fact, affordability multiples are significantly above historic norms.

The ongoing house-price boom, which originated in the mid-1990s, has taken its toll on the overall rate of UK home ownership. For a century, the share of households owning their own home grew, from 18 per cent in 1919, to 32 per cent in 1933, reaching 50 per cent in the early 1970s. Home ownership peaked at 73 per cent of all households in 2007 but has since declined to 63 per cent.

FIGURE 2.6: HOUSE-PRICE-TO-EARNINGS RATIO (BY REGION, 2018)

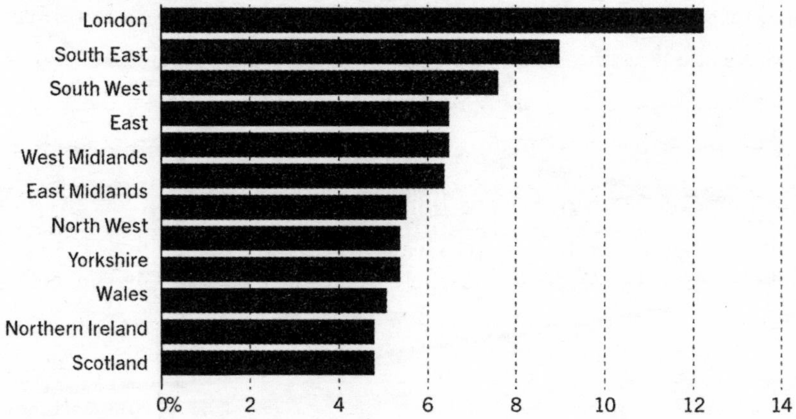

Region	
London	
South East	
South West	
East	
West Midlands	
East Midlands	
North West	
Yorkshire	
Wales	
Northern Ireland	
Scotland	

0%   2   4   6   8   10   12   14

Source: Nationwide and ONS

That means UK home ownership is now lower than in Spain, where 77 per cent of households are homeowners, the EU average of 69 per cent and 65 per cent in France.[30] Home ownership in Canada is 68 per cent and is 67 per cent in Australia and 64 per cent in the US.[31] So the UK is no longer what it has traditionally been – a society of high home ownership. This country has the fourth lowest rate of owner-occupancy among all EU nations and ranks below many non-European nations including the US, Australia and Canada. What's far more shocking than this decline of overall home ownership, though, is the plunge in the share of young adults, even well-paid professionals, who can afford to buy their own home.

GENERATION RENT

This steady fall in overall UK owner-occupancy, to levels still comparable with similar countries if now slightly lower, masks a far more dramatic and alarming decline in home ownership among young people.

FIGURE 2.7: HOME OWNERSHIP (BY AGE, ENGLAND, 1991–2016)

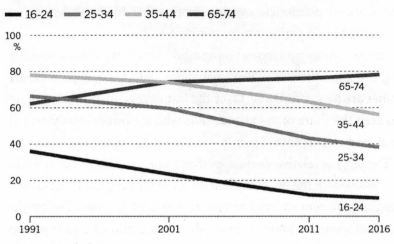

Source: English Housing Survey

In 1991, over one third of 16–24-year-olds owned their own home – either a flat or house. That share of young owner-occupiers has fallen to just a tenth on the most recent numbers – as shown in Figure 2.7. The proportion of slightly older adults with their own home, those aged 25–34 years old, has meanwhile collapsed from 67 per cent to just 38 per cent over the same period. Well over half of the current generation of young adults, then, is locked out of the property market at the age when couples most commonly look to have children. This is nothing short of an economic and social disaster.

There is evidence, as mentioned in the previous chapter, that this lack of home ownership is now impacting the rate at which, and even whether or not, families are choosing to have children. The UK's chronic housing affordability crisis, then, is weakening the country's broader demographic profile and, as such, our fiscal strength and growth potential.

Moving into middle age, some 78 per cent of 35–44-year-olds

were homeowners in the early 1990s, but only 56 per cent are now. The share of pensioners owning a home has, meanwhile, soared from roughly 60 per cent to 80 per cent.

Home ownership among young adults has fallen right across the UK, but the impact has been felt more sharply in regions where homes are least affordable. Over the last twenty years, every region has seen the share of 25–34-year-olds who are owner-occupiers fall by at least 10 percentage points – as shown in Figure 2.8.

The biggest relative decline, perhaps unsurprisingly, has been in London, where the ownership share among young adults has fallen from 46 per cent in 1996 to just 20 per cent in 2016. The southeast has seen the same measure drop from almost two-thirds to less than a third over the same twenty-year period. And in Yorkshire and Humberside, just 35 per cent of those aged twenty-five to thirty-four are now owner-occupiers, compared to 63 per cent two decades ago.[32]

FIGURE 2.8: HOME OWNERSHIP AMONG 25–34-YEAR-OLDS (BY REGION)

● 1995-96   ● 2015-16

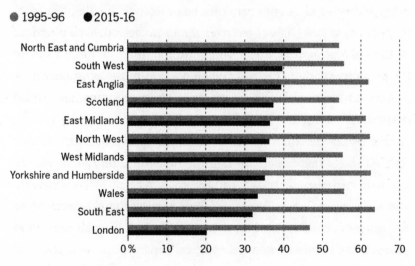

Source: Institute for Fiscal Studies

The smallest drop in home ownership among young adults has been in the north-east and Cumbria, the south-west and Scotland – but the fall has still been rather substantial. Across every single nation and region of the UK, in fact, the share of 25–34-year-olds who own their own home is now lower than it was in 1996 in London, where housing is always the least affordable.

Since 2008, banks and other lenders have restricted mortgage availability for young adults. Home loans for FTBs dropped sharply after the financial crisis, from around 100,000 to 40,000 per quarter. While that number has recovered to around 85,000, it remains well short of the 1985–2000 average – when 125,000 FTB mortgages were granted each quarter.[33] Industry data shows that the average income multiple lenders are granting on FTB mortgages in 2018 is 3.6 times – the highest on record.

The Nationwide Building Society calculates an affordability index specifically for FTBs who are generally looking for smaller homes and apartments. The UK-wide average house-price-to-earnings ratio for FTBs in March 2018 was 5.2 times – far higher than the average income-to-debt multiple offered to FTBs by lenders. The price multiple faced by FTBs rises to 6.0 times in the south-west and 9.8 times in London. Across the Midlands, too, the FTB price-to-earnings multiple is again historically high – approaching 5.0 times.[34]

The combination of house prices outstripping earnings growth and more limited mortgage availability means today's FTBs find it far harder than previous generations to amass the deposit needed to get that fabled 'foot on the housing ladder'. Such chronic unaffordability explains why around half of all FTBs across the UK now rely, to some extent, on their parents to help them get on the property ladder, rising to two-thirds in London and the south-east – a contentious issue that will be explored in more detail in Chapter III.

For young adults who don't have access to family money to buy their first home, the obstacles are formidable. Assuming they save a tenth of their gross income, up until the mid-1990s, FTBs needed to save for just two years to generate the necessary deposit on an average FTB home. By 2018, they would have needed to have saved for an average of ten years – five times longer.[35] At the same time, low interest rates mean that renting is currently far more expensive, from month to month, than paying a mortgage. This compounds the advantages of being able to buy, and the disadvantages of renting – with renters finding it ever harder to save up a deposit given low interest on their savings and high rental costs, as house prices rise ever further out of reach.

When those born in the 1940s were between the ages of twenty-six and thirty, they spent an average of 10 per cent of their income on housing costs, whether they rented or were paying a mortgage – as shown in Figure 2.9. By the time those born in the 1950s were in the same age range, house price rises had increased their housing costs to 15 per cent of income – with rising interest rates meaning mortgage-holders paid slightly more.

FIGURE 2.9: HOUSING COSTS AS SHARE OF INCOME (26–30-YEAR-OLDS, BIRTH DECADE)

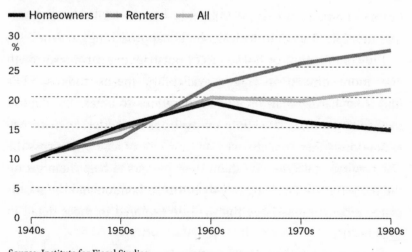

Source: Institute for Fiscal Studies

The cohort born in the 1960s spent around 20 per cent of their income on housing in their late twenties, as did those born in the 1970s. In the 1970s, though, the monthly cost of servicing a mortgage fell, relative to renting, as inflation eroded the real value of outstanding debts.

The steep house price rises of recent decades mean that those born in the 1980s – today's young adults – are spending 22 per cent of their incomes on housing, not much more than those born the decade before. But this average figure masks a large and fast-growing discrepancy between renters and those who have been lucky enough to buy.

Homeowners now in their late twenties and early thirties are spending just 15 per cent of their income on housing, reflecting low interest rates – as Figure 2.9 shows. If you can amass the large deposit now needed to buy, mortgage service costs are relatively low.[36] But housing costs for young adults in rented accommodation have soared towards 30 per cent of their income – and are much more in London and other hotspots with the most attractive employment opportunities. Renting, then, makes it so much harder for young tenants to save towards a deposit on a home of their own – which means family money is all the more important, particularly for those who lack access to such funding through no fault of their own.

Today's young adults have less chance of owning their own property than any post-war generation – which seems perverse. Only 40 per cent of those born in the mid-1980s were owner-occupiers by the age of thirty. This compares with 55 per cent of the 1940s and 1970s cohorts and over 60 per cent of the 1950s and 1960s cohorts.[37] The result is that, while the chances of home ownership are low for today's young adults, their overall housing costs are higher than any generation for almost a century – with unfortunate renters, rather than lucky homeowners, driving that unfortunate trend.

The increase in the ranks of private renters over the last two decades really is quite striking – as shown in Figure 2.10. No fewer than four out of every ten thirty-year-olds now lives in private rented accommodation, compared to just one in ten as recently as 1996. This is 'generation rent'. Not only is the incidence of renting among young adults so much higher now than in the past, but these would-be homebuyers are spending a much higher share of their total incomes on housing costs – paying rent approaching 30 per cent of their incomes, compared to just 15 per cent spent by the 'baby-boomers' born in the late 1940s and 1950s.

While often an acceptable form of tenure when 'footloose and fancy free', there is overwhelming evidence that private renting is far less desirable, and can be incredibly frustrating, as people move beyond young adulthood – bringing considerable insecurity and limiting life chances and choices.[38]

FIGURE 2.10: POPULATION SHARE IN RENTED HOMES BY AGE

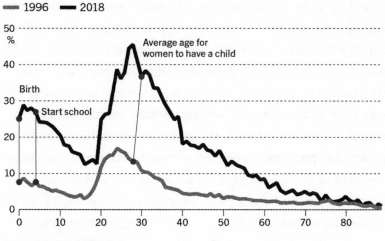

Source: Resolution Foundation

In 1996, just 8 per cent of babies were born to families living in rented accommodation. Twenty years later, that share has risen to 25 per cent – as Figure 2.10 shows. Almost 40 per cent of women at the average age to have a first baby in the UK are still renting, often against their will, compared to less than 15 per cent in 1996.[39]

While renting works well for some young adults, for countless others it provides low security of tenure and is particularly unattractive as they contemplate having children. Private renting is not just the least secure form of housing but also that with the worst record for housing quality. The sheer scale of young adults renting in the UK, and the sense of injustice they feel at being denied the same chance to buy a home which their parents enjoyed, is one of the cardinal political developments of our time. 'Generation rent' is coming of age, they are voting more, and – as their chance of ever buying their own home seems to slip away – getting increasingly angry.

ANTI-SOCIAL AND ANTI-SOCIETY

Another striking feature of the UK housing market is the sharp fall in the share of the population living in social housing – down from around 30 per cent in the late 1970s to 17 per cent in 2018. This fall has been driven, in part, by the astonishingly sharp decline in the extent to which local authorities are building homes for subsidised rental by low-income households and other vulnerable groups.

Back in 1969, when *The Times* wrote its 'Housing Anguish' editorial cited at the start of this chapter, local authorities built, or had built on their behalf, almost 140,000 homes that year. From the mid-1970s onwards, that source of new homes collapsed – falling to just a few hundred per annum during the 2000s, and an average of only 2,500 each year from 2010.[40] This striking fall in social housing provision, partially mitigated by the activities of non-profit housing associations, is at the heart of the UK's current epidemic of homelessness and rough sleeping.

The UK's chronic social housing shortage is, to a large extent, the result of this collapse of local authority building activity – Figure 2.11. This building slow-down has, in turn, been partly driven by the sky-high land costs faced by the state when buying land for social housing. For so long a largely forgotten part of public policy, barely mentioned by the mainstream media, social housing has of course become politically far more sensitive since the 2017 Grenfell Tower tragedy.

FIGURE 2.11: DWELLINGS BUILT BY LOCAL AUTHORITIES (1969–2016)

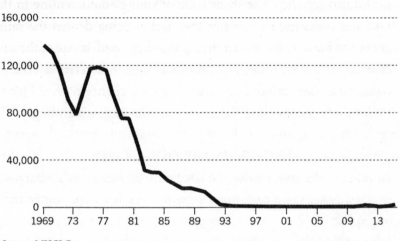

Source: MHCLG

What is less widely understood than the lack of social housing, and the impact of that on poverty and homelessness, is the extent to which our social housing shortage means the UK places much more reliance on, and hands increasing influence to, commercial housebuilders. In the late 1960s, the private sector accounted for just 49 per cent of all newly built homes. By 2017/18, that share of commercial provision had risen to 81 per cent, with the private housebuilding sector now far more concentrated, and less exposed to genuine competition, than it was fifty years ago.

Commercial housebuilders have and always will be very important to the UK's housing supply. They should account for the bulk of new-build homes in a nation like Britain – and incentivising them to deliver good-quality, keenly priced products in sufficient numbers to prevent prices spiralling, bringing affordability and market stability, is absolutely central to solving the UK's housing shortage.

But our current heavy over-reliance on private sector developers has, particularly since the 2008 financial crisis, allowed the large 'volume' builders to exert far too much political influence and unreasonably game the system, while successfully facing down significant supply-side reforms. It is vital that we have a mixed economy of housing provision, not only to provide the social housing that will always be needed for those on low incomes and other vulnerable groups, but also to prevent private housebuilders from becoming too powerful.

What's also vital is that space is found, on which planning permission is then granted, to build more homes – to buy and to rent, on behalf of both the private and the public sector. It is often said that the UK is a small, crowded country – and that our moribund planning system and serious homes shortage is a function of our geography.

The reality is rather different. According to the 2011 National Ecosystem Assessment, just 2 per cent of all land in England is covered with actual buildings.[41] The 'green belt', in comparison, covers 13 per cent of England's total acreage. Even maintaining today's average UK building density, which is rather low, releasing just 3 per cent of the green belt would provide space for almost two million new homes.[42]

Domestic buildings cover a mere 1.1 per cent of this country's land mass, with commercial buildings taking up another 0.6 per cent and roads and rail accounting for 2.2 per cent. Only around 11 per cent of total land across the UK is developed in any way, with another 3 per cent within our coastal borders covered by water.[43] All the rest – well over 80 per cent of the country – is 'space'.

Some UK land, of course, is mountainous, too remote or otherwise uninhabitable. Other parts are ecologically sensitive or of outstanding natural beauty. Yet Britain is still blessed with many, many acres of land eminently suitable for development that is being barely used, much of it within easy commuting distances of towns and cities. It is by no means environmentally irresponsible to observe that there is ample scope, while protecting areas of natural beauty and leaving ample space for wildlife and our own recreation, to build the homes that we need – for today's young adults and those of many generations to come.

The 'Britain is full' argument is often accompanied by the claim that 'we're concreting over the countryside'. Both are arrant nonsense. Given that the 25 million homes in the UK cover little more than 1 per cent of the land, you could increase the housing stock by a fifth – another five million homes – and use only another 0.2 per cent of our land mass. In addition, building density across Britain is very low by international standards, certainly in urban areas – as shown in Figure 2.12. So if we increase such density by developing more apartments, particularly in the UK's big cities, we would need even less than 0.2 per cent of our land mass to solve our chronic housing shortage.[44]

In London, there are just fifty-five inhabitants per hectare on average, rising to 101 per hectare in inner London. The population density of Bristol is fifty-two per hectare, while in Oxford it is thirty-five and in Peterborough just five.[45] By contrast, there are 213 people per hectare in inner Paris and 286 people per hectare in central Madrid.[46] The UK's relatively low urban density results from the lack of low-rise multi-storey apartment buildings that are common across the US, continental Europe and Asia. So we can maximise the use of already developed land and related infrastructure in our cities by building more intensely and building up – which, if done thoughtfully, can significantly enhance rather than blight urban and semi-urban districts, from both an aesthetic and economic point of view.

FIGURE 2.12: URBAN POPULATION-WEIGHTED DENSITY (2014)

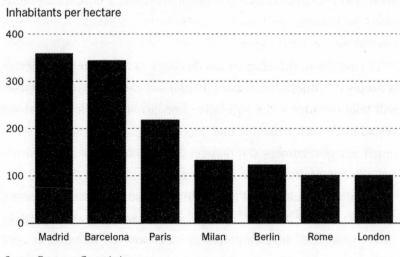

Inhabitants per hectare

Source: European Commission

It is clear that many of the barriers and key challenges we face in delivering more homes are linked to the same root cause – not the lack of land *per se*, but the lack of land made available for residential housebuilding. That takes us back to our planning system – and the manner in which the 1947 Town and Country Planning Act was partially dismantled, leaving us with a system heavily stacked towards private landowners, who have every incentive to develop land only very slowly, whatever the impact on broader society.

'Housing has not yet achieved the place of priority in official policy justified both by the social suffering involved and by the public concern that has been aroused,' wrote *The Times* in its 1969 editorial. Over the fifty years since then, as the policy responses of successive Conservative, Labour and coalition governments have become less and less adequate, the social suffering caused by our housing shortage, and related public anxiety, has become ever more intense.

The UK's long-standing shortage of homes, apparent half a century ago, is now far more acute. With house prices consistently outpacing earnings, we are now in the midst of a near-nationwide affordability crisis. Today's generation of young adults are spending more on housing, and are less likely to be owner-occupiers, than any cohort since the 1930s.

The graphs in this chapter tell the story of a housing market that is deeply dysfunctional. Solving Britain's chronic shortage of homes will take decades – the legislative hurdles are significant and the vested interests formidable that need to be faced down. There is not much any government can do over the course of one single Parliament dramatically to improve the situation.

But it is absolutely vital our political class demonstrates, beyond doubt, that it is finally taking radical and consistent steps to make sure commercial housebuilders are incentivised to build at least 250,000 homes each year, while providing far more social housing. Only then will younger voters feel they have a chance of buying their own home, with low-income workers able to secure decent social housing, so that society as a whole feels 'the system' is working for them.

Some say home ownership no longer matters. But that view is not shared by the vast majority of the UK population – and certainly not by 'generation rent', the millions of hard-working, aspirational young adults, living their lives under the shadow of the UK's cruelly dysfunctional housing market.

III

A PLACE OF OUR OWN

The vast majority of people have aspirations to own their home.
It is only by rethinking how the housing market works
that those aspirations will be achieved.[1]
SIR EDWARD LISTER, 2017

'It's a constant concern,' says Whitney Joseph, as we sip tea in a bustling café in Barking, on the outskirts of east London. 'As each year passes, and house prices rise – I'm worried it will just get worse.'

'The average salary in the south-east is around £34,000,' says her fiancé, Aaron Senessie, 'while the average house price is well over £400,000 – eleven or twelve times more.' Aaron looks at Whitney, then back at me. 'Even applying jointly, no lender will give us a mortgage anywhere close to that,' he says. 'We're saving hard and holding down good, professional jobs – but still we have no chance.'

This is the plight of two successful, highly motivated graduates, both of whom earn good money. Whitney is a 29-year-old trainee at a London law firm. Aaron is thirty and teaches mathematics at a leading secondary school. Having been a couple for several years, they are keen to get married and, while pursuing their respective careers, eventually start a family. 'Our natural next step is to buy a home,' says Whitney, the frustration visible on her face. 'We're putting as much aside as we can each month but there's no hope – the housing market is failing ordinary people like us.'

To help save, Whitney still lives with her parents. Aaron, meanwhile, rents a small bedroom in a shared house – lacking privacy and even the space for a proper desk to mark his pupils' books. 'We're not after hand-outs or an extravagant property,' he says. 'We've studied hard and we work hard – and now we desperately want, and feel we deserve, the opportunity to buy a place of our own.'

The story of Whitney and Aaron is the story of a generation – across not just the south-east but large parts of the UK. That's because our housebuilding industry represents one of the most important failures of capitalism in Britain today. Such is the scale of the dysfunction, in fact, and the extent of the economic and social fallout, that it is provoking – for Whitney and Aaron's generation – a crisis of confidence in 'the system' itself.

In her October 2017 Conservative Party conference speech, Theresa May spoke in soaring rhetorical terms about the 'British Dream' – a vision built around home ownership for the masses, with each generation being better off than the one before. 'I will dedicate my premiership to restoring hope, to renewing the British Dream for a new generation – and that means fixing our broken housing market,' the then Prime Minister told delegates gathered in Manchester.[2] Labour leader Jeremy Corbyn, too, while wanting more social housing to be built and owned by the state than his Tory opponent, has similarly often argued that 'everyone who works hard should be able to own their own home.'[3]

UK home ownership peaked at 73 per cent of all households in 2007, as mentioned in Chapter II. Since then, the share of owner-occupation has fallen to 63 per cent, rising among pensioners, but dropping very sharply among every other age group. While 36 per cent of all 16–24-year-olds owned their own home in 1991, by 2016 it was just 10 per cent. The share of 25–34-year-old owner-occupiers fell from 67 per cent to 38 per cent over the same period – with well over half a generation locked out of the property market at this crucial family-forming age. Moving into middle age, 78 per cent of 35–44-year-olds were homeowners in 1991, but just 56 per cent twenty-five years later. The share of pensioners owning a home, in contrast, soared – from roughly 60 per cent to 80 per cent.[4]

Whitney Joseph and Aaron Senessie, then, are part of the 62 per cent of 25–34-year-olds who are not owner-occupiers, often despite their desires, aspirations and concerted efforts to buy their own home. As such, around three-fifths of an entire generation is now locked out of the UK's property market. Even professional youngsters, who may have grown up in owner-occupied houses in leafy suburbs, are routinely failing to achieve the certainty and security that comes with buying suitable basic accommodation as they look to have a family, let alone purchase a property similar to their childhood home. Such a sudden and stark reversal in generational fortunes, on such an overwhelming scale, tears at the social fabric.

Some 71 per cent of those living in rented accommodation in the UK aspire to own their own home, with 86 per cent of the population as a whole viewing home ownership as superior to living as a tenant.[5] Home ownership is still widely perceived as an important life ambition, one that previous generations have enjoyed and future generations should too. The available evidence overwhelmingly points to the vast majority of people wanting to be owner-occupiers.

With overall home ownership now below two-thirds, that suggests a large slice of the population – a majority across several younger age groups – wants to buy but, like Whitney and Aaron, have had the steel door of unaffordability slammed in their face.

NO RIGHT TO BUY

This desire to be an owner-occupier should not be surprising. Property ownership, repeated studies show, makes people feel more happy and secure. Buying a home is, for millions, an important rite of passage, as well as a strong incentive to gain skills, work hard and live responsible, stable lives.

At the most basic level, renting is typically far more expensive than owner-occupancy. Tenants across all age groups spend an average of 35 per cent of household income on rent, while owner-occupiers spend 17 per cent on mortgage payments.[6] This helps explain why, during the decade after the financial crisis, average household incomes after housing costs for those renting have risen by just 4 per cent, while those for mortgage-holders have gone up 17 per cent.[7]

So renting costs more each month than servicing a mortgage – and rented homes also tend to be smaller and of inferior quality. The average rented home is 76 square metres, while the average owner-occupied residence is 108 square metres. Some 28 per cent of homes in the private rental sector failed to meet the government's Decent Homes Standard in 2016, compared to 18 per cent of owner-occupied homes.[8]

While providing better homes, owner-occupancy also frees families from the inherent insecurity of tenancy agreements, while encouraging them to maintain and invest in their properties – which benefits the broader economy. And those paying off their own home loans, of course, rather than paying rent 'down the drain' to service their landlord's mortgage, will ultimately benefit from tax-free capital gains and the outright ownership of a valuable asset. Being an owner-occupier, then, has traditionally given ordinary working people, even those on modest incomes, a chance to accumulate capital, providing them with an ability to leave money to their children, a tangible 'stake' in the economy and more control over their lives.

Academic research has also consistently shown a positive link between owner-occupancy and participation in community organisations and broader civic engagement, with ownership speaking to a visceral human instinct.[9] Broad owner-occupancy, then, makes societies not just more productive, but more stable. As such, property-owning democracies are less prone to populism and even radicalisation – as Lloyd George well understood at the end of the First World War. Individuals are more likely to believe in and support capitalism, after all, when they own some actual capital.

The UK's chronic home shortage, though, means millions of young adults are now 'priced out' of the housing market altogether – unable to rent or buy. One sad result is that young adults are increasingly unable to leave their childhood home. The number of 20–34-year-olds living with their parents rose no less than 47 per cent from 2006 to 2016, reaching 3.4 million according to ONS data – including 20 per cent of women in that age range and an astonishing 32 per cent of men.

In addition to single adults living with their parents, the affordability crisis has also driven up the number of 'concealed households' – that is couples, with or without children, living within another household. Internal government estimates indicate that the number of concealed households rose by 50 per cent from 2006 to 2016, to 2.5 million – an extremely significant number, pointing to frequent over-crowding, given that there are around 28 million UK households in total. And the number of concealed family units living within other households in London soared by no less than 80 per cent over the same period, to an estimated 720,000.[10]

Despite spending more than previous generations on housing, today's young adults also endure longer commutes to work – as the lack of homes, and related high housing costs, push them further away from city centres. There are now 3.2 million workers with daily commutes exceeding two hours each way, some 34 per cent more than in 2007.[11] As people move to less central locations in a bid to buy or rent an affordable home, the resultant longer journeys not only lower productivity but, clearly, negatively impact family life, health and general wellbeing.

And, of course, as prices spiral way ahead of wages, ever more young adults – including those holding down professional jobs – need financial help from their family if they are to buy their first property. This is one of the major property market trends of our time.

In 2017, family and friends contributed an estimated £6.5 billion to help FTBs, up no less than 30 per cent on the previous year, supporting almost 300,000 transactions.[12] With mortgage rates still close to record lows, few struggle to make the monthly repayments once, with family assistance, they have bought their first home. The biggest obstacle is amassing a deposit – with 70 per cent of those who received parental help admitting, had they not had such assistance, they would still be renting.

Taking such a route is only possible, of course, for those from relatively wealthy backgrounds. This lays bare an uncomfortable truth – the growing gulf between Britain's 'property haves' and 'property have-nots', a gulf that is now increasingly likely to be maintained from one generation to the next, seriously undermining the notion that Britain is a progressive society. That's why the UK housing market, traditionally a source of social mobility and financial security, is now fuelling social immobility and resentment.

With this affordability crisis pricing out successive generations of young adults, more and more people are being forced into a life of renting. Since 1997, the numbers of households in the private rented sector has risen substantially, from 2.1 million to 4.7 million.[13] Some nine million working-age adults, and around 870,000 retirees, now live in rented homes. The vast majority of this privately rented accommodation is owned by the UK's 2.5 million buy-to-let landlords, each of whom owns an average of 1.8 rental properties.[14]

FIGURE 3.1: TRENDS IN HOUSING TENURE

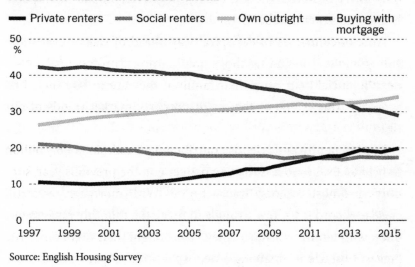

Source: English Housing Survey

This shift away from ownership and towards renting caused by the overall lack of homes and the related affordability crisis has very significantly changed the shape of the housing market – as shown in Figure 3.1. Less than 30 per cent of homes are occupied by a household paying off a mortgage, down from 43 per cent back in 1997. Since 2013, a home has been more likely to be owned outright, often by retirees. At the same time, the gap between the share of owner-occupiers still paying off their home loan and those renting has fallen from well over 30 percentage points to less than 10 percentage points.

While the number of homes purchased by people aged twenty-five to forty-four with a mortgage dropped by over 1.6 million over the last decade, the number of homes owned outright by those above sixty-five has increased by more than 1.4 million. Such trends, with young adults owning relatively fewer homes and the older generation owning more, are set to become more acute. A major reason is because almost three-fifths of those who haven't yet bought a home are saving nothing whatsoever towards a deposit for their own property. In many cases, this is hardly surprising – given low wage growth and the shortage of rental properties, which drives up the cost of rent, making monthly saving extremely tough.[15]

With house prices generally still rising faster than earnings across much of the country, 'generation rent' is set to keep expanding. Having more than doubled to 4.7 million since 1997, the number of households in private rented accommodation is set to increase to 7.2 million by 2025, according to projections by PwC. By then, the accountancy firm predicts, just 26 per cent of 25–34-year-olds will own their own home, down from 38 per cent in 2016.[16] The harsh reality is that increasing numbers of well educated, hard-working people who want to start a family, people like Whitney and Aaron, will never fulfil their dream of becoming owner-occupiers.

While the UK is most definitely a nation of aspirational home-owners, those aspirations could soon be thwarted for the majority of our entire population – with owner-occupiers set to become a minority overall. From 2010 until 2016, the share of owner-occupant homeowners fell by 5 percentage points while those in the rental sector rose by 5 percentage points. Should this trend persist, by 2039 the scale will tip, with homeowners accounting for less than half of all households for the first time since the early 1970s. That, in the eyes of the vast majority of the population, would amount to a major reversal in our national fortune.

THE ECONOMY, STUPID

The rate at which the UK has been building homes has slowed significantly over recent decades, particularly when compared to other nations across the EU. During the 1980s, the total UK housing stock grew by just 1 per cent a year, compared to average EU growth of 1.4 per cent. The following decade, Britain's housing stock increased by just 0.7 per cent per annum, with EU nations chalking up a much higher 1.7 per cent annual growth rate. From 2000 to 2004, that very slow 0.7 per cent UK housing stock growth rate was repeated, as the EU average rose to 1.8 per cent.[17]

This ultra-slow rate of housebuilding clearly contributes to far more costly housing – with the average UK house price rising 219 per cent in real terms between 1985 and 2015, compared to just 10 per cent in Germany, 28 per cent in Italy and 120 per cent in France.[18] By channelling far too high a share of savings into housing rather than more productive assets, this contributes to economic stultification. While longer commutes harm productivity, health and wellbeing, high housing costs also hinder the ability of firms to attract workers to the industrial, tech and service-sector clusters vital for future UK innovation, growth and broader economic prosperity.

UK employment growth is dominated by London, which accounts for more than one in three new jobs.[19] But sky-high housing costs make it hard for people to move not just to the capital, but smaller cities too.[20] That's why we're seeing more over-crowding and even the emergence of modern-day slums – including the 'Beds in Sheds' phenomenon described in Chapter I – in London and other regional centres.

One of the defining features of British life, in fact, the pattern of young people moving from small towns to bigger cities to build their careers, is now in dramatic decline. Over the last two decades, the number of 25–34-year-olds who move home and start a new job each year has fallen no less than 40 per cent, with high housing costs in employment hot-spots increasingly wiping out the financial gains of such moves.

Research from the Resolution Foundation shows that a young adult making the relatively short move from the coastal town of Scarborough to the city of Leeds, both in Yorkshire, would in 1997 have seen a 29 per cent rise in their income after housing costs, given relative average wages and rents in each place. But the subsequent increase in Leeds rents, and stagnant wages, mean the same move in 2018 results in a financial gain of just 4 per cent.[21]

For a young adult moving from the UK regions into London, the economics are even more daunting. A 25–34-year-old renting in Corby in Northamptonshire who wanted to move to the outlying London suburb of Barnet stood to gain a 6 per cent rise in their income in 1997, with higher London wages outweighing higher housing costs. By 2018, though, that net income gain had become instead a 22 per cent net loss, with rents having risen far faster than wages.

Whereas previous generations were able to move to big cities such as London, Manchester and Leeds, or regional hubs like Bristol to develop their careers, the 'millennials' are enduring a slump in geographic mobility, ultimately caused by the slow pace of house-building over decades and the resulting affordability crisis. Bigger salaries in cities are not as big as they were – and they are, in many cases, being entirely swallowed up by higher housing costs.

So the UK's chronic lack of homes is reducing labour mobility, leading to shortages in areas with high house prices – as talented people struggle to move close to the job opportunities best allowing them to develop their careers and potential. This drives down average wages in places where workers are 'left behind', while pushing wages up where skilled labour is needed most – hindering business development and further exacerbating regional inequalities. Our housing crisis, then, isn't only impacting general wellbeing and the environment by causing longer commutes, and undermining opportunity and ambition, it is also stifling broader UK growth and prosperity given the chronic shortage of homes within easy reach of the most potentially productive jobs.

In 2015, Enrico Moretti and Chang-Tai Hsieh, two talented US economists, attempted to estimate the impact of America's housing shortage on productivity. They concluded that US growth between

1964 and 2009 was no less than 50 per cent lower than it would otherwise have been had enough housing been built in the right place.[22] This reflects the fact that the parts of the US with the highest productivity, like New York and San Francisco, also have the most stringent restrictions on building more homes – which raises business rents and prevents many well-qualified workers from moving to fill the best job opportunities, limiting the expansion of companies that could otherwise have employed them.

Despite the clear implications of Britain's housing shortage on productivity, the author is aware of no serious study which attempts to measure this important phenomenon across the UK. Consider, though, that the value of land upon which US houses are built is estimated at around $10,000 billion, or 10 per cent of total US wealth.[23] This reflects the vast difference between the cost of farmland and land made available for residential building, which in turn demonstrates the value of the official permissions and other planning consents. In the US, the scarcity value of such permissions is extremely high – amounting to approximately a tenth of the total wealth of the world's biggest economy. And that is reflected, in turn, in the very high estimated impact such restrictive planning constraints have had on the US economy over recent decades, with growth no less than 50 per cent lower than it would have been between the mid-1960s and the start of the global financial crisis, had such restrictions been lighter.

It turns out that the value of the land on which UK houses are built is, in relative terms, even higher than the US – suggesting that Britain's planning system hinders growth to an even greater extent. Figures from the ONS imply the land under UK dwellings is valued at £4.1 trillion – equivalent to around 40 per cent of this country's net wealth, a share approaching four times that of the US.[24] The clear implication is that Britain's restrictive planning laws are doing even more to prevent people and businesses moving to the most productive places than in America, damaging UK growth to an even greater extent than Moretti and Chang-Tai estimated in the US.

The scale of the monopoly 'rents' generated in the UK, the 'dead-weight' loss to GDP, as reflected in the extent to which land values are artificially boosted by residential planning permission, is clearly vast. And this huge sum is then included in the price which ordinary people, often young adults hoping to start a family, then face when trying to buy a home. The costs of our housing shortage, then, are not solely felt in terms of stress, health and the environment. The UK's affordability crisis also stymies productivity, seriously undermining growth and future prosperity.

Britain's chronic lack of homes therefore has major economic drawbacks. It is fuelling not only inter-generational tensions, but also compounding regional income disparities – both of which are contributing to political resentment and a shift away from moderate, centrist politics. The constrained supply of housing and land for development reduces choice for homebuyers, with over-powerful developers building some of the smallest homes in Europe, often with inadequate regard to quality and design – an issue that will be explored in later chapters.

More generally, falling home ownership is hindering the ambition and life chances of millions of young adults, undermining family formation as couples delay and even decide against having children due to a lack of adequate housing while, at the same time, reducing freedom and increasing the power and influence of the state. Given the traditional volatility of the UK's property market, and with house prices having grown so much more than earnings over recent decades, it is also worth pointing out the current affordability crisis, on top of everything else, has increased the risks of another financial collapse.

Back in July 2014, Bank of England deputy governor Sir Jon Cunliffe issued a stark warning, saying that the housing market poses

the 'biggest risk' to the UK economy. 'Prices rising faster than people's incomes,' he said, 'leads to a big increase in the amount of debt
in the economy,' which then poses a danger.[25] The previous month,
the International Monetary Fund had warned that accelerating
house prices were the greatest threat to the UK's economic recovery. 'House price inflation is particularly high in London, and is
becoming more widespread,' said the IMF. 'A steady increase in the
size of new mortgages compared with borrower incomes suggests
that households are gradually becoming more vulnerable to income
and interest rate shocks.'[26]

Since these mid-2014 warnings, the average UK house price has
risen by almost 20 per cent – from £178,124 to £215,910 at the time
of writing.[27] Lenders have started to offer so-called 'monster mortgages' once more – loans amounting to 95 or even 100 per cent of
the value of the property being bought, on multiples of five times
earnings or more, with only a 5 per cent deposit.

Such products, ahead of the financial crisis, were widely viewed
as reckless and irresponsible. After the 2008 collapse, the multiple
of annual earnings lenders could extend to homebuyers was immediately slashed. But multiples have since returned to pre-crisis
levels – pointing to renewed dangers that lenders are creating yet
another dangerous house price bubble. The largest new mortgages
are actually even more of a burden than those offered prior to
the crisis – with repayment periods stretching over thirty or even
thirty-five years, rather than the traditional 25-year term, to allow
larger loans to be made for a given monthly payment.[28]

What has also changed since the last crisis is that consumers have
become even more indebted. In 2017, UK households as a whole
saw their annual outgoings surpass their income for the first time
in thirty years. Even in the run-up to the financial crisis of 2008 and
2009, the country did not reach a point where the average household was a net borrower.

In 2017, though, households took out nearly £80 billion in loans while depositing just £37 billion with UK banks, according to ONS data – accumulating more debts than assets (including pensions and other personal investments) for the first time since such records began in 1987. 'If this were to continue,' the ONS warned, 'households could risk lacking enough collateral to cover their debts.'[29]

Borrowing has become elevated in part because interest rates are low, with the Bank of England's base rate at just 0.75 per cent at the time of writing, compared to 15 per cent in the early 1990s. The implication is, though, that interest rates have a long way to rise – which would, of course, increase the cost of debt service for many households. That's why the Bank of England in May 2019 raised a red flag over the state of the mortgage market, warning lenders that stricter minimum capital requirements could be imposed, to help avoid the kind of risks that led to the 2008 financial crisis.

'We, together with many others, have done a huge amount to make the financial system safer over the last ten years,' said Sam Woods, the Head of the Bank of England's Prudential Regulation Authority, in an address to the Building Societies Association. 'But the lesson of financial history is that unless we are absolutely vigilant ... then this safety can easily slip through our hands.'[30]

In sum, a major increase in the rate of UK housebuilding would bring very significant benefits in terms of consumer happiness and wellbeing. Housing costs would fall, for both renters and buyers, with more young adults in particular able to fulfil what for many is a natural ambition to buy their own home. Cheaper housing – or at least a slow-down in the rate of price growth, allowing wages to catch up – would promote labour market flexibility and higher productivity, while spreading wealth across the regions. It would also significantly reduce the chances of yet another damaging house price collapse, and the related economic and financial fallout.

On top of all that, a sizeable housebuilding drive would provide the UK economy, after several years of Brexit-related uncertainty, with a much-needed economic boost. Every UK recovery from recession over the past century has been associated with a sharp rise in the number of homes built – with the exception of the post-2008 recovery. It is no coincidence, given the slow pace of housebuilding since the financial crisis, that we have just lived through the longest and slowest recovery in British history.

YOUTHQUAKE

In June 2017, the wealthiest 10 per cent of UK adults owned around half of Britain's wealth, with the richest 1 per cent controlling no less than 14 per cent.[31] Even these shocking numbers are surely an underestimate, given the difficulties in identifying the assets of the super-rich. An unfortunate 15 per cent, by contrast, have no or negative wealth.

Some inequality is inevitable, and even desirable, under a capitalist system. But having fallen steadily during the decade from 1997 to 2007, wealth inequality has spiralled upward since the 2008 global financial crisis – not least due to the overall fall in home ownership, linked in turn to the inability of increasing numbers of young adults to buy their own home.

In the May 2015 general election, David Cameron's Conservatives gained 36 per cent of votes among 30–39-year-olds, compared to 34 per cent of the same age group who backed Ed Miliband's Labour Party. In the election of June 2017, that position was transformed. Jeremy Corbyn's more hard-line Labour Party attracted 55 per cent of voters in their thirties, while Theresa May's Conservatives trailed badly, with just 29 per cent.

With even high-achieving professionals now often facing a locked door of housing unaffordability, a growing number of voters are concluding that capitalism isn't working for them. Just as owner-occupiers are more likely to vote Conservative, young adults desperately upset they are unable to buy a home as their parents did are increasingly prone to vote for politicians offering to 'shake things up' – hence Corbyn's strong showing in 2017.

Heavy Labour support among students and twenty-somethings isn't unusual. What is new – and potentially disastrous for the Conservatives – is that those in their thirties and early forties, missing out on the security and invested wealth of home ownership, in turn driving lower family formation, are proving themselves far less likely to 'graduate' to the Tories.

Polling conducted by YouGov in 2018 found that almost one in five 18–24-year-olds thought it would be at least two decades before they could own their own home. Almost one in ten thought they could never afford it, even at that young age. Making housing more affordable was their top priority for government, chosen by 41 per cent of this cohort as the most immediate way the state could improve their lives.[32]

Among the 25–34-year-old age group, too, housing affordability featured strongly in their policy concerns, second only to the overall cost of living. And across both age groups, there was an overwhelming preference for policies designed to increase the chances of home ownership, rather than reducing the cost or increasing the security of renting.

Broad and largely accessible UK home ownership has, for many decades, guarded against an unhealthy and potentially destabilising concentration of wealth. Yet this long-standing feature of British society, a natural corrective, is now going into reverse. The UK's housing affordability crisis has been instrumental in convincing a growing number of voters that capitalism is unfair – from low-income workers to high-achieving professionals. With many people's capacity to buy a home now determined by their parental wealth rather than their own hard work, the UK housing market is entrenching wealth inequalities, rather than providing an opportunity for ordinary working people, over the course of their lifetime, to amass some wealth by taking ownership of a valuable asset.

Some commentators saw the link between the UK's dysfunctional housing market and a possible Corbyn premiership ahead of the June 2017 election.[33] But it was only after Labour came within a whisker of power that Theresa May's rhetoric began to reflect the reality that millions of voters in their thirties and forties who should be natural Tory-supporting property owners were instead unhappily renting or living with their parents – and therefore prepared to vote for something more radical.

In March 2018, the Prime Minister once again identified the UK housing market as 'the biggest threat to the British dream – that every generation has a better future than the last'. Addressing the National Planning Conference, May admitted that the June 2017 election campaign had showed her 'that many people, particularly younger people, are angry' about the housing shortage. She warned that if large housebuilders failed to 'do their duty to Britain' and build more homes more quickly, then 'the government would step in to make sure enough new homes are built'.[34] In her October 2018 Conservative Party conference speech, May reiterated that 'solving the housing crisis is the biggest domestic policy challenge of our generation', once again stressing that 'we will only fix this broken market by building more homes'.

Despite widespread opposition to development among so-called Not In My Back Yard (NIMBY) objectors, there is growing support for more homes to be built.[35] Polling in September 2018 indicated that voters overwhelmingly think house prices are now too high, supporting more housebuilding in their area by a margin of 48 per cent to 33 per cent – a sharp turnaround on just five or six years ago. Today's NIMBYs are starting to realise that it is their children and grandchildren who are being penalised by the UK's chronic housing shortage.

Falling UK home ownership among young adults, then, continuing as they move into middle age, has become a source of inter-generational conflict. But there are the very early signs of a growing consensus that the housing market is everyone's problem. Those who already own their home, after all, are ultimately dependent on someone else buying it. A Burkean inter-generational contract needs to be restored between those who wish to own their home, those that already do and those who perhaps want to sell up to leave money to their descendants and/or finance their retirement.[36]

• • •

Lenny and Yolande Joseph are sitting in the living room of their house in Barking, on the far reaches of east London. For thirty years, Lenny has been an engineer with British Telecom. Yolande helps at a local primary school. With them are their daughter Whitney and her fiancée, Aaron. Despite their qualifications and promise, after years of searching and putting money aside, these bright, hard-working young adults remain 'priced out' of the property market.

Lenny was 'about twenty-six or twenty-seven' when he and Yolande bought their first home. 'It was a struggle, but achievable,' he tells me. 'We were just an ordinary couple, we had no fancy qualifications, but we worked, saved and did it – and after that, instead of paying rent to someone else, we had the security of our own home.'

Yolande looks fondly at her daughter, then back at me. 'We felt, right, this is it: we're putting down foundations, a solid base for our children,' she says, her pride in this achievement still obvious, decades on. 'We bought a home and hoped our children would grow up to do the same.'

Whitney is certainly trying. But as hard as she and Aaron save towards a deposit, as house prices keep rising, they are unable to reach their goal. 'It's crazy,' says Lenny. 'These kids have university degrees and great jobs, far more than we ever had – but when it comes to property, they can't afford a matchbox.'

Whitney, who is twenty-nine, has two siblings in their mid-thirties, both of whom bought homes when they were younger than she is now. Since then, as property prices have spiralled ahead of wages, homes have become even more unaffordable for countless young adults. 'If I had the job I have now five or ten years ago, we wouldn't be having this conversation,' Whitney says, with genuine frustration. 'Me being on the housing ladder wouldn't be an issue – because I'd already be on it.'

'It's an uphill struggle, we're saving as much as we can but always battling rising prices,' says Aaron, taking Whitney's hand.

'Actually, it's really upsetting – and constantly on my mind,' Whitney continues. 'However hard we try, the market pulls away from us,' she says, her eyes now moist with tears.

IV

A BROKEN MARKET

I have always felt that the best security for civilization is the dwelling – and that upon properly appointed and becoming dwellings depends, more than anything else, the improvement of mankind.[1]

BENJAMIN DISRAELI, 1874

The government's Housing White Paper of February 2017 opens with the following statement: 'The housing market in this country is broken, and the cause is very simple: for too long, we haven't built enough homes.'[2]

Over many years, the UK's private sector housebuilding industry has failed to respond to higher house prices by significantly raising output – that is, the number of homes being completed and made available for sale. The resulting housing supply shortfall, by pushing prices even higher and increasingly ahead of earnings, has sparked a now chronic affordability crisis, that is causing widespread economic and social damage.

This chapter outlines the 'speculative' business model that dominates UK housebuilding – and identifies seven inter-related characteristics of the housing market that prevent supply from responding adequately to higher prices. These seven features, taken together, have helped create a shortage of homes which has grown far more acute since the 2008 global financial crisis – resulting in rising numbers of would-be homebuyers being priced out of the housing market.

Britain's 'broken housing market' is a market failure with very significant societal implications indeed. Residential construction has, particularly over the last decade, become ever more dominated by large 'volume' housebuilders – those producing over 2,000 homes a year, which are well placed to access land and able to exert market power by controlling local 'build-out' rates.

Given the importance of housing not only as a place to live and raise children but as a traditional generator and store of long-term wealth and security for the majority of families, the UK's chronic housing shortage, unless it is seriously addressed – and soon – could upend British politics.

RISKY BUSINESS?

The UK's private sector housing industry revolves around a 'speculative' or 'current trader' model of housebuilding. This is essentially a cyclical process of raising finance, buying land, securing planning permission, constructing the homes and then selling them. The developer is acting 'speculatively' because they are not building for a known purchaser or selling at a known price. They build, instead, for sale on the open market to whomever is prepared to pay the most for the new home.

Speculative developers are exposed to big risks but often glean big rewards. The major risk they take is on their land purchases, which they make at prices based on the estimated sale price they believe they will get for the homes they eventually build, as long as they can secure planning permission – which, itself, can sometimes be uncertain.

This is known as the 'residual valuation' method of determining land prices – under which the developer's profit is the margin between the sale price achieved and the total amount spent on the entire development process, including the land purchase, which is often the first and largest cost that developers incur.

The cardinal feature of the UK housebuilding industry, then, is that whichever firm is able to most squeeze future building and other costs is able to pay the most for the land, and thus generally ends up securing the land. Because of the often intense competition for acreage likely to gain planning permission, the resulting pressure on building and other costs is also fierce.

As such, the speculative building model drives out and intrinsically fails to deliver the aspects of housebuilding which matter most for those buying new homes and the broader community – including value for money, the size of the house or flat offered for sale and build quality, along with the provision of affordable housing and local infrastructure as part of the condition of planning permission.

At the same time, speculative housebuilding pushes up land prices – and, therefore, the eventual price paid by homebuyers for what are often small, sub-standard homes. This, in turn, means that sellers of land – who will not sell their site willingly unless they feel they are getting the best possible return – will, as a rule, sit on their land for many years and watch prices rise ever more. This applies whether the landowner is a private individual such as a farmer, a speculative land trading company or even the state itself.

Obtaining planning permission can be a complex, unpredictable process, often exposed to the vagaries of fraught local politics and endless appeals. So there are often long time-lags between a developer buying land and the sale of finished homes, during which considerable amounts of capital are at risk. This creates high barriers to entry for new housebuilding firms and can push out SME builders as they struggle to raise and then finance debt to invest in such a highly competitive, risk-prone land market, characterised by high prices.

Large, well-established developers meanwhile consolidate their advantages by prioritising risk-reducing strategies such as amassing large strategic land banks and seeking to dominate local new-build markets – keeping house prices high and rising by building out sites very slowly, 'drip-feeding' supply by adding only gradually to the housing stock.

With SMEs unable to mount a serious challenge, particularly after so many smaller builders were wiped out after the 2009 banking collapse, the UK's speculative housebuilding model is clearly failing to deliver the homes required, both in terms of numbers and affordability. Large developers now have serious market power, allowing them to slow down total housing output to such an extent that prices in most localities have kept rising over the last decade, and are now very high by historic standards, despite sluggish wage growth.

This gets us to the conundrum at the heart of the UK's broken housing market. When prices are weak, powerful developers suspend land acquisitions and cut build-out rates sharply in order to avoid selling into a falling market. When prices are rising, in contrast, the same developers compete even more fiercely to acquire land – which means that, once acreage is secured, it becomes even more important to supply homes only very slowly to achieve eventual sale prices that maintain a healthy margin, having paid elevated initial land costs. Unchecked by a much higher number of homes coming to the market, then, prices continue to spiral upward.

If residential construction is left almost entirely to private developers operating on a speculative model – as has been the case since housebuilding by local authorities largely ceased in the 1980s – the industry forms what, from a societal perspective, has been dubbed a 'negative loop'.[3] As affordability gets worse, there are fewer housing market transactions overall, which leads to the construction of fewer new-build homes by speculative developers. So prices rise further, making homes even less affordable, which lowers the number of transactions – and thus the number of new-build homes – even more.

Property prices are determined by more than the supply of new homes and the number of new households being formed, of course. Credit availability, the extent to which banks are willing and permitted by the regulatory authorities to extend mortgages to prospective homebuyers, is also very significant. But a housebuilding model has emerged in the UK which sees housing output drop rapidly during a recession, as the industry moves to prevent prices from sharply falling. During each subsequent recovery and credit boom, though, as housing supply fails adequately to respond to rising purchasing power, house prices are ratcheted up even more.

The result is that, over the last fifty years, during each housing cycle, the volume of peak private sector housebuilding has been lower and the average house-price higher than during the previous cycle. The UK's private construction industry built over 200,000 homes in 1968, before falling back, but just 176,000 when it peaked again in 1988. The next peak in private sector housebuilding was in 2007, when 154,000 homes were built. And, at the time of writing, the latest data shows the private developers built 135,000 homes in 2018.[4] During this fifty-year period, the average UK house price went up more than three-fold in real, inflation-adjusted terms.[5]

In countries including Germany, Taiwan, South Korea and in parts of the US, the state plays more of an interventionist role in the market for residential land – actions which help drive urban development, influence house prices and can have a major effect on national growth strategies, as will be discussed in later chapters of *Home Truths*. In the UK, the overwhelming predominance of the speculative development model exposes the entire housing industry to an ultra-competitive land market – which means it is practically impossible to run a business specialising in 'low cost' homes, producing large volumes at lower margins.

That's because in order to secure land, almost all developers – whatever their preferred business model, and however large a gap they see between demand and supply – need to make the same hard-nosed assumptions about future high sale prices, relatively low quality and the deliberately slow roll-out of homes while being determined to incur the minimal possible costs to provide affordable housing, available at sub-market prices to certain groups – whatever promises they have previously made to local planning authorities.

A failure to make such assumptions would see any developer lose out, with the land going instead to a buyer that does. And a failure to act on such assumptions would see a developer, having paid such high land prices, quickly go bankrupt.

As such, anyone who wants to run a UK housebuilding firm offering homes at lower prices and higher volumes, while cheerfully fulfilling affordable housing obligations, would be consistently outbid when trying to buy land suitable for residential building. That's the reality of the 'residual valuation' method which predominates in the market for such land, under the 'speculative' housebuilding model.

The large developers which provide a disproportionately high share of UK homes are, in essence, land-buying, land-holding and land-trading firms first and foremost, with deep pockets and access to capital, able to manage risk over long periods of time. Such firms are extremely profitable when house prices are rising, but also relatively well protected from the inevitable market downturns which the speculative development system unavoidably generates from time to time.

The UK's housebuilding model is competitive only in the sense that the market for land is competitive – but the benefits of such competition accrue not to millions of prospective homebuyers, or even those trying to access a rental property. They accrue, instead, to the still massively powerful vested interest of landowners – whether individuals, developers or land agents – who are able to sit on land and extract vast windfall returns.

By tying up large amounts of capital for long periods of time, the UK's speculative system intrinsically encourages an unhealthy over-concentration within the private housebuilding industry. The logical outcome of this arrangement is an ever smaller number of large developers exercising undue market influence, to the detriment of consumers. This model also, by definition, produces homes for sale at a rate deliberately set so as not to challenge the upward trajectory of local property prices. It would be hard to conceive of a system skewed in favour of landowners and the housebuilding industry to a greater extent than the one we have, and to the detriment of ordinary homebuyers.

The UK's large housebuilders cannot be blamed for the current housing shortage, which has emerged over several decades. Senior executives of these firms are required, within the law, to maximise the return on capital for shareholders. The problem lies instead with the existing set of complex regulatory incentives and the broader legislative framework which encourages landowners to bide their time and severely restrict the supply of available land.

This underlying reality combines with the UK's still often overly complex planning system to drive up house prices faced by potential buyers, who are then forced to borrow rising multiples of their annual incomes if they are to secure even a modest home of their own, often far from their place of work.

A 'mixed economy' of housebuilding is required, as argued in Chapter I. Local authorities and housing associations should provide a far greater number of subsidised homes each year, for certain low-income workers and other vulnerable groups, than they currently do. Commercial housebuilders, though, will always be more important, providing the vast bulk of the UK's new homes. What's vital is to design legal and regulatory structures which make sure landowners and commercial providers are properly incentivised to sell land and deliver good-quality, keenly priced homes in sufficient numbers adequately to address this country's chronic housing shortage. Under the current framework, they most certainly are not.

BREAKING IT DOWN

For several decades, major landowners and large 'volume' developers have used their political influence to resist supply-side reforms that would take some of the speculative heat out of the market for residential acreage, while ensuring more finance is made available for affordable housing and the kind of local 'place-making' infrastructure that makes new homes acceptable to existing local communities and desirable places to live.

Since the 2008 financial crisis, the UK's private housebuilding industry has become far more dysfunctional. While rates of home-building have increased lately, they remain historically low, despite spiralling prices and fast-growing demand. That the housing market requires major reform is now beyond contention, the stuff of mainstream political discourse – yet the nature of such reforms is widely debated.

In order to accurately diagnose the problem, it is instructive to describe the UK's private housebuilding sector, and the broader market, with reference to seven distinct characteristics – all of which need to be addressed if the market is to function so as to deliver more homes. Housing is a very complex issue – and breaking down the problems which beset the industry into distinct features will be useful to formulate and recommend necessary reforms.

I) SLOW BUILD-OUT

It is often argued that the UK's planning system holds back housebuilders and prevents them providing the homes that Britain needs. It is certainly true that strict planning laws and a tangle of complex regulations, particularly in England, have previously hindered development. Our planning laws put significant power in the hands of local communities to block construction. And local planners are, to some extent, at the mercy of the communities they serve – with the politics of planning sometimes making it tough for elected councillors to permit developments without facing a voter backlash.

Since the National Planning Policy Framework was introduced in 2012, though, there has been a presumption 'in favour of sustainable development'. The NPPF reduced some 1,300 pages of official planning guidance down to a 65-page document and a 27-page technical annex.[6] While planning law is still overly complex, the 2012 simplification has helped significantly to increase the number of planning permissions granted.

In 2010, for instance, local authorities granted permission for just 155,637 housing units – way below the 250,000 housing completions required each year, as recommended by the 2004 Barker Report. Yet in 2015, three years after NPPF was introduced, 272,500 planning permissions were granted, rising again in 2017 to permission for 370,400 housing units.[7] By 2017, no less than 80.5 per cent of all applications to build residential housing were being accepted – suggesting the planning system has become much less of a barrier in recent years. Even in 2010, though, the approval rate for planning applications submitted was still relatively high – at 73.5 per cent. As such, the planning system alone, while often expensive and troublesome to navigate, particularly for SMEs, may never have been the formidable barrier to building homes which large housebuilders often claim it to be.

This view is supported by the pattern over recent years of housing completions rising far more slowly than the number of permissions granted – with 'build-out' delays getting longer. Between 2010 and 2015, for instance, the number of planning permissions given each year, on the figures cited above, rose by 75 per cent – not least due to the 2012 introduction of NPPF. But the number of homes completed each year and made available for sale went up from 106,980 to 142,470 over that five-year period, an increase of just 33 per cent. Similarly, between 2015 and 2017, when we saw a 36 per cent increase in planning permissions granted per annum, the number of homes actually built rose by only 15 per cent.[8]

A Local Government Association survey reported in 2013 that once detailed planning permission had been granted, developers took an average of 1.7 years to complete each home.[9] By 2017, an equally authoritative industry study pointed to a delay of 'at least four years on average' from detailed planning permission to completion – a 2.4-fold increase over just four years.[10]

The growing delay in build-out rates is undeniable and very significant. It has happened at a time when house prices have risen steadily, the number of concealed households has increased sharply (as outlined in Chapter I) and net immigration has soared – from 176,000 in 2012 to 342,000 in 2015 – pointing not only to a marked increase in the demand for housing but also ample labour supply to carry out the construction work required to build more homes.

With housing completions having risen far more slowly than the rate at which planning permissions have been granted, the stock of outstanding permissions has ballooned by over 40 per cent – from 496,000 residential units across England in December 2012 to 684,000 by July 2016.[11] This reflects the greater extent to which large developers have been sitting on viable building land, with permissions to build in place, but drip-feeding new homes onto the market to keep prices high and rising, leading to wider margins and greater overall profitability.

Between 2010 and 2017, in fact, the author calculates that 1,943,125 new planning permissions were granted in England. Of these, some 932,335 homes – or 48 per cent of permissions awarded – were not built. Over a seven-year period, then, in which the UK's housing shortage became chronic, and unaffordability spiralled, the residential construction industry applied for and was given permission to construct almost one million new homes that it chose not to build.

Unused planning permissions are valuable, of course, adding to the net worth of the developer's balance sheet – and, if the company is listed, to its share price and related executive bonuses. Granting permission for a certain number of housing units to a large housebuilder also means that a particular local authority, having fulfilled its 'housing plan', is then less likely to grant further permissions to a range of SME builders – which, evidence shows, are more likely to build quickly to aid cashflow.

The UK's most powerful developers, then, can use their large, well-resourced legal departments to obtain planning permissions which they may have no intention of using – not only to boost their stock market valuation but also effectively to hinder the efforts of SMEs to obtaining permission to build elsewhere in the same locality.

Securing planning permission is expensive, of course – particularly if permissions remain unused. But large developers are more than compensated for this expense by the boost to their balance sheet and their enhanced ability to control the rate at which homes come to market in a particular part of the country, while keeping smaller rivals at bay.

II) BIG PLAYERS TOO DOMINANT

During the 1930s, over 300,000 homes a year were built – many of them in the Metro-Land London suburbs such as Brent, Harrow and Barnet described in the Introduction. These homes were constructed, for the most part, by local SMEs, which built countless units for both local authorities and commercial sale.

From the inter-war years up until the mid-1980s, in fact, small housebuilding companies were able to start up, grow quickly and

establish themselves as significant contributors to regional economies.[12] As such, the UK residential construction industry was
characterised by a large number of small and medium-sized firms –
which were able to access land and finance at reasonable prices and
on reasonable terms, allowing them to compete on quality, price
and overall value for money.

In 1960, the ten biggest UK housebuilders accounted for just 9
per cent of all new homes built – with a large number of competing
SMEs operating on relatively thin margins and striving to build as
many homes as they could.[13] When the UK last consistently built
over 250,000 homes a year, in fact, during the early and mid-1980s,
SMEs accounted for two-thirds of all such completions.

Since then, the industry has significantly changed. In 1988, around
12,200 active small building firms were responsible for nearly 40 per
cent of housing completions. By 2014, though, there were just 2,400
such companies, and they were building just 12 per cent of new
homes.[14] By 2016, the UK housebuilding sector had become even
more consolidated – with the three largest developers accounting
for a quarter of homes built each year and over half provided by the
biggest eight firms.[15]

This shift partly reflected the move by local authorities to a more
'plan-led' system of planning, with housing schemes that were
granted permission tending to involve a larger number of housing
units – making them less suitable for SMEs. The attitude of banks
towards SME builders also changed during this period, gradually
squeezing their access to finance. And during the 2008 financial
crisis, no less than a third of the UK's active small housebuilders got
into difficulty and ceased to trade.

The increase in industry concentration since the financial crisis
has been striking – as shown in Figure 4.1. Over just seven years, between 2008 and 2015, the market share controlled by large 'volume'

developers (those building more than 2,000 homes a year) practically doubled – to almost 60 per cent. The share accounted for by SMEs, meanwhile, which favour fast build-out, plunged from 68 per cent to 41 per cent.

FIGURE 4.1: MARKET SHARE BY HOUSEBUILDER SIZE

● Small builders   ● Medium-sized builders   ● Volume builders
    (1-100 units)   (101-2000 units)   (2000+ units)

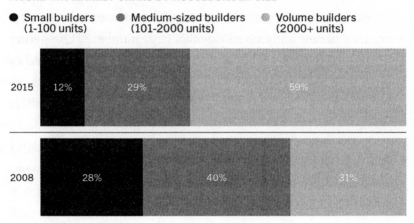

Source: NHBC Registrations

Within that SME total, small developers – those completing fewer than 100 units annually, typically family firms with considerable local knowledge – were still building over a quarter of all new homes when the 2008 crisis took hold. By 2015, that share had fallen to just 12 per cent. The actual number of units such firms completed collapsed from 44,000 to 18,000 during that period, with small builders accounting for fewer homes in 2015 – a year of relatively buoyant UK growth – than they did in 2009, during the most severe period of the post-crisis recession.

Those SMEs which survived the financial crisis can now barely compete with the volume developers that increasingly dominate the UK housebuilding industry. In the struggle to raise finance, then secure and develop residential plots, SME have, quite literally, lost considerable ground since 2008 – as large stock market-listed builders have acquired smaller operators, in order to access their land holdings and, in turn, limit future competition. Across the UK housebuilding sector, studies have shown that such takeovers, rather than driving efficiency, have resulted in fewer units being built each year compared to the amalgamated pre-merger output. This has been a major source of market failure.[16]

In what is now a highly consolidated industry, with SMEs lacking access to finance and finding it hard to source land, powerful large operators are able to use 'contrived scarcity' to prioritise profitability per unit over volume.[17] In doing so, they are putting home ownership beyond the reach of the majority, and an increasing majority, of the UK's young adult population. Housebuilding is not complicated. Builders buy land, secure planning permission, put up structures involving very basic and long-standing technology and then sell them. The barriers to entry should be low and the competition among rival developers fierce – to the benefit of consumers.

Instead, increasingly dominant big players in the UK housebuilding market boast profit margins that resemble those of path-breaking high-tech start-ups. Between 2012 and 2016, while the annual rate at which planning permissions were granted increased by 53 per cent, private sector housing completions each year rose by just 22 per cent. Over this same period, the profits of the UK's five largest housebuilders soared by 388 per cent, reaching £3.3 billion.

A recent inquiry by the House of Lords concluded that the UK's highly consolidated housebuilding industry now displays 'all the characteristics of an oligopoly'.[18] A former Housing Minister privately told the author that the sector 'has lately been acting like a cartel' – a charge implying illegal restrictive practices, which large developers deny.

Keen to build fast to aid their own cash flow, SMEs can in theory quickly translate planning permissions into marketable homes. The current weakness of the UK's SME housebuilders is not only seriously limiting industry-wide competition. It also means fewer small plots are developed – the kind that large firms find far less economically and logistically attractive. The serious demise of the UK's SME builders since the mid-1980s, and particularly since the 2008 financial crisis, is a major reason why the housing market is so dysfunctional, failing to supply good-quality homes in sufficient numbers and at reasonable prices.

III) THE GREEN BELT

The third feature of the UK housing market which contributes to our chronic shortage of homes is the green belt. While the government has awarded many more planning permissions in recent years, the less restrictive NPPF rules introduced in 2012 did not change green belt designations – which continue to prevent development in many parts of the UK where there is a very acute need for housing. The reality is that responsible and environmentally sensitive planning and the construction of enough homes adequately to accommodate the UK population are by no means antithetical.

Many parts of the green belt, much of which derives from the 1947 Town and Country Planning Act, are clearly valuable and important.[19] But many other parts are farmland with no public access or urban scrub of no environmental or aesthetic merit whatsoever. Outdated green belt classifications are too often being used to protect disused sites in areas of intense housing demand, that are far from green and pleasant and which should be developed.

Although the green belt surrounding London covers, for instance, the rolling hills of the Chilterns, it also includes litter-strewn railway sidings and much scruffy wasteland. It should also be remembered that the prettiest and most environmentally important parts of our countryside are anyway designated as 'areas of outstanding natural beauty' or as 'National Parks' – so would remain protected even if the entire green belt was scrapped.

According to the 2011 National Ecosystem Assessment, just 2 per cent of all land in England is covered with actual buildings – as mentioned in Chapter I of *Home Truths*.[20] The green belt, which surrounds London, Birmingham, Manchester, Bristol and many other urban areas – including smaller conurbations such as Derby, Nottingham, Gloucester and Stoke-on-Trent – covers an area almost seven times bigger.

Since it was created, the green belt has very significantly expanded. Back in the late 1970s, the total area amounted to 721,500 hectares. But with local authorities often keen to deter development, particularly in the English shires, by 2016 this figure had ballooned to 1,634,700 hectares – around 13 per cent of the land area of England.[21] The area covered by Surrey's green belt has grown by 20 per cent since 1979, with similar growth figures applying in Buckinghamshire and Kent. As a result, development has been severely thwarted, which has damaged economic vitality and forced workers to endure longer journeys – as they leap-frog the green belt to areas where housing is more available, resulting in lower productivity and more carbon emissions.

No less than 88 per cent of the area of Guildford, the largest town in Surrey, is devoted to green belt. More of Surrey, in fact, is covered by golf courses than by residential housing.[22] That helps to explain why Surrey is regularly rated as England's most expensive county in which to buy a property.

Supporters of urban containment argue that the UK is a small island, warning against 'concreting over the countryside'. We are a very long way from that. Green belts cover one and a half times as much land as all our towns and cities put together – and then we have National Parks (accounting for around 9 per cent of the country's land mass) and Areas of Outstanding Natural Beauty (15 per cent) as well.[23] While there is some overlap between these categories, the economist Kate Barker estimates that 'up to 25 per cent of England is protected in some way'. On top of that, local political opposition to development remains widespread, and is often decisive, in many of the areas which are not formally protected and where new housing is needed most.[24]

After years of expansion, the green belt surrounding London – a massive thirty-five miles wide in places – is now three times bigger than the size of the capital itself. The designated land around Oxford – officially the UK's most unaffordable city, with the average house costing no less than 11.5 times the average local wage – is larger than the university town, where houses are in desperately short supply.[25] The same is true in York and Cambridge too, where the green belt is bigger than the place it is supposedly protecting.

Local authorities are able to give planning permission on green belt sites if they decide that is the only way to meet housing need, by demonstrating 'exceptional circumstances' that are 'fully evidenced and justified' and having 'examined fully all other reasonable options for meeting its identified need for development'.[26] Yet this rarely happens, not least as local MPs, even those who reach high office and repeatedly declare it their 'personal mission' to 'fix the housing crisis', tend to object.[27]

Despite her declared support for building more homes, Theresa May has a long track record of opposing development in her Maidenhead constituency, which is part of the green belt surrounding London.[28] The Conservative manifesto on which she took her party into the 2017 general election also pledged to 'maintain existing strong protections on the green belt'.[29]

It is worth stressing that the green belt is only rhetorically 'green'. More than half of it is used for intensive farming which, given that it involves the extensive use of chemicals and provides little refuge for wildlife, generates a negative net environmental benefit.[30] There is often greater biodiversity in our towns and cities, given that the biggest land use within them is parks and gardens. Yet a determination to treat the green belt as sacrosanct means school playing fields are sold off for housing and transport systems overflow as commuters are forced to make ever-longer journeys between a home they can afford and their place of work – both of which seriously detract from public welfare, the environment and broader wellbeing.

The reality is that the UK's various green belts are only truly valuable to those who own houses within them.[31] As such, they amount to 'a very British form of discriminatory zoning', according to Professor Paul Cheshire of the London School of Economics, 'keeping the urban unwashed out of the Home Counties – while helping to turn houses into investment assets instead of places to live'.[32]

Between 1970 and 2015, house prices in Canada, Australia, New Zealand and the UK all rose by well over 200 per cent in real (inflation-adjusted) terms, with the UK experiencing a real-terms price rise of close to 300 per cent.[33] These nations have experienced the highest house price inflation, and most serious affordability issues, of any OECD members over the past half-century. All have planning systems modelled on that of the UK, with extensive green belts around urban areas.

The green belt amounts to a huge and growing distortion in a market for land which is already deeply dysfunctional. There is no need to 'concrete over' the countryside, but we must stop severely constraining the growth of housing in places where people really want and need to live.

IV) VIABILITY LOOPHOLE

Since 2012, the 'viability loophole' has allowed large, powerful developers who have been granted planning permission to evade related obligations to provide affordable housing and other community-focused contributions. Introduced as a way of boosting developer profits to support housebuilding in the aftermath of the 2008 global financial crisis, the continued existence of this loophole at a time when large developer profitability is so high is entirely unjustified – and is the fourth underlying cause of the UK's 'broken' housing market.

The viability loophole dramatically impacts the number of affordable homes being built, for both rent and purchase, while further inflating the cost of land – seeing as developers overbid in the struggle to buy acreage knowing they can save money later by using the viability loophole to shirk their affordable housing and other social obligations.

Under so-called Section 106 Agreements, housing companies make legal commitments to the council granting them planning permission to build a particular development.[34] Such commitments typically include a requirement to provide a certain number of 'affordable homes'. The government's definition of 'affordable' in terms of renting is that a home should cost no more than 80 per cent of the average local market rent. When it comes to homes built for sale, the definition is far less clear cut – with official guidance indicating that mortgage payments on such a property should be more than the rent that would be paid on social housing, but below market levels – clearly a very broad range.[35]

Viability tests allow developers to reduce their affordable housing commitments if profits slip below 'competitive' levels – which the major housebuilders define as around 20 per cent. That means developers overpay for land in order to guarantee they win sites, safe in the knowledge they can recoup the costs later by going back on their commitments and squeezing out affordable housing. Such viability assessments are also largely conducted behind closed doors, with all parties citing 'commercial confidentiality'. This is astonishing, given that the viability loophole allows developers to tell councils that it's not possible to deliver the affordable homes they'd previously agreed to deliver, all because they've subsequently decided they paid too much for the land.

The campaign group Shelter undertook research across eleven local authorities in 2015, covering nine of England's biggest cities. Where viability assessments were used, just 7 per cent of the homes on new sites were affordable housing, far below the average 28 per cent requirement set in the planning permissions granted by the councils involved in the study. This amounted to a loss of 2,500 affordable homes in just one year across less than 3 per cent of the UK's 406 councils. Viability tests saw a 79 per cent reduction in affordable housing compared to the levels required by council policies across the parts of the country Shelter examined.[36]

The reality is that, with councils under enormous pressure from Whitehall to 'fulfil housing plans' and get a certain number of homes built, and the completion of those homes largely in the hands of a small number of powerful firms, it is often the private housebuilding industry which calls the shots in Section 106 'viability' negotiations. The updated NPPF, completed in 2019, sought to address this gaming of the planning system, by handing local councils more powers. New guidance makes clear that the price paid for land must account for councils' affordable housing requirements, suggesting developers receive a 'reasonable' rather than a 'competitive' return. The updated rubric also repeatedly uses the phrase: 'Under no circumstances will the price paid for land be relevant justification for failing to accord with relevant policies in the plan.'

In theory, this should leave less room for landowners' profit expectations to reduce affordable housing on individual schemes through viability assessments. Yet there is still no clarity when it comes to how affordable housing and other Section 106 obligations should be determined in the first place. So these will remain subject to negotiation between councils, landowners and developers – with the agreement of all three required if any particular housing scheme is to get off the ground.

Also, the definition of 'affordable housing' itself remains, in the eyes of many, extremely weak – with 80 per cent of market rent well out of reach for many, and the criteria on homes for purchase still extremely vague. And while viability talks are now meant to be public by default, developers can still request they are private, which councils, desperate for homes to be built to fulfil their Whitehall-monitored housing plan, may be forced to accept.

Councils with acute housing targets are, indeed, highly likely to remain at the mercy of powerful developers – even under the new 2019 NPPF viability test guidance. It is arguable, in fact, that the Housing Delivery Test, also introduced as part of the NPPF update, is far more significant than the new language relating to the viability test. The new test puts local authorities under even more pressure to get homes built, tipping the balance of negotiating power back even further in the direction of landowners and developers and away from council officials – and, ultimately, those trying to buy or rent a home they can afford.[37]

V) LANDBANKING

In an international context, British housebuilders are unusual in that they combine the acquisition and long-term development of land with actual construction.[38] It has been officially recognised for some time that the large UK developers are primarily land speculating firms that build houses on the side. As the 2007 Callcutt Review acknowledged: 'identifying, acquiring, preparing, developing and selling land is the key activity of all [UK] house building companies'.[39]

A 2008 inquiry by the Office of Fair Trading was even more blunt in its assessment. 'Rather than thinking of homebuilders as construction firms that have integrated upwards into land development, it may be more realistic to think of land developers who have integrated downwards into home construction,' the OFT said. 'Home-builders deliver new homes as fast as they can sell them, not as fast as they can build them.'[40]

Some view landbanking as a rational response by developers to future market uncertainty. The biggest risk facing speculative housebuilders is that they invest capital into a piece of land based on estimated selling prices for the resulting housing units which they then fail to achieve. This is a major structural barrier to private housebuilders ever delivering as many homes as are needed under the UK's speculative model. It also militates against the provision of affordable homes, of course – as such houses not only sell for less, they also undermine local prices if made available in significant numbers.

Others see landbanking as a method used by a cynical building industry to constrain housing supply and speculate on rising land values, with the very act of supply constraint pushing prices up further. As the large developers have become far more dominant in recent years, it is clear that the scope to use land banks in a deliberately restrictive and anti-competitive manner has been singularly enhanced. 'Landbanking, sitting on plots while the value of the land rises, is clearly endemic and compounds the overall supply difficulties we're facing,' according to one senior civil servant in conversation with the author.

What's clear is that large speculative developers amass huge land banks to help them control the flow of new housing onto local markets. Having land in reserve also helps strengthen the negotiating position of developers as they engage with landowners in a bid to acquire acreage suitable for residential housing.

In 2015, the biggest three housebuilders – Persimmon, Taylor Wimpey and Barratt – completed 44,000 homes between them. But they had planning permission to build another 200,000

– permissions which have, in recent years, been built out into saleable homes at a decreasing pace, as discussed earlier in this chapter. On top of that, though, Persimmon, Taylor Wimpey and Barratt also owned 'strategic land holdings' between them with enough capacity to build somewhere approaching half a million more homes.[41] And that's only the top three builders.

The Home Builders Federation, the main lobby group for large developers, denies that slow build-out and landbanking are devices to raise profitability. 'Delays can be caused by overly prescriptive planning permissions which fail to reflect prevailing market conditions,' says the HBF. 'Where this has occurred, renegotiations will usually take place which can result in lengthy delays.'[42] But housing academics Tom Archer and Ian Cole refute this, suggesting that such practices are largely about maximising profit. Their evidence is discussed in more detail in Chapter V.[43]

Consider, also, that much of the land-banked land across the UK isn't even held by builders – but instead by so-called land promoters and land agents. Stock market-listed housebuilders like Persimmon and Taylor Wimpey quietly disclose their land-holdings in their annual reports, as large land banks point to a high 'book value' and healthy future profits – keeping share prices and, in turn, executive remuneration high.

But land promotion companies don't routinely disclose what they own and have no obligation to do so. They are not generally listed on any stock market, so have no public shareholders they are obliged to inform or have need to impress. As well as acquiring vast acreage, land promoters also are adept at obtaining planning permissions, allowing them to sell on 'shovel-ready' land to developers at a vast profit.

In 2012, it was estimated that 45 per cent of all residential planning permissions in London were granted on land controlled by firms that had never built anything.[44] The clear implication is that many such firms exist only to speculate on future rises in land values – at the expense of ordinary workers struggling to buy a home. Such companies have every incentive to negotiate extremely hard with local authorities to lower Section 106 obligations – making their sites more valuable still.

In fact, the 'viability' loophole outlined above encourages land promoters, for whom delay costs nothing, to retain sites until councils get desperate to see planning permissions they have granted become homes that local people can rent or buy. The longer land promoters wait, the more such homes are needed, and the greater their chances of further diluting affordable housing obligations and other previously struck Section 106 requirements, making their sites more valuable still.

Alongside the land banks held by the large housebuilders, non-building land promoters are estimated to own an astonishing 55 per cent of all land with full planning permissions across the UK, and no less than 87 per cent with outline planning permission.[45] Such holdings are gradually auctioned off to developers at vast profit, all of which is obviously reflected in the price the homebuyer ultimately pays – the size of the deposit needed to buy the home and the scale of the mortgage that the household will need to service over twenty-five years or more.

Ultimately, all the cards are held by landowners and their agents. If a landowner decides not to sell but has a piece of land vital to the growth of a local area, intense competitive pressure within the system will bid up the price of that land. And such upward price pressure is at the expense of the quality and affordability of houses that are ultimately built for the local homebuyers.

Ministers have begun to express concern that the growing concentration of the UK housebuilding industry, combined with delays between planning permission and build-out and more intense land-banking, are harming consumers and broader society, contributing to the 'pricing out' of countless young adults. 'The big developers must release their stranglehold on supply,' said Communities Secretary Sajid Javid in October 2016. 'It's time to stop sitting on land banks and delaying build-out – the homebuyers must come first.'[46] 'There is definitely some hoarding of land by developers,' Javid then told *The Times* in early 2018. 'The government needs to play a more active, more muscular role.'[47]

Developers and non-building 'land promoters' are able to thrive, then, in a market for residential acreage which is opaque and deeply dysfunctional. Information on land values, ownership, planning status and policy is not easily available, which means both landowners and local planners are often in the dark about what the right value should be for a plot of land – or how much affordable housing can reasonably be expected.

As well as buying up land directly, developers and land promoters also strike options agreements with farmers and other landowners – then spend years developing potential housing plots, navigating labyrinthine systems of planning applications and appeals and capturing massive financial gains when permission is granted. While an acre of agricultural land may sell for £5,000 to £10,000, land with residential planning permission can be worth £1 million to £4 million per acre, or much more, depending on location.

Large developers and promoters often pay for the right to buy from a landowner at some future point, once planning permission has been granted. They undertake to seek planning permission while the landowner agrees not to sell the land to anyone else. Such options agreements mean the housing industry avoids the risk of paying for land before it has planning permission, with the builder and landowner then sharing the 'planning gain' or 'uplift' – the massive increase in the value of land once planning permission is in place.

The amounts of land controlled by large developers and

promoters in this way are vast – far exceeding the land they own directly – but are ultimately unknown. The UK's Land Registry remains extremely patchy and there is no legal requirement to register the widespread options agreements between promoters, developers and landowners – so no one knows who controls some of the UK's prime potential housing acreage.

The market for residential building land – on which housing supply and house prices ultimately depend – is closed and opaque and effectively stitched up between landowners and large housebuilders. This not only drives land prices and, in turn, house prices much higher, leading to chronic affordability issues, it also gives developers and promoters enormous influence over how many houses get built, where, by whom and when.

VI) SPECULATIVE INFLOWS

Speculative demand for housing, and the land on which homes stand, is the sixth dysfunctional aspect of the UK housing market. The compelling impulse felt by so many to buy their own home stems in part from the observation, over successive decades, that while house prices can be volatile, they generally rise. As such, buying a home with a mortgage allows ordinary working people to secure a modest but all-important degree of financial security and accumulated wealth, ultimately taking ownership of an asset worth far more in real terms than the original purchase price.

Problems emerge, though, when house prices race so far ahead of earnings that the majority of young adults are unable to buy and, in turn, benefit from rising property prices. With the median house price approaching eight times the median wage, UK homes have never been less affordable. Rising real house prices do leave owner-occupiers feeling richer, but they also leave young homebuyers with homes of poor quality and size as land prices are bid up, if they can afford any property at all. Homes are effectively transformed, then, from places to live into investment assets in their own right – and by far the most important investment asset for the vast majority of owners.

As such, house prices are then partly influenced by their expected value compared to other financial assets. And, since the crash of 2008, with interest rates at historic lows and much uncertainty on global markets, UK residential property – its price bolstered by a fundamental demand–supply shortage – has become a very attractive asset indeed.

One manifestation of this is the buy-to-let phenomenon, with millions of not particularly wealthy UK households now owning two or more homes, as an alternative to the perceived uncertainty of low-yield pension saving. Another is the growing, and in some developments very significant, share of new-build properties that are now bought 'off-plan' for rental by non-UK-based institutional investors. This trend has extended beyond central London to the capital's suburbs and also to parts of Manchester, Birmingham, Oxford, Cambridge, Brighton, Leeds and other areas of acute property shortage.

The bottom line is that the more tightly our still too complex planning system and oligopolistic developers control the supply of homes, the more those homes, and the land on which they stand, will be treated as investment assets. This, in turn, encourages owners of multiple homes and extensive acreage to hold on to both, for longer, as prices are driven up, generating a self-reinforcing upward spiral.

None of this behaviour can be blamed on individual owners of buy-to-let properties, institutional investors acting within the law or even large developers. What is at fault here is the UK's long-standing housing policy, which sets incentives that will inevitably result in what are, for millions, entirely miserable and deeply regressive outcomes. By far the most significant of these deeply counter-productive regulatory features is the 1961 Land Compensation Act, which generates massive 'planning gain' windfalls when acreage is sold, encouraging land-owners and developers to sit on their holdings for as long as possible.

As such, the rules and regulations surrounding the market for residential-building land, and our broader housing market, are so badly designed that they have transformed a good which is relatively easy to produce, and the supply of which should respond directly to price incentives and which is of vital importance – residential property – into a scare and fast-appreciating investment asset that, to growing numbers of people, is increasingly inaccessible.

This reality becomes obvious when we consider the behaviour of UK land prices and house prices prior to the early 1960s – when the demand for housing was very strong, but prices rose only gently and housing remained broadly affordable. It is obvious, also, when we study countries like the Netherlands, Switzerland and Germany, where policy is designed to encourage residential building land to come to market in a relatively steady and orderly manner and at reasonable prices, in stark contrast to Britain.

Such nations have varying rates of home ownership – some higher than the UK, some lower. But in all of them, property prices are far less volatile and housing, to both buy and rent, is much more affordable. Access to relatively cheap land also means governments in these countries are able to provide decent and spacious social housing – which, again, in the UK is far too rare.

VII) LOBBYING POWER

Gallagher Estates is, according to its own website, 'one of the largest strategic land companies in the UK'. In October 2016, the company's billionaire founder Tony Gallagher hosted a fiftieth birthday dinner for former Prime Minister David Cameron, at Sarsden House – Gallagher's seventeenth-century mansion near Chipping Norton in Oxfordshire. The year before, Gallagher had given over half a million pounds to the Conservative Party.

Large developers and land promoters benefit handsomely from the chronic market failure across the UK's housing market. Highly resistant to potentially corrective policies, such as those outlined in later chapters, some leading industry figures take steps to influence lawmakers in a bid to make sure nothing changes. Industry research shows that the property sector accounted for over a third of the Conservatives' corporate donations between January and May of 2017.[48] Electoral Commission data then confirmed that the Tories received large donations from property and construction companies ahead of the June 2017 election as well.[49]

Just before the 2010 general election, as Leader of the Opposition, Cameron gave a speech warning that 'corporate lobbying' was 'the next big scandal waiting to happen'. He said that 'ex-ministers and ex-advisors for hire, helping big business find the right way to get its way' were central to this 'scandal'.[50] Yet under Cameron, and his successor Theresa May, Britain's property industry was second only to financial services in terms of political donations to the Conservative Party.

In addition, Cameron's Chancellor, George Osborne, went on to secure a £650,000-a-year post at BlackRock, the world's biggest fund manager. BlackRock controls significant investments in many of the UK's largest residential housebuilders, which have benefited handsomely from Help to Buy – the multibillion-pound homebuyers subsidy scheme introduced by Osborne in 2013, described in detail in the next chapter. Cameron, May, Osborne and Gallagher deny any wrongdoing and political donations received by the Conservative Party are all cleared by the Electoral Commission.

The right to own property – including land – is central to the idea of a liberal society, not least a leading democracy like the UK. But the right to land ownership should not include the right to capture the entire uplift in value when that land is granted planning permission. Such gains are often vast, given that agricultural land prices can jump 100- or 200-fold and more after permission to build is secured. The vast bulk of this money often accrues to developers and land agents who own or have optioned the land – with the use of complex tax structures keeping the state's share of the planning gain extremely low.

This injustice – which Winston Churchill condemned as long ago as 1909, as we shall explore in Chapter VIII – lies at the heart of our housing affordability crisis. It's a crisis which is crushing the very ideal of a property-owning democracy. Rather than tackling this clear problem, successive governments continue to side with lucky landowners and property developers, at the expense of ordinary renters and homebuyers.

At the same time, ministers for the most part deny that the huge backlog of unused planning permissions is clear evidence that big developers are deliberately restricting housing supply to keep prices high – and that the incentives structure and broader regulatory and legal framework that governs our housebuilding industry needs fundamental change to prevent that from happening.

One reason these necessary reforms aren't proposed, and these challenges aren't met, is inertia. Housing is still seen as a Cinderella portfolio among senior politicians, a step towards more senior Cabinet positions and the great offices of state. That needs to change, with the appointment of a Secretary of State for Housing, whose job is focused entirely on tackling our chronic housing shortage.

Another obstacle to change is the raw political power of the land-owning lobby, land agents and property developers – as indicated by their political donations, together with the revolving door between public sector positions of influence, from local planning officers right up to the Cabinet, and private sector players whose business is affected by policy decisions.[51]

It would be naïve in the extreme to ignore the influence of political donations on public policy. It would also be wrong. The fact is that such lobbying tactics matter and are an important factor, the seventh, in explaining the UK 'broken' housing market. It's a deeply dysfunctional market that suits large developers and landowners very well, allowing them to make vast amounts of money, but is doing a major disservice to an ever rising share of Britain's broader population.

IRON TRIANGLE OF INTERESTS

Homes in the UK are currently built mostly by large builders operating on a speculative development basis – with land promoters or developers buying up acreage years before they start building. This model isn't delivering. Residential construction in the UK is rigged heavily in favour of powerful developers at the expense of the home-buying public. This market distortion has become far worse since the 2008 financial crisis, as the industry has become much more concentrated.

Strong demand for homes should mean developers build more and sell at a competitive price. The fact that planning uplift on privately owned land accrues entirely to commercial players leads to speculative bidding by developers. Those developers then maintain big profit margins despite soaring land costs by building homes that are small and low-quality, as well as over-priced.

Very high-cost land also acts as a barrier to SME builders, who struggle to raise up-front finance. The lack of competition from smaller builders, in turn, allows land agents and large developers to assemble sizeable land banks, exerting considerable control over the number of homes coming to market – giving them every incentive to sit on sites and reap additional gains, as an inherent shortage keeps prices rising.

The market is 'broken', then, in that developers building the lowest-quality homes at the cheapest cost get the land, while smaller firms cannot compete – with homebuyers facing sky-high prices for a sub-standard product. This status quo can only be disrupted if housebuilders can access land at steady, reasonable prices, so the homes they build can then compete on quality and price. Land access is the formidable barrier to entry for all but the largest, most powerful developers – who exploit that reality by building low-cost homes in limited numbers, for which buyers then over-pay.

The bad news for young 'priced-out' adults struggling to buy their own home is that the seven egregious features of the UK housing market described above work in favour of three enormously powerful interest groups. Between them, they form a hugely powerful coalition – an 'iron triangle of vested interests' – that supports the restriction of new housing supply. The powerful developers that now dominate our housebuilding are just one of those groups.

The second group comprises existing property owners themselves. While the government pays lip service to more housebuilding, the reality is that homeowners vote in large numbers and still, just about, form a majority. In general, ministers are extremely mindful that rising house prices garner the support of 'middle England' – where elections tend to be won and lost. Contentious planning decisions can swing elections in key marginal constituencies, with the potential significantly to impact the composition of the House of Commons.

As concern about the UK's property apartheid grows, though, the political geometry is starting to shift. Young adults are increasingly angry and more and more older voters, having bought a property themselves, are upset and alarmed that their children and grandchildren are unable to do the same. But for now, the electoral arithmetic still means the 'property-haves' rule – with rising house prices leading to lots of re-mortgaging and related consumer spending by owner-occupiers, in turn bringing buoyant GDP numbers and more likely electoral success. This 'feel-good factor', though, is increasingly at the expense of 'generation rent'.

The third side of this iron triangle of vested interests is the banking sector. Following the 2008 financial collapse, the UK's still rather fragile banking solvency apparently remains closely linked to housing. More than three-quarters of all outstanding UK bank loans are property related and, the argument goes, if housebuilding ramps up significantly and prices flat-line or even fall, there are fears bank balance sheets could suffer.

It has become, in the author's experience, a near orthodoxy among senior HM Treasury officials in recent years that a significantly higher build-out rate of UK residential property will spark another banking collapse. This warning has been issued to several ministers who have shown a serious interest in tackling our housing shortage, with whom the author has subsequently spoken. As an argument, the HM Treasury view strikes me as nonsense – and probably has more to do with the fact that senior Treasury officials, often with substantial homes in attractive parts of Surrey, Buckinghamshire and other Home Counties, have conveniently elided their 'judgement' of what is good for the economic stability of the country with their inner NIMBY.

Yet, this is the orthodoxy that pervades Whitehall's most powerful ministry and, however often senior ministers issue rallying cries to 'get Britain building', it is a view that has thwarted countless attempts by other departments over recent years – and even No. 10 – to implement policies designed to make UK housing supply more responsive to price.

While some will dispute that, what's unanswerably true is that UK banks, heavily exposed to property as they are, have absolutely no incentive whatsoever to challenge the growing concentration of the housing industry. As such, unless compelled to do otherwise, leading banks will continue to extend little in the way of finance to the SME builders that have, in previous generations, kept UK housebuilding relatively competitive, so contributing to more modest price rises.

This iron triangle of interests, and the seven housing market features within it outlined above, form a formidable coalition against change. As such, attempts to 'fix' this market – making it more competitive, with the supply side meeting rising prices with significant increases in the completion of new homes – will need to be coherent, determined and sustained.

If the UK is to thrive during the decade after Brexit, with a relatively buoyant economy, it is vital that the government puts housebuilding at the heart of its economic strategy. If we fail to build more homes, ordinary working people will find it ever harder to keep a roof over their heads, and the damage to the wider economy, and society, will only get worse.

On top of that, though, a major programme of housebuilding will bring significant benefits in terms of future labour market flexibility and rising productivity, along with a more general economic boost.

So what policies has the government implemented since 2010, as the unaffordability of housing has spiralled?

V

HOW MINISTERS MADE THE
HOUSING CRISIS WORSE

*Politics is the art of looking for trouble, finding it whether it exists or
not, diagnosing it incorrectly and applying the wrong remedies.*[1]

ERNEST BENN, 1944

'Hopefully we will get a little housing boom and everyone will
be happy as property values go up,' quipped George Osborne,
to his colleagues around the Cabinet table, in early 2013.[2] The then
Chancellor was about to launch Help to Buy – a controversial
scheme, designed to make it easier for those having trouble raising
a big deposit to get on or move up the housing ladder.

Osborne's quip went down badly, with some Cabinet colleagues
worried about the prospect, just a few years after the 2008 financial
crisis, of generating another dangerous housing market bubble.
Other senior ministers and party activists were already warning
that house prices, having bounced back from their post-crisis
slump across most of the UK, were surging to new heights. As such,
the adult children even of well-heeled families were already finding it increasingly difficult to buy their first home, and not only in
London and the south-east.

Help to Buy (HTB) was introduced in April 2013. It was an extension and major expansion of a previous programme called FirstBuy,

also launched by Osborne, in 2011.[3] Like FirstBuy, HTB allowed a limited number of aspiring homeowners to take out a mortgage for 75 per cent of the cost of a property, provided they could put down a 5 per cent deposit. Up to 20 per cent of the cost of the home would be funded by a government-backed shared equity loan (later raised to 40 per cent in London), interest-free for the first five years.

But while FirstBuy was launched as a £250-million scheme, HTB was on a much bigger scale. Osborne pledged in this 2013 spring Budget to spend £3.5 billion on HTB.[4] And while HTB loans, like FirstBuy, were made available only on new-build homes, the HTB price cap for properties eligible was as high as £600,000, with the scheme open to all, not just first-time buyers.[5]

Colleagues warned from the outset that Osborne's HTB policy was politically dangerous, as the traditional 'feel-good factor' associated with rising house prices risked being eclipsed by a broader discontent driven by the rising number of young adults 'priced out' of the market, the vast majority of which would not gain access to the Chancellor's HTB scheme. Stoking up house prices, then, could be a net political negative.

In the autumn of 2013, though, six months into the scheme, Osborne quickened the pace, bringing forward the second phase of HTB. Advised to introduce some safeguards to prevent the housing market from overheating, he handed oversight to Bank of England Governor Mark Carney, promising to bring HTB to an end if the bank deemed it to be too destabilising. But Carney later admitted that, although the bank's Financial Policy Committee would monitor the scheme and report annually, Osborne had not granted the bank a veto.[6]

Vince Cable, then Liberal Democrat Business Secretary, voiced doubts about HTB in public, as did former Tory Chancellor Nigel Lawson, who said it should not be available in London, given the capital's already over-heated property market.[7] Andrew Tyrie, a former Treasury advisor and chair of the Commons Treasury Select Committee, warned that HTB would raise house prices, rather than stimulate new building. He also worried aloud that, once introduced at scale, the housing market could become too dependent on HTB. 'The political pressure to extend the scheme could be immense,' Tyrie predicted.

And so it has turned out. HTB has, since 2013, been repeatedly enlarged and extended. In June 2019, the National Audit Office confirmed that almost two-thirds of homebuyers who used HTB could have bought a home without it. The scheme 'helped inflate' already high property prices and boosted the profits of building firms, the NAO reported.

'The government's greatest challenge now is to wean the property market off the scheme with as little impact as possible,' the NAO report concluded. The suspicions of many when HTB was launched – that it was designed for short-term political benefits, rather than long-term economic progress – have been more than justified.

Yet, still, this scheme is scheduled to remain in place until 2023, by which time the government will have pumped almost £30 billion of public money into HTB – rather more than the £3.5 billion to which Osborne said he would limit the programme when it was announced.

GORGEOUS GEORGE

'I'd argue quite strongly that most of our housing problems have their origins in supply or, rather, a lack of supply – that's what my economics training tells me when I see prices rising in the face of rising demand.' These are the words of a very senior Whitehall official, written in early 2018. 'This under-supply of housing has made it less affordable, increasing the number of concealed households and contributing to declining home ownership rates.'[8]

Ministers have long been advised that the roots of the UK's

chronic housing shortage lie in the 'supply side' – with developers failing to build enough homes, either due to a lack of planning permission or, more recently, a tendency to restrict new supply to keep prices, and profitability per unit, high. Since 2010, though, as affordability issues have become particularly acute, successive governments have taken 'demand-side' measures – arguably boosting prices even further.

Instead of injecting even more taxpayer cash into a severely imbalanced market, the government should take drastic steps to ensure more homes are built. That means not only loosening up the planning system, but ensuring permissions granted are actually used.

The seminal 2004 Barker Review suggested around 250,000 new homes were needed each year to match UK household formation. For decades, construction has fallen way short. When the UK last built 250,000 homes a year, back in the mid-1980s, two-thirds were supplied by SME builders – who develop plots quickly to aid cashflow. With many such firms wiped out during the 2008 financial crisis, the UK housebuilding sector is now dominated by a handful of extremely powerful developers.

Rather than tackling the supply-side constraints outlined in Chapter IV, Theresa May continued with Osborne's misguided approach – pumping tens of billions of pounds into HTB. That's been a cash bonanza for large developers, helping them offload small, low-quality new homes, often racked with faults and on disgracefully punitive leaseholds – with the buyer not owning the property outright, but paying the freeholder an annual ground rent. House prices have meanwhile been driven up for the vast majority of would-be buyers unable to access the HTB scheme.

The danger that HTB would simply subsidise buyers to afford high prices – and for a temporary period – was apparent from the outset. The scheme was always likely to generate favourable short-term headlines but do little to increase housebuilding over the long term. As HTB was being introduced in 2013, Sir Stephen Nickell, a distinguished economics professor and senior official at the Office for Budget Responsibility (OBR), was asked for his view. 'Is it just going to drive up house prices? By and large, in the short run, yes,' Sir Stephen told the Treasury Select Committee. 'In the medium term will the increased house prices stimulate more housebuilding? A bit, but the historical evidence suggests not very much.'[9]

In 2016, three years after HTB was introduced, a government-commissioned study argued it had generated a 14 per cent rise in annual housebuilding – well short of the significant uplift needed.[10] And the government's flagship housing policy was otherwise slammed by a range of credible analysts. The Adam Smith Institute, a free-market thinktank, compared HTB to 'throwing petrol onto a bonfire ... adding more demand without improving the supply of houses is just going to raise prices and make homes more unaffordable for people who don't qualify for the subsidy'.[11]

The respected housing charity Shelter was similarly critical. 'HTB has completely missed the mark, doing barely anything to help first-time buyers, and nothing to help those most in need of an affordable home,' Shelter said. 'By inflating house prices and subsidising huge corporate payouts it is actually making matters worse.'[12]

There are legitimate concerns that the main impact of HTB, rather than helping young adults buy a home, has been to strengthen further the powerful developers who already dominate the UK housebuilding industry. In 2014, half the homes bought under HTB were sold by the UK's five largest housebuilders.[13] HTB sales constituted 53 per cent of all Taylor Wimpey homes sold in 2014, helping generate a 54 per cent increase in profits, to £481 million.[14] The scheme drove 40 per cent of Persimmon sales that year and 57 per cent by 2016. Some 31 per cent of Barratt homes were sold under HTB in 2014, rising to 44 per cent two years later. Shelter concluded, meanwhile, that HTB added 3 per cent to UK-wide house prices in a single year.[15]

From 2013 to mid-2017, 135,000 homes were sold under HTB. There is evidence the scheme, designed to help cash-strapped FTBs, also channelled hundreds of millions of pounds of public subsidy to thousands of already very wealthy homeowners. An analysis of government figures in 2018 suggested that over 5,500 existing homeowners earning above £100,000 a year benefited from taxpayer-funded HTB loans.[16]

An even bigger worry is that 32,266 HTB homes, or almost 25 per cent, were sold with leaseholds, many of which are seen to be extremely harsh. While flats are often sold with a lease, involving an annual charge for the servicing and maintenance of communal areas, leases on new-build houses were long considered a thing of the past. Yet almost a fifth of houses purchased under HTB in 2017 were sold leasehold. There is growing outrage that large developers have been marketing new HTB houses with contract clauses allowing ground rents to rise dramatically in later years, before selling these leases on to investors at huge profit.

Campaigners say young families are 'trapped as prisoners' in homes with escalating ground rent bills, that then become difficult to sell – not least as mortgage providers often won't lend against them. After six years of HTB, an estimated 100,000 families now live in leasehold properties with spiralling ground rents – an issue that will be further explored in Chapter VII.[17]

Despite such concerns, the government unveiled another £10 billion of HTB funding in October 2017, similar to the amount spent since 2013. Immediately after this announcement, the UK's biggest housebuilders saw their stock market valuation rise by well over £1 billion in a single day – illustrating the extent to which HTB has been a cash bonanza for already powerful developers.[18]

Since HTB began, UK Finance (previously the Council of Mortgage Lenders) estimates it has helped just 9 per cent of all FTBs, while resulting in higher prices for the 91 per cent of those it hasn't helped and potentially pricing out countless more. The National

Audit Office said in June 2019 that HTB, as well as being misdirected, has 'tied up significant public financial capacity', while most of the people it has helped did not need that assistance. The report confirms the scheme leaves the taxpayer on the hook, exposed to falling house prices, having inflated prices in the first place. Homeowners also face 'negative equity' when they come to sell – given that new-build homes generally command a 15 per cent premium.

In general, by juicing up demand, without tackling supply bottlenecks, HTB has simply boosted prices further, making homes even more unaffordable for the vast majority of would-be buyers who don't qualify. Yet, under Theresa May, this deeply flawed scheme was repeatedly expanded. And there is every possibility that future governments, lured by the easy headlines of another short-term boost to the housing market, will extend this counter-productive scheme once again.

The other main demand-side measures of recent years have related to stamp duty. In December 2014, Chancellor Osborne rationalised the stamp duty regime, so those buying homes worth under around one million pounds paid less, with higher bills for buyers of top-end homes. The following year, he imposed a 3 per cent stamp duty surcharge on purchases of rental properties or second homes, which again probably helped FTBs to some degree – although buy-to-let lending remained steady, at about £8 billion a quarter both before and after this change.

The most eye-catching move, though, was in November 2017, when Osborne's replacement Philip Hammond abolished stamp duty altogether for FTBs on homes under £300,000. Just months after Labour came within a whisker of power thanks to support from younger voters, the Chancellor received positive headlines for helping FTBs get on the housing ladder. The danger remains, though, that without a very significant rise in new homes built, the main impact of this change will be to bid property prices up even further. 'This measure is expected to increase house prices,' said the OBR in its budget commentary, ascribing Hammond's policy a 'high uncertainty rating'.[19]

The government's demand-side policies, then, may well have worsened affordability for the vast majority of aspiring homebuyers. The Institute for Fiscal Studies suggests that 'pricing out' has become more acute not just since the 2008 financial crisis but particularly since HTB was introduced. Just 25 per cent of those born in the late 1980s owned their own home by the time they turned twenty-seven years old, says the IFS – covering the years 2013 to 2017, the first years of HTB. That compares with 33 per cent of those born in the early 1980s and 43 per cent of early 1970s births at the same age.[20]

SUPPLY GO-SLOW

Over the last four years, the number of residential permissions out-standing – granted but not built – has more than doubled. Powerful mega-builders deliberately drip-feed the market to keep prices and profits artificially high. Drastic measures are needed to break this stranglehold, namely imposing heavy fines on large developers who create undue delays while reserving land for SME builders.

Making such changes means tackling formidable vested interests – including developers and land agents that make large campaign donations. The scale of this challenge perhaps explains, without condoning, why successive Housing Ministers, Chancellors and Prime Ministers have resorted to the short-term expedient of demand-boosting schemes, rather than addressing the supply-side realities of our broken housing market.

Some 155,637 housing units were granted permission in England in 2010, rising to 272,500 in 2015 – as shown in Figure 5.1 and re-ported earlier in Chapter IV. That's a 75 per cent increase, reflecting the introduction of the National Planning Policy Framework in

2012. Yet housing completions over that same period went up by far less, from 106,980 to 142,470 – a rise of just 33 per cent.

FIGURE 5.1: HOUSING COMPLETIONS AND PERMISSIONS (2008–16)

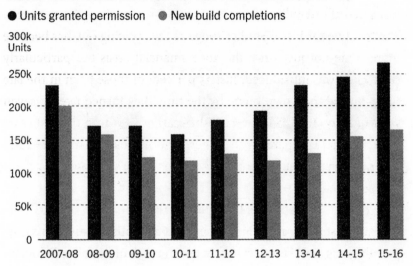

● Units granted permission   ● New build completions

Source: MHCLG, Glenigan

This illustrates how market-dominating developers have been allowed to engineer a deliberate housebuilding go-slow, putting further upward pressure on prices, so boosting profitability per unit. This prioritisation of profit over output is shown in Figure 5.2, which is based on research by Tom Archer and Ian Cole, both at Sheffield Hallam University. From 2012 to 2015, the rise in the number of homes built by the nine largest UK developers was consistently outstripped by revenue growth. Over this four-year period, housing completions increased 33 per cent but revenues no less than 76 per cent. As such, these large developers saw a three-fold increase in profits, while building only a third more homes. Over a slightly longer period, from 2010 to 2015, profits at the top five housebuilders surged more than five-fold – from £372 million to over £2 billion.[21]

FIGURE 5.2: COMPLETIONS AND REVENUES (TOP NINE FIRMS, 2012–15)

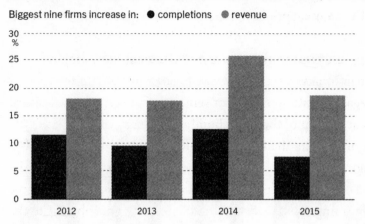

Source: Annual Reports, Archer and Cole

The 'volume' housebuilders, in particular, have been able to sell homes at a growing premium to the average sale prices since 2012 – see Figure 5.3. This reflects their domination of high-value localities, given the lack of SME competition, and their overwhelming role in delivering HTB homes, often sold at a premium.[22]

FIGURE 5.3: AVERAGE PRICE AND 'VOLUME BUILDER' PRICE (2009–15)

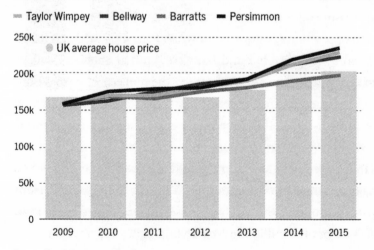

Source: Land Registry, annual reports

In 2015, the biggest five housebuilders returned an enormous 43 per cent of their annual profits to shareholders, no less than £936 million – as shown in Figure 5.4. These firms are, to an enormous extent, foregoing the chance to reinvest in order to build more homes. It is rational for any company to maximise profits within the law – it is the legal obligation, in fact, of senior executives. But the scale of returns at the top of the housebuilding industry, and the far faster growth of revenue than output as affordability worsens, points to super-normal profits. It's clear that the growing concentration of the UK housebuilding sector is now restricting competition to a degree that is harming consumers and broader society, contributing to the 'pricing out' of countless young adults.

FIGURE 5.4: DIVIDENDS AS SHARE OF PROFITS (TOP FIVE FIRMS, 2010–15)

Dividend as a percentage of yearly profit

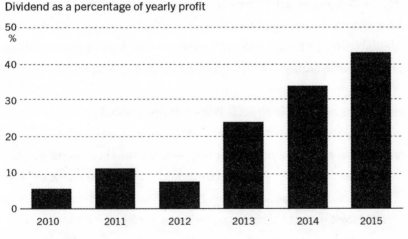

Source: Archer and Cole

The 2017 Housing White Paper highlighted the 'large gap between permissions granted and new homes built'. It pointed to 'concern that it may be in the interest of speculators and developers to snap up land for housing and then sit back for a while as prices continue to rise'.[23] The 'may' in this sentence speaks volumes. It is, in fact, very clearly in the interests of speculators and developers to sit on their land holdings and, given existing rules and regulations, it is very clearly happening.

Amid the growing dominance of just a few large developers, the government has done nothing to encourage planning permission to be used promptly. Under current circumstances, large, cash-rich housebuilders and the land promoters described in Chapter IV have every incentive to let permissions lapse, usually after three years, then make fresh applications. They can sit on sites and wait for prices to rise, the gains massively outweighing re-application costs. And that will remain the case as long as no threat or penalty exists that makes it not worth their while.

The MHCLG now estimates up to 40 per cent of permissions granted are allowed to lapse, with 20 per cent never being used at all. As dominant developers and promoters build up permissions, those permits and the land they are linked to clearly remain un-available for SMEs to build the homes for which there is such strong demand – retaining upward pressure on house prices.

NOTHING TO WRITE HOME ABOUT

Since 2010, then, having further stoked housing demand with HTB, successive governments have done nothing to alter the incentives of large developers to boost broader housing supply. Those supply-side reforms we have seen appear piecemeal and, when it comes to 'fixing' the housing market, somewhat insignificant. An example re-lates to the sale of public land for residential use – another way the government could theoretically influence the rate of housebuilding, particularly if such sales were made contingent on land being built-out by developers within a given timeframe.

The state owns enormous amounts of land – almost one million hectares, much of it suitable for development. Network Rail, Trans-port for London, the NHS and various ministries, particularly the

Ministry of Defence, all have major land holdings, sections of which could be made available for housing. Given that the average density of new-build housing in the UK is around 45 units per hectare, releasing just a tenth of state land for development could provide acreage for over a million homes.

From 1997 until 2010, while ministers talked a lot about using state land for housing development, the amounts sold were negligible – enough to build an average of fewer than one thousand homes a year. An increased effort was made between 2010 and 2015, under the coalition government, resulting in somewhat higher state land sales. But ministerial inertia and a lack of Whitehall follow-through meant that very few homes were actually built on these sites – with the acreage, for the most part, being added to the land banks of large developers, land agents and others with an incentive to sit on such holdings for years, as land prices rise.

The government could do a great deal to ease the UK's housing shortage by preparing state land for housebuilding and selling it with outline planning permission in place – using the proceeds to build schools, hospitals, roads and other forms of 'place-making' infrastructure that are necessary to create desirable and economically vibrant localities. Yet very little state land is ever sold, with or without planning permission. This amounts to a major missed opportunity – which will be explored in later chapters.

Various other supply-side schemes have been announced in recent years, including a £3 billion Home Building Fund in 2016. But just £1 billon of this subsidy was targeted at SMEs, with £2 billion directed towards large sites. This seems perverse, seeing as large developers can already access capital. The Accelerated Construction programme, meanwhile, created a partnership between the government, investors and contractors to target the use of off-site construction and new models of building. Again, this is welcome, but with even rosy government estimates of just 15,000 new homes over four years, the scheme will do nothing to address the UK's urgent housing affordability crisis.

Another initiative that is yet to deliver relates to brownfield sites – that is, previously developed land that has the potential to be redeveloped. In 2016, the government legislated to introduce a 'zoning-like' system for brownfield land – allowing local authorities to grant 'permission in principle' (PiP), a form of advance residential permission.

Two years later, as PiP was about to be introduced, a study by the Royal Town Planning Institute raised significant doubts that this initiative would spark more housebuilding, as such permissions remain vulnerable to legal reversal by later political and public opposition.[24] The RTPI also warned PiP could trigger land speculation, ultimately driving up the price of new homes. At the time of writing, PiP has barely been used, with only four councils across the UK, less than 1 per cent, opting to offer this form of planning permission.[25]

After the June 2017 election, in which Jeremy Corbyn made considerable gains, Theresa May vowed to take 'personal charge of fixing the housing market' and, in his November 2017 budget, Chancellor Hammond unveiled an eye-catching '£44 billion home-building fund'. Yet this package of capital funding, loans and guarantees added just £630 million to the Home Builders Fund for SME builders. Some £8 billion of financial guarantees were made available, though, 'to support private housebuilding' – designed for use, once again, by the 'volume' developers.[26]

Hammond also stated that 300,000 new homes a year would be built by the mid-2020s – what he called 'the biggest annual increase in housing supply since 1970s'. The OBR said it was making no changes for its forecast for new homes based on the Chancellor's budget pledge.

What does seem to be on the political agenda, if you believe the rhetoric, is one very obvious supply-side policy – a major increase in building by both local authorities and housing associations, independent non-profit bodies that often receive public funding. Over the last two decades, only a few thousand new homes have been built by local authorities each year, falling to just a few hundred per annum under Tony Blair.

The Grenfell Tower tragedy of June 2017, in which seventy-two people lost their lives, highlighted the poor quality of much of the UK's social housing stock, And in 2016, prior to Grenfell, the House of Lords Select Committee on Economic Affairs concluded that 'the government must recognise the inability of the private sector, as currently incentivised, to build the number of homes needed'. Without far more new building by local authorities and housing associations, the committee argued, there is no chance of providing the homes needed over the coming decades.[27]

The UK needs 300,000 new homes annually, to meet household formation and start addressing the long-standing supply backlog. With commercial developers having failed to build 200,000 homes for almost half a century, it seems inevitable that non-commercial suppliers will need to provide some 100,000 new homes each year. These would be split between 'social housing' (that is, council homes, typically available at 40–50 per cent of market rents) and other forms of 'affordable housing' (to rent or buy at up to 80 per cent of market rates). In 2017, housing associations built 30,180 such homes while local authorities built 2,960 – so we're talking about a very substantial combined three-fold increase.

The reality is, though, that for over a decade, and even post-Grenfell, there has been little additional state funding to build more social and affordable housing. This, again, has been a major failure of UK housing policy – and the case for more such housing, and reforms that could help bring it about, is presented in Chapter IX.

The May government did suggest that housing association debt might be taken 'off the books', allowing them to borrow more to build additional social and affordable housing in high-demand areas. But these ideas remain vague and are a long way from producing results. And on the basis of the current evidence – not least the structure, organisation and recent performance of major developers – the private sector alone will fail to build the homes we need in adequate numbers.

Over the last decade or so, the combination of Help to Buy, a lack of effective supply-side measures and a clear failure adequately to fund more social housing means successive governments have done very little to address our chronic housing shortage. In fact, ministers have made this crisis much worse.

That's why radical and disruptive policies are now needed to re-incentivise the private sector and spark a boom in housebuilding by both commercial and non-commercial providers – as shall be outlined in later chapters. But first, we need to examine and challenge the argument put forward, with increasing force and determination, by a number of economists and large developers who claim there is no need to increase the rate at which homes are built in Britain because there is, in fact, 'no shortage'.

VI

'NO SHORTAGE' NONSENSE

Happiness grows at our own firesides.[1]
DOUGLAS JERROLD, 1842

As the UK's housing shortage has become more serious, the subject has rocketed up the political agenda. Ministers, and MPs more generally, have become acutely aware of the disquiet among young adults, and their parents, that so many people wanting to settle down and start a family are now unable to afford their own home.

As well as affordability for would-be homebuyers, the sharp rise in the number of families in temporary accommodation and the escalation of outright homelessness due to a lack of social housing, as highlighted by respected campaigning charities such as Shelter and Crisis, has focused yet more attention on Britain's chronic shortage of homes.

While over a third of 16–24-year-olds owned their own home in 1991, by 2016 this figure had fallen to just a tenth – as we have already seen. The share of 25–34-year-old owner-occupiers similarly collapsed over the same period, from 67 per cent to just 38 per cent – with well over half a generation locked out of the property market at this crucial family-forming age. This stark reality has fuelled resentment among millions of 'priced-out' youngsters – not least those with parents lacking the means to help them.

A separate but similarly serious issue is that the affordability crisis means there are parts of the country where nurses, teachers, emergency services personnel and other vital public sector workers can barely afford to live – impacting everyone in such localities. A report by the Halifax Building Society published in June 2019 suggested that in only 8 per cent of towns across the UK is it feasible to buy a home on the wages offered by mid-ranking, but crucially important public sector jobs.[2]

While house prices rose 32 per cent between 2014 and 2018, public sector earnings increased just 7 per cent over the same period. In this context, Halifax analysed average house prices and average earnings for nurses, teachers, police officers, firefighters and paramedics across 515 towns – including thirty-one London boroughs.

Based on a four-times price–earnings multiple representing the threshold of affordability, just one in twelve – or 8 per cent – of the localities examined was affordable in 2018, down from one in four in 2014. Halifax found that just 3 per cent of towns offered affordable housing for nurses in 2018, compared to 12 per cent four years earlier. Meanwhile, only 9 per cent were affordable for teachers, 15 per cent for paramedics, 18 per cent for police officers and just 5 per cent for firefighters.

The decisive swing towards Jeremy Corbyn in the June 2017 general election marked a political watershed. Support for Labour surged among 25–34-year-olds – in large part because millions of young adult voters, locked out of the property market, were being forced to make high rental payments or remain living with their parents.

A hard-left Labour administration almost clinched power, the Conservative Party rightly concluded, because 'generation rent' was coming of political age and, angry at the affordability crisis, was willing to vote for someone offering to challenge 'the system'. Post-election analysis shows that Corbyn could have entered No. 10 and formed a government had his party won just a few thousand additional votes, spread across certain constituencies.[3]

Following this election, senior ministers, including the Prime Minister herself, upped their rhetorical game on housing. While Brexit has obviously dominated the political headlines, increasingly so after May lost her Commons majority in June 2017, much of the Tory leadership and broader Parliamentary party has, behind the scenes, become convinced that radical changes are needed to make the housing market less dysfunctional.

As such, some within the previously described 'iron triangle of vested interests' – including large residential developers and leading banks – have become increasingly concerned that a housing status quo which suits them could soon be disrupted.

CRISIS? WHAT CRISIS?

Housing is the most pressing domestic policy challenge facing Britain today. Several million too few homes have been built over the last thirty years. Relentless demand, in the face of inadequate supply, has seen prices spiral upward. Millions of hard-working people – even well-educated professionals, who should be natural Tory voters – are being denied the security and stability of home ownership.

Despite that, for some years now, and particularly since ministers began contemplating bold action, some of the UK's large house-builders have publicly downplayed the link between the historically low residential building rates and sharply rising unaffordability. Senior executives at some large developers and their in-house economists have gone to great lengths to try to shape the public narrative. The centre-piece of this 'no shortage' effort was the Redfern Review – written by Pete Redfern, chief executive officer of Taylor

Wimpey in 2016. This report claimed that increasing the supply of housing 'does not directly improve the home ownership rate'.[4]

The modelling work for the Redfern Review was carried out by the consultancy Oxford Economics, under the direction of Ian Mulheirn, a former Treasury economist. Mulheirn has since gone much further, forcefully arguing that 'there is no housing shortage' and 'the obsession with supply is a red herring'.[5] Such claims are now being repeated by prominent political commentators.[6]

The government Housing White Paper of February 2017 was a clear official admission of the urgent need to build more homes. 'Since the 1970s, there have been on average 160,000 new homes built each year in England,' it stated. 'The consensus is that we need from 225,000 to 275,000 or more homes per year to keep up with population growth and start to tackle years of under-supply.'[7] The 'no shortage' argument directly denies this need. 'To many this sounds like Mission Impossible,' Mulheirn writes, referring to government aspirations of more than 250,000 new homes a year. 'In fact, it's Mission Unnecessary.'[8]

The central plank of the 'no shortage' argument is that the government has been relying on estimates of the increase in the number of households each year which are far too high. Whitehall has been producing what Mulheirn refers to as 'repeatedly exaggerated' official forecasts of annual household growth. It is true that, since 2008, actual household formation has averaged only 152,000 per year, as Mulheirn points out, far below the MHCLG estimate of 235,000. The implication is that because around 80,000 fewer households are being formed each year than policymakers expected, the shortfall in housing supply is being overstated.

Yet the reason fewer households are being formed than officially predicted by demographic trends is because, for many people, the necessary physical home to create that household, either to rent or buy, is unaffordable and therefore unobtainable or otherwise doesn't exist. Or, if the individual concerned would ordinarily qualify for social housing, again, that local-authority-supplied flat or house may have not been built.

Such people do exist, though – and they often end up either living with their parents as adults, or as part of a 'concealed household', not counted in official household numbers. The extent to which this is happening was noted in Chapter III. But the figures warrant further examination in this context.

From 2006 to 2016, the number of 20–34-year-olds living with their parents in the UK rose no less than 47 per cent, to 3.4 million people – including 20 per cent of women in that age range and an astonishing 32 per cent of men.[9] Some young adults in this age range may willingly choose to stay with their parents. But, as housing has become less affordable, the share doing so has risen from less than a fifth in the mid-2000s to more than a quarter. It can surely be assumed a significant share of the 1.1 million rise in 20–34-year-olds still living in their childhood bedroom over the last decade are doing so because they are unable to rent or buy.

The rise in 'concealed households' during the ten years to 2016 – at least two adults (with or without children) living within another household – has also been very significant, rising 50 per cent to 2.5 million. In London alone, concealed households rose from 400,000 to 720,000.[10] Again, while some couples may choose to live within another household, it seems reasonable to assume the vast majority are doing so because they lack the means to buy or rent in order to form a discrete household of their own, or otherwise cannot access social housing.

Mulheirn says that because, over the last decade, around 800,000 fewer households were formed than MHCLG predicted, rising to 1.2 million fewer if you use earlier Whitehall forecasts, 'there doesn't appear to be a housing shortage'. Yet, over that same decade, the number of adults aged between twenty and thirty-four living with their parents grew by over a million and there were 830,000 more concealed households.

Given that each concealed household comprises at least two adults and some couples will have children, over three million people under these two headings are currently living in the UK who – in many cases against their wishes – have over the last ten years not formed the 'households' that officials previously predicted they would form. They are unlikely to agree with Mulheirn's conclusion that 'UK housing needs look to be far below [official] forecasts'.

There is clearly, as Professor Steve Wilcox points out, 'a circularity between household formation and the number of houses we provide, in that households cannot form if the houses are not there for them'. Wilcox, an academic at the Centre for Housing at the University of York, made this point to the House of Lords Economic Affairs Select Committee in 2016.[11] 'In the crudest terms,' he said, 'if we do not supply the 200,000-plus dwellings a year, fewer households will form – and there will be more sharing, more young people living at home with their parents and more concealed households.'

'The number and the frustrations, over-crowding and social disruption of concealed households is growing,' said property manager Martin Grubb, in evidence to the same committee. 'The disappearance of prospects for owner occupation for the young, even with substantial incomes, denies them housing stability and the ability to build an asset and credit base against future family security and ambitions,' Grubb wrote. 'This is the inevitable consequences of population increase overwhelming supply and it is a very sad policy failure.'[12]

Daniel Bentley, of the thinktank Civitas, makes a similar point. 'An under-supply of homes is likely to curtail the number of households actually formed,' he says. 'This may take the form of young adults not moving out of their parents' home when they previously would have done, or people joining house-shares, or people becoming homeless – even if those households are not actually formed, however, the pressure for housing will remain.'[13]

Mulheirn's 'no shortage' argument rests on the assumptions that higher housing costs 'have no impact on household formation, which most find hard to believe', according to Nick Boys Smith, co-chair of the government's Building Better, Building Beautiful Commission.[14] And that's the fundamental point – households can only form if there is a household space available for them to move into, and they can afford to do so.

Lindsay Judge, a Senior Research and Policy Analyst at the Resolution Foundation, argues that 'the household is not the right unit of analysis to explore many a housing question' – seeing as the concept captures everyone living at the same property, as long as they share common facilities, regardless of their circumstances and inter-relationships. 'Contained within the definition,' she says, 'is the supply constraint in that a household can only form if there is a building in which to do that.' As such, Judge rightly concludes that comparing the increase in the number of households each year to the growth in the number of homes – the central analytical assertion of Mulheirn and other 'no shortage' advocates – is 'a tautological exercise that tells us very little about the real pressure for housing'.[15]

Judge prefers to look at the number of available homes not per household, but per *family* (which could mean a single adult, or a couple with or without children). Using official data to estimate family numbers, Judge demonstrates that while there were 1,045 homes across the UK for every 1,000 *registered households* in 2016 (suggesting a small surplus of available homes), there were only 825 homes for every 1,000 *families* (revealing a very considerable deficit).

What's more, the number of homes available per 1,000 families has fallen consistently since 1997, coinciding exactly with the UK's third big post-war house price boom. The median price paid for residential property in England and Wales increased by 259 per cent between 1997 and 2016, while median individual annual earnings increased by just 68 per cent over the same period – resulting in chronic affordability issues in many parts of the country, for both aspiring homeowners and those looking to rent.[16] As such, 'it's hard to conclude that housing supply and demand are happily aligned' concludes an admirably understated Judge.

The second main pillar of the 'no shortage' argument rests on the fact that the headline number of 'permanent dwellings completed' – the total number of new houses and flats built each year by the private sector, local authorities and housing associations – is generally lower than 'net additional dwellings'. This second figure includes conversions of houses into separate flats, and shops and office blocks into homes – as discussed in earlier chapters. So, as long as the demolition of existing homes is relatively low, 'net additional dwellings' is generally a larger number than 'permanent dwellings completed'.

As such, Mulheirn and others argue that because housing 'demand' is *over-stated* (fewer households are formed than official predictions) and 'supply' is *under-stated* (with more new homes once conversions are included) there is 'no shortage of homes'. We countered this first assertion earlier in this chapter, so what of the second?

It is certainly true, as shown in Figure 6.1, that the number of 'net additional dwellings' has recently pulled significantly ahead of 'permanent dwellings completed' – that is, the number of newly built homes. A major reason is that in 2013, 'automatic' permitted development rights (PDRs) were granted to convert offices into residential properties – and since then, 'change of use' additions to the housing stock have nearly doubled, from around 20,000 in 2007 to 37,000 in 2017. That helps explain why, while there were 147,930 new homes completed in England in 2017, there were 217,350 net additional dwellings.[17]

FIGURE 6.1: PERMANENT DWELLINGS COMPLETED AND NET ADDITIONAL DWELLINGS (1992–2017)

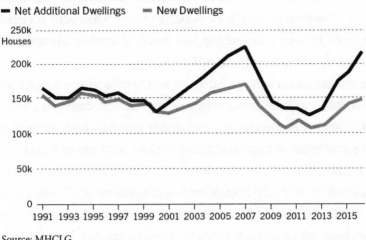

Source: MHCLG

In some localities, converted shops or office buildings can indeed make suitable and even attractive additions to the UK housing stock. There is certainly merit in encouraging 'change of use' as the government has done under certain circumstances, not least in city centres where housing demand can be acute, particularly for apartments. Some such conversion schemes may end up revitalising particular urban neighbourhoods.

But that does not mean that 'net additional dwellings' are, as Mulheirn argues, the 'bigger picture'.[18] Yes, we are in the midst of a conversion boom, but that does not amount to a permanent and sustained upward shift in the long-term rate of UK housebuilding. For one thing, the sharp rise in conversions over recent years is largely due to the one-off legislative change in 2013. The current high conversion rate is likely soon to fall away as the availability of commercially attractive buildings to convert reduces, as the Nation-wide Building Society has pointed out.

Changes of use from existing premises are, by definition, finite and one-off. 'While this is an encouraging development, we shouldn't overstate its significance,' says Nationwide. 'The growth in change of use may well slow in future years, as developers have probably con-verted the easiest sites and the stock of suitable commercial property will reduce … the quality and long-term suitability of some of these changes of use remains to be seen.'[19]

In early 2019, councils, architects, social housing providers and charities came together to urge the government to reconsider meas-ures that enable homes to be built under the widened permitted development rights legislation of 2013 – effectively outside the plan-ning system.

In a letter to Housing Secretary James Brokenshire, the groups argued that such measures sacrificed the construction of thousands of affordable homes, which councils would normally require as a condition of planning consent. Two of the signatories, Shelter and the Local Government Association, calculated that if homes built under PDR between 2016 and 2018 had been built through the normal planning process, an additional 10,000 affordable homes would have been constructed. Meanwhile, just 6,463 homes for social rent were actually built in 2018, while 1.2 million households are on councils' housing waiting lists.[20]

Concerns have also been raised about homes constructed under PDRs being of poor quality and often too small – seeing as such schemes are exempt not only from affordable homes requirements but also official space standards. Around a third of office-to-residential conversions have been in London – with more in Croydon than any other borough. 'We are seeing hundreds of substandard units in what were already fairly poor-quality office buildings,' says Paul Scott, Croydon's council cabinet member responsible for planning and regeneration. 'To pretend that this is somehow responding positively to the housing crisis is a farce – we are seeing units with no windows and building the slums of the future in Croydon now.' Two years after the 2013 change in PDR legislation, Croydon council was so alarmed by the low quality of homes being produced it used its powers to override new PDR provision, so that office-to-residential conversions once again needed regular planning permission.[21]

While some office conversions have been successful, producing decent homes, many have resulted in multiple units that don't meet space standards normally enforced through the planning system. A 2018 study by University College London examined five local authorities with high rates of PDR schemes – Camden and Croydon in London, together with Leeds, Leicester and Reading. After site visits to 568 buildings, the study found that only 30 per cent of the units delivered through PDRs met regular national space standards.[22]

The 2013 extension of PDRs 'was probably the worst housing policy mistake in the post-war era', says Hugh Ellis, of the Town and Country Planning Association, a group that campaigns for planning reform. 'Left to their own devices, real estate investors will see opportunities to deliver cheap, profitable developments to low standards.'

In one permitted development scheme at Newbury House in Ilford, north-east London, an office block just yards from a busy six-lane highway has been turned into sixty flats measuring as little as thirteen square metres each. According to national space standards, the minimum floor area for a new one-bedroom, one-person home is thirty-seven square metres. The local MP and councillors ended up publicly blaming each other for 'the worst new flats in Britain'.[23] Critics warn that such shoddy schemes can be damaging to residents' mental wellbeing and conducive to crime. In the neighbourhood of Terminus House – a fourteen-storey converted office-block in Harlow, Essex – crime jumped 45 per cent during the first ten months after people moved in.[24]

The low quality and small size of many homes built under PDRs has become such a scandal that in April 2019, Labour vowed to scrap the 2013 legislation, which it said had 'led to the creation of slum housing and rabbit-hutch flats'. The policy has 'seen the loss of countless affordable homes', said Labour, and meant that 'flats just a few feet wide were now being counted in the official statistics as new homes'.

'This Conservative housing free-for-all gives developers a free hand to build what they want but ignore what local communities need', said John Healey, Labour's shadow Housing Secretary. 'Labour would cut housebuilding and put a stop to people achieving home ownership', replied Marcus Jones, Conservative vice-chair for Local Government. 'We're backing permitted development rights, which are converting dormant offices into places families can call home.'[25]

A CONVENIENT NARRATIVE?

There is clearly a willing and receptive audience, a market in fact, for the 'no shortage' argument. For those opposed to a significant rise in the pace of UK housebuilding – whether powerful developers, environmental campaigners and/or ordinary homeowners not wanting more dwellings 'in my back yard' – this is a convenient narrative. These lobby groups can use it to claim that nothing needs to be done to address the unaffordability of housing – or, at least nothing that involves building more homes.

It is wrong, though, to interpret lower-than-expected household formation rates as evidence of less demand and need for housing. Household formation has been lower than expected over recent years in large part because homes simply aren't available to allow their creation – as the large increase in the number of concealed households and young adults living with their parents makes abundantly clear. And it is wrong to present a one-off 'change of use' conversion boom as a structural increase in the output of an industry dominated by a few powerful developers who benefit massively from 'contrived scarcity'. This is particularly true when the easing of PDRs results in housing units, many of which are smaller than would, under normal circumstances, be legally permissible.

Perhaps the most serious weakness in the 'no shortage' argument, though, is that it is based entirely on national numbers, ignoring that many homes, new and existing, are in the wrong place, a long way from where people work. Aggregate housebuilding data, whether 'permanent new dwellings' or 'net additional dwellings', takes no account of the local bottlenecks – either in planning or 'build-out' once permission has been given – that create supply imbalances in areas where homes are needed most.

We've already established that the number of households formed each year does not amount to 'demand'. A family of four living in a one-bedroom flat is housed, but very far from satisfied. A couple camped semi-permanently in a friend's attic is a 'household', despite not being registered as such. A priced-out thirty-something professional, unhappily living in his parents' basement, has no desire and no need to buy or rent his own place, according to those promoting the 'no shortage' creed.

But on the supply side, too, the headline number of new homes does not amount to 'supply'. Such aggregate data ignores location, quality, size, tenure, transport links, amenities and everything else that matters to a house. And when you take a good-sized family home and put in countless partitions, dividing it into grotty leasehold bedsits, the 'net additional dwellings' number rises sharply even though total living space is reduced.

Those asserting 'no shortage' sometimes point to the number of empty homes as additional evidence for their case. Why build more when the UK has so many empty homes? Yet again, though, many empty homes are a long way from where people live and work. And while in 2010 there were around 300,000 homes in England stand-ing empty for over six months, by 2016 there were around 200,000 – a decline of well over 30 per cent. This represents just 0.8 per cent of the total housing stock, the lowest since records began.

The treatment of empty homes, in fact, is a rare recent example of relative housing policy success. Local authorities were given powers and incentives to tackle empty homes as part of the 'New Homes Bonus' introduced by the coalition government, which extended the same financial reward for bringing an empty home back into use as building a new one. Councils were also granted the flexibility to impose a council tax premium of up to 50 per cent (on top of the council tax bill) on properties empty for over two years. And powers to raise that premium to 100 per cent of council tax were announced in November 2017.

Of course, more should be done to bring empty homes back into use. But their number has fallen sharply over the last decade, as af-fordability has become worse – suggesting the reason that millions of young adults are priced out of the UK property lies elsewhere.

Ian Mulheirn goes as far as to claim that the historically low rate of homebuilding across the UK during the twenty years from 1996 did nothing to increase housing costs, and actually put downward pressure on prices. 'Housing supply did not contribute to the 150 per cent increase in house prices between 1996 and 2016,' he told a conference held at the National Institute for Economic and Social Research. 'It was, in fact, a drag on price growth as the stock [of homes] rose faster than the number of households.'[26]

This conclusion stands in direct contrast to a vast body of aca-demic research over many years – to say nothing of common sense. Rather than counting up simplistic headline totals of new homes and households formed each year, successive generations of economic analysts have tried instead to get to the root of why house prices are so high. One approach compares the cost of physical construction to the cost of an existing home in order to capture the impact of planning constraint on house prices. A related method considers the price of land with planning permission to that without.

In a celebrated paper written in 2002, for instance, US academics Edward Glaeser and Joseph Gyourko attributed half the cost of new Manhattan apartments to restrictive planning rules.[27] In the UK, Christian Hilber and Wouter Vermeulen similarly identified the lack of new-build housing as a leading factor in house price inflation from 1974 onwards, demonstrating that prices could have been 35 per cent lower in 2008 in real terms had building kept place with latent housing demand.[28]

It is certainly true that there is more to the soaring rise in UK housing costs since the mid-1990s, and particularly since the 2008 global financial crisis, than the lack of supply. Low wage growth has certainly made affordability issues far more acute, particularly for young adults and many working in our public services. Falling interest rates have also pushed up prices, with many viewing even their own residential property as a financial asset. As the Bank of England itself acknowledged in 2018, quantitative easing has, since 2009, raised housing costs, explaining an estimated 22 per cent of the increase in UK house prices since 2009.[29]

In general, this 'financialisation' of housing, there can be no doubt, means that housing demand also reflects speculative pressure, on the part of both homeowners and property investors, going beyond practical residential needs. The liberalisation of mortgage lending in the 1980s and 1990s clearly boosted the UK housing market. And the advent of buy-to-let mortgages in 1996 similarly made it easier for individual investors to speculate on property by becoming landlords – which they, in turn, have been incentivised to do by low interest rates on conventional savings instruments.

It must be added, though, that aside from all these reasons and under all these scenarios, it is the intrinsic and ongoing limit on housing supply – resulting from the UK's unpredictable planning system, dysfunctional land market and highly concentrated house-building industry – in the face of growing underlying demand that ultimately preserves and enhances the value of residential property, making houses and flats such attractive financial assets.

CIRCULAR ARGUMENT

In January 2017, a couple of months after the Redfern Review, it was announced that official household projection numbers – of vital importance in the ongoing 'no shortage' debate – would no longer be calculated by MHCLG but instead by the Office for National Statistics.[30]

It was later disclosed, in September 2018, that the number of households in England is set to rise much more slowly than previous projections suggested. Between 2016 and 2041, around 159,000 new households will form each year if recent trends continue, the ONS says. This is much lower than the previous MHCLG projection, based on long-run trends going back to 1971, that an additional 210,000 households would annually be formed over the same 25-year period. These new ONS figures, then, seriously challenge statements from government, based on modelling work by MHCLG, that around 300,000 new homes are required each year to keep pace with household formation, make inroads into the UK historic housing shortage and ease the affordability crisis.

The revised figures mean the total number of households in England is projected to rise from 22.9 million in 2016 to 26.9 million in 2041 – an increase of 17 per cent. Previous projections, made in 2014, estimated there would be 26.9 million households eight years earlier, in 2033. Critics of the government's housebuilding aspirations seized on the new ONS data, claiming that it proved that the UK had no housing shortage. 'We have been over-estimating housing need for over twenty years,' said Ian Mulheirn, in response.[31]

The new lower ONS household projections partly reflect changing population trends, with the ONS predicting slower gains in life expectancy and lower net migration than it did before. Life expectancy at birth in 2041 is projected to be 83.6 years for men and 86.4 years for women, compared to the earlier estimate of 84.4 years and 87.2 years respectively. The long-term average number of children per woman is slightly lower in the new estimates and there is also a reduced assumption for long-term net migration, possibly reflecting the UK's Brexit referendum – with net immigration of 152,000 per year from mid-2023 down from 170,500.

What's alarming, though, is that the ONS also appears to have legitimised the spurious argument confusing official growth in the number of households with housing need. The new figures, remarked ONS statistician Joanna Harkrader, reflected 'lower projections of the population ... and more up-to-date figures about living arrangements, such as living with parents or cohabiting'.[32]

While it is a statistician's primary task to measure, rather than interpret, this blithe official acceptance that the huge increase in the number of concealed households and young adults living in their childhood bedroom amounts only to 'more up-to-date figures about living arrangements' is concerning. It is even more troubling that the UK's new official household formation figures could now be used to downplay and even ignore the reality of such 'living arrangements' – and the huge human misery they represent.

There is, at the very least, a danger that officialdom – with this very significant reduction in forecasted household formation, based in part on behaviour that itself reflects our chronic housing shortage, at a time when the policy debate is at a critical point – could be accused of trying to gloss over that housing shortage. It is also noteworthy that the ONS consultation process on household projections took evidence from the Home Builders Federation and other powerful property developers, which have an incentive to downplay the UK's crisis, in a bid to resist radical changes to land-use law and other aspects of our dysfunctional planning system to which they owe their dominant market position and ongoing high profits.[33]

In some sense, the new ONS household projections have institutionalised the 'no shortage' argument. On paper, the UK's housing shortage, our most chronic domestic policy problem, the source of massive discontent to millions of people, has suddenly been significantly eased. In the real world, of course, this is totally untrue. As such, the downward revision of headline numbers that previously made uncomfortable reading for powerful vested interests, but which now justify less urgent action to solve a national crisis, is an act that can only corrode public trust.

The cost of housing in many Western nations is one of the great economic and political problems of our age. In Canada, Australia, the US and across much of the UK itself, housing costs are creating vast inter-generational inequalities and preventing people moving to good jobs, impacting productivity and the broader quality of life for millions. These costs derive, as discussed in Chapter IV, from highly restrictive land use and planning rules. The status quo, in turn, sees enormous benefit flow to landowners and large property developers with the means and political connections to navigate the planning system to their advantage, allowing them to restrict supply so keeping property prices artificially high. And these benefits, of course, are derived largely at the expense of millions of ordinary workers – who either can't afford a home of their own, who must pay an elevated price for any property they do manage to buy or rent who are otherwise excluded from social housing because high land costs discourage the construction of such homes.

As such, there is a ready if somewhat tasteless demand for economic analysis which attempts to justify the continuation of such deeply iniquitous arrangements – arrangements which work well for property industry interests and the politicians to whom they give campaign donations, along with others who want less house-building, but which are nothing short of a personal and financial disaster for a growing proportion of our population, not least the younger generation.

In Vancouver, where the average house costs 11 times the median household income, the academic John Rose has written a paper called 'The Housing Supply Myth'.[34] Academics at the Australian National University estimate that their housing market had an over-supply of 164,000 homes between 2001 and 2017, with the surplus most pronounced in the phenomenally expensive cities of Brisbane, Melbourne and Sydney.[35] And in the UK, where the average house price is now eight times average earnings, Ian Mulheirn argues there is no housing shortage, not even in London, and that the UK's slow pace of housebuilding over the last twenty years has actually put downward pressure on prices.

These studies, while seized upon eagerly by people who do not want new houses built, are entirely wrong. They are based on a wholly erroneous approach to housing which treats headline national demand and supply numbers as the whole story – ignoring living conditions, local economic factors and housing size and quality, to say nothing of basic human desires.

'The current backlog of households with housing need is four million in England or 4.7 million across Great Britain,' according to an authoritative 2018 study carried out by the Chartered Institute of Housing and Heriot-Watt University. Of course, the most important failing of the 'no shortage' argument is that it deals only in current annual estimates of demand and supply, taking no account of the UK's large backlog shortage of homes.

'Over a fifteen-year time horizon, the total level of new house-building required is estimated at around 340,000 *per year* for England and 380,000 for Great Britain,' the Heriot-Watt study said. 'These numbers include significant allowances for suppressed household formation by younger adults resulting from previous inadequate supply and unaffordability, as well [as] necessary provision for more demolitions and vacancies.'[36]

There are plenty of legitimate things to say about the role of falling interest rates in pushing up house prices – I agree with Mulheirn and other 'no shortage' advocates on that. It is also true that low wages have aggravated affordability issues, particularly since the 2008 financial crisis, and that high house prices in part reflect the use of residential property as an investment asset.

What should not be in doubt, though, is that the single biggest problem with the UK housing market, and the main driver of affordability issues, is the underlying homes shortage. It is clear to the author – and the vast majority of academics, policymakers and other analysts working in this area – that the UK is suffering from a chronic lack of homes. It makes no sense to interpret lower than expected household formation rates as evidence of less demand and need for housing – it is an insidiously circular argument. Household formation has been lower than expected over recent years because homes simply aren't available to allow their creation – as the large increase in the number of concealed households and young adults living with their parents makes abundantly clear.

'This notion there is no homes shortage in the UK is utter nonsense,' one recent UK Housing Minister told me. 'The Treasury loves it, though, as they're fixated on the idea that building more homes will cause a banking collapse.'[37] There are many vocal interest groups that want to prevent a sharp rise in UK housebuilding, of course – and they are no doubt a willing audience for, and will vigorously promote, 'no shortage' claims. But such arguments – whether they result from genuine independent research, or as part of a lobbying effort by large developers – are disproved by a cool analysis of the facts.

IMMIGRATION NATION

Another highly contentious issue within the housing debate is the link between immigration and high UK house prices. To what extent has high net immigration in recent years contributed to the UK's housing shortage and made affordability worse? Would lower immigration mean we could solve our housing supply problems without having to tackle the difficult issues relating to planning consent, finance and land transactions outlined in this book?

Immigration has long been a net positive for the UK. The British economy and our broader cultural life have benefited enormously, over many centuries, from successive waves of immigration – from continental Europe, Ireland, the West Indies, Africa, Asia and elsewhere. Immigration has brought numerous talented and hard-working people to the UK.

This country, for the most part, has strong interracial and multicultural relations. In a Pew Global Attitudes survey conducted in 2018, 62 per cent of British people agreed with the statement 'Immigrants make our country stronger', while just 29 per cent thought 'Immigrants are a burden'. This authoritative study of public opinion indicated, in fact, that the UK is more welcoming of and tolerant towards immigration than any other European nation – rather undermining the notion that the Brexit vote somehow makes Britain bigoted or narrow-minded.[38]

Very sharp increases in annual net immigration over recent years, though, have raised difficult questions. Backed by many large employers as an easy way to recruit, high immigration has suppressed wages among low-income workers, making their financial insecurity more acute.[39] It has also deterred investment in staff training and, in certain localities, created tensions by, in the words of a 2016 government report, putting 'extra pressure' on the public services upon which lower-income communities disproportionately rely – not least the NHS, social housing and other low-cost accommodation.[40]

From 48,000 in 1997, annual net immigration rose to 177,000 in 2012 before peaking at 342,000 in 2015 – a figure larger than the population of Cardiff.[41] So immigration doubled during the three years ahead of the Brexit vote, having increased seven-fold since 1997. While immigration clearly has benefits, both economically and culturally, the pace and scale in recent years has become a legitimate concern for millions of British voters. The Leave majority in the June 2016 referendum undoubtedly represented, in part, a vote of no confidence in the handling of immigration by successive governments.

In 2018, Housing Minister Dominic Raab argued that immigration had pushed up property prices by around 20 per cent between 1991 and 2016. Several days later, his department published a study backing that view.[42] Though a long-standing advocate of the merits of immigration – whose father came to Britain from Czechoslovakia as a Jewish refugee in 1938 – Raab argued that lower net immigration after Brexit would ease the housing crisis. 'You've got to deal with demand as well as supply,' he said. 'If we delivered on the government's target of reducing immigration to the tens of thousands every year, that would have a material impact on the number of homes we need to build.'[43]

Raab's intervention echoed the words of Theresa May. Back in 2012, as Home Secretary, May had suggested immigration was behind a third of all new UK housing demand. 'There is evidence that without the demand caused by mass immigration, house prices could be 10 per cent lower over a twenty-year period,' she said.[44]

Responding to Raab, pro-immigration commentators countered with reference to an authoritative study from the government's own

Migration Advisory Committee. 'The impact on house prices of the accumulated increase in Tier 2 type (skilled) immigrants over a five-year period is likely to be well below one per cent,' the study concluded.[45] Another academic investigation found that, at the local level, immigration may reduce house prices slightly – as the arrival of relatively less-affluent immigrants to an area lowers prices that buyers are willing to pay.[46]

About 80 per cent of immigrants who have been resident in the UK for less than five years live in the private rented sector, compared to around 20 per cent of the UK-born population. Migrants with over a decade of residence, though, show the same owner-occupancy levels as the broader population. But when it comes to the impact of immigration on housing demand as a whole and, in turn, on house prices, the verdict of a detailed House of Commons investigation is that the evidence is inconclusive.[47]

Despite that, and notwithstanding the UK's liberal attitude towards immigration, much of the public has made up its mind. A 2016 poll by Opinium Research found that 69 per cent of UK adults think Britain is in the midst of a housing affordability crisis and, among those, more than half – 54 per cent – view immigration as the largest contributory factor.[48]

Since 1960, the UK population has risen from 52.4 million to an estimated 66.6 million at the time of writing. For the first forty years of that period, annual population growth was just over 150,000. From 2000 onwards, the population has grown by around 410,000 a year on average – in part, of course, due to rising net immigration. This population acceleration over the past two decades has clearly boosted the number of homes required.[49] Since 1960, in addition, the average household size in the UK has fallen from 3.01 people to 2.33, further increasing the latent demand for more homes.

A major reason for recent high immigration, is the accession to the EU of the 'A8 countries' in 2004.[50] The year before that, official forecasts suggested that migration to the UK from these Central and Eastern European former Soviet nations would be 5,000 to 13,000 a year.[51] Actual annual inflows turned out to be over twenty times the upper end of that estimate – a pace of immigration which, under the EU's freedom of movement rules, the UK's border authorities, and voters, could do nothing to control.

Given such a sharp and unexpected rise in immigration, the UK government clearly struggled to make adequate provision – in terms of schools, hospitals and, indeed, social housing – for this rise in population. That then resulted in understandable discontent among some communities particularly reliant on relatively low-wage work and scarce public services – even those with a history, over previous generations, of relatively successful immigration absorption.

It is the author's view, though, that the UK has a housing supply problem, and a related and chronic affordability problem, not because of immigration. The underlying reason is that our increasingly concentrated housebuilding industry, along with housing associations and local authorities, faced with growing demand, have spectacularly failed to build enough homes – not just in response to the A8 immigration spike, but over a very long period of time. During the 1950s, there were five new homes built in the UK each year for every thousand people living in the country. By 2017, that figure had fallen to less than three per thousand.

Over the past twenty years, UK population growth has been driven both by immigration and by a 'natural' increase – as births have outpaced deaths. This increase has clearly been faster than the growth rate of UK housebuilding. Why? Because our broken housing market has not produced the supply needed to meet this rising demand. Even worse, in fact, the warped incentive structure within our housebuilding system – encouraging land price speculation, industry consolidation and 'contrived' scarcity, as ever more planning permissions go unused and homes are 'drip-fed' onto the market – has actually served to reduce supply over the last decade, in a deliberate ploy to boost prices and profitability as demand pressures have cranked up.

In 2000, the UK was building homes each year at a rate of 0.7 per cent of the existing housing stock. By 2016, the annual housebuilding rate plunged to just 0.49 per cent of existing housing. That placed Britain in twenty-seventh place out of thirty-one industrialised nations, according to a study by the Organisation for Economic Co-operation and Development – behind Lithuania, Estonia and Cyprus among OECD members and ahead of only Latvia, Portugal, Bulgaria and Hungary.[52]

This issue isn't immigration. The issue is that we are not building nearly enough homes. This could be remedied, but that would mean our political class summoning up the necessary courage, intellectual grit and focus to challenge the iron triangle of vested interest outlined earlier in *Home Truths*, altering laws and regulations in a way that realigns incentives to promote greater housing supply.

It's not as if the UK lacks space to build – again, as highlighted in previous chapters. Residential buildings, including gardens, cover little more than 1 per cent of our land mass. Setting aside just 3 per cent of the green belt – the acreage of which has doubled over the past forty years and much of which is anyway urban scrubland – would provide space for almost two million new homes. Selling just one twentieth of state-owned land for development would, at average building densities, be space enough for well over two million more.

The problem, then, isn't population growth. The problem is the deeply dysfunctional supply side of the UK housebuilding sector, our 'broken market' which singularly fails to respond – indeed, is designed to fail to respond – to rising demand. This point was illustrated starkly by Professor Paul Cheshire of the London School of Economics, giving evidence to a House of Lords Committee.

'The population of London since 1951 has increased by less than 5 per cent,' Professor Cheshire told peers. 'Yet real house prices in London – that is, house prices, allowing for inflation – have increased six-fold over the period, so it is not population that drives house prices.'[53]

The UK and France have roughly the same size population. Between 1970 and 2015, their rate of population growth has also been almost identical, with the French population actually expanding slightly faster – at 0.5 per cent a year compared to 0.4 per cent in Britain. Over the same period, the broader French and British economies have grown at the same pace – chalking up average annual GDP growth of 2.3 per cent. Since 1970, though, France has built 16.7 million new homes, a 91 per cent expansion of the French housing stock, while Britain has built just 8.9 million, increasing the UK housing stock by only 46 per cent.

Between 1970 and 2015, real house prices in France grew by 232 per cent, while UK house prices grew more than twice as fast, by 480 per cent.[54] And twice as many people in Britain as in France are now spending 40 per cent or more of their income on housing costs.[55]

Since 1970, house prices in the UK have grown faster than in any other OECD country. This cannot be explained by financial liberalisation, globalisation or lower global interest rates, as the 'no shortage' advocates claim – seeing as these factors have affected and continue to affect many other countries apart from Britain. Other nations have also combined higher rates of immigration than the UK with much lower house prices growth.

The overwhelming reason for the UK's housing affordability crisis is, instead, our chronic homes shortage – with the UK, as stated above, performing very poorly in terms of housing supply over the long term, languishing near the very bottom of the OECD house-building league table, far below other large industrialised countries.

When it comes to social housing, it is often asserted that immigrants 'jump the housing queue'. There is certainly a widespread perception, particularly among some white working-class communities, that migrants enjoy positive discrimination regarding social housing allocation. 'The level of discrimination perceived by white Britons in social housing is higher than that perceived by any other group in social housing', according to a 2014 paper from the London School of Economics. 'The only other ethnic groups reporting higher levels of perceived discrimination with any part of the state is the black community with the police, criminal justice and immigration authorities, a relationship that we know to be very troubled.'[56]

The available evidence, though, points away from such discrimination. Less than a fifth of migrants are in social rented accommodation, similar to the rates for the broader population, according to stock data.[57] Official figures indicate that, in 2017, around 91 per cent of all new social tenancies were taken up by households with a UK-born 'lead tenant' – a share which has remained steady for several years. As such, just 9 per cent of social housing was allocated to households headed by a non-UK citizen.[58] In 2017, the share of the UK population accounted for by such citizens was 9.6 per cent, up from 5 per cent at the time of the A8 EU enlargement in 2004.[59]

BUILDING DREAMS

In some senses, immigration can make a big contribution towards solving our housing crisis – given the important role immigrant labour plays in the construction industry. The Chartered Institute of Building points out that a low immigration cap could harm housebuilding rates, given the lack of UK-born nationals trained in construction skills.[60] Some 7 per cent of the UK's construction workforce are EU27 nationals, rising to 28 per cent in London.[61]

Some fear that Brexit could create a gap in the construction labour force, unlikely to be filled any time soon – which would make solving our housing shortage harder.

The reality is that Brexit could exacerbate but certainly did not cause the UK's lack of construction labour. This skills shortage has been decades in the making and will be solved by a combination of employer-based and non-employer-based apprenticeships, rather than by staying in the EU contrary to the June 2016 referendum result.

It is right that Britain is taking back control of its borders, like many other successful, broadly open and liberal economies – including Australia, Canada, New Zealand and the US. The UK can continue to be pro-immigration, championing diversity and tolerance, while recognising that the process needs to be managed, or that very tolerance will come under threat.

Net immigration did need to fall from the 2015 high of 342,000 – and, to some degree, it has, reaching around 240,000 in 2018. Reducing net inflows too drastically, though, risks doing economic damage. Decades of under-building, and our massive backlog shortage of homes, means a sharp immigration cutback would do nothing to make homes affordable for 'generation rent', or impact significantly the availability of social housing. Only more building can do that.

Even if net immigration were to fall below 100,000 in the coming years – harking back to David Cameron's 2010 pledge that 'net immigration will be capped at tens of thousands' – that would do nothing to address the chronic shortage of homes that has built up in the UK since the late 1960s.[62] Net migration could fall to zero, but there would still be millions of concealed households, serious over-crowding and a nationwide lack of affordability. Too tight or too rapid a restriction on immigration, in fact, could do harm when it comes to building the homes needed to ease the shortage, given the significant role previous waves of semi-skilled immigrants have played in earlier UK housebuilding booms.

While immigration brings net benefits, both economically and culturally, if it proceeds too quickly, low-income communities suffer disproportionately – which can spark social tensions. Although net immigration has fallen since its 2015 peak, and will likely fall further as and when the UK leaves the EU, that does not mean that future governments can dodge the bold and, to some interest groups, no doubt, uncomfortable actions needed to revitalise the supply side of the UK housing market, if our housing shortage is to be addressed.

The MHCLG paper cited by Housing Minister Raab in 2018 did suggest migration had added 21 per cent to house prices over the period 1991–2016. But the same paper also noted that house prices had increased by 284 per cent over the same period overall. Immigration may have some impact on housing affordability, but it is rather small as a share of the overall upward price pressure.

The key to solving our housing shortage and the related affordability crisis is simply to build more homes. There is ample space to do so and, of course, a pressing demand. What stands in the way is the dysfunctional supply side of the UK's broken housing market, which needs bold and radical reform. Such reforms will be tough and will make life difficult for a powerful housebuilding, landowning lobby that is doing very well out of the status quo. That's why our housing problem is so often blamed on other causes, such as immigration – and why there is now a concerted effort to convince politicians, policymakers and economic commentators that there is no housing shortage at all.

The same opinion poll conducted by Opinium Research in 2016 which cited immigration as the leading cause of our housing crisis also asked survey respondents for their preferred solution. The most popular answer was 'build more social housing' – cited by 58 per cent of those surveyed, far more than the share who chose 'immigration restrictions' – again, pointing to the UK's relatively liberal attitude towards immigration.

The same poll also indicated that no less than 89 per cent of 18–34-year-olds who don't own a property would like to buy their own home one day. And across all age groups, two-thirds of non-homeowners have aspirations to buy. The reality is, though, that while Britain still sees itself as 'a nation of homeowners', our rate of home ownership is now below the EU average, with only three of the twenty-seven EU member states below us.

Those locked out of home ownership are now paying over 30 per cent of their disposable income on rent, rising to 40 per cent in London – up from an average of 10–15 per cent during the 1960s, 1970s and early 1980s. At the same time, the share of UK households that live in privately rented accommodation has doubled since 2000 – from around one in ten to one in five across all age groups, which means more people are spending this sharply increased income share on their housing costs.[63]

This is part of the reason there is such a clamour to buy residential property – and why, perhaps, David Cameron's Conservative government launched its Help to Buy scheme in 2013. The trouble is that by subsidising aspiring property owners to buy new-build homes, the scheme allowed some powerful housebuilders to raise prices and abuse often desperate homebuyers by selling them sub-standard homes. These 'New-Build Nightmares' are an illustration of much that is wrong with the supply side of the UK housing market.

VII

NEW-BUILD NIGHTMARES

We shape our buildings – thereafter, they shape us.[1]
WINSTON CHURCHILL, 1943

Becky Williams is a 24-year-old events manager from Yorkshire. Smart, hard-working and ambitious, she was keen from a young age to buy a place of her own. So Becky knuckled down and saved up for a deposit, as she strove to get her foot on the property ladder and establish some financial independence. But she still needed assistance from the government's Help to Buy (HTB) scheme if she was to buy a property, which meant she could only choose a new-build home.

Keen to live relatively close to her parents, Becky decided to buy a two-bedroom house being built on an estate in Wakefield by Persimmon, the UK's second-largest housing developer.[2] 'After paying my deposit, arranging a mortgage and then waiting several months, I was told, at short notice, that my home was ready and I'd be moving in just before Christmas,' says Becky.

'That was back in 2017 – and I was so thrilled at the idea of moving, for the first time, into my own place,' she recalls. 'I wanted it to be a happy and exciting moment, but it was far from that,' Becky says. 'In fact, the whole experience has been awful.'[3]

Becky's problems began as soon as she picked up her keys from the Persimmon site office on her estate. 'I walked into my new home and the first thought I had, rather than joy, was "What's going on? Why are there still builders in my house?"' Becky quickly realised that she was part of a biannual process in which, ahead of reporting results in December and June, Persimmon rushes homebuyers into their new-build houses, securing as many 'completions' as possible, even though the properties may not always be finished – certainly in the eyes of their new owners. Confirming a raft of sales as each set of financial results is announced helps elevate the Persimmon share price, of course, keeping executive bonuses as high as possible.

'It was December 22nd, three days before Christmas, and lots of people were moving in,' says Becky. 'It was chaos, the whole estate was gridlocked with cars.' She had expected to open the door on her new home to find a fresh, high-quality property, with all her carefully selected, bought-and-paid-for 'finishing touches' in place – including the new kitchen cabinets she had picked out, fitted and ready to be used, painted in her chosen colour. She had expected, throughout the entire property, the 'deep sparkle' clean that Persimmon had promised.

'The first time I walked into my living room, I was faced with a builder's workbench and there was dust everywhere,' says Becky. 'The kitchen, in particular, was so filthy I literally couldn't tell what colour the cabinets were.' Her new home was in such an unfinished state, in fact, that Becky felt she couldn't even bring in her furniture. 'We had a van outside the house, full of my things,' she says. 'But we couldn't put anything down on the floor, because there was rubbish, building materials and filth all over the place – it was disgusting.'

Becky was determined not to let the state of her property ruin her sense of achievement that she had bought her first home. 'I really wanted to spend Christmas in my new house, that meant so much to me,' she says. 'But I put up a few decorations and then lost heart – it was all so grim and disappointing that I just went back to stay with my parents.' That inauspicious beginning to life in her Persimmon new-build home was the start of long, drawn-out process – 'an absolute nightmare that just got worse over months and months' – as Becky pleaded with the developer to conduct repairs and finish off the property she had worked so hard to buy.

'We couldn't put the flooring down in the kitchen, as it was still rough concrete and far from level,' she says. 'The whole staircase looked as though it had dropped because of the size of the cracks down the side … doors wouldn't shut …. bricks on the drive started falling away … when my friends came over, it was just embarrassing.' Becky says she was 'often in tears' about her new-build house and ended up 'hating' the home she had bought. 'For a long time, I didn't like coming back from work – I'd pull up outside and think about all the outstanding issues, issues which shouldn't exist seeing as I had bought a brand-new property, and I just didn't want to go inside.'

So why did Becky buy a new-build? 'The main reason was Help to Buy,' she says. 'I couldn't stretch my income enough to buy my own place otherwise. And I also liked the idea of a blank canvas, a new house that I could decorate as I liked.' But after Christmas 2017, Becky spent 'hours and hours' chasing Persimmon to address the 'countless faults' in her home and 'days and days' waiting for workmen to show up. 'I used up most of my holiday leave sitting on my sofa, waiting for Persimmon's maintenance people to arrive, long after they said they would,' she says. 'I felt this company was laughing at me, not taking me seriously … it was horrendous.'

Sixteen months after she moved in, does Becky now think that Persimmon has finally completed her new-build home? 'To some extent, yes,' she says. 'But the finish on this house is still really scruffy in lots of places – which is not how it should be with a new-build.' Persimmon was 'very attentive' during the sales process, Becky says, but not afterwards. 'They did everything they could to convince me to buy this house,' she says. 'But once the sale was done, and I was effectively forced to move into a home that wasn't finished, it was as if I'd been forgotten about – I don't think Persimmon knows what customer care really means.'

NEW HOME, LESS STRESS?

In Pembroke, Wales, another owner of a Persimmon home has had an even worse experience. Kelsey Alldritt moved in to her new-build property in November 2018. Soon after, she became so concerned about the 'multiple problems' with the house that she hired an independent surveyor to inspect her new property. Kelsey was 'horrified' when, after a thorough inspection, her surveyor listed 167 issues, including a lack of fire-barriers in some of the property's cavity walls. Also, the gable-end wall of her new home – the property's tallest exterior wall – had been constructed 30mm off the vertical, far exceeding the 8mm industry standard tolerance. 'We don't have snags with this house – snags suggest issues that are minor,' says Kelsey, sitting on her living room sofa. 'No – this house has had major problems from the moment we moved in – including a lack of adequate fire protection and a twisted gable-end wall.'[4]

When I meet Kelsey, she is six months pregnant. She and her partner, Theo, are expecting their first child. It's a high-risk pregnancy and Kelsey's doctor has told her to avoid stress. 'It really angers me that Persimmon has given us such a defective house,' says Theo, sitting next to Kelsey, holding her hand. 'Nothing is built right in this house – and I don't want her to be stressing, worrying about chasing down Persimmon to do repairs, not at a time like this.' Visibly upset, Theo's grip on Kelsey's hand tightens.

'This house is our house,' says Kelsey quietly, after a pause, her voice shaking with emotion. 'And we're proud to own our own property,' she says, looking at Theo. 'This is our place, the dream that we've worked for, to have a nice home together and raise a family.

But the trouble is we don't feel we can make this house into our home, because the house itself is so broken.'

Buying a new property is 'less stressful than buying a second-hand home', Persimmon tells prospective customers on its website. 'We pledge to make the experience enjoyable.'⁵ The reality is that Persimmon has been widely criticised in recent years for building sub-standard homes and for poor after-sales care – as well as for the massive £75 million pay packet of Chief Executive Officer Jeff Fairburn, who left the company in November 2018. This has happened while Persimmon has been the main beneficiary of the government's £20 billion HTB scheme – under which the developer sells around half the 16,000 homes it completes each year.

Launched in 2013, HTB was sold by ministers as a way to encourage UK housebuilders to build more homes as the residential construction industry recovered from the 2008 global financial crisis. The evidence is that HTB has, instead, turbocharged the profits of a handful of powerful housebuilders, without leading to a significant increase in the number of homes actually built compared to the pre-crisis average – as outlined in Chapter IV.

Across the housebuilding industry, the combined profits of the UK's seven largest housebuilders – Barratt, Persimmon, Taylor Wimpey, Bellway, Redrow, Berkeley Group and Bovis – surged from £1.1 billion in 2012, the year before HTB began, to £4.4 billion in 2017. Five of the biggest developers have sold between them a greater total of properties under the HTB scheme than the whole of the rest of the UK housebuilding industry combined. So HTB has disproportionately benefited the largest builders, significantly increasing their market share, profitability, and broader power. Persimmon alone accounted for 15 per cent of all HTB homes sold between 2013 and 2018, according to the National Audit Office.⁶

Five years after HTB began, each of the five biggest developers was selling well over a third of their new-build properties under the scheme, with Persimmon using HTB to drive 48 per cent of its sales. This helped fuel massive increases in profitability, particularly among the biggest three developers – with profits up 271 per cent at Taylor Wimpey between 2013 and 2017, 318 per cent higher at Barratt and up 329 per cent at Persimmon.

Given that housebuilding involves very long-standing, widely available technology, such a sharp increase in profitability points to a distinct lack of genuine competition. At the same time, the combined annual salaries of the chief executives of the seven largest UK housebuilders increased three-fold during this period, from £22.9 million to £68.7 million, rising from an average of £3.3 million to almost £10 million a year.

Fuelled by HTB, the UK's five largest housebuilders made an average profit of £57,000 on each house they sold in 2018, compared with an average of around £29,000 in 2007 – the last full year before the financial crisis.[7] Yet these firms built just 70,890 houses between them in 2017, significantly below their combined output of 77,813 in 2007 – when there was no HTB subsidy and the UK population was some 10 per cent smaller.[8]

Of the big three builders, Barratt doubled its profit per house built, from £24,918 in 2007 to £47,528 in 2018. But the number of actual homes it built increased only marginally, by just 2 per cent, from 17,198 to 17,579. Taylor Wimpey's profit per house soared from £29,407 to £54,709 over the same period. Yet it built just 14,842 homes in 2017 – 28 per cent fewer than in 2007, despite benefiting hugely from HTB.

Profitability at Persimmon, though, was the highest among the big housebuilders, with the firm making £60,219 on each house it sold in 2018, up from £36,787 in 2007, a 63 per cent rise. But the number of homes Persimmon built was just 3 per cent higher than in 2007, at 16,449, despite the firm benefiting from HTB to a greater extent than any other developer.

In 2018, Persimmon made £1.1 billion in profits, up from £225 million in 2012, the year before HTB was introduced.[9] This was the biggest profit ever made by a UK housebuilder, on a record 30.8 per cent margin. Jeff Fairburn was awarded a bonus of over £100 million but after a widespread political backlash, he agreed to reduce that sum to £75 million – still by far the biggest annual bonus paid by any UK publicly listed company.

Fairburn then walked out of a BBC interview after being questioned on whether his pay-out was reasonable, given that Persimmon's profits were linked to a taxpayer-funded scheme. Amid more public outcry, the Persimmon chief executive then left the company. 'We believe that the distraction around his remuneration,' said a statement from the Persimmon board, 'continues to have a negative impact on the reputation of the business and consequently on Jeff's ability to continue in his role.'[10]

In early 2019, Vince Cable accused Persimmon of 'pinching their profits from the public purse'. The Liberal Democrat leader said: 'Far from benefiting first-time buyers, the major effect of Help to Buy is to drive up demand while having no effect on supply – the result is not help for those who need it, but a boost to the profits of big developers.'

'Persimmon represents everything that is wrong with the house-building system,' said Greg Beales, the campaign director of the housing charity Shelter. 'The firm has generated huge profits from taxpayer subsidies whilst doing very little to help solve the housing crisis we face.'[11]

In May 2019, Persimmon paid Fairburn an additional £39 million, after he had left the company. His successor as CEO, David Jenkinson, was awarded £25 million and Persimmon Finance Director Mike Killoran got a £26 million bonus.[12] These payments were approved a month after Persimmon was suspended from the government's Prompt Payment Code (PPC) – because the company was paying only 65 per cent of supplier invoices within sixty days, much less than the 95 per cent demand by the code.[13]

The most serious charge against Persimmon, though, relates not to executive pay, but the poor quality of the homes it produces. The Home Builders Federation satisfaction survey ranks developers by the number of stars that new buyers give them in response to the question 'Would you recommend your builder?' In the March 2019 survey, Persimmon was among the bottom five builders in the country – alongside four other much smaller developers.[14] The UK's second-largest housebuilder, in fact, has managed only a three-star rating in this survey, regarded as the bare minimum, since 2014.

The National House Building Council runs yearly 'Pride in the Job' awards for the best site managers – who are automatically entered if working on a site registered for an NHBC warranty. In 2018, Persimmon was bottom of the table with two awards, compared to, for example, eighty-three for Barratt and sixty-seven for Taylor Wimpey, the other two of the UK's three biggest housebuilders. Since 2012, Persimmon has won just forty-two NHBC awards, compared to 507 won by Barratt.[15]

On the website snagging.org, those who have recently bought new-build homes post their complaints about housebuilding companies. Persimmon attracts the most threads and posts, by a long way.[16] Complaints typically range from poorly fitting windows, cupboards and appliances, wobbling walls, exposed sewage pipes, staircases held in by a couple of pins and little or no insulation fitted. Some residents have taken to threatening class-action lawsuits or putting posters in their windows to warn off potential buyers.[17]

FIRE AND BRIMSTONE

Persimmon has also generated negative publicity related to potentially life-threatening fire safety issues. The case of Kelsey and

Theo described above is not an isolated incident. Numerous tim-ber-framed Persimmon homes were found to have missing or in-correctly installed fire barriers, which are fitted in cavity walls to guard against the spread of fire. Building regulations require by law that new homes are built with fire protection measures to delay fire spreading and allow crucial time for escape. In timber-framed new-build homes, fire barriers are a vital part of this protection.[18]

In 2017, a Persimmon building in Coventry, West Midlands, con-taining some forty-eight apartments was evacuated, following the discovery of a number of defects including missing fire barriers. Then, in April 2018, a fire started by a cigarette dropped at ground level spread very quickly at a Persimmon home on the Greenacres development in Exeter, engulfing the roof of a house and spreading to adjacent properties. A subsequent investigation by Persimmon found missing fire barriers at 37 per cent of homes on the Green-acres estate.

This triggered a huge inspection programme of thousands of homes across the south-west region, where more than 650 Persim-mon homes were found to have missing or incorrectly installed fire barriers. While the company has taken some action to remedy this situation, at the time of writing not all identified issues have been rectified – and countless Persimmon homes in the region have yet to be inspected.

As well as carrying out investigations across the south-west, for which Persimmon has set up a 'dedicated team', the developer says it is also implementing fire safety 'spot checks' at homes it has built across the country. In the case of Kelsey Alldritt mentioned earlier in this chapter, once a lack of adequate fire barriers was identified in a post-purchase survey that she paid for, Persimmon did then retro-fit fire barriers in Kelsey's home.

The trouble is, though, that 'a post-construction inspection for fire barriers will only allow a very limited view,' says Greig Adams, an experienced chartered building surveyor. 'Even if you drill into walls, and insert specialist cameras, you cannot state that all the fire barriers are there and installed correctly, because you need to inspect during the construction phase.'[19] The author asked Adams, who acts as an expert witness in legal disputes across the construction sector, why fire barriers might not be fitted while a home was actually being built. 'The only reason that people would miss them out is to save costs and to get the house up and built as quickly as possible,' he says. 'That's really the only reason not to install them, to try to do things quicker and more cheaply, with site supervision not being up to standard to check.'

Persimmon has been criticised under other headings too, not least on numerous social media sites set up by disgruntled owners of new-build homes.[20] There are many complaints about the extent to which potential buyers are pressured to use mortgage brokers and solicitors appointed by Persimmon. Complainants report those solicitors are not always forthcoming or even transparent about the existence and effects of ongoing ground rent liabilities under leasehold agreements and other covenants.

Persimmon, along with some other large developers, has been bitterly criticised by MPs for selling new-build houses with rising leasehold charges which can make such properties expensive to live in, and very difficult to sell on. Almost a fifth of houses purchased under HTB in 2017 were sold leasehold, as reported in Chapter V. The sale of HTB houses with contract clauses allowing ground rents to rise dramatically in later years has caused public outrage.

Repeated surveys show that such leasehold contracts have often been sold to unsuspecting buyers of new-build homes, using solicitors appointed by the developer. Contractual rights under such leaseholds, including future payments for which homeowners are liable, have then been sold on to private equity companies and other third-party financial investors, from which developers have made huge profits.

There is no explicit UK law to limit the level of ground rents and no independent body which oversees their management. But in December 2017, amid growing outcry about punitive leasehold terms, the government issued a consultation paper saying it wants to prohibit residential leases both on existing freeholds and new-build properties. At the time of writing there has been no significant change.[21] In the meantime, such leases mean homeowners are often compelled to pay not just regular ground rents, at a rate set by the freeholder, but may also be charged when they want to extend or re-mortgage their new-build property.

The problems associated with selling on such properties when owners want to move have been highlighted by the National Association of Estate Agents – made up of firms which clearly have considerable property-selling experience. In September 2018, an NAEA survey reported that 94 per cent of 1,000 homebuyers who purchased leasehold new-build homes regretted their decision – and 65 per cent used the developers' own solicitor.[22]

Almost half the people who bought a new-build home during the decade before 2018 had 'no idea about the trappings of a lease-hold contract until it was too late', said the NAEA. The report found leaseholders paid an average of £277 per year in ground rent when they moved in, and as of 2018 were paying £319, with most having been in their properties for three or four years.[23] Freeholders typically charged homeowners £1,422 to install double glazing, £887 to change kitchen units and £689 to replace the flooring, the survey found. Some homeowners faced bills of £527 for changing their blinds and £411 for installing a new front door. Along with the 94 per cent of new-build homeowners with leaseholds who regretted their decision, the study showed that 62 per cent felt their homes had been mis-sold.

Those considering the purchase of new-build homes were faced with misleading marketing terms like 'virtual freehold' – 'which gives buyers the perception of total ownership, control and stability, but is anything but,' the NAEA reported. 'Buyers were assured they would have the same rights and responsibilities as a freeholder or have all the freedoms associated with being a freeholder, but this is not the case.'[24]

The NAEA dubbed the sale of new-builds with leaseholds the 'PPI of the property sector' – a reference to the Payment Protection Insurance scandal during the run-up to the 2008 financial crisis. PPI amounted to a serious fraud involving unnecessary mortgage and loan cover which resulted in a Competition Commission inquiry, legal action and, as of 2019, some £36 billion being repaid to customers.[25] In February 2019, after an extensive investigation, the Leasehold Knowledge Partnership (LKP), the secretariat of the All-Party Parliamentary Group on Leasehold Reform, a cross-party body of MPs and peers, concluded that Persimmon had been 'the main offender' when it comes to 'spreading leasehold houses around the country, creating homes which include an investment asset for someone else'.

LKP remarked that 'taxpayers have been subsidising the investments of private equity speculators in residential freeholds, who hide their beneficial ownership behind nominee directors and are often based offshore'.[26] The LKP study, which considered the circumstances of 2,800 leaseholders, also found a direct correlation between feelings of dissatisfaction among customers and those who had used solicitors recommended by the developer.

In mid-2019, more than forty housebuilders – including Persimmon, Barratt, Taylor Wimpey and Bovis – signed a government-backed pledge to scrap the most exploitative 'doubling' clauses in leases which can see ground rents soar over a short period.[27] The government also finally said it wanted to ban the sale of houses with leaseholds under HTB. This move is designed to stop 'taxpayers' money from directly supporting the unjustified sale of leasehold houses', said a statement from the Ministry of Housing, Communities and Local Government.

Yet in early 2019, Communities Secretary James Brokenshire said the restriction won't come in until 2021, giving large developers another two years to use HTB to sell leasehold homes to often young, unsuspecting buyers that then cause such bitter resentment.[28] The restriction will also only apply to new-build houses and not flats – which account for around a fifth of HTB properties. At the time of writing, several months after Brokenshire's announcement, the relevant legislation has yet to be passed by Parliament – so, as far as homebuyers are concerned, nothing has actually changed.[29]

LACK OF PROTECTION

'When you come into your new home you should be thinking "Oh, I can do such and such in this room, my favourite picture can go on that wall" – it should be fun,' says Richard Day, nursing a mug of tea at his kitchen table. 'But, instead, we had a minefield to walk through – there were holes in the ceiling, electrical wires hanging out, all we were thinking of was the faults we saw.'

Sitting next to Richard is Lukas Platts. 'In terms of snagging we had just over 200 issues, five of them majors – it's been a nightmare,' says Lukas. 'There are problems everywhere – here in the kitchen, for instance, none of the units are straight – it's all on a slant.'

Richard and Lukas live on the same Persimmon estate in Wakefield as Becky Williams. Having decided to set up home together, they put down a deposit on a new-build property being built by the developer, then paid out thousands of pounds more for bespoke 'finishing touches' to be added to their property before completion. 'We understand everyone has their own sense of style and wants to create a home unique to them,' says Persimmon's marketing brochure. 'That's why we created the *Finishing Touches* range – your new home, styled by you, ready to move into.'[30]

For Richard and Lukas, though, the sense of expectation and excitement they felt at the prospect of owning their first home together turned to bitter disappointment – as it did for Becky. They, too, took possession of a home they maintain was 'sub-standard' and, ahead of Persimmon reporting their end-of-year results, they were, they say, 'forced' to move into a property before it was ready and which they were not given time to inspect.

'Just before Christmas, I received a call saying our house was done and we needed to pick up the keys and sign the final paperwork by 5 p.m. that day,' says Richard. 'Well, I got the call around 4.30 p.m. and was at work in Leeds – so that put me under enormous pressure.'

Richard and Lukas say Persimmon told them that if they didn't complete by 5 p.m. they would incur a £50 charge, every day, for ten days. After that, the developer said, they were at risk of legal action and could lose their new home, along with their deposit and the extra money they had already paid for their 'finishing touches'.

'Persimmon said the build is done, it's finished, you need to be here by 5 p.m. to sign for the keys,' recalls Richard. 'But there had been no letter, no email or text – I was in the middle of a meeting and this phone call came out of the blue.' Lukas says he felt 'emotionally pressured' into accepting a house he had barely seen. 'There was no inspection, no time for the walk-around the house that we'd been promised – nothing,' he says. 'They pushed this house onto us, in a totally unfinished state.'

Richard says 'fear' was the main emotion when he and Lukas signed for the house. 'They hit us with endless legal jargon,' he says. 'We're not solicitors, we're not a legal firm,' says Lukas. 'When you buy something and invest your time and money, trying to achieve your dream, you expect to be treated fairly and told the truth – and that simply never happened.'

Once they had signed, for the next three months Richard and Lukas felt unable to move in, as their property was in such a bad state. 'We asked Persimmon to send people to fix our house – but it wasn't right after they came, so they had to come again – we were wading through endless bureaucracy to get the most simple things done.'

During that time, Richard and Lukas were paying the mortgage on a house they say they couldn't live in. 'Eventually, when it looked like we were getting somewhere, Persimmon then said, "Oh we're not doing all these repairs now, as we think the house is liveable,"' says Lukas. 'Well, maybe by that stage you could technically live in the house, but you wouldn't expect a brand-new car to have dents and scratches all over it – and, similarly, we expected to get what we purchased, which was a brand-new house.'

One reason so many owners of new-build homes find themselves in unfinished, sub-standard properties is that many developers prevent new-build buyers from hiring their own independent surveyor, prior to purchase. 'It's a problem across the industry,' says chartered surveyor Greig Adams. 'If you try to get a survey done before you move in to a newly built home, most of [the big housebuilders] will block it'.[31] Buyers of new-builds are also not automatically covered under the Sale of Goods Act or the Consumer Rights Act, as you are when you buy normal domestic appliances. So, as Adams observes, 'consumers enjoy more protection buying a toaster than when they buy a new-build home, probably the biggest purchase of their life'.

Paula Higgins is a former civil servant who set up the Home-Owners Alliance (HOA) – an advisory service for homeowners and aspiring homebuyers. 'It's quite shocking, actually, because when you buy a new-build home you have a contract that's written by the developer which generally provides very little control over when you complete the purchase,' she says. 'You can't delay it if you think your house isn't ready and there's no mandatory right to inspect the property before you finalise the purchase – that is the default position in the industry.'[32]

This is an astonishing state of affairs – which speaks volumes about the market power of the UK's housebuilders, and their ability to resist the most basic legislation regulating their product. And by presenting such developers with thousands of often young, first-time buyers who, having been lent money by the state, are then limited to buying only new-build homes, HTB has served to increase that market power – with an obvious negative impact on the level of true competition and related customer service.

Some people claim that buyers of new-build homes have peace of mind because such properties come with a ten-year warranty from the National House Building Council (or similar body). Fixtures and fittings and snagging issues are generally covered for just two years by the developer's guarantee – which may give housebuilders like Persimmon an incentive to drag out repairs after homebuyers have moved in. But the ten-year NHBC warranty for structural problems – including plumbing, wiring and roof coverings – is often presented as much more reliable.

There are concerns, though, that NHBC controls over 80 per cent of the warranties market for new homes. Eyebrows have also been raised that the organisation annually pays millions of pounds a year to big developers, rewarding those who register the most new-build homes with NHBC – in what is, effectively, a profit-sharing agreement.[33]

The NHBC says it operates 'to robust, independent and transparent governance practices and is committed to protecting homeowners and raising the standard of new homes in the UK'.[34] Yet campaigners have previously pointed to close links between large developers, the Home Builders Federation lobby group, and the governance of NHBC – including the warranty organisation's board of directors.[35] And there are certainly frequent complaints from buyers of new-build homes, via local newspapers and social media, who claim in disputes about snagging, and rectifying structural flaws, that the NHBC too often acts more in the interests of developers than consumers.

HOLDING BACK

For a long time, the construction of residential property in the UK has been fundamentally a sellers' market. Under the 'speculative development' model, described in Chapter IV, the vast majority of properties are built in a way that largely accommodates the constraints of producers rather than the aspirations of consumers. 'Housebuilders do not have to deliver a good product or high levels of customer service to win market share,' stated Kate Barker, in her seminal 2004 report, ten years before HTB was introduced.[36]

The lack of a meaningful producer-consumer relationship between large homebuilders and homebuyers often results in badly designed housing and means the best developers are not always rewarded. If this was the case when Barker wrote her report, at a time when the 'volume' housebuilders constructing over 2,000 homes each year built less than 30 per cent of all new homes, it is far more so in 2019, when such large developers account for around 60 per cent of homes built.[37]

Since HTB began, the public's view regarding the quality of new-build homes has significantly deteriorated – increasingly so over the last two or three years. The annual HOA survey for 2019 shows fears over the quality of new-build homes at a five-year high, with 88 per cent of new-build homeowners calling for a system to withhold funds from housebuilders until they rectify faults.[38] The New

Homes Review, another independent advisory body, dedicated solely to new-build homeowners, found in its 2019 survey that 91 per cent of new-build homes have snags and defects.

'We are inundated with calls about shoddy workmanship and flawed properties, about developers who fail to fix faults ranging from poor finishes and ineffective insulation to dangerous electrical and structural problems,' says Paula Higgins. 'But it's currently very hard to hold developers to account – especially once you have parted with your money.'

In March 2019, faced with a public relations crisis, Persimmon announced a homebuyers' 'retention' scheme – under which buyers could withhold a share of the purchase price until the developer has fixed any faults. It was an eye-catching gesture, designed to combat Persimmon's reputation for low quality, customer discontent and corporate greed, as embodied by Fairburn's notorious £75 million bonus. Persimmon pointed to their new retention policy as 'an unambiguous signal of cultural and operational change'.[39]

Yet pressure to change had come not just from the media, but also major shareholders – given reports that the government was considering excluding Persimmon from HTB because of concerns about the quality of the homes it was building. Such a move would seriously dent Persimmon's bottom line.

The developer's proposed retention share, though – a mere 1.5 per cent of the purchase price – amounts to just £3,600 on the average Persimmon home. That would finance the correction of only a few snags – and is far from what would be needed to fund the installation of fire barriers or carry out other structural works. The HOA believes the standard contract of new-build developers should allow for an automatic snagging retention of 2.5 per cent of the purchase price, with the homebuyer having at least six months after their move-in date to identify and report any faults.

Not only is Persimmon's 1.5 per cent retention share much lower but when the legal details of its retention policy were quietly published in April 2019, it turned out that the retained funds could only be used to address faults 'identified at the point of key release'. In other words, people moving into a new home, with all the logistical complexity and activity that involves, would be given *at most only a single day* by Persimmon to identify faults with their new property.[40]

'Moving into a new home should be a positive experience enhanced by all the benefits of a new build that is designed for modern living,' declared CEO David Jenkinson, when announcing Persimmon's new retention scheme. 'We are determined that the experience is not overshadowed by teething problems and providing a homebuyer's retention is an important step towards achieving this.'[41]

So the Persimmon CEO claims he is 'determined' that the experience of moving into one of his company's new-build homes should not be 'overshadowed by teething problems' – and yet, as he makes that announcement, he launches a retention policy which says that, unless homebuyers detect and report faults to Persimmon on the very same day they move in, the developer will refuse to use retained funds to put right 'teething problems' of the firm's own making.

During June 2019, while the author was investigating Persimmon for an episode of Channel 4's *Dispatches*, we asked Persimmon why it had granted homebuyers only a single day to identify snags with their new-build property. The developer refused to grant *Dispatches* an interview or discuss this issue. But in early July, less than two weeks before the documentary was broadcast, Persimmon quietly announced, via a line buried in its regular trading statement, that it would extend the length of time customers can check for faults in their new homes from the first day to the first week of occupation.[42]

David Jenkinson eventually said, since announcing the retention scheme, the firm had 'been in discussions with stakeholders' and decided to extend the retention 'to cover faults identified in the first week after moving in, not just by the moving-in day itself'. The Persimmon CEO added, though, that use of the retention scheme 'may be determined by which mortgage lender the customer chooses' – casting further doubt on the extent to which the scheme will be accessible or useful for a broad range of Persimmon homebuyers.

RABBIT-HUTCH BRITAIN

Living rooms in new-build homes in the UK are almost a third smaller than in similar homes built in the 1970s. The average living room in a house built since 2010 is 17.1 square metres, compared with 24.9 square metres in 1970s new-builds – a 32 per cent contraction. Bedrooms and kitchens are also significantly smaller. Overall, homes built since 2010 are barely the same size as those built during the 1940s, a decade ravaged by a desperate post-war shortage of building materials, capital and labour.[43]

A separate study found that newly built homes in England are the smallest by floor area in Europe, at an average of 76 square metres. This was some way behind the next worst, in Italy and Portugal, at 81.5 square metres and 82.2 square metres respectively. Homes in Denmark were by far the most spacious, at 137 square metres, followed by Greece, with an average floor area of 126.4 square metres. Some 55 per cent of dwellings in England were found to fall short of the accepted internal space standards.[44]

The reasons for this are complex, but relate in part to the removal of minimum space standards through the 1980 Local Government, Planning and Land Act – another example of the housebuilding lobby's raw power. The small size of new-build homes also reflects the high value of land and the low number of houses built by public authorities and housing associations – which means commercial housebuilders face less competition.

The combination of the 2008 financial crisis crushing so many

SME builders, then HTB disproportionately benefiting large developers since its 2013 launch, has resulted in a much more concentrated UK housebuilding industry. As such, dominant builders, operating in an environment of limited competition, have been able to squeeze room dimensions to push up profits. The size of new-build gardens has also significantly diminished, so more properties can be packed onto a development.

At the same time, the 2013 relaxation of Permitted Development Rights referred to in the previous chapter, automatically allowing the conversion of offices into residential properties, has since almost doubled the 'change of use' additions to the housing stock – with 30 per cent of such homes failing to meet designated living space standards, from which PDR homes are exempt.

The controversy over 'rabbit-hutch Britain' is clearly becoming more intense, as new homes and conversions produce ever more crowded living spaces, even for those who are fortunate enough to be able to buy their own homes. It is against this stark reality that the government launched its Building Better, Building Beautiful Commission in November 2018, with its stated mission of easing the UK housing crisis with homes that reflect the character of existing communities. More weight should be placed on attractive housing developments when giving planning permission, suggests the Commission's July 2019 report, called 'Creating Space for Beauty'.[45]

This is clearly a laudable aim – with which few could disagree. Yet as the country struggles to build the homes it needs, there's certainly an argument that such concerns as size and character will be sacrificed for the goal of getting more units to market, with a focus on quantity, not quality. 'Some housebuilders, knowing they have access to Help to Buy, believe they can build any old crap and still sell it,' said one housebuilding executive to the Building Better, Building Beautiful Commission. It's a shame that this highly newsworthy quotation was reported only anonymously by the commission in its Interim Report, buried in a footnote at the very back of the document.

Many owners of new-build properties are perfectly happy with the homes they have bought. There are UK developers who consistently build high-quality new homes. But it is clear there is far too much dissatisfaction, which is serious and widespread, with the quality of new-build homes. Over recent years, a constant stream of social media postings and local news reports have told of growing frustration and fear of financial ruin among those who have bought properties from a variety of developers, with owners of recently acquired new-builds fearing their homes may never be finished or will be very difficult to sell.

Since HTB was introduced, powerful developers have clearly used the demand spike to sell a slew of small, low-quality houses, racked with faults and often on extremely punitive leasehold ownership terms. The scheme has been a huge cash bonanza for already extremely powerful big developers that dominate the housing industry, consolidating their grip and allowing them to restrict competition to an even greater extent. Ahead of Theresa May's party conference speech in October 2017, when it was reported the Prime Minister was about to announce that an additional £10 billion of taxpayers' money was to be channelled into HTB, the shares of the UK's biggest housebuilders gained no less than £1 billion in value in a single day, as we learnt in a previous chapter.[46]

The reality is that the housebuilding industry is delivering massive shareholder returns while often providing a deeply sub-standard product. Bumper profits have coincided with a catalogue of failings by some of the UK's major housebuilders, including poor design, miserable space standards and defective workmanship. Such developers are also systematically delaying build-out to keep prices high, sitting on planning permissions to prevent SMEs obtaining permits to build and consistently exploiting a loophole in the planning process to renege on their obligations to provide affordable homes and other forms of community infrastructure.

The increasing dominance of the large developers enables them, under intense pressure from the banks and other large financial investors that own them, always to prioritise high profits over the number and quality of new homes. 'Since the 2008 financial crisis, shareholders have become the main priority for housebuilders,' says Neal Hudson, housing expert and founder of Residential Analysts. 'The overarching factor has been big pressure from the City, for whom the priority is the profit margin not the number of homes built.'[47]

The Scottish academic Professor James Sommerville has decades of experience as both a property industry analyst and practitioner. 'The large housebuilders no longer understand or focus on their customers – it's all about their institutional investors demanding a return,' he says. 'So housebuilders have no incentive to hand over quality finished homes … what it's all about instead is getting signatures on dotted lines so, come result season, they can include more sales in their figures.'[48]

Persimmon – due to a combination of its size, bloated executive pay, consistently poor quality ratings and alarming fire safety issues – has become, in the minds of many MPs and more broadly, the major culprit when it comes to poor customer service and shoddy new-build homes. Public outrage has been heightened by that fact Persimmon has used HTB more than any other developer – so, while selling countless low-quality unsafe homes, often on punitive leaseholds, the UK's most profitable housebuilder has also been the main beneficiary of the billions of pounds of taxpayers' money channelled into this scheme.

In early 2019, Housing Secretary James Brokenshire expressed 'increasing concern' about Persimmon's build quality and 'their leadership seemingly not getting [that] they're accountable to customers', amid speculation the developer may be excluded from the next round of HTB – which, at the time of writing, is set to extend to 2023.[49] In response, Persimmon was forced to reassure shareholders, as well as the government, that build quality and customer service would improve.

In April 2019, the developer announced an 'independent review' of its 'customer care, culture and operations, and on eliminating cases of poor workmanship'.[50] The review, which includes fire safety, is being chaired by a QC – and the final findings will be published. Persimmon is also introducing a number of other customer care initiatives, including more accurate moving-in dates, weekend appointments for snagging and out-of-hours customer care access – and adds that its independent fire risk assessor is inspecting cavity barriers at a lower level in properties, not just via the attic space. Since then, Persimmon has said customer satisfaction will be one factor in deciding future director remuneration. 'The incentive pay for senior operational management also includes customer care performance conditions,' the developer insists, 'aligning their interests with this priority for the group'.[51]

In July 2019, three months after this review was announced, Channel 4's *Dispatches* commissioned an experienced snagging expert to inspect a brand new Persimmon home – after the owners had completed the sale, but before they moved in. He found 292 faults, including a defective fire door and a full set of leaking sinks – with over 70 per cent of the snags 'below building regulations tolerance'.[52]

Persimmon still refused to be interviewed. In response to the programme, which revealed ongoing quality-control and safety issues, the developer apologised 'without reservation' to the disgruntled homebuyers featured in the film. 'We can and will do better,' said Persimmon, pointing to 'profound change under new leadership' via a written statement. 'We fully accept that on too many occasions in the past we have fallen short on customer care and the speed and empathy with which we dealt with problems.'

Two days after the *Dispatches* film was broadcast, Persimmon was the subject of a blistering attack at Prime Minister's Questions by Harlow MP Robert Halfon. 'I met a group of Harlow residents, many of them on the government's Help to Buy scheme, who moved into homes built by Persimmon that are shoddily built with severe damp and crumbling walls,' said Halfon. 'In the eyes of my residents, Persimmon are crooks, cowboys and con artists.'[53]

It must surely make sense for the government to introduce a mandatory right for homebuyers to inspect new-build properties, appointing their own independent surveyor, before they agree to complete their purchase. The absence of this basic right, and the paucity of broader legislation protecting the buyers of new-build homes, is a telling indictment of the overbearing power of the housebuilding lobby. It is nothing short of disgraceful that successive governments have failed to put in place these most rudimentary safeguards for countless ordinary people making the biggest purchase of their lives.

Clearly, ministers should also keep up the pressure on Persimmon, and other developers building shoddy homes, amassing legal evidence to exclude them from Help to Buy unless their performance sharply improves. 'I expect all developers to deliver good-quality housing on time, and to treat buyers fairly,' said Housing Minister Kit Malthouse in May 2019. 'The government will be considering carefully how the developers who work with us meet the standards and quality that customers expect and deserve.'[54]

'We will take care of you,' says Persimmon to prospective homeowners, 'not just when you're buying but after you've moved in.'[55] Lukas Platt remains scarred by how Persimmon treated him, rushing him into a home full of faults which he viewed as unfinished. 'I felt victimised, used as nothing but a cash cow,' he says. 'They say buying your first home is stressful – but in our case the most stressful thing was the people building the home.' His partner, Richard Day, is equally upset. 'It's not OK to treat people like this,' he says. 'We invested ourselves, our hard-earned money, our hearts into a dream of buying a home together – and the way Persimmon treated us was simply not OK.'

Becky Williams feels the same way, having also moved into an unfinished Persimmon house full of snags. 'Once the sale was done, it was as if I'd been forgotten about,' she says. 'If I could turn back time, would I go with another developer? One hundred per cent.'

And Kelsey Alldritt, with her twisted gable-end wall, wonders if she'll ever be able to sell her Persimmon home. 'This house isn't worth what I paid for it – not with all these problems,' she says. 'And given that they'll show up in a survey, who'll buy my house when I want to move?' says Kelsey. 'Who wants to buy a broken house?'

VIII

FAT OF THE LAND

The incomes of landowners are rising while they are sleeping,
through the general prosperity produced by the labour
and outlay of other people.[1]
JOHN STUART MILL, 1871

On many measures, the UK is a laudably modern, progressive society. This country boasts universal education and healthcare, of course – both free at the point of use. In 2018, Britain was judged to be 'the best place in the world to do business' by *Forbes* magazine, which ranked 153 nations on fifteen different factors including innovation, taxes, technology, corruption, red tape and investor protection.[2] And Britain has traditionally been a society with a high degree of social mobility – although a recent government report concludes that social mobility has been 'virtually stagnant' during the five years up to 2019.[3]

On one very important measure, though, British society remains positively feudal. There are around 60 million acres of land across England, Scotland, Wales and Northern Ireland – and around two-thirds of it is owned by fewer than 6,000 people. In previous centuries, landowners paid tax on their sprawling acreages. In recent decades, thanks in part to their formidable lobbying power, and the EU's Common Agricultural Policy, large landowners have for the most part avoided land taxation and received huge subsidies instead.

Each month, then, ordinary homeowners cough up hefty rates of council tax, paid out of hard-earned income. And after working a lifetime to pay off a mortgage, even those with relatively modest homes are then taxed heavily on any property inheritance they leave their children – who themselves, as discussed at length, are often struggling to buy a home.[4] The owners of large country estates, in contrast, somehow use 'family trusts' to pass on to their gilded off-spring chunks of our green and pleasant land joyously free of tax. As a young, undergraduate economist, the discovery of these iniquitous realities was an affront to my student sensitivities. Now older, and hopefully wiser, my sense of outrage, if anything, has grown.

THE LEAST BAD TAX

In the aftermath of the 2008 financial crisis, as central banks engaged in so-called 'quantitative easing', artificially expanding their balance sheets, asset prices – particularly for land and real estate – ballooned. As more and more gains accrued to those who were already asset-rich, UK wealth inequality rose. During the five years after 2010, the wealth of the richest 10 per cent of UK households has increased three times faster than that of the bottom 50 per cent.

While fat-cat salaries and the visible wage gap between senior executives and rank-and-file workers attracts most media attention, the real driver of growing discontent with capitalism is widening wealth inequality – typified, above all, by the millions of young adults now priced out of the property market. It was these discontented voters of 'generation rent', of course, who brought Jeremy Corbyn to within a whisker of Downing Street during the June 2017 general election.

With wages taxed at up to 45 per cent, and national insurance contributions on top, almost half of all UK government revenue derives from income tax and NICs – in other words, taxes on labour. Capital gains tax, in contrast, is levied at just 20 per cent on assets and 28 per cent on residential property – with CGT and other property taxation raising only 14 per cent of total government revenue.[5] So, at a time when wealth inequality is widening, we continue to tax 'earned income' at a far higher rate than 'unearned income' stemming from capital gains or broader speculation – which widens wealth inequality even more. This is not only inefficient, discouraging effort and enterprise, but could easily be seen as immoral.

As the UK tax system becomes increasingly complex, with ever more loopholes, the case for levying charges on tangible, immovable assets, as opposed to easily re-domiciled liquid cash and other financial holdings, grows stronger. And as more and more young adults strive to buy their own property, amid a chronic housing shortage, there is an increasingly compelling argument to use the tax system to encourage building on land otherwise left undeveloped. These interrelated needs – addressing wealth inequality, making the tax system fairer and more transparent and encouraging the release of more land for housebuilding – can all be met by using some variant of a land value tax.

Nobody made the land. It is nature's bequest. By farming it, or building on it, land may be made more valuable, but it was always there. If landowners want to own and occupy a plot of land, with the government protecting the title, then there is an argument a payment should be made that reflects that land's value. If landowners don't want to pay such a levy, and use the land accordingly, they should sell it to someone who will. This is the principle behind a land value tax (LVT), a policy which the Nobel Prize-winning economist Milton Friedman – no left-winger – called the 'least bad tax'.[6] LVT has been praised and promoted by a broad range of thinkers, not least the eighteenth-century economist and philosopher Adam Smith – a leading figure of the Scottish Enlightenment.[7]

'The tax on land values is the most just and equal of taxes,' wrote the nineteenth-century US economist Henry George, stressing that the value of land derives not just from its inherent existence, but from the needs of households, firms and communities for food, shelter and space, combined with their efforts to work in and develop the economy and infrastructure of any particular locality. So levying an LVT is 'the taking by the community, for the use of the community, that value which is the creation of the community', wrote George in his celebrated work, *Progress and Poverty*, in 1879.[8]

George called the LVT 'the single tax' because, for him and many other academic proponents, it should be levied at such a rate that allows it to replace all other taxes. Under a 'Georgist' school of economic thought, the income you earn from your labours is yours entirely to spend in whatever way you like, with government revenue deriving entirely from LVT.

A classical LVT works by levying a percentage tax on the imputed rental value of the land. So, as the needs of a community push up rental values, part of that gain is transferred from landowners to broader society. Those owning houses and other real estate also pay LVT – based on market valuations of the land underneath their home or business, which can be derived by comparing residential and commercial rents between different parts of the country. But that would be the only tax they pay.

The idea of scrapping all taxation and replacing it with LVT is, of course, pie-in-the-sky. The Labour Party, in its 2017 manifesto, said it would 'consider options such as a land value tax to ensure local government has sustainable funding for the long term', but clearly in addition to other taxes.[9] The Liberal Democrats, too, pledged at that same election to 'consider the implementation' of LVT, as did the Green Party – but, again, without scrapping existing forms of tax.[10]

While an LVT-only world makes theoretical sense, appealing to an undergraduate economist perhaps, no sizeable nation – to say nothing of a world-ranking economy such as the UK – would upend its entire system of revenue collection to adopt Henry George's 'single tax' LVT. Yet the general idea which underpins the LVT remains highly relevant and, if introduced by a government determined to enact reform, could still be used to help tackle the UK's endemic housing crisis.

The failure of large developers to build enough homes, at sufficient pace, even when planning permissions have been granted, is, as we have seen, a crucial issue. Despite the sharp increase in residential planning permissions granted by local authorities each year since 2010, an astonishing 30–40 per cent of such permissions remain unused – with hundreds of thousands now outstanding.

This reflects a concerted ploy by an increasingly concentrated UK housebuilding industry. Large developers sit on usable plots in a rising market, accruing wealth as such plots become more valuable – while ordinary workers save desperately, as prices rise, in a bid to be able eventually to afford a home. And, of course, as speculative pressure builds, and land prices increase, new-build houses become smaller, with quality and customer care suffering; as SME builders are squeezed out, 'volume' developers become even more dominant and genuine competition is further reduced.

In this context, a targeted LVT should be used to impose a direct cost on developers that hold building plots in their 'strategic land banks' for more than a certain number of years without using them. Once planning permission has been granted, such land becomes far more valuable – so should then attract a much higher charge if it remains unused. The levy on any building delay should fall away not when a development is started but only when the homes are completed and available for sale directly to potential homebuyers. Applying the LVT principle in this way, to alter the financial incentives faced particularly by large developers, would help address the worst excesses of deliberately slow build-out and related restrictive practices across the UK housebuilding industry.

But bolder reforms are required. The LVT idea should be used to capture for local government part of 'planning uplift' more generally – that is the often very considerable difference in 'existing use' land valuations (generally related to agriculture) and the same land once planning permission is in place. In some parts of the country, such is the backlog of housing demand, in the face of restricted supply, that the administrative act of bestowing permission to build residential property increases the price of a hectare of land 100-fold, 200-fold or even more. At present, that entire valuation uplift goes to the landowner, land agent and/or the developer that has optioned the land – resulting in windfalls of tens or even hundreds of millions of pounds.

When planning permission is granted, a share of this considerable uplift should be ring-fenced, accruing to the local authority which has granted the related permission. The resulting funds could then be channelled into providing new or enhanced schools, hospitals and other infrastructure at no net cost to the Exchequer. This would provide the social amenities that new-build housing requires, removing a lot of the reason for local people to object to a new housing development. In fact, the judicious use of planning uplift could considerably improve the provision of local facilities and other public services for everyone, including existing residents – reversing local opposition to additional housing entirely.

Local authorities should be empowered to go further, in fact, forming Local Development Corporations (LDCs) which have the legal authority to use the threat of compulsory purchase orders (CPOs) to buy land at close to 'existing use' value – plus some additional compensation to those selling land. LDCs could then grant themselves planning permission, parcel up the now far more valuable acreage into building plots, then sell them at significant profit to a variety of developers – including SME builders who are generally incentivised to build quickly.

Again, the value accrued could be ring-fenced within the LDC, earmarked specifically for local 'place-making' infrastructure relating not only to resulting housing developments, but across the locality. Using the spirit of the LVT in this way, in a process known as land value capture (LVC), could have a significant, indeed transformative, impact on local attitudes towards housing development, and related local politics.

LVC could also be used, of course, to fund far more adequate social and affordable housing, providing a mechanism not only to allow local authorities to obtain land for social housing at a reasonable cost, but potentially with the resources to build such homes as well – all without recourse to central government and without raising taxation on local residents either. An economy-wide LVT, implemented in its purest form with all other taxation disappearing, is a utopian dream. But the lessons and principles of LVT – with unused planning permissions resulting in high bills for developers, and the state channelling 'planning uplift' into local infrastructure and other public goods using LVC – could be harnessed to make sure land is available, to a variety of developers, and the state itself, at reasonable prices.

While no silver bullet, the reforms outlined above could go a long way towards fixing the UK's broken housing market. They represent, though, a significant departure from the status quo – and would be fiercely resisted by powerful vested interests. Large landowners and big developers would strenuously object, not least on legal grounds. Yet the UK's housing shortage is now causing such economic and social damage, and the reasons behind it are so deeply entrenched, that it is no longer acceptable to hope that the situation will change without radical reform.

A STAKE IN THE GROUND

Since the 1947 Town and Country Planning Act, the UK has been regulated by a system designed to prevent 'urban sprawl'. This land-mark piece of post-war legislation has, in many ways, worked too well. For decades, it has been almost impossible to construct any new residential property without permission from local councils. And in the places where people most want to live – often suburbs at the edge of big cities – locally elected councillors have been reluctant to allow that to happen.

Ministers have periodically tried to override often bitter objections from local NIMBYs. Labour governments under Tony Blair and then Gordon Brown set regional housebuilding targets and bullied councils to accept high allocations. The subsequent Tory–Liberal Democrat coalition scrapped that approach in the name of local democracy – but soon resorted once again to pushing local councils into granting more planning permissions, as have successive Conservative governments since.

The way to get more houses built is to give local people – and, in turn, local councils – bigger incentives to allow them to be built. Nimbyism, while often characterised as unreasonable and small-minded, is not always irrational. Housebuilding can be, for those living nearby, a messy and noisy business. New developments, once built, can spoil views, put more pressure on already over-crowded local schools and hospitals and result in more traffic congestion. Yet, even though land prices often soar once planning permission has been granted, local councils are unable to extract much of the increased value to spend on services, amenities or other infrastructure that local communities may want.

Only a very small part of that gain currently accrues to local councils, and ultimately local communities, mainly via 'Section 106' planning agreements. These are often exhaustive negotiations where councils try to claw back tiny slices of planning uplift via one-off developer contributions to social housing and local infrastructure – a lengthy and expensive process, involving countless lawyers and other professionals, paid for by taxpayers and homebuyers. Since 2011, local councils have also used the Community Infrastructure Levy (CIL) – a tariff-based payment calculated on the total floor space of a development – for a similar purpose.

In practice, large developers often wriggle out of even rather limited Section 106 obligations, using the 'viability loophole' outlined in Chapter IV. Alternatively, they may drag their feet in order to secure extra concessions, knowing councils will be penalised by central government if previously agreed numbers of new homes fail to appear in a given time frame. And given that CIL is charged at each local authority's discretion, it is also frequently negotiated away by powerful developers – which is why it raises, across the entire country, just a few hundred million pounds each year.[11]

The bulk of the huge gains, then, when planning permission is obtained, go to the seller of the land and/or the land agent or developer who optioned the land before permission was granted. Because very little of this 'planning uplift' goes to local communities, those same local communities – rationally – often vehemently oppose development, as to them there are only downsides.

The very heart of the problem, as outlined in Chapter I, is that the UK's post-war planning system was semi-dismantled – and, to this day, we have one side of it operating, but not the other. While the 1947 Town and Country Planning Act introduced the need for planning permission, it also required that land be sold at 'existing use' value – ensuring there would be a plentiful supply of acreage, at reasonable prices, allowing a competitive market in housebuilding that would produce decent-quality homes at affordable prices.

Within just a few years of this landmark legislation, during the early 1950s in fact, the UK's carefully constructed post-war planning system was semi-dismantled, as land-owning vested interests lobbied politicians to neuter the 'existing use' sale requirement. The result was a system that requires planning permission, but without the resulting gains to local communities – leading to rampant speculation among landowners, resulting in only a restricted supply of acreage at enormously inflated prices. This is the root cause of the current crisis – with high prices for land with residential planning permission contributing significantly not only to chronic affordability obstacles faced by millions of would-be homebuyers but the under-provision of decent social housing too.

Back in the 1930s, when my childhood home was built in London's Metro-Land, land costs accounted for just 2 per cent of the price of an average home.[12] After the Second World War, the 1947 planning reforms kept land prices low, helping to drive a building boom. By the late 1950s, though, as the post-war planning settlement began to unravel, land prices began to rise sharply, accounting for 10 per cent of the total cost faced by homebuyers by the mid-1960s. By the mid-1990s, land had soared, accounting for 40 per cent of the average house price.[13] Between the mid-1950s and the mid-1990s, in fact, the average price of residential land spiralled from about £150,000 a hectare to £1.3 million, before surging again to £5 million a hectare by 2007 – with all these numbers expressed in 2016 prices.[14]

This is the main explanation behind escalating UK house prices over the last sixty years. Ever-rising land costs also largely explain why local authorities (and, later, housing associations) have found it increasingly difficult to finance the building of social and affordable housing. On average, land now accounts for well over half of the sale price of an average home. Between 1995 and 2017, little more than two decades, the total value of UK residential land, on government figures, exploded by no less than 580 per cent.[15] Over the same time period, prices across the economy as a whole rose just 50 per cent.

Such rampant land speculation began in the late 1950s. Prior to the Second World War, residential building land was abundant, as there was almost no need to get planning permission – so prices were cheap. This facilitated the 1930s building boom, which produced millions of eminently affordable, good-quality homes – which remain perfectly serviceable to this day. After the 1947 legislation, prices remained low despite the need to obtain building permission, as landowners were only entitled to 'existing use' value – allowing the UK's building boom to continue. But a series of legal changes throughout the 1950s, unpicking the 1947 legislation, culminating in the 1961 Land Compensation Act, meant land prices were once again unrestricted, but with the planning system still strictly controlling building permission – and, therefore, the supply of building land.

The housing historian Stephen Merrett refers to the end of the 1950s as a 'price watershed', as the semi-dismantling of the UK's planning system sparked land price speculation, which fed into the price of finished homes.[16] Referring to successive pieces of legislation passed after 1947, up to 1961, the historian Andrew Cox says: 'As long as owners could expect to receive only existing use value, there was little point in buying land to hold in anticipation of a price rise – but when development values were given back to private sellers, the prospect of speculative profits emerged again.'[17]

This is the nub of the UK's broken housing market – the incompatible combination of a highly controlled, deeply unpredictable supply of residential building land, combined with a rampant free market when it comes to demand. This is the central problem we face – one with its origins in the fact that, to this day, we're using only half of the carefully designed 1947 planning system and have been for six decades.

Legislation passed during the 1950s, together with the pivotal 1961 Act and a raft of resulting case law, enshrined a landowner's right to so-called 'hope value' when selling acreage, including in the case of compulsory purchase by a public body. As such, from then onwards land prices reflected, and still do, the likelihood the plot might one day be used for a highly lucrative housing development, creating a price floor based on the most profitable use imaginable – which, in turn, generates an incentive to sit on land until the price goes higher still. As a result, many forms of potential development – from social housing financed by councils, to homes built by SMEs, struggle to break through the financial barrier represented by the 1961 Act. Which means they simply don't happen.

The Federation of Master Builders found that in 2018 'a lack of available and viable land' was the most commonly cited barrier to building cited by SME developers, for the fourth year in a row – with 'viable' meaning affordable.[18] Joint research from the campaign group Shelter and the Local Government Association shows that the high cost of land is the single biggest barrier that local councils face in getting social housing built.[19]

Similarly, a council wanting to build an ambitious new settlement, in the style of Letchworth Garden City for instance, would only be able to buy the land at a price that made it impossible to deliver the scheme – at least without massive public subsidy. Housing associations, too – not-for-profit organisations that have been the engine room for new affordable housing delivery since the decline of local authority housebuilding – also cite acquiring land as their biggest barrier to more building.[20]

Under our current system, landowners, for their part, face a choice between selling now at current prices, inflated by the prospect of future planning permission, or holding their land back from development, in the knowledge they will almost certainly get an even better price in the future. In a strict business sense, waiting is the rational choice. As such, in order to secure land in a highly competitive bidding process, prices offered by developers escalate to tempt landowners to sell. But such bids are only possible if developers envisage housing schemes with the highest prices and almost no social housing, while cutting back on the size and quality of the homes and investment in local infrastructure. And once the land has been bought at that price, the envisaged scheme is the only one that then makes commercial sense. This is why house prices consistently spiral ahead of wages, why developers build far more luxury flats than are needed and far too few decent-quality family homes. This is why the market for homes which are affordable to ordinary people on ordinary incomes, despite enormous demand for such homes, is so desperately under-supplied.

The current arrangements, then, encourage speculation by landowners. That, in turn, encourages land agents and volume developers to consolidate and, amid rising prices, amass huge land banks. This is the context in which, as we saw in Chapters IV and V, large developers are increasingly obtaining planning permissions but deciding not to build out permitted homes. Such permissions are extremely valuable – so they sit on the balance sheets of the volume builders, enhancing their share prices and, in turn, the bonuses payable to top executives. But claiming these permissions also uses up 'quotas' in the housing plans of local authorities, often preventing SME builders, incentivised to build out quickly, from obtaining permission to build. In this way, large developers exert even more control over local housing markets – determining what gets built, where, and at what price, to the detriment of ordinary homebuyers.

It is only with the reintroduction of 'existing use' value rules, largely scrapped in the 1950s and 1960s, that we can remove the incentive for landowners to hoard their acreage and stoke speculative pressure in the hope of larger future windfalls. Were such a change to happen, SME developers could once again routinely obtain reasonably priced land, injecting much-needed competition and encouraging quicker building across the entire industry, as smaller housebuilders reclaimed substantial market share.

With cheaper land, houses sold on the open market would then be priced more reasonably, and there would be scope to oblige developers to provide more affordable homes, while still allowing for healthy profits and steady shareholder dividends. All this requires, though, what would be a highly controversial reversal of the 1961 Land Compensation Act – a radical shift returning us to the original vision of Uthwatt, Barlow and the other founders of the UK's post-war planning system.

Using 'existing use' pricing would allow the reinstatement, too, of 'planning uplift' capture by local authorities. This would provide funding for local infrastructure and amenities which could not only revolutionise local attitudes to housing development, as described, but also help raise UK productivity. After decades of under-investment, Britain's infrastructure stock is worth just 57 per cent of GDP, compared to 71 per cent in Germany.[21] The World Economic Forum recently ranked the quality of UK infrastructure as only twenty-fourth in the world, towards the lower end of the group of G7 countries, and mid-ranking in terms of other industrialised nations.[22]

Highly developed economies like the UK should be spending around 3.5 per cent of GDP a year on infrastructure, according to the OECD – but as recently as 2016, Britain's spending total was just 1.7 per cent, as defined by public sector net investment, rising to 2.1 per cent in 2017 and 2018. This helps explain low UK productivity, which bears down on growth and living standards.

In many other advanced countries, regional infrastructure investment is funded not via general taxation, but by municipalities investing directly, having raised money from bond markets. Bond-holders, in turn, are often paid back from revenues directly stemming from the uplift in land values when planning permission is granted, shared with the state. This mechanism has funded large-scale infrastructure around the world, from the Hong Kong metro to the recent expansion of Hamburg. Such funding is largely absent in the UK, though, as the 1961 Land Compensation Act requires the uplift in land values to flow directly and in their entirety to landowners instead – notwithstanding the grossly unequal distribution of land referred to at the beginning of this chapter.

The value of unearned uplift accruing to landowners, which could otherwise be channelled into social housing, schools, hospitals and local infrastructure, amounts to around £9 billion a year, according to analysis by the cross-party Centre for Progressive Policy. Were the 1961 legislation changed, that would not only facilitate the construction of lots more affordable homes, but also generate a significant permanent increase in UK infrastructure spending. Public sector net investment would rise close to 3 per cent of GDP – far nearer the OECD target.[23]

On top of that, countless homebuyers would be living in homes with less mortgage debt, allowing them to allocate more to both consumption and saving. Lower land prices would also boost the provision of social housing, lowering the UK's housing benefit bill. The Centre for Progressive Policy estimates that using LVC in areas benefiting from Crossrail 2 – the proposed underground Surrey–Hertfordshire railway, running from north to south through London – would generate an uplift in land values from 200,000 new houses of £69 billion. That would self-finance the entire project, with no need for additional funding from general taxation.

Since the 1961 Act, repeated efforts have been made to reintroduce the combination of 'existing use' land prices and LVC mechanisms to ensure more homes are built that are affordable, while generating funds for spending on local and regional infrastructure. In 1967, Labour introduced a 'betterment levy' – using Uthwatt's original term – but it was dropped by the Tories in the early 1970s. Again, in 1976, Labour introduced a 'development land tax', set at 80 per cent of the increase in land value. This was originally maintained by Margaret Thatcher's government from 1979, at 60 per cent, but then scrapped in 1985. Property taxes that capture land value are central to the planning system in many countries around the world – from Australia, to parts of the US, Denmark, Taiwan, Germany, France, the Netherlands and Hong Kong. Yet in the UK, despite being introduced three times over the last seventy years, they never seem to survive the political pushback from the large landowners and powerful developers who thrive in such an opaque, dysfunctional land market.

'Three times since 1947, Labour governments have legislated on land,' write historians Peter Hall and Colin Ward.[24] 'Each time, the legislation they drafted ran into well-nigh insuperable difficulties; each time a succeeding Conservative government more or less promptly repealed all or part of the legislation ... we need to start asking why.'

In many parts of the UK, particularly where the housing shortage is at its most acute, the price differential between agricultural land and land with planning permission is staggering. Yet, in recent years, there has been no genuine attempt to introduce an effective LVC mechanism – and until that happens, our planning system will inevitably remain broken and inextricably tied to land speculation.

The reason is that soaring land and, in turn, house prices are at the heart of the business model for all the major housebuilders – and, to a significant extent, also benefit existing homeowners. These two powerful lobbies, together with a banking sector heavily exposed to property loans, form the 'iron triangle of vested interests', referred to in Chapter IV, that sustain our current, malfunctioning housing market. Over recent years, though, as the housing crisis has worsened, and affordability issues have become both more widespread and acute, there have been unmistakeable signs of support for root-and-branch reform. Close observation of UK politics and policymaking suggests, in fact, that a return to 'existing use' land prices and the capture of planning uplift by local government in various forms, could soon be in the offing.

PRESSURE BUILDING

The phrase 'fat of the land' first appeared in the King James Version of the Bible, published in 1611. 'Lade your beasts, and go, get you unto the land of Canaan,' the Pharaoh tells Joseph. 'Come unto me: and I will give you the good of the land of Egypt, and ye shall eat the fat of the land.'[25] This expression is often used to refer to desirable resources, especially those that have been acquired with little or no effort.

Landowners and developers made estimated windfall profits of £13.4 billion in 2016/17 as a result of acreage being granted planning permission, only a fraction of which was returned in regular taxation and via Section 106 agreements and the CIL.[26] This represents unearned gains equivalent to around £75,000 for each home built that year. As such, 'fat of the land' seems an apt way to describe the considerable unearned value that could, in part, routinely accrue to local government, to be channelled into local infrastructure and other amenities that housing developments require, after residential planning permission has been granted.

For some years now, the idea of the state once again playing an active role in the land market – reinstating 'existing use' prices and using land value capture, as it did immediately after 1947, while buying up acreage, granting itself planning permission, then selling plots on – has been quietly gaining momentum. 'Windfall profits otherwise known as development gains often arise as a result of development decisions,' said Kate Barker back in 2004, in her influential government-commissioned housing review. 'The Government should actively pursue measures to share in these windfall gains, which accrue to landowners, so that these increases in land values can benefit the community more widely.'[27]

Ten years after Barker, the Lyons Review, another authoritative official inquiry, pointed out that 'in many European countries, local authorities play a proactive role in assembling and promoting land and getting it ready for development', in contrast to the UK where local authorities 'to a large extent rely on developers'. Lyons called, instead, for 'a strong leadership role from local government' with councils playing 'a more energetic and active role in assembling land and driving development through partnership to deliver the type, number and quality of homes their communities need'.[28]

There is growing recognition that, far from Britain being 'full', we are in fact blessed with copious land that is suitable for housing development – given that only around 10 per cent of England's land mass is classed as urban, and just 1 per cent is covered with residential buildings.[29] In addition, a consensus has emerged that the main problem is the price of building acreage, resulting from the combination of land speculation on the one hand and the UK's planning system on the other – the heart of our broken housing market.

In 2015, an influential joint-report by Shelter and KPMG highlighted that developers engage in 'fierce' competition for land 'while remaining uncertain as to what planning permission they will be able to secure' – resulting in high prices and formidable barriers to entry for would-be housebuilders. Huge gains in value when planning permission is secured 'encourage strategic land trading, rather than development', Shelter/KPMG observed, in turn forcing down the quality and size of new homes while preventing SMEs from competing. 'Competition is focused on acquiring land, rather than satisfying consumers', the joint-report said. 'The result is a vicious circle in which high land prices ensure housing output remains low and house prices high – which in turn feedbacks to sustain higher land prices'.[30]

In 2018, the New Economics Foundation argued that unaffordable land is 'at the heart of the housing crisis' and that 'any solution will never succeed unless it takes major steps to address our broken land system'. This left-leaning thinktank called for mechanisms 'to redistribute unfair gains which accrue to landowners through public investment and land value increases'.[31]

In the same year, the right-of-centre thinktank Civitas came to a similar conclusion, arguing that local councils should be allowed to buy sites at valuations that exclude potential future planning permission. This, Civitas argued, could reduce upfront development costs for 100,000 social housing units from an estimated £24 billion to £15 billion – stressing how LVC can be used to encourage both commercial housebuilding and the development of social housing on behalf of the public sector.[32] Also in 2018, the National Housing Federation – representing the UK's housing associations – called specifically for reform of the 1961 Land Compensation Act to enable 'a fairer proportion of the uplift in land value to be shared with the community, not least for affordable housing'.[33]

Again from the centre-right, Nick Boles MP has expressed support for radical reform. The government should 'change our laws on compulsory purchase, specifically the 1961 Land Compensation Act, and give local councils (and their development corporations) the power to buy land at its current use value', wrote the former Housing Minister in November 2017. 'We should seek cross-party support for a broad reform to the land market which ensures the interests of the community in meeting housing need and maintaining high-quality infrastructure are balanced against the rights of landowners to receive fair value for their property'.[34]

Neil O'Brien MP, too, writing for the Conservative thinktank Onward in June 2018, argued to 'give councils borrowing power to buy land and grant themselves planning permission, to enable councils to capture more of the gains from development'. A former special advisor to both Downing Street and the Treasury, O'Brien is widely viewed as one of the Conservative Party's most influential policy thinkers. 'Reform the 1961 Land Compensation Act,' he argued, 'to clarify that local and central government can purchase land at current market use values, not inflated or speculative "hope" values.'[35]

And, in a seven-month period between December 2017 and July 2018, the Centre for Policy Studies, arguably the most influential centre-right thinktank, published three separate proposals, by three different Conservative MPs, exploring different ways of directing a far greater share of 'planning uplift' away from landowners and developers and towards local communities.[36]

These well-researched interventions, by a series of highly respected campaigners and policymakers, follow much academic work in this area. Oxford economist John Muellbauer has long advocated a UK 'public sector land bank', empowered to acquire land at 'existing use' value. 'Changes to the 1961 Land Compensation Act are needed,' he confirms, allowing 'far more of the uplift in land values when planning permission is given to accrue to society (rather than to the landowner) and be available to fund infrastructure and affordable housing'. Government budgetary rules should target net liabilities, says Muellbauer, subtracting from overall debt marketable land assets. 'Then, if the government borrows to buy land for the public sector land bank, this would not add to net debt,' he observes. 'Eventually, it would actually reduce net debt, as land was revalued with change of use.'[37]

In the US, public sector land banks have worked successfully in certain states and, says, Muellbauer, have 'driven urban development and played a major role in national growth strategies' in Asian countries including South Korea, Singapore, Taiwan and Hong Kong. 'The UK could learn a great deal from the comparative experiences of South Korea and others,' he concludes.[38]

In related work, Tim Leunig, an economist from the London School of Economics, who was on the advisory panel of the Barker Report, has been writing about 'community land auctions' since 2007. These provide another route to LVC, which could be used to create local-level land banks, facilitating incremental additions to housing supply. Under Leunig's scheme, local councils ask willing landowners to name the price at which they would sell their land – but doing so gives councils the right to buy at that price for eighteen months. Councils then decide what land they want developed and auction it to housebuilders, keeping the difference between the price named by the original landowner and that paid by the developer.

Leunig's community land auctions pose less of a challenge to existing property rights. 'Everyone can offer their land, or not, and can name any price they like,' he explains. 'But landowners have to compete against each other to be chosen, so keeping acceptable prices quite low ... Equally, when the local authority comes to sell the land to developers ... there are many potential purchasers, which means it will receive a full price for the land.'[39]

Another variation is offered by Professor Richard Layard, also of the London School of Economics. He offers 'two-interlocking recommendations – one carrot and one stick'. Whenever the price of building land outside the green belt exceeds £2 million per hectare, Layard says 'planning permission in principle should be automatic', unless the local authority can persuade the inspectorate that the amenity value of the land exceeds the residential building valuation. This is the 'carrot' to developers.

At the same time, though, when any new housing scheme is completed, Layard argues the local authority should receive a development charge – the 'stick'. This would be calculated as 40 per cent of the final value of the completed development minus £100 per square foot of housing space, to reflect the cost of construction. 'This levy will be paid by the developer, who will reduce the price he offers for the land by an equal amount,' explains Layard. He says developers would not defer projects, hoping this LVC levy might be abolished by a subsequent government, as has happened through-out history, as other developers would press ahead with building homes, taking market share, having received planning permission under the 'carrot' proposal.[40]

In August 2018, following a wide range of policy reports, the po-litical discussion about LVC stepped up a gear. A range of organi-sations with interests in and links to the housing market published an open letter to Communities Secretary James Brokenshire. 'The root of England's housing crisis lies in how we buy and sell land', the letter began, observing that agricultural land 'typically becomes at least 100 times more valuable' when residential planning permis-sion is granted.

'More of this huge uplift in value should be captured to provide benefits to the community … to be invested in better landscaping; in attractive green spaces; and in affordable housing and public ser-vices like new doctors' surgeries and schools,' the letter said. 'That would result in less opposition to new development and much better infrastructure.'[41]

The signatories included an array of housing charities and thinktanks from across the political spectrum – Shelter, the New Economics Foundation, the Institute for Public Policy Research, Onward and the Campaign for the Protection of Rural England among others. Additional groups that signed, representing young adults unable to buy homes, included Generation Rent, Priced Out and Yimby (which stands for 'Yes in my back yard').[42]

Local government should have 'a stronger role in buying and

assembling land for housing, allowing them to plan new developments more effectively, share the benefits for the community and
approve developments in places local people accept,' the letter
continued. 'Most importantly, government should reform the 1961
Land Compensation Act to clarify that local authorities should be
able to compulsorily purchase land at a fair market value that does
not include prospective planning permission, rather than speculative "hope" value.'

This powerful statement was signed, in addition, by a range of
Conservative and Labour MPs, including former ministers, as well
as the Local Government Association plus countless leaders of local
councils and city mayors – again from across the political parties.
Other signatories included the Chartered Institute of Housing, the
leading body for housing industry professionals and, on behalf of
housing associations, the NHF.

'Too often in Britain, new housing is not good enough and comes
without the infrastructure and public services required to support
it,' the joint letter concluded. 'Other countries do a better job of
making attractive new places to live, by making sure that development profits the community as a whole – unless we learn from
them, Britain's housing crisis will remain.'

The following month, in September 2018, the Housing, Communities and Local Government Select Committee of MPs, having
heard from multiple expert witnesses, published a detailed report
into LVC, together with recommendations. There is scope for central and local government to claim a greater proportion of land
value increases through 'reforms to existing taxes and charges,
improvements to compulsory purchase powers, or through new
mechanisms of land value capture', said the committee.[43]

'The present right of landowners to receive "hope value" – a value
reflective of speculative future planning permissions – serves to dis-
tort land prices, encourage land speculation, and reduce revenues

for affordable housing, infrastructure and local services,' this influential cross-party committee concluded, pushing for radical action. 'We believe that the Land Compensation Act 1961 requires reform... and there is a clear public interest and proportionality case to make this change.'[44]

Responding to the committee in November 2018, James Brokenshire agreed that 'there is scope to claim a greater proportion of land values'. Referring to Section 106 agreements and the CIL, though, he said the government wants to 'evolve the existing system of developer contributions to make them more transparent, efficient and accountable'. Having said that, the committee was told there is an intention to 'continue to explore options for further reforms to better capture land value uplift, providing it can be assured that the short-run impact on land markets does not distract from delivering a better housing market'.[45]

Given the head of steam that has built behind the idea of reintroducing 'existing use' land prices and LVC during the five years ahead of this Brokenshire statement, particularly during 2018, this amounted to a weak response from government. But that by no means suggests these ideas won't make it back onto the statute book.

RIGHT POLICY? RIGHT TIME?

Some may balk at the idea of the state getting involved in the process of buying and selling land, while capturing 'planning gain' that currently flows directly to landowners, using CPOs if necessary. Surely, nobody should be forcibly deprived of their property at a discount to its potential value? And don't free markets produce the best outcomes?

One problem is that, if every piece of land were residential, where would offices, shops, roads and train stations be located? More specifically, the value of any particular piece of land is largely driven by its surroundings – including local commerce and public amenities provided and sustained either by the local community or the state.

This is a long-standing principle, recognised not just by economists such as Adam Smith in late eighteenth-century Scotland and Henry George in late nineteenth-century America, but also by politicians like Winston Churchill in early twentieth-century Britain. 'Roads are made, streets are made, railway services are improved, electric light turns night into day,' declared Winston Churchill, promoting Lloyd George's radical 1909 People's Budget.[46] 'Water is brought from reservoirs a hundred miles off in the mountains … and all the while the landlord sits still … To not one of these improvements does the land monopolist as a land monopolist contribute, and yet by every one of them the value of his land is enhanced.'

Land is a public good, which cannot be replicated. While it can clearly be privately owned, how land is used is of legitimate interest to everyone. Why should vast planning gains, which reflect a combined public effort to enhance a locality, be limited exclusively to those who have 'land-banked' farming acreage, often big developers and land agents using opaque subsidiaries and unregulated options agreements, holding out for years for the highest price while local communities suffer from acute housing shortages? These entirely unearned returns are financed, of course, by millions of ordinary homeowners over future months and years, as they service hefty mortgages on modest yet ridiculously expensive and often low-quality properties built on vastly over-priced land.

And while markets generally know best, much of the supply side of the UK housebuilding industry is not a market at all. It is a dysfunctional set of relationships that restrict genuine competition, producing consistently sub-optimal, often deeply unsatisfactory and quite frequently utterly galling outcomes for millions of individuals and their families. Britain's housebuilding industry, and above all the land-trading activities on which it is based, needs drastic modification – lest support for democratic politics, and even capitalism itself, be severely undermined.

The 1961 legislation, as it stands, is clear – ensuring land is valued at a price that 'could reasonably have been expected to be granted' at a later date. So private developers, and local councils seeking to build social housing, are forced to pay prices as if planning permission has already been granted. This principle was famously ratified in a legal battle over a CPO connected to the 2012 Olympic Park.

In 2007, the London Development Agency bought a goods depot in Stratford, east London, owned by Rooff, a building contractor, as industrial land. Yet, four years later the Court of Appeal quashed a previous High Court ruling, effectively overturning a decision by the Secretary of State. The upshot was that the LDA had to compensate Rooff, as if the land already had residential planning permission.[47] A change to the underlying statute is essential, then, if LVC is to happen on any significant scale.

Some say CPOs have historically been reserved for really critical pieces of infrastructure – such as railways, motorways or regenerating a large derelict brownfield site like the London Docklands. This ignores the historic role CPOs and certainly LVC played in the post-war building boom – sparking the construction of literally millions of homes, for both social housing and for private sale, built on reasonably cheap land, making them affordable for governments to fund and ordinary people to buy.

Re-establishing the right of the state to use CPOs to purchase land for housing does not mean this power should be used routinely. Having the option available, though, would 'incentivise landowners to release land for development in advance of any application of the compulsory purchase', according to the Chartered Institute for Housing. CPO would serve as 'a credible threat … as a last resort', according to Shelter, so landowners sell their land at a fairer value, as opposed to 'holding out for the wildest possible value based on the wildest possible calculation of what they could possibly get in future'.[48]

Fair market value would continue to be paid – which could be determined as it is in Germany and the Netherlands, where land is acquired by local municipalities at a price that offsets the cost of providing the infrastructure and services associated with making a development viable, as determined by an independent expert panel.

Another option, recommended by the Town and Country Planning Association, the organisation originally set up to develop New Towns, is that where large developments are envisaged, local landowners are paid a flat rate of compensation based on existing use value plus a share of the planning uplift.[49] Or, landowners could be given the option, as an alternative to CPO, to invest their land in a development scheme as equity, yielding a long-term rental income stream, as opposed to today's vast upfront windfall returns.

Everyone has the right to a fair price for their land – but that price should reflect the use to which land will actually be put, building reasonably priced homes with the local infrastructure that is required for the land purchase to make sense. And it is not true to say that altering the 1961 legislation would contravene the European Convention on Human Rights, as some large developers claim.

After detailed consideration, MPs now see 'a clear public interest and proportionality case to make this change', as the Commons Housing, Communities and Local Government Select Committee reported. And in France, the Netherlands and Germany, all ECHR signatories of course, local authorities routinely purchase land without considering future development value.[50] In the Netherlands, in fact, around 90 per cent of uplift value is captured to help fund infrastructure and affordable housing. And, since the mid-1970s, the Netherlands has built nearly 70 per cent more housing units per capita than the UK.[51]

Public support for housebuilding is growing, even among those who have traditionally been opposed. Figure 8.1 shows backing for 'more housebuilding in my area' rising from 30 per cent in 2010 to

56 per cent in 2017.[52] The rise is significant across all age groups, with the largest increase among 18–34-year-olds. But even among pensioners, often characterised as the most vociferous opponents of development, support for more housebuilding has risen from little more than a quarter to well over a half in just seven years.

FIGURE 8.1: 'DO YOU SUPPORT MORE LOCAL HOUSEBUILDING?' (2010–17)

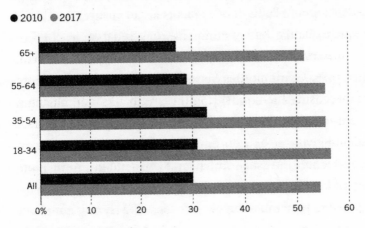

Source: British Social Attitudes Surveys

If planning gain was shared, and the resulting funds ring-fenced, a new local housing development could guarantee local public infrastructure and services were significantly enhanced, adding to rather than blighting the value of existing properties. Finance for new schools, hospitals, roads, leisure facilities, and even temporary reductions in council tax, could turn increasing general support for more housebuilding into local support in specific instances, among those directly affected – which is what counts.

There are, though, signs of further political breakthroughs. An April 2018 Labour Party Green Paper contains proposals to establish a 'Sovereign Land Trust' that would 'work with local authorities to enable more proactive buying of land at a price closer to existing use value'. Shying away from a full commitment to reforming the 1961 legislation, the paper says Labour will 'consider changes to the rules governing the compensation paid to landowners'.[53]

The Liberal Democrats have gone further. 'To acquire land, there will have to be amendments to the 1961 Land Compensation Act,' wrote party leader Vince Cable in June 2018. 'By eliminating the 60 per cent or more of the cost of homes absorbed in prohibitive land costs and developers' profits, it becomes easier to ensure that homes are of adequate quality, safety and insulation standards.'[54]

Senior Conservatives are also inching towards radical reform. In October 2016, Communities Secretary Sajid Javid rattled large developers, accusing them of 'sitting on land banks' and having a 'stranglehold over supply' which 'prices out' young homebuyers.[55] 'There is definitely some hoarding of land by developers,' Javid then said in January 2018. 'When you have a lack of supply, developers feel confident land prices will keep rising.'[56]

Determined to reform the supply side of the UK housing market, Javid appointed former Cabinet minister Sir Oliver Letwin to conduct a review into landbanking and slow build-out rates – which was published as part of the October 2018 Budget Statement.[57] Yet the review 'found no evidence that speculative land banking is part of the business model for major housebuilders'. That same day, Chancellor Philip Hammond announced another multibillion-pound expansion of Help to Buy, extending the scheme from 2021 to 2023 – giving the UK's volume housebuilders double cause to celebrate.[58]

Letwin's report, though, indicated his agreement that build-out rates were too slow. He focused on large sites, defined as 1,500 homes or more – which Letwin said took an average of 15.5 years to build out, and longer in London. The main reason, he concluded, was the 'homogeneity' of homes that private builders were developing, with the answer being 'increased diversity'. This related not only to the size and type of the homes, but also the tenure, meaning more shared ownership and more houses for social and affordable rent.

Such diversity would be achieved, said Letwin, by new planning rules for large sites in 'areas of high housing demand', requiring developers to provide a range of offerings – meaning lower profits, as requirements for social and affordable homes would go up. A national expert committee would be established to advise local authorities and arbitrate inevitable disputes – given that developers would try to split large sites into smaller units, while contesting definitions of 'high housing demand'. The government responded to the Letwin Review in March 2019.[59]

The Letwin Review and related official conclusions and actions proposed 'sidestepped the issue', according to a joint response by the same core group of campaigners and thinktanks behind the joint letter of August 2018 – including Shelter, Civitas and the Centre for Progressive Policy. 'This analysis is flawed,' they argued. 'Meeting the government's ambitions of building more than 300,000 homes a year by the middle of the next decade will require harder thinking and much greater urgency.'[60]

Specifically, the government indicated that there would be no changes to primary legislation to facilitate Letwin's proposals – with Brokenshire suggesting 'new planning guidance' would be sufficient to convince volume housebuilders to accept the obligation to build a 'more diverse' and therefore less profitable range of homes on large sites. 'This is a mistake,' said the campaign groups' joint response. 'Without legislative reform, specifically to the 1961 Land Compensation Act, the Letwin plans will be shrouded in uncertainty until their attempted implementation and are at that point at serious risk of failure.'

Later statements from Letwin, though, indicate he may be having second thoughts himself. 'We've made a fundamental mistake, handing over to private builders the development of very large sites,' he said in April 2019, a month after the government's response to his review, reacting to questions from the author. 'We've sleep-walked into this and no other European country has,' Letwin remarked. 'I have nothing against developers, but they are business-people and that is not how public policy in developing housing and places can possibly succeed.'

Letwin pointed to the 'more muscular' role for the state previously indicated by Javid, but not endorsed by Javid's successor as Communities Secretary, given Brokenshire's reliance on changes only in planning guidance. 'We need people acting in the public interest to direct these vital things, not people acting as commercial operators – local government has a huge role to play,' said Letwin. 'We've focused on planning guidance so far, which is fine, but that remains very far from going all the way to the solution we need – our aim is land value capture and that will require primary legislation.'[61]

In his response to the author, Letwin pointed to the imbalance between the volume housebuilders on the one hand, and cash-strapped local council planning departments with high staff turnover on the other. 'The developers have lots of professionals and expertise, yet they face under-staffed planning departments, where the officers involved change often – that is not a sensible situation,' he said.

But the 'big problem', Letwin told the author, 'is that we have handed over an enormous amount of power to developers who shouldn't have it ... Land value capture could unleash phenomenal amounts of money to spend on schools, parks and everything else ... and if we get this issue right, the problems of oligopoly and all the rest of it will disappear over the horizon.'

IX

BEYOND GRENFELL

Yo! Theresa May – Where's the money for Grenfell?[1]
STORMZY, 2018

On 14 June 2017, a tragic fire at the 24-storey Grenfell tower block in central London left seventy-two dead – the UK's worst residential fire since the Second World War. There were seventy other people injured and 223 escaped unharmed. The tower, which opened in 1974, was built as social housing, although fourteen of the 129 flats had been bought from the council by their tenants, some of whom had rented them out privately.[2]

Events at Grenfell, at the time of writing, remain under investigation as part of a public inquiry. It is well established, though, that the tragedy started on the fourth floor, with a faulty fridge-freezer, then rapidly spread up the exterior of the building. This fatal escalation of the fire has been attributed to the cladding affixed to the tower during a renovation in 2015/16 – in part to enhance the tower's external appearance.[3] Made of flammable material, this cladding was of a type used on countless other tower blocks across Britain, many of them built as social housing.

Grenfell Tower burned for around sixty hours before being finally extinguished. More than 250 London Fire Brigade firefighters and seventy fire engines from stations across the capital helped control the fire and rescue residents. In the immediate aftermath, the London Fire Brigade won huge plaudits. 'Hats off,' read a headline in the *Evening Standard*, London's daily newspaper. 'Praise for heroic firefighters who dashed into burning Grenfell Tower to save lives.'[4]

During the public inquiry, though, lawyers for the Grenfell victims and their families have bitterly criticised the LFB, referring to 'dreadful failings'. Complaints have focused on the advice given to distressed residents to stay in their flats as the fire spread, amid claims of 'overwhelming evidence' the LFB had failed to plan for such a scenario. Commissioner Dany Cotton and her leadership team have been accused of being 'not fit to run' the emergency service.[5]

The LFB insists, in response, that the Commissioner gave 'direct leadership' during efforts to control the blaze and ensure the safety of residents – and says it is 'unfair' to reach a final judgment before all the evidence has been heard. There is also evidence that, in May 2017, following an incident at a 1970s social housing tower block in Shepherd's Bush, west London, the LFB warned all thirty-three London councils to review the use of external cladding on tower blocks and 'take appropriate action to mitigate the fire risk'.[6] A first report from the public inquiry is expected in October 2019, as this book goes to press, with hearings scheduled to resume in 2020.

LACK OF URGENCY

There has been a history of disasters involving flammable cladding materials on buildings across the British Isles. In 1973, the Summerland Leisure Centre on the Isle of Man caught fire, with fifty people losing their lives.[7] The eleven-storey Knowsley Heights tower block on Merseyside went up in flames in 1991, but residents thankfully escaped unharmed.[8] In both cases, the gap between the cladding and the main structure acted as a chimney, causing fire rapidly to spread.

External cladding also played a role in the notorious 2009 Lakanal House fire, in Camberwell, south London – a fourteen-storey block in which six people died. In the aftermath of the Grenfell disaster, the Lakanal House incident was widely referred to as 'an unheeded warning'. It was sadly ironic that it took Southwark Council eight years finally to plead guilty to breaking four counts of fire safety regulations at Lakanal – and that Grenfell happened just four months after that admission.[9] 'The failure to act on the warnings from the fatal Lakanal House fire in 2009 in time to stop Grenfell represents one of the greatest policy failures of our time,' remarked *Inside Housing*, the highly respected trade journal.[10]

While the Grenfell fire was clearly an accident, the fact that countless other social housing tower blocks across Britain are covered in similarly flammable external cladding caused widespread concern in the aftermath of the tragedy. As clear evidence emerged that Grenfell residents had repeatedly registered safety concerns, and been ignored, the public mood shifted to outrage and anger – moving social housing up the political agenda.

In November 1966, a television play was broadcast on BBC One – *Cathy Come Home*, directed by Ken Loach. Decades later, the cultural reverberations of that single programme are still with us. A 1998 *Radio Times* readers' poll voted *Cathy Come Home* the 'best single television drama' ever made.[11] Two years later, the British Film Industry judged it the second-best television programme of all time – across all categories.[12] In 2005, *Broadcast Magazine* said *Cathy Come Home* was the single most influential television drama in British history.[13]

The play tells the story of a young couple who marry and start a family before descending into poverty and homelessness. Initially,

Cathy and Reg are doing well, renting a modern flat. But just as Cathy becomes pregnant and stops working, Reg gets injured at work and loses his job too. With little income, they have trouble finding anywhere affordable – but are taken in by a kindly landlady and have two more children. After the landlady dies and they're evicted, Cathy and Reg struggle to access housing through the local council. When Reg goes away to find work, Cathy endures a series of cold and judgemental brushes with social services and their children are brutally taken away. Filmed in a gritty, highly realistic documentary style, and produced with great skill, the film caused public outrage.

Cathy Come Home generated enormous support for Shelter, a homelessness charity founded in 1966, the same year the programme was broadcast.[14] Another housing charity, Crisis, was formed the year after. Both organisations remain highly influential to this day. Yet, despite the huge cultural impact of *Cathy Come Home*, in the words of Ken Loach himself 'it didn't change much at all' in terms of public policy.[15] It was eleven years later that the Housing (Homeless Persons) Act 1977 was passed, imposing on local authorities the legal duty to house homeless people in priority need.[16]

A similar dynamic seems to be at play following Grenfell. The tragedy certainly struck a deep chord across the country. 'Public investment enriches lives; here it would have saved them,' wrote the social housing expert John Boughton on his influential *Municipal Dreams* blog, a few days after the tragedy. 'The best memorial to all those who have lost their lives in Grenfell is that we as a nation choose collectively to invest in safe and secure public housing for all who need it.'[17] In writing this, Boughton certainly captured the post-Grenfell national mood. Yet a palpable sense that the Grenfell tragedy warrants and requires a meaningful response seems to have translated into little apart from political rhetoric.

'We are two years on from the Grenfell Tower disaster and the

Government is far behind where it should be in every aspect of its response,' said Clive Betts, Chair of the Housing, Communities and Local Government Committee Select Committee, in July 2019. Safety reforms introduced after the Grenfell disaster have been too slow and are 'simply not good enough', concluded a report by this cross-party group of MPs.[18] Local authorities are clearly taking too long to remove potentially dangerous cladding from hundreds of other housing blocks. And, despite promising in July 2017 to 'urgently assess' building regulations, it took central government twenty-three months to merely publish proposals for consultation.[19]

Official figures revealed that, by July 2019, more than two years on, there were still 328 high-rise social housing blocks in England fitted with cladding similar to that which burned with such ferocity at Grenfell. As such, tens of thousands of people are living in flats wrapped in materials that the government says breach building safety rules.

In October 2017, less than four months on from Grenfell, Theresa May took to the stage in Manchester to address the Conservative Party conference and made what was, in her words, 'a bold housing offer'. If the UK is to build the 250,000 new homes needed each year, she said, then that needs to include some 50,000–100,000 units of social housing. From the conference stage, the then Prime Minister pledged 'an extra £2 billion in funding for affordable homes'.[20] Yet that would pay for just 25,000 new homes – or 5,000 a year from 2022 onward, the period over which the new funding was pledged. At the time there were 1.2 million households on the council house waiting list. A year later, in September 2018, May made exactly the same announcement again.[21]

During the 1960s, the era of *Cathy Come Home*, some 150,000 social housing units were built in England by local authorities each year. During the ten years ahead of 2017, and the Grenfell tragedy, the average annual figure was 1,423 – less than 1 per cent of the 1960s equivalent. It's true that not-for-profit housing associations built an average of 31,000 homes each year during the ten years up to 2017 – but the majority of these were for private sale or 'affordable' rent that is often far from affordable, rather than traditional social housing. The construction of new social housing is, undeniably, at a historically low ebb. And despite the heartfelt call for more and better social housing provision since Grenfell, there still seems to be little urgency at the top of government.

In April 2019, LBC radio presenter Iain Dale was interviewing Housing Secretary James Brokenshire as part of a panel discussion. 'We have made progress – last year 222,000 new homes were de-livered,' Brokenshire told Dale's countless thousands of listeners. The new homes figure he cited was 'net new dwellings', not newly built homes. As such, it included around 30,000 converted offices and shops, many of which are too small to satisfy standard building regulations, as explained in Chapter VI.[22]

'How many of that total are social housing?' Dale then asked. After some prevarication, it became clear Brokenshire didn't know. 'I haven't got the specific breakdown of the numbers,' he admitted. 'James, you are Secretary of State for Housing, you should know how many of the 222,000 total new homes are social housing,' said Dale. 'I'm astonished that you don't know the figures – apart from Brexit, this is the most important issue facing government and you can't tell me the figures for council house builds or even affordable housing out of the 222,000 new homes you cite,' said the radio host. 'I think that's shocking.'[23]

A SOLID PHYSICAL HOME

'I'm a child of social housing,' declared Marvin Rees, his audience paying close attention. 'Living in a refuge with my mum, and then a council house, was massively significant for me'. As Rees talks about his childhood, his body language displays poise, confidence, even fond nostalgia and pride. 'Yes, I carried the stigma of council housing, but when I was growing up all my friends lived in social housing,' he says. 'The bottom line is that my mum's council house, our own front door, gave me a vital sense of stability in my childhood that far outweighed any stigma I might have felt.'

Marvin Rees is, in his own words, 'the son of a Jamaican father and a white single mother'.[24] In May 2016, he became Europe's first mixed-race directly elected mayor – for his hometown of Bristol. The star turn at a 2019 housing policy conference, Rees scans the crowd from the speaking platform, sits forward in his seat, puts his elbows on his knees, and clasps his hands. 'We need to make sure that basic housing is there, just like health and education,' he says. 'If the public sector under-performs on housing, then under-performance on education and health will surely follow, and we'll end up with more crime – which then turns up as a cost elsewhere in the public sector.'[25]

Rees points out that Bristol has over 11,000 people on the housing waiting list and 500 families in temporary accommodation – and is seeing a rise in rough sleeping. 'Looking at how housing interacts with health, skills, economic inclusion, it is the key policy tool,' he says. 'It cannot sit separately from the need to build communities, to improve urban security, to address the dangers of knife crime.'

Taking his time, Rees makes eye-contact with individual audience members before continuing. The audience knows they are in the hands of a gifted public speaker. 'Of all the educational policies you can think of, I'll tell you what one works best,' he says. 'What we need to do, above all, is guarantee that every child of primary school age has a kitchen table,' Rees continues, to smiles and spontaneous, scattered applause. 'Yep, that's the best intervention we can make on education, on mental health, on building communities, the lot – provide vulnerable people with a platform for their aspiration, a solid physical home.'

The documented history of social housing in Britain starts with almshouses, established from the tenth century onwards, the earliest recorded example of which was founded in York by King Athelstan.[26] As industrialisation took off in the eighteenth and nineteenth centuries, and rural labourers flocked to cities, public workhouses became the final fallback for the destitute.

Britain's first social housing was built at Vauxhall in north Liverpool in 1869. It was established on the advice of the city's pioneering medical officer, Dr William Duncan, who had established a link between unsanitary housing conditions and poor health, which risked the spread of disease, broader public health scares and labour shortages. During this period, some industrialists provided housing in tenement blocks, while a handful of philanthropic factory owners built entire worker-villages – including Saltaire, Port Sunlight and Bournville.[27]

In 1900, London County Council opened the Boundary Estate, a 'block dwelling' of tenements in Tower Hamlets, built on the site of the notorious Old Nichol slum.[28] Before the First World War, social housing provision relied on philanthropists and a small number of far-sighted 'corporations' – the forerunners to modern-day local government. They attempted to deliver humane habitation in response to the disease and degradation of Victorian-era working-class housing.

Soon after troops returned from the First World War, Lloyd George's Liberal government passed the 1919 Housing and Town Planning Act, providing councils with subsidies to build houses in areas where there was high demand. This amounted to the first government-backed, council-led building programme of affordable homes. This landmark legislation was known as the 'Addison Act' – after the Minister of Health Christopher Addison who brought it to Parliament. Another doctor, Addison was also well aware of the potentially transformative health impact of decent social housing.

The 1919 legislation was driven in part by the authorities' alarm at the ill health of many of the working-class men conscripted during the war, which raised concerns about manpower for any future military campaign. Fears of political extremism also played a part, given the spread of radical politics across Europe. 'When we talk of expense and cost, let us realise that everything is comparative and let us measure the cost of our housing proposals by the cost of Bolshevism to the country and the cost of revolution,' Waldorf Astor told fellow MPs as the 1919 legislation went through Parliament. 'The money we propose to spend on housing is an insurance against Bolshevism and revolution.'[29]

There were some notable initial successes, including slum clearance and the construction of the Becontree Estate in Barking and Dagenham, east London, which became the largest council housing estate in the world – built specifically for returning soldiers. But the 'Homes fit for Heroes' programme soon began to peter out, leaving Addison feeling aggrieved. 'Contented people are easy to govern, for they are prepared to govern and control themselves,' he wrote, in his 1922 book, *The Betrayal of the Slums*. 'But a wretched home does not allow of contentment.'

The provision of quality affordable housing may be 'drab and unattractive in its detail, but in its nature and in its fulfilment, it is heroic', Addison argued. 'It is worthy of sacrifice and of all the powers of discipline and statesmanship that we possess.'[30] The UK's social housing effort continued, if in fits and starts, with local councils building a total of 1.1 million homes during the twenty years after the First World War. By 1939, around 10 per cent of households were living in social housing, up from 1 per cent prior to 1914.

After the Second World War, Britain entered the 'golden age' of social housing, embarking on a building boom of low-cost, state-owned accommodation that lasted until the end of the 1960s. Fuelled by the vision in the 1942 Beveridge Report, Clement Attlee's post-war Labour government launched a council-house building programme that was sustained by consecutive administrations, both Conservative and Labour, with central government subsidising local authorities to build millions of new homes.

Throughout the twenty-five years from 1945 to 1970, some 3.1 million council homes were built by local authorities, almost 70 per cent of the 4.5 million such homes ever constructed across England.[31] Many were sited on land secured by the state at 'existing use' cost, under the 1946 New Towns Act and the 1947 Town and Country Planning Act, which kept building costs reasonably low.

Then, during the 1970s, another one million social housing units were constructed, increasingly in tower blocks, as speculative pressure drove up land prices and local authorities looked for lower-cost options. By 1979, just over a third of the British population lived in local authority housing.[32] After over three decades of sustained housebuilding by and on behalf of the public sector, ministers were finally able to point to a crude surplus in housing – but it was an achievement that owed its success to both private and public sector initiative.[33]

The 1980s marked the beginning of the end of mass-building of social housing, as subsidies from central government were reduced, borrowing caps were imposed on local authority housing revenue accounts and councils concentrated instead on maintaining their now aging housing stock. Only 311,000 units were built by local authorities during the entire decade, less than a third of the previous decade's total. The introduction of Right to Buy (RTB) under the Housing Act 1980 was a watershed, forcing councils to sell off their social housing stock, at heavy discounts, to tenants who had lived in properties for a certain period of time. The building of new social housing quickly lagged behind numbers sold, reducing the number of local authority homes.

Prior to the 1980s, council housing was seen as a step up the social ladder for working-class families. But with better-quality homes more likely to be those bought by tenants, and particularly houses rather than flats, RTB altered the balance of the stock of council housing – towards a greater concentration of the poorest and most vulnerable households, known as the 'residualisation' of the social rented sector.[34]

During Margaret Thatcher's time in office, from 1979 to 1990, some 1.5 million homes were sold under RTB. This policy remains divisive, with some viewing it as a great success, providing access to an appreciating asset that many would otherwise not have had. Others say RTB has exacerbated the UK's social housing shortage – even though the families who bought their homes, in many cases, continued to live in them. Another argument is that the scheme was a bad deal for taxpayers as a whole – seeing as homes built by the state, then sold at a discount, would no longer generate rental income, cutting off a revenue stream to build and maintain more local authority homes.

Thatcher herself described RTB as 'one of the most important revolutions of the century'.[35] And by the end of the twentieth century, it had helped drive the share of UK owner-occupancy above 70 per cent of all households. Yet the promise that councils should replace social housing sold off, in order to maintain the overall stock of social homes, was never honoured. Under Thatcher, almost 1.2 million of the social homes sold off weren't replaced.

During the 1990s, the construction of social housing by local authorities effectively stopped. Local authorities in England built just 30,050 homes during the entire decade – an average of around 3,000 a year, less than a tenth of the amount built during the 1980s. This total then plunged again during the 2000s, averaging under 250 a year. There has been a slight uptick since 2010, with 15,950 homes built by local authorities during the nine years from 2010 to 2018 inclusive, a still paltry annual average of 1,772.

From 1990 to 2018, then, fewer than 50,000 local authority homes have been built. But, over the same period, around half a million more social homes have been sold off under RTB, bringing the total to almost two million.[36] The sell-off accelerated after 2012, when David Cameron's government 'revamped' RTB, increasing the discounts available. Despite a renewed pledge that housing stock sold under RTB would be replaced one-for-one with new social housing, that has not happened.

The peak year of RTB was 1983, when 167,000 social homes were sold in England in a single year, rising to almost 200,000 including Scotland and Wales. That year, just 29,420 homes were built by local authorities, with only around one in every seven homes being replaced. In 2017, 17,760 local authority homes were sold under RTB, but just 1,740 built – an even worse replacement rate of under one in ten. Efforts to replace social housing have not been helped by HM Treasury's insistence, since the inception of RTB, that local authorities retain only around a third of the sales revenue, with the rest going back to central government.

During the 1950s, around 148,000 social homes were built by local authorities each year across England, accounting for 63 per cent of all new-build homes. By 2017, local authorities accounted for barely 1 per cent of the total. This striking fall in social housing provision has been mitigated, to some extent, by the activities of housing associations. In the early 1970s, legislation granted the extension of subsidies to housing associations to build homes for sub-market rents, and this sector subsequently expanded rapidly. Housing associations are private sector non-profit-making bodies – any trading surpluses they generate are reinvested into building and maintenance. As well as collecting rents and subsidy finance, some housing associations also receive charitable donations and issue bonds. The sector is heavily regulated and central government has a big say in determining rent levels. Some housing associations have proud histories, tracing their origins to the mid-nineteenth-century philanthropic and voluntary organisations – such as Guinness Trust and Peabody Trust.

Under Thatcher, local authorities prevented from subsidising housing directly also began channelling money to housing associations – which now receive the majority of the public subsidies for housebuilding. Facilitated by the Housing Acts of 1985 and 1986, councils then started to transfer the management of some of their existing housing stock to housing associations. By 2017, of around four million homes rented from councils or housing associations, some 2.4 million were accounted for by housing associations.

The reduction of central government capital grants for non-market housing means that the number of 'additional affordable homes' made available has fallen from 61,089 in 2011 to 47,124 in 2018.[37] This total is made up of affordable homes built by housing associations and local authorities and also property acquired as affordable housing. It includes, in addition, homes built under Section 106 agreements by commercial developers. Of this 2018 total, in fact, some 47 per cent of affordable homes were built under such agreements (involving no government grant).[38]

What's more significant than the headline drop in the numbers, though, if we're thinking about housing for the vulnerable, is the definition of 'affordable'. This includes 'shared ownership' homes and other homes to rent at up to 80 per cent of market rates. So while the reported 'affordable housing number' which ministers cite for 2018 is 'still close to 50,000', the reality is very different. 'Shared ownership' is impossible for many on low wages or otherwise vulnerable, as it requires obtaining a mortgage. And in places of high and even mid-range housing demand, four-fifths of market rent is out of the question for anyone in the bottom two-fifths of the income bracket.

Delving into the data, the situation becomes even worse.

Traditional 'social housing' is pegged not to market rents but, instead, to local incomes – and 'social rent' generally equates to 40–50 per cent of market rents. Back in 2011, of the 61,089 new affordable homes, over three-quarters were for 'social rent' – that is, council housing in the traditional sense, for low-income families and other vulnerable tenants. Of the 47,124 affordable homes built in 2018, a mere 14 per cent were for 'social rent' – amounting to 6,434 homes. Over less than a decade, then, between 2011 and 2018, while the headline number of 'affordable homes' built each year fell 22 per cent, the share of new homes built for 'social rent' nose-dived no less than 86 per cent.

Looking deeper into the official numbers reveals that of those new 'social rent' homes built in 2018, the vast majority were funded either via Section 106 agreements or by housing associations using non-grant income. The government, it seems, has all but abandoned building homes for traditional council house tenants, available at genuinely sub-market rents. The total number of 'social rent' homes built by local authorities in 2018, funded by government, was just 970 – less than 0.6 per cent of all homes built. Even that paltry total was down from 1,081 in 2017, the year of the Grenfell Fire.[39]

GROUNDS FOR CHANGE

In the aftermath of Grenfell, Stormzy featured on a charity single which was sold to raise money for the families of victims. Several months later, at the 2018 Brit Awards, the iconic rap artist delivered a furious attack on the Prime Minister. Having picked up the prize for 'Best British Male Solo Artist' and for 'Best British Album', Stormzy was asked to perform as the awards ceremony closed. He took the opportunity to remind a huge live audience, and millions more watching on television, of the frustration felt by countless Grenfell survivors:

Yo! Theresa May – Where's the money for Grenfell?
What, you thought we just forgot about Grenfell?
You're criminals – and you got the cheek to call us savages,
You should do some jail time, you should pay some damages,
We should burn your house down and see if you can manage this.

By July 2019, as mentioned earlier in this chapter, hundreds of high-rise social housing blocks across England were still fitted with flammable cladding similar to that which contributed to seventy-two deaths at Grenfell more than two years previously. Tens of thousands of people, then, are living in flats wrapped in materials now breaching official building safety rules. Stormzy had a good point.

More generally, the actual amount of money the government spends on social housing each year is not always easy to ascertain – particularly how much is allocated for the building of new social and affordable housing. For some reason it is, in the words of the House of Commons Library, 'difficult to produce a consistent estimate of public spending on new housing supply'.[40] It's almost as if the figures are presented in the national accounts in a deliberately opaque manner.

Untangling the numbers, though, it is clear that since the 1970s, successive governments have very significantly reduced spending on new housing – while presiding over an enormous corresponding rise in the housing benefit bill. Capital spending on social housing fell by more than half between 1975 and 2003, from around £14 billion to £5.4 billion (in 2003 prices), which includes rent paid by local authority tenants. During this period the number of dwellings built by local authorities and housing associations plunged from nearly 130,000 in 1975 to fewer than 13,000 in 2003.[41]

At this point, state housebuilding subsidies amounted to just 0.5 per cent of GDP. Since then, government spending on housing development has fallen even more, to just 0.2 per cent of national income in 2017, rising to 0.3 per cent in 2018, or £6.9 billion. This was still well down from the 0.7 per cent of GDP spent by the government on housing development as recently as 2009.[42] But just as government spending on building new social homes has dropped heavily over recent decades, spending on housing benefit, supporting low-income households to live in rental properties, has gone sharply in the other direction.

Between 1996 and 2017, the housing benefit bill rose by 51 per cent, from £16.6 billion to £25.1 billion, in constant prices.[43] Some three million working-age households receive a combined total of around £18 billion per year in housing benefit, with the rest going to pensioner households. There has been a deliberate switch away from 'supply-side' to 'demand-side' subsidies – from building social homes for genuinely sub-market rents and towards using housing benefit to help low-income and unemployed tenants meet rental costs in so-called 'affordable' homes and on the private rental market.

Successive governments have remained committed to the idea of targeting support at individuals, rather than investing in bricks and mortar.[44] Back in 1975, 82 per cent of the money the government spent on housing subsidies went towards building homes, with the rest spent on housing benefits – a ratio of over four to one in favour of supply-side subsidies.[45] By 2017, the balance was completely in the other direction, with subsidies four-to-one towards the demand side, with far less money going towards housebuilding.

The UK government now spends more on housing benefit than on police, road-building and buying military hardware combined. The state allocates billions towards tenants renting in the private sector – a direct transfer from taxpayers to landlords. Keeping low-income tenants in private rental accommodation is 23 per cent more expensive, per head, than local authority or housing association housing, according to the National Housing Federation.[46] And, of course, while social landlords are legally obliged to reinvest rental income into new social homes and maintenance, private landlords most certainly are not.

As the UK's housing shortage gets worse, and prices faced by homebuyers rise, so does the demand for sub-market affordable accommodation, including social housing, but also private sector rents. This helps explain the very steep rise in total housing benefit spending over recent years – as private rents rise, so do the numbers of people who need housing benefit, and the degree of support each requires. So, unless there is a drastic change in approach, housing benefit is set to spiral even more – as rents and the number of priced-out renters keeps going up.

There are many good reasons to now shift housing subsidy back towards the supply side and away from the demand side – 'from benefits back to bricks'. For one thing, even though local authority social rents have gone up sharply, they remain far more affordable for low-income families than private rents. Back in 2010, families paying social rent were spending 10 per cent of their income on housing costs, net of housing benefit. That share rose to 16 per cent by 2017. But private renters who receive housing benefit are now spending 34 per cent of their non-housing-benefit income on accommodation costs – cutting deeply into the spending power of vulnerable families.[47]

Social housing is also of better quality than much of the private rented accommodation provided to recipients of housing benefit. While 25 per cent of private rented homes failed to meet the 'Decent Homes Standard' in 2017, the equivalent number for social rented homes was just 13 per cent, down from 29 per cent in 2006. This reflects the fact that while the social housing stock has become smaller, government funding has been somewhat effective in raising the standard of local authority housing.[48]

In 1980, almost 30 per cent of all families were renting from local authorities or housing associations. By 2017, that figure was 13 per cent of families – or 17 per cent of the population. Yet social housing is not only more likely to provide a decent home for a low-income household, but living in such accommodation is also more likely to leave them with more disposable income. These benefits are in addition to the security of tenancy enjoyed by social housing tenants.

As UK home ownership falls, and more and more people end up renting as pensioners, the lack of social homes means they will end up needing state support to rent on the open market. As such, the plunging rates of owner-occupancy among people in their thirties and forties are storing up a future fiscal crisis, as successive generations of non-property owners are forced to rent beyond their working lives and will be unable to afford to do so. This explains why city consultancy Capital Economics projects that, on current trends, the housing benefit bill will increase by two and a half times by 2065, to more than £62 billion in today's prices, with at least £40 billion of that money being paid straight to private sector landlords.[49]

Some say that the return on shifting government social housing subsidy back from 'benefits to bricks' is low – given that a single social housing unit may cost upward of £70,000 to construct, and often much more, while the benefit saving when a family moves back from private rented accommodation to social housing is just £2,000 to £3,000 per year. This simple arithmetic ignores the non-financial benefits of social housing – affordability, security and dignity for the tenant – outlined above.

And, while it's true that benefits to bricks is a long-term financial game, serious consideration must also be given to factors going beyond the direct annual cost comparison. Because there are far, far bigger benefits costs looming in future decades as ever more people who have been unable to buy a home during their working life then carry on renting into old age – and are unable to afford market rents when they are no longer working.

Analysis carried out for Shelter suggests that the economic benefits of building much more social housing would ultimately outweigh the initial costs. A programme to deliver three million new social homes over a twenty-year period would require an average yearly investment of £10.7 billion during the construction phase, according to the Shelter study, initiated after the Grenfell tragedy. But an average of two-thirds of this annual cost could be recouped through housing benefit savings and increased tax revenue each year. On this basis, the net additional cost to government would be £3.8 billion per year over the twenty-year construction phase. That's a fraction of an overall capital expenditure budget that was £62 billion in 2017/18 and considerably less than the £4.2 billion the government is due to spend every year, for ten years from 2019/20 onward, on the HS2 rail link – the benefits of which are hotly contested.[50]

Within forty years, the Shelter analysis concludes, the construction of three million extra social homes, expanding the stock from around four million to seven million, would have paid for itself completely.[51] The additional accommodation could include 1.3 million homes for those in greatest housing need – homeless households, those with a disability or long-term illness, or living in very poor conditions. Another 1.2 million new social homes would be for 'trapped renters' – younger families who cannot afford to buy and face a lifetime in expensive and insecure private renting. The remainder would be for older private renters – those over fifty-five struggling with high housing costs and insecurity beyond retirement.

High and rising house prices mean the majority of successive generations now look unlikely ever to buy a home. A lack of affordable homes, to buy or rent, means more and more couples are delaying have children – undermining fertility and future economic growth. As young adults struggle to pay for housing, a third of men aged twenty to thirty-four are still living with their parents. And, some 300,000 people across the UK are homeless – a ten-fold increase over the past half-century.

Just 6,463 homes for social rent were built in 2018, providing accommodation for barely 0.5 per cent – one in every two hundred – of the 1.2 million households on councils' housing waiting lists.[52] Of those waiting, around half were in preference categories, including 250,000 occupying unsanitary or over-crowded accommodation, and others with medical and welfare issues. There is a very real and serious crisis across the UK's housing sector – and it doesn't only involve young professionals not fulfilling their ownership ambitions in their twenties or being forced to buy outside their preferred neighbourhood. This housing shortage is causing harm, above all, across the social housing sector – where the related human suffering is most acute, and the potential fiscal and, indeed, political consequences are the most serious unless significant changes are made.

SHARING THE GAINS

With the Conservative Party now supporting a new generation of council housing, the three main parties in England agree on the need for a local-authority building programme. Yet, as of 2019, one hundred years on from the Addison Act, the government's ambitions remain limited to council building in the low thousands per annum, with a high proportion of those resulting from long, drawn-out negotiations with private developers under Section 106 agreements.

Describing the UK's pioneering mass-building programme of social housing, Addison himself spoke of its 'utmost importance from the point of view not only of the physical wellbeing of our people, but of our social stability and industrial content', as he piloted the legislation through the House of Commons. 'This sentiment is not lost in the context of the current housing crisis,' says housing historian John Boughton. 'The lessons of the Addison Act are not merely historical: its ideals, objectives and means remain as relevant today as ever.'[53]

If the building of social housing and other genuinely affordable accommodation is to be scaled up, it will indeed require a substantial increase in levels of government spending on housing development. That is not to say that commercial finance can't be involved along the way. But far too many billions of pounds of taxpayers' money are currently being spent on often sub-standard private sector rental accommodation. Those billions should be diverted, instead, back towards developing and maintaining social homes, that could house low-income and other vulnerable households more securely and with more dignity than most private accommodation, while offering better taxpayer value.

So, at the very least, state spending on housing subsidy needs to be rebalanced, away from benefits, and towards investment in housing stock. And, given the chronic forty-year slowdown of the building of social homes, the overall size of that stock will need to be increased – requiring capital investment on a scale not seen since the mid-1970s. Housing has been on the political agenda for years, increasingly so since the 2008 financial crisis. But it was only after Grenfell that the need for more and better social housing returned to mainstream political debate. That was wrong. Social housing should have been there all the time – for there is no genuine solution to the UK's housing emergency that doesn't include building a lot more social homes each year.

As well as money, though, reform is needed – specifically to the 1961 Land Compensation Act, as has been argued elsewhere throughout this book. For it is only by reforming the broken land laws at the heart of our current housing crisis, we can begin to control the costs of development and make room for significant social housing supply alongside the commercial housebuilding that should always provide the bulk of new homes each year. Social homes are needed too, though – because a mixed economy of housing supply is vital. Without it, there is no way the UK will build the 300,000-plus homes needed annually, to begin to fill our chronic supply backlog, not least of social homes.

Land is usually the single biggest cost in residential building homes in the UK, currently accounting for 70 per cent of the cost of a home bought on the open market.[54] And it was rising land prices that were responsible for three-quarters of the increase in UK house prices between 1950 and 2012.[55] But things weren't always this way. Social housebuilding in the immediate post-war period benefited from legislation which decoupled its land costs from those prevailing for market housing.

This stabilised the costs of developing social housing, avoiding land market inflation and providing a secure supply of affordable land on which truly affordable housing could be built. As a result, social housing providers achieved high-quality, well-planned developments that were able to build out at record speeds, and are still well loved by residents today. In the three and a half decades after the end of the Second World War, councils and housing associations between them built 4.4 million homes, at a sustained average rate of more than 125,000 a year. While public money has built many social homes over the years, since the 1961 Land Compensation Act and subsequent case law, local authorities have often been forced to compromise on quality, design and density to cope with escalating land prices.

Over the last fifty years, whenever governments have invested more public money in social housing, land prices have increased sharply because landowners have known they can charge as much as the government is willing to pay. The system-built tower blocks of the 1960s were in part a way of coping with rising land prices by fitting as many homes as possible on the same amount of land. In

1963, Hackney Council pleaded that the 'lack of building sites and the ever-increasing cost of site purchase left the Council with no alternative but to build higher.'[56]

Compromises on conditions and quality – and, most tragically, on safety – were made to bridge the gap between land sold at market prices and the ambition to deliver homes at affordable prices. Aspirational social housebuilding programmes require rules to make sure land comes into development at a price that isn't inflated by laws guaranteeing landowners the highest possible return.

Today, access to land is a major constraint on social housebuilding in England. A recent Savills survey of housing associations found that 'availability of land' was by far the biggest constraint on them building more homes.[57] For councils not currently delivering housing, 'lack of land' is the leading reason.[58] Councils that are delivering housing cite 'lack of land' as the second most important barrier to delivering more, just slightly behind the Housing Revenue Account borrowing cap, which government recently scrapped.[59]

Social housing providers in 2019 either need an unusually affordable source of land – for example, acreage owned by a public body with an interest in seeing social housing built, such as a local authority – or they must find the money to compete with those buying land to build the most profitable kinds of homes for commercial sale. Evidence gathered by the NHF shows that providing social housing is often impossible under these circumstances.

The levels of direct investment which would be needed to purchase land at today's market prices and then use it to build social homes at affordable prices would be considerable. In reality, if government increased grants for social housing without also reforming the land market, this additional demand would simply push land prices up further.

It makes no sense to launch a new programme of social housebuilding until the rules surrounding land sales are changed. Public funding for social housing must be used to build urgently needed homes – not siphoned off into an already bloated land market. The potential gains are great. Work from Civitas has estimated reforming the Land Compensation Act 1961 could slash 38 per cent off the total development costs of a new scaled-up programme of social housebuilding across England.

To move forward and improve our ability to capture rising land values for the benefit of communities, we must change the incentives in the land market by reforming the 1961 Land Compensation Act so compensation is much closer to the value of land in its existing state. The effects would be felt far beyond land purchased using CPO.

Because land traders know that 'hope value' is protected in current legislation, they price it into their trades. A reformed compensation code, though, would remove the 'hope value' floor from the land market. Valuations would then reflect the risk of CPO without 'hope value', with land prices falling from their current high.

As such, the world created by this reform would not be one in which CPO is widely used to purchase land for development – which both sellers and purchasers of land have strong incentives to avoid. Without the high bar of 'hope value', landowners have far more incentive to compromise with communities who want to see their local areas developed with their interests at heart. This will result in more reasonably priced land – not just for commercial housebuilding for sale on the open market, but for social housing and mixed developments too.

Commercial housebuilders are vital, of course. They should provide the bulk of new-build homes in a nation like Britain, of course. But they must be incentivised to deliver good-quality, keenly priced products in sufficient numbers to prevent prices spiralling.

This country's current over-reliance on private sector developers has, particularly since the 2008 financial crisis, allowed large 'volume' builders to exert far too much political clout and un-reasonably game the system. Above all, large housebuilders have successfully faced down significant supply-side reforms – resulting in ever-higher prices and, at times, blatant customer abuse. It is vital that we have a mixed-economy of housing provision, not only to provide the social housing that will always be needed for those on low-incomes and other vulnerable groups, but also to prevent private housebuilders from becoming too powerful.

'The consequences of any stigma are not nearly as bad as the con-sequences of failing to deliver social housing,' says Bristol Mayor, Marvin Rees, recalling his childhood home. 'I'd have preferred the stigma of being a council house kid than not having a stable home, with a front door I could close, and a kitchen table and security.'

Rees goes further, looking back on his formative years with fond-ness, judging them as crucial in his future success. 'Having some trials in your childhood, if they don't crush you, and if you get other positive inputs, plus your health and mental stability, can make you stronger later on – a source of strength and power.'

Marvin Rees argues that solving the UK's social housing crisis – while encouraging stronger communities, and better health and education outcomes too – is all about unashamedly building many more social housing units and genuinely affordable homes each year, just like the one in which he grew up. 'We can deal with the hearts and minds stuff as we go along,' he says. 'In the meantime, we need to put in place hard bricks and mortar.'

X

A MANIFESTO FOR CHANGE

Too much capitalism does not mean too many
capitalists but too few capitalists.[1]
G. K. CHESTERTON, 1920

Tackling the UK's chronic housing shortage clearly requires a multi-faceted response. There is, as the saying goes, no 'silver bullet'. Since 2010, the government has focused for the most part on 'demand-side' measures – such as 'Help to Buy'. Injecting billions of pounds of taxpayer cash into a property market already over-squeezed due to long-standing demand–supply imbalances has helped some homebuyers but, on balance, has done more harm than good. The thrust of our efforts must, instead, be on the 'supply side' – namely the building industry itself and, above all, the provision of land and planning permission. While the rhetoric of successive governments has been strong, there has not been nearly enough resolve to tackle the entrenched supply-side vested interests benefiting from the status quo.

The UK's housebuilding industry has become far too concentrated, dominated by a small number of powerful companies. Bold measures are needed to allow competitive pressures to reassert themselves in an industry, the healthy operation of which is vital not just to our economy but broader society. The most vital component of a competitive housebuilding industry is access to land at reasonable prices. Yet the UK's market for land is 'broken'.

On the one hand, there is a rampant free market when it comes to the demand for residential building acreage, the result of years of under-building. On the other hand, the supply of land suitable for building is highly restricted and deeply unpredictable – resulting in sky-high prices which are, in turn, the main driver of unaffordable homes. Land accounts for 70 per cent of the cost of a home bought on the open market and rising land costs were behind three-quarters of the increase in UK house prices between 1950 and 2012.[2] This is the central problem we face – and it's one with its origins in the fact that since 1961, we've been using only half of the carefully designed planning system introduced in 1947.

Accessing land, then obtaining planning permission, amounts to the most formidable barrier to entry for all but the largest, most powerful housebuilders. Even dominant builders end up paying very high prices for acreage. This results in them building low-quality homes which are very expensive to buy. Large builders then exploit their local monopolies by 'drip-feeding' homes onto the market to push prices even higher. Facing little competition, some of the residential construction giants go as far as widening their margins by blatantly exploiting consumers – skimping on safety measures and cutting corners during construction, with some homes, while already of inferior design and incorporating poor materials, then being built in a manner which fails basic industry standards.

To break this impasse, incentives need to shift – so land is more accessible, at reasonable cost, with owners less likely to sit on acreage for years, waiting for a better price. Measures are also needed to make sure that sites with planning permission are built out at a steady pace – so there is genuine competition, putting an end to the 'contrived scarcity' created by the large over-dominant 'volume' housebuilders.

BACK TO THE FUTURE

For some years now, the idea of reinstating 'existing use' prices when land is sold, then using 'land value capture' (LVC) to divert funds so local authorities can build infrastructure, has been gaining support. During 2018 and 2019, this debate has become far more energised, as described in Chapter VIII, with leading policymakers and thinkers from across the political spectrum arguing to upend the 1961 Land Compensation Act. This legislation, along with related case law, altered the 1947 planning settlement, which had kept land prices reasonable, facilitating the mass-building of both commercial and social housing during the 1950s, while generating resources to fund the schools, roads and hospitals that were needed to support a commercial building boom.

There are also now calls, again from across the political spectrum, for the government to become a bigger player in the land market – as it is in many other advanced capitalist economies. This would involve the state not only bringing forward more existing publicly owned acreage for housebuilding, but granting local authorities powers to fine developers who delay the build-out of sites with planning permission, while using the threat of compulsory purchase orders (CPOs), if necessary, to encourage landowners to sell in areas of high demand for housing.

The awarding of planning permission dramatically increases agricultural land values – from an average of £22,520 per hectare to £6.2 million per hectare, based on average residential values for new builds across England in 2016/17 – an increase of more than 275 times.[3] This huge 'planning gain' currently accrues almost entirely to the landowner and/or land agent and developer. Such gains should, instead, be fairly and efficiently shared with the state, providing local authorities with the funds to build new amenities and infrastructure. This would significantly lessen local objections to new housing developments – and could even make them popular.

Local authorities should also be allowed to form Local Development Corporations (LDCs) to buy land relatively cheaply at 'existing use' value, grant outline planning permission, then sell land parcels on to developers at a profit. Variations on this model are successfully used in Germany, the Netherlands, Singapore, South Korea and elsewhere. The sale price should be high enough to fund local infrastructure and social housing. But land prices under such circumstances will be far lower than current open-market valuations which, thanks to the 1961 legislation, are based on the highest possible 'hope value' of any future development – which ramps up the cost of development acreage and, in turn, final prices faced by homebuyers. A high proportion of LDC plots could be prioritised for SME builders, ensuring more competition – and time limits on build-out would be a condition of sale.

At present, Section 106 agreements are used by local authorities to try to claw back some of the massive planning uplift accruing to landowners and/or developers, along with the Community Infrastructure Levy. But, as we've seen, related obligations to build social and other affordable housing, along with communal infrastructure, are often negotiated away by powerful developers, who face down under-resourced planning departments, overseen by local politicians under enormous pressure to deliver more housing. And cash payments under S106 and CIL often turn out to be far lower than initially calculated and reported. Our existing LVC mechanisms, then, are inadequate and failing. This is another reason to reform the 1961 legislation – not only to take the speculative heat out of the UK's bloated market for residential building land, but so planning gain is shared in a meaningful, more systematic and more predictable manner.

Many will be unsettled by the idea of the state getting involved in the land market, while capturing 'planning gain' that currently flows directly to landowners, using CPOs if necessary. Along with the enormously powerful lobby of landowners and developers themselves, others will object on a point of political principle – insisting that free markets know best. The UK housing market, though, with the market for land at its heart, is deeply dysfunctional. It produces consistently bad outcomes for millions of ordinary people. What's more, the value of any particular piece of land is largely driven by surrounding public amenities provided and sustained either by the state or local commerce.

So why should vast planning windfalls, which reflect a combined public effort to enhance a locality, be limited exclusively to those who have 'land-banked' farming acreage? Why shouldn't they be shared? And with land costs now accounting for 70 per cent of the price of a new-build home, can we keep ignoring the impact of entirely speculative land transactions? While generating hundreds of millions of pounds for individual landowners and/or developers, such transactions drive soaring rent payments for millions of unwilling tenants, while rendering home ownership entirely unaffordable for the majority of successive generations. High land prices also explain the severe lack of decent social housing across the UK – which, in turn, is driving an epidemic of over-crowding and homelessness.

We learnt in Chapter VIII that former Cabinet minister Sir Oliver Letwin, who published a government investigation into 'landbanking' in October 2018, has since said that 'our aim is land value capture and this will require primary legislation'. Sajid Javid, too, while Communities Secretary, worked on proposals to reform the 1961 legislation, returning to a system of 'existing use' prices, while splitting planning uplift between sellers of land and local authorities. 'When I was Secretary of State, we worked on a fifty–fifty split of the valuation between local government and landowners,' said Javid, in an interview with the author. 'This would be an efficient and morally justifiable tax,' he said. 'The state is expected to create the infrastructure around new housing, and that needs to be paid for – so fifty–fifty makes sense.'

Javid, who at the time of writing is Chancellor of the Exchequer, was 'frustrated' when Theresa May removed such radical policies from the 2017 Housing White Paper, produced by the department which he then ran. 'She just didn't get the impact of this housing crisis on ordinary families, ordinary working men and women – so the White Paper was gutted, all the strong ideas removed,' he says. 'It is vital we now take radical steps – once Brexit is done, housing is easily the most important domestic policy issue we face.'[4]

There are signs that some of Britain's big housebuilders also support the systemic sharing of planning gains between landowners/developers and local authorities. Tony Pidgley is the founder and chairman of Berkeley Group, one of the UK's leading developers. A former Barnardo's boy, later adopted by a gypsy family, he has a reputation as a shrewd judge of the UK property market whose company builds high-quality homes.[5]

Pidgley had a long track record of sometimes volunteering to share planning gains to an extent far exceeding any S106 or CIL obligations, to unlock political stand-offs, secure planning permission and get housing developments built. 'I've done about fifteen or twenty deals like that over the years,' he says. 'I think they make a lot of sense for everyone.'[6]

Pidgley talks about a piece of land he bought near Effingham Junction Railway Station – in the prime Surrey commuter belt. He got the land 'for a song – about three million pounds', largely because no one thought that residential planning permission would ever be granted. But, after initial applications were turned down, Pidgley made contact with a local school, Howard of Effingham, that was in dire need of redevelopment. 'The head was brilliant, a real leader, but the fabric of the school was sub-standard,' says Pidgley. 'So I made the council an offer – that I'd spend £25 million on the school, plus do 20 per cent affordable housing.'

Eventually, Pidgley agreed to spend £32 million on the Howard of

Effingham School and, after an appeal that went all the way to the Secretary of State, got planning permission in 2018 to build 295 new homes.[7] 'It was good business,' he says. 'I make my normal margin of around 20 per cent, they got a fantastic new school – why does this need to be so difficult?'[8]

Pidgley agrees that the UK land market, more broadly, is in 'dire need' of reform. 'We need a central body that can buy land, award planning permission, then pass on the returns to society,' he says. 'The local community, the whole of society should capture that value – it's about decency.' Pidgley is 'not squeamish' about the wider use of CPOs to ensure land is bought and sold at reasonable values. 'We're in the building business – and that's where we should be competing, not in trading land,' he says. 'As long as there is room to make a decent margin on housebuilding, bring it on.'

Pidgley's views on housebuilding and all manner of property development have been, for many years, sought and taken seriously across government.[9] It is striking, then, that he has added his voice to those calling for a reversal of the 1961 legislation and the introduction of meaningful LVC, as a means of dampening down land prices and funding 'place-making' infrastructure. This policy is now backed not just by campaign groups like Shelter and the Centre for Progressive Policy, but also by leading centre-right thinkers and policymakers – including, it transpires, Sajid Javid and Sir Oliver Letwin.

Keith Joseph was a Conservative Cabinet minister who played a very significant role in the development of economic policy under Margaret Thatcher. In the mid-1970s, he worked with the future Prime Minister to set up the free-market thinktank the Centre for Policy Studies. When Joseph was Housing Minister, he also recognised the importance of the state taking an active role in the land market and continuing to use LVC to fund infrastructure.

'Land planned for major development should be bought well in advance by a public authority for disposal to private enterprise or to public enterprise as required,' said Joseph, to the House of Commons, in 1963.[10] 'What is our plan for tackling high land prices – first and foremost, to tackle the cause, the shortage, and then be prepared to undertake large-scale acquisition by the public sector in order to get the building we need, as and where we need it, and to gather the value so created in helping to meet the cost.'[11]

Few would describe Margaret Thatcher's future economics guru as an enemy of free markets – and yet, here he is arguing for government intervention in the market for residential building land. It is significant, also, that Joseph was speaking soon after the dismantling throughout the 1950s of LVC mechanisms in the 1947 Town and Country Planning Act, a process which culminated in the 1961 Land Compensation Act – which ensures to this day that land prices remain elevated, with sellers legally entitled to 'hope value'.

'The consequence of this legislation ... was the property boom of the early 1960s, making it difficult for local authorities to acquire land,' the relevant Cabinet papers make clear. This stymied the construction of social housing at a time when 'housing was a serious political issue'. Within government, Keith Joseph argued 'for the large-scale acquisition of land in areas where housing was scarce, but this was unacceptable to other Cabinet members', the Cabinet papers record. 'Joseph put forward a plan for a "betterment" or development tax to assist with funding, but Cabinet decided against this.'[12]

Joseph had watched as successive Conservative governments had, during the 1950s and early 1960s, stripped away the state's ability to use LVC to share planning gain with powerful landowners. Yet, just two years after the pivotal 1961 legislation, by arguing within Cabinet for a 'betterment' tax, he was effectively calling for the law to revert to a version of the post-1947 regime. Those on the right of politics who instantly reject the idea of LVC or a more active state role in buying and parcelling land for residential development should consider that the idea was championed, at a time when it directly contradicted his own party's policy, by the man who, in the words of political scientist Vernon Bogdanor, later became 'the most articulate and powerful of the post-war exponents of the market economy … providing the ideological dynamic for what came to be called Thatcherism'.[13]

One problem with the post-1947 system of 'betterment' was that LVC was levied at 100 per cent – so there was little money to be made by landowners selling their land for development. The system was also introduced at a time when many land-owning families were under severe financial distress – after the 1945 Labour government had set the top rate of tax at 98 per cent and ratcheted up death duties twice in four years. Crucially, though, the 100 per cent levy actively disincentivised land sales – and landowners sat on their hands, hoping the law would change which, thanks to the fall of Attlee's government in 1951 and successive Conservative administrations, it soon did.

At that time, various voices advocated setting the 'development charge' at a more moderate level. Planning Minister Lewis Silkin had initially suggested 70 or 80 per cent of the planning uplift to ensure there was something for landowners to incentivise sales, while Chancellor Rab Butler later argued to reduce the charge to 60 or 70 per cent.[14] Instead, it was abolished altogether, shifting from 100 per cent to zero.

There were subsequent attempts to reintroduce an explicit LVC mechanism to capture planning uplift – including the 'Betterment Levy' (introduced by the Land Commission Act 1967 and initially charged at 40 per cent), the 'Development Gains Tax', introduced in 1973, and the subsequent 'Development Land Tax', introduced in 1976. The Mandatory Tariff was proposed in 2001, but not implemented, and the Optional Planning Charge was partially implemented in 2004, then abandoned.[15] The same year, Kate Barker's

Review of Housing Supply proposed a new 'Planning Gain Supplement' – which was never introduced.[16] The key feature of all these post-1961 attempts to reinstate significant LVC is that they were either blocked by landowners' lobbying efforts or, if they were introduced, landowners would just sit on their holdings, waiting for the measure to be reversed. This became an established pattern, with Labour introducing new LVC mechanisms, then subsequent Conservative governments scrapping them.

History suggests, then, that a new system of significant LVC is unlikely to be effective unless the planning uplift is shared between landowners and the state – so, not a 1947-style 'betterment levy' where the state takes the entire planning gain. Also, unless LVC measures are introduced by a Conservative administration, and with the threat of CPO in the background, landowners are likely to judge they can just sit on land and wait for the law to be revoked, as has always happened in the past. A system which splits planning gains evenly, though, introduced by a Conservative government with cross-party support, has a good chance of working, winning popular consent, and becoming an established part of the UK's legal landscape – as it is in nations ranging from Germany and the Netherlands to Singapore and South Korea.

A 'Georgist' land value tax requiring high annual payments from all landholders, while scrapping most other taxes, would not help to solve the UK's housing shortage. Many landowners do a superb job of looking after our rural environment and are far from wealthy – caring for the land in part from a sense of obligation and duty. They should not be taxed simply for land ownership. Similarly, a vindictive 100 per cent LVC scheme would be counter-productive – it would not only disincentivise land sales but, being an extreme measure, would struggle to attract widespread mainstream support. As such, returning to the 1947 legislation, in its precise 'full capture' form, would be ineffective in terms of bringing land forward and would also be vulnerable to legislative reversal.

But introducing a comprehensive LVC mechanism that entitles local authorities to a fixed split of the vast planning gains when residential planning permission is granted is an entirely reasonable policy that is long overdue. The LVC measures we currently have – namely S106 and CIL – are eminently avoidable and capture far too little of the uplift.

There is an argument that not all of the state's share of planning gains should accrue to local authorities. Some parts of the country – those with high housing demand – will generate more uplift gain than others. Part of the proceeds could be redistributed, then, via central government, to fund social housing or housing-related infrastructure elsewhere. It is vital, though, if the local politics of housing are to change, that communities can be confident that if housing developments are approved, the provision of local infrastructure – such as schools, hospitals and transport links – that the new housing requires, will soon follow. This is the only way engrained Nimbyism can be overcome.

The bulk of LVC proceeds claimed by the state, then, on particular land sales for residential development, must be retained and controlled by local politicians within the local authorities involved – away from the political vagaries of central government. For it is only by forming an unbreakable bond between additional local housing and additional local amenities and infrastructure, from which the same community benefits, that the growing general support for more housebuilding can be translated into acceptance in specific instances – which is what counts. And it is only proper LVC measures that can take some of the speculative heat out of the UK market for land – unlocking the door not only to a more competitive housebuilding sector, with more affordable and better-quality properties to rent or buy on the open market, but more social housing too.

MANIFESTO FOR CHANGE

I) LAND VALUE CAPTURE

Landowners, land agents and developers currently have a strong incentive to sit on land that has planning permission, waiting for the price of both acreage and homes built on it to rise. As such, a targeted land value tax should be used to impose a direct cost on failing to build out plots where permission has been granted. If a home has not been completed, and made ready for sale, within two years of permission being given, the developer should become liable to pay full council tax on the unfinished property, rising to double then triple council tax in subsequent years until a home is ready for sale.

Planning permission should be viewed as a contract to build, between developers and the community. Penalties should be payable by either side – the developer or the local authority – if they cause the process to be unduly delayed. Applying the LVT principle in this way, to alter the financial incentives faced particularly by large developers, would help address the worst excesses of deliberately slow build-out.

'Planning uplift' should be captured more generally – split on a fifty–fifty basis between landowners, agents and/or developers on the one hand, and the state on the other. Four-fifths of the state's share of the land value capture (LVC) should automatically accrue to the relevant local authority, to be channelled into new or enhanced schools, hospitals and other infrastructure. The remaining fifth should be ring-fenced within the Treasury for social housing and/or housing-related amenities in other parts of the country.

Local authorities should be empowered, in addition, to form

Local Development Corporations (LDCs) with legal authority to use the threat of compulsory purchase orders (CPOs) to buy land. LDCs then grant themselves planning permission, parcel up the now far more valuable acreage into building plots, then sell them at profit to a variety of developers – earmarking at least half the plots for SME builders, who are generally incentivised to build quickly.

Again, the value accrued should be retained within the LDC, being used for local 'place-making' infrastructure relating not only to resulting housing developments, but across the locality. Using LVC in this way could have a transformative impact on local attitudes towards housing development, and related local politics. In addition, land bought by LDCs should score on the national accounts as an asset – the value of which increases once planning permission is granted. If local authorities borrow to buy land at existing use value, then grant planning permission, local authorities balance sheets could even be strengthened.

The UK should not be relying solely on speculative builders to carry out vital land-assembly functions – upon which the entire development and character of a locality depend. Public-led land assembly is the norm across many other countries – which not only raises money for local infrastructure, but also significantly lowers barriers to entry for SME builders, ensuring that high-quality houses are built for commercial sale and rent in a competitive and timely manner, resulting in far better outcomes for consumers.

LDCs will effectively act as land banks owned and controlled by local authorities that generate benefits that are channelled back to the community. They allow the value stemming from the inherent scarcity of development acreage to be harnessed for both private and public benefit, with landowners and the broader community sharing in the crystallisation of gains when planning permission is granted and land is sold. In many parts of the UK, where valuations between agricultural and residential land are massive, the scope for

LDCs to give existing landowners a fair price – while contributing significantly to enhanced local infrastructure – is vast.

LVC is an internationally recognised, widely used mechanism to keep land prices reasonable while funding infrastructure investment. It was used successfully in the UK during the late 1940s and 1950s, sparking the construction of millions of private and public sector homes. Analysis by the Centre for Progressive Policy indicates that planning uplift of some £18 billion was created across England in 2016/17, of which £5 billion accrued to the state via S106, CIL and general taxation. This LVC split of just 27 per cent should be much more in the favour of the state, with time-consuming S106 and CIL negotiations being scrapped, replaced instead by a transparent fifty–fifty split.

A broad political coalition has emerged in favour of reversing the 1961 Land Compensation Act, which ended the UK's previous system of significant LVC by enshrining landowners' entitlement to 'hope value'. But LVC can be re-introduced, on a shared basis, to fund both local and national infrastructure, including Crossrail 2, Northern Powerhouse Rail and much of the infrastructure investment along the proposed Oxford–Milton Keynes–Cambridge corridor, while also providing a subsidy for more affordable homes.[17]

For decades, UK politicians have been far too timid in challenging increasingly powerful landowners and developers. But this rentier system is now at the heart of a chronic housing shortage, while preventing a more equitable form of economic growth. Unless this system is not only challenged, but dismantled, it will result in increasing support for a more extreme form of politics, including far more invasive market interventions that are not only ineffective, but deeply counterproductive.

II) NEW TOWNS

The UK's New Towns programme, which lasted from 1946 to 1970, took inspiration from the two garden cities of the early twentieth century – Letchworth, built from 1903 onward, and Welwyn, begun in 1920. Both were sited on land purchased at agricultural use value – which allowed the later sale of plots for development at higher prices, generating funds to build local amenities and infrastructure.

The 1946 New Towns Act similarly gave new 'development corporations' powers to CPO land at 'existing use' value if it could not be bought by voluntary agreement. This, again, made possible the building of settlements with relatively low land costs, facilitating the delivery of other public and community benefits. Built between the designated green belts of long-established cities, some thirty-two New Towns were developed across the UK over a 25-year period. They are now home to three million people, around 5 per cent of all UK households.

It is ridiculous that, over the last fifty years, a time of fast population growth, almost no sizeable additional towns have been created in Britain. Restoring 'existing use' land value rules, though, would make it much easier and cheaper for local authorities to launch a 21st-century generation of New Towns. While the quality of housing in New Town developments is sometimes maligned, there is no reason such settlements cannot be characterised by high-quality housing, especially if land is acquired and prepared by an LDC, then sold on to a range of developers at competitive rates, allowing them to vie for customers on both quality and price when building new homes for sale and rent.

'The first generation of New Towns owed much of their success to the ability of development corporations to acquire land at, or near to, existing use value and capture uplifts in land value from the infrastructure they developed and subsequent economic activity to reinvest in the local community,' concluded the Commons Housing, Communities and Local Government Select Committee in September 2018.[18] 'Reform of the Land Compensation Act 1961, alongside enhanced CPO land assembly powers, would provide a powerful tool for local authorities to build a new generation of New Towns,' said this cross-party group of MPs. This model has 'worked well in the past ... and would lead to a significant, and much-needed, catalyst for housebuilding'.

The winners of the 2014 Wolfson Economics Prize, David Rudlin and Nicholas Falk, wrote about the need to extend existing New Towns, with LVC at the heart of their proposals.[19] For all the government's enthusiastic talk about garden cities and New Towns, though, this vital financial aspect of what made them possible is rarely considered. Across much of Britain, the price differential between agricultural land and land with planning permission is staggering. Yet, in recent years, there have been no serious attempts to introduce an effective LVC system – despite strong evidence that it could generate a building boom that would do much to address the UK's chronic housing shortage, while providing much-needed social housing too.

In June 2018, the government quietly legislated to allow local authorities to set up 'New Town Corporations'.[20] This change was encouraging but did not go nearly far enough. The proposed development corporations are still stymied by the 1961 Land Compensation Act, so are unable to capture the planning uplift so crucial to the original New Towns.

When Milton Keynes was built, the cost of the land amounted to just 1 per cent of total construction costs – compared to a UK average of around 70 per cent today.[21] What's more, Milton Keynes – while often disparaged by *bien pensant* commentators – has been a huge economic success.[22] Now a city of 250,000, it boasts a business start-up rate that's twice the national average, has a gross value added measure per worker that outstrips Oxford and Cambridge, and generates the most taxes per worker of any UK city outside London.[23]

The reality is, though, that without revoking the 1961 Act,

building a fresh wave of New Towns is not going to happen. The slow progress of Ebbsfleet 'garden city' in Kent demonstrates the problem well. In March 2014, almost twenty years after the idea was first mooted, the government announced its intention to construct a New Town at Ebbsfleet, with up to 15,000 homes. At the time of writing, over five years later, little more than 1,000 of those homes have been built.[24] This is because the project is controlled largely by private developers, who own the land – allowing them, under the current regulatory framework, to build out at their own slow pace. As such, the misnamed Ebbsfleet 'development corporation' is largely powerless, with only limited abilities to influence the pace of building or use any form of LVC to fund the provision of local amenities and infrastructure.

Without meaningful LVC, declaring the launch of a 'garden city' or 'New Town' is disingenuous. The original New Town Development Corporations had powers to threaten the use of CPOs to obtain land without sellers being legally entitled to 'hope value' – a land valuation that assumes the most lucrative future development imaginable. In the event, CPOs were rarely required, as landowners came to the table willing to accept a reasonable price. An updated, somewhat more moderate variant of this mechanism would see landowners and genuinely empowered LDCs splitting planning uplift fifty–fifty. That would still provide ample scope for LDCs to sell on land to developers at a healthy profit, so funding local infrastructure, while allowing for the production of high-quality yet still commercially profitable homes.

Following suitable changes to the 1961 Land Compensation Act, such a mechanism should be introduced – with powerful LDCs and NTDCs extending and reinvigorating existing New Towns (many of which already have good transport links), while encouraging completely new settlements to be established as well.

III) SOCIAL HOUSING

Between 1945 and 1970, some 3.1 million council homes were built by local authorities, almost 70 per cent of the 4.5 million such homes ever constructed across England.[25] Many were sited on land secured by the state at 'existing use' cost, under the 1946 and 1947 legislation, which kept building costs reasonably low. During the post-war period, then, social housing providers benefited from rules allowing them to access land at an affordable price. So they were able to build relatively high-quality, well-planned, low-density accommodation at record speeds – much of which is still perfectly serviceable and sought-after to this day.

However, from the early 1960s onwards, changes to land compensation rules meant local authorities found it far more expensive to buy land, which resulted in high-rise building. Another one million social housing units were constructed during the 1970s, but they were increasingly in tower blocks, as speculative pressure drove local authorities to look for lower-cost options.

One hundred years on from the 1919 Addison Act, which kick-started the first mass provision of social housing, there is a chronic shortage of social housing, resulting in an epidemic of over-crowding and homelessness. As such, in the aftermath of the 2017 Grenfell tragedy, there are widespread calls for a new generation of social housing. Research conducted by Heriot-Watt University on behalf of NHF estimates that England needs 340,000 new homes a year to tackle its housing shortage, including 90,000 for social rent.[26] Shelter has called for some 150,000 social housing units to be built every year for twenty years, upward of three million more homes for social rent in total.[27]

At the time of writing, the government has a target of 300,000 housing completions per year by the middle of the 2020s to address our housing shortage and tackle affordability. The private sector has failed to build anything like that in living memory. Since the late

1960s, in fact, commercial housebuilders have averaged little more than 150,000 new homes each year across the UK as a whole – less than half the government's stated aim.

There is no way we can possibly build enough homes, then, without a marked increase in the construction of social housing – which now stands at a very low single-digit number of thousands of homes each year, despite waiting lists totalling around 1.2 million applicants. Almost forty years on from Margaret Thatcher launching the Right to Buy (RTB) in 1979, attitudes toward social housing are now changing, with all the main political parties agreeing on the need to build much more. The Conservatives' 2017 manifesto said they would support 'a new generation of council homes right across the country'.[28] Labour's manifesto committed to 500,000 more council homes by 2022.[29]

Under current circumstances, though, local authorities face a 'very hostile environment' if they try to construct a viable business model to build new housing, according to the Localis thinktank. The ongoing use of RTB, for instance, means 'there is a big risk attached to building a home: they may have to sell it at a significant discount'. Also, 'a local authority's capacity and intention to build is very much dependent on the attitude of its members and officers,' observes Localis. 'And a depressing number of local authority members will work against new homes and investment in their area'.[30]

In 2017, fewer than 1,500 new homes were started by local authorities – with almost a third of those being built in just three. Of the 326 local authorities with responsibility for housing, 286 built no homes at all. This situation is only likely to change if the question of expensive land is addressed, allowing local authorities to launch new development in a cost-effective manner.

As demands grow to change the 1961 Land Compensation Act, there is an increasing recognition that, as well as encouraging the building of more housing for commercial sale and rent, such a shift could also facilitate the far more cost-effective construction of social housing too. In June 2019, Shelter published 'Grounds for Change' – a collection of essays reflecting 'the cross-sector consensus that land reform is now the foundation for a new generation of social housing in England'.[31] Drawing on a survey of Chief Council Planners, the study highlighted that 'the cost of land is the biggest barrier to council housebuilding – two-thirds of respondents said it prevents them building more social or affordable homes'.

While more direct investment will be needed to fund a new wave of social housing, this should only happen after land reform has happened. If not, the additional demand for land sparked by a new social housing programme would instantly be factored into land prices, bidding them up and making land even more expensive. 'Because of this, the problems of financing social housing are bound up with the problems of accessing the land on which to build it,' argues Rose Grayston, a co-author of 'Grounds for Change'. 'It is not enough to pour more money into a broken system … as we increase public investment in social housing, government must also act to reform the broken market for land.'[32]

Between 1995 and 2018, the value of land across England rose no less than 550 per cent – more than ten times the rate of general economy-wide inflation. This explains much of the current affordability crisis among those trying to buy or rent a home on the open market. But sky-high land prices are also a major reason that so few social homes have been built by local authorities over the same time period – an average of less than 1,400 a year since the mid-1990s. Reforming the 1961 Land Compensation Act could slash around 40 per cent off the total development costs of a new scaled-up programme of social housebuilding, according to the Civitas thinktank.[33] Building high-quality homes on a mass scale, whether for private ownership or social housing, requires reasonably priced land – and that is only going to happen with significant and radical reform.

In October 2018, Prime Minister Theresa May said she would scrap the Housing Revenue Account borrowing cap, which had been in place since 2012. This would allow local authorities to borrow more to fund new social housing. By March 2019, 94 per cent of councils affected said they planned to take advantage of this reform to invest in more housebuilding.[34] The problem remains, though, that the dynamics of the land market are coming into play – and, as various local authorities look to buy land, having borrowed heavily, prices are simply rising by the same amount, not only for public sector buyers, but private developers too.

Lifting the borrowing cap is, theoretically, a sensible move. At the time of writing, central government can raise money for ten years at 0.48 per cent and for thirty years at 1.16 per cent. Local authorities building physical homes, which would generate rent, should be able to access credit on similarly favourable terms. Yet, unless land reform comes first, and prices are no longer bid up by 'hope value', it makes no sense for local authorities to borrow simply to invest in over-priced land.

There is much scope to be innovative in the provision of social housing. The government could, for instance, use newly empowered LDCs to buy land which it could then offer to developers with planning permission and at relatively low cost, on condition it is used to build, within a certain time, primarily social housing. As an alternative to conventional borrowing, such a project would generate a return for developers and their co-investors in the form of low, regulated but steady rental payments – that could be shared by the various stakeholders.

The UK also has very considerable pension fund wealth which, for many years now, given the negative returns on government bonds, has been searching for moderate yields to match long-term liabilities. There is surely scope, with the required regulatory and administrative acumen, to connect this investment requirement with the need to finance and build social housing on behalf of local authorities. To expand the provision of sub-market-rent homes for sale and rent, local authorities should consider joint ventures with institutional investors, with the state putting forward as equity either existing public land, or land acquired at 'existing use' value.

Housing associations also have a key role to play. Set up in the 1960s to provide low-cost homes for workers, these non-profit bodies are now the leading providers of social housing in Britain. Housing associations currently manage 2.7 million homes, with some six million residents, while employing 150,000 people. In recent years, though, in response to deep cuts in government grant funding, many housing associations have become much more commercial, seeking to sell upmarket homes to cross-subsidise social housing. At the same time, despite still receiving billions of pounds of central government funding, housing associations are increasingly paying top executives as if they are fully commercial organisations. In 2018, almost 200 housing association executives were paid over £150,000 – which is more than the Prime Minister.[35]

The reality is that, after years of funding squeezes, many housing associations are struggling to provide their core services. Meanwhile, large-scale mergers and diversification have magnified financial risks.[36] With the government ultimately on the hook for the provision of social housing, some housing associations have now ballooned into multibillion-pound entities, with a combined total debt of around £70 billion, suggesting the sector may have a 'too-big-to-fail' problem.[37] And much of the 'affordable' housing produced by housing associations is not affordable at all, at up to 80 per cent of open-market prices.

Housing associations have built more in recent years, with their output rising from an average of 22,465 homes per annum during the eight years ahead of the 2008 financial crisis, to 30,483 from 2010 to 2018. As we saw in Chapter IX, though, while some three-quarters of 'affordable housing' was for 'social rent' in 2010 – typically 40–50 per cent of market prices – that share had fallen to just 14 per cent by 2018.

Genuine land reform could significantly strengthen the UK's housing associations – giving them access to acreage at reasonable prices. And when a government-run LDC buys land, on which it grants planning permission before selling it on, a share could be reserved for housing associations. But the government must make such land access, and further government grants, strictly contingent on housing associations staying true to their original purpose.

Also, the right to buy should be curtailed in England, as it already has been in Scotland and Wales – not just for housing associations but for local authorities too. Until we reach a point where the building of new social housing is once again widespread, and homes sold under RTB are heavily outnumbered by new stock, RTB should not be used. As and when it is reintroduced, sale proceeds should accrue in full to local authorities or housing associations, under the condition that the money is fully reinvested into more social housing.

The UK needs to aim for a mixed-economy of housing supply, with commercial builders, housing associations and local authorities each playing their part to build the 300,000-plus new homes we require each year. There will always be a need for subsidised housing in any advanced economy – and the UK's policy of increasing reliance on private landlords to house social tenants is, as rents rise, causing the housing benefit bill to spiral. This will continue unless we decisively reverse the long-term decline in social housebuilding.

The massive shift to private renting in the past decade reflects not just the inability of much of 'generation rent' to buy a home. It also stems from a seriously diminished stock of social housing – which has brought far more low-income and otherwise vulnerable households into contact with the sharp end of housing insecurity and unaffordability.

The social housing sector could also, if well managed, play an important 'counter-cyclical' role. As the commercial property market goes through cycles, local authorities should be able to scale their own housebuilding programmes up or down to maintain a relatively even output across the entire sector and preserve capacity – particularly in terms of skills and the provision of construction materials. There are signs that the Conservative government is now thinking along these lines.[38]

More fundamentally, the UK's distinct lack of social building in recent years means we are far too dependent upon and handing increasing influence to commercial housebuilders. In the late 1960s, the private sector accounted for just 49 per cent of all newly built homes. By 2018, that share of commercial provision had risen to 81 per cent, with the commercial housebuilding lobby now far more concentrated, less exposed to genuine competition and much more politically powerful than it was fifty years ago.

Private developers have been and always will be very important to meeting the UK's housing supply. They should account for the bulk of new-build homes in a nation like Britain. They must be incentivised, though, to deliver good-quality, keenly priced products in sufficient numbers to prevent prices spiralling. Yet the abject lack of social housing, and subsequent over-reliance on private sector developers, has handed them far too much influence, allowing them to resist meaningful and long-overdue supply-side reforms. Unless we break this impasse, Britain will continue to suffer from a near-nationwide affordability crisis stemming from a chronic housing shortage.

IV) BETTER PLANNING

Back in 2010, local authorities granted permission for just 155,637 housing units – way below the 300,000 or so new homes we need each year. By 2015, after the introduction of the more lenient

National Planning Policy Framework, 272,500 planning permissions were granted, rising to 370,400 two years later.[39] By 2017, in fact, over 80 per cent of all applications to build residential housing were being accepted – suggesting the planning system hasn't been too much of a barrier to more housebuilding in recent years.

In 2013, though, according to a Local Government Association (LGA) survey, developers took an average of 1.7 years to complete each home once detailed planning permission had been granted.[40] By 2017, an equally authoritative industry study pointed to a delay of 'at least four years on average' from detailed planning permission to completion – a 2.4-fold increase over just four years.[41]

Based on such data, and increasing evidence of slow build-out rates, the LGA now argues that 'the planning system is not a barrier to building … councils are approving almost nine in every ten planning applications'.[42] Instead, the LGA is calling for councils to have more powers to deal with unbuilt land where permission to build has already been granted. This makes sense – which is why this book recommends using a targeted land value tax to impose a direct cost on failing to build out plots with planning permission. If a home is not ready for sale within two years of permission, the developer should pay full council tax on the unfinished property, rising to double then triple rates of council tax in subsequent years that the home isn't ready. Planning permission must be seen as a contract to build, between developers and local authority – with penalties payable by either side if they delay building unduly.

Even though more permissions are being granted, though, our planning system is still a significant hindrance to the building of new homes. That's because, unusually for an advanced industrialised economy, UK planning is not rules-based, as it is across continental Europe and much of the US, but takes a case-by-case approach instead. Planning decisions in this country are highly discretionary and, therefore, highly politicised. This results in much greater planning risk and, once permission is secured, higher land prices – acting as a barrier to entry to SMEs and those who wish to self-build. What we need is a system where the right to develop is clearly regulated, but with much greater clarity about what is and is not permissible. The huge uncertainty and related cost in our system means that many otherwise viable projects do not get built. The discretion involved in our specific forms of LVC – namely S106 and CIL – adds very significant additional uncertainty and provides little in the way of fiscal rewards for communities that approve development.

'To get planning permission to build houses on a plot of land requires expertise on a huge range of subjects and takes a lot of time,' says Nick Boles, a former Housing Minister. 'As a result, the number of suppliers of new houses has collapsed – and, instead of a free market with a potentially unlimited number of suppliers, we have created an oligopoly, with utterly predictable results.' Boles rightly argues that, partly due to our planning system, 'a small number of large housebuilders produce between them far fewer houses of a lower quality and at a much higher cost than the free market would'. Such large firms are 'sheltered by the planning system from competition by new entrants,' he says, so they 'fail to innovate or invest in new, more efficient ways of building houses' – and consumers just have to take what they're given. [43]

Nicholas Boys Smith, the co-head of the government's Building Better, Building Beautiful Commission, goes further. 'In historic and comparative terms, the UK has a very strange planning governance and process – and this really matters,' he says.[44] It makes no sense, Boys Smith argues, to run a bespoke system (with discretionary decision-making) for a mass product such as housing. Rather than treating individual sites on a case-by-case basis, there should be a broader use of zoning rules for what is, and is not, permissible.

Boys Smith argues, like Boles, that the planning system 'poses a major barrier to entry for smaller developers and self-builders'. Certainly, in the UK, less than a third of all homes are built by SME builders, compared to 50 per cent in Germany and 73 per cent in Denmark, where the planning system is far more predictable. And less than a tenth of UK homes are self- or custom-build (versus a European average of around half).

The UK's planning system should be radically simplified, easing height restrictions, with much more zoning. In locations where rapid development is needed, 'pink zone' status should be declared – which designates broad permitted-build parameters, such as maximum height, density, affordable housing requirements and so on. Within a 'pink zone', specific planning applications are granted within two months and are deemed granted if no decision is made.[45]

Alongside this liberalising move, the use of Permitted Development Rights (PDRs) to convert office buildings and shops into residential property, in place since 2013, should be modified. It is wrong that PDRs allows homes to be created that don't conform with basic requirements relating to space, daylight and ventilation – as described in Chapter VI. Dropping such requirements under the guise of PDRs, in the name of boosting the headline number of 'new dwellings', is myopic in the extreme.

V) GREEN BELT

The 2011 NPFF did not change green belt designations – which continue to prevent development in many parts of the UK where there is a very acute need for housing. Yet responsible and environmentally sensitive planning and the provision of adequate housing need not be incompatible.

Many parts of the green belt are valuable and important. But other parts are farmland with no public access or urban scrub of no environmental or aesthetic merit. Outdated green belt classifications are too often used to protect land in areas of intense housing demand that should clearly be developed – as outlined in Chapter IV. The most aesthetically and environmentally important parts of the UK are already designated 'Areas of Outstanding Natural Beauty' or 'National Parks'. And consider that the fifteen green belts, surrounding seventeen cities, now take up 13 per cent of all the land in England – having expanded by no less than 126 per cent since 1979. The green belt now covers an area of England that is almost ten times bigger than the total acreage taken up by residential housing and gardens. This has severely thwarted development in areas close to cities where people want to live, resulting in much longer commutes, lower productivity and more carbon emissions.

Since 2011, local authorities can grant planning permission on green belt sites if they decide this is the only way to meet housing need, by demonstrating 'exceptional circumstances' that are 'fully evidenced and justified' and having 'examined fully all other reasonable options for meeting its identified need for development'.[46] Yet this rarely happens, not least because local councillors and MPs so often step in to object.

Over half the green belt is used for intensive farming – which involves the heavy use of chemicals and provides little refuge for wildlife, so is not 'green' at all. What it amounts to, instead, is a huge and growing distortion in a market for land which is already deeply dysfunctional – a distortion used by millions of lucky homeowners to stymie much-needed development under the guise of environmental virtue. There is no need to 'concrete over' the countryside, but we do need to stop severely constraining the growth of housing in places where people really want and need to live.

'The philosophy of preventing urban sprawl is a good one and ought to ensure that real green space – some of it green belt, some of it metropolitan open land – is protected where it provides real beauty and utility to the community', says former Liberal Democrat leader Vince Cable. 'Yet there are some parts of the green belt which have disused petrol stations or abandoned warehouses and could hardly be called areas of natural beauty,' he observes. 'Nobody who is serious about resolving the housing crisis would argue such sites should be off-limits.'[47]

Rather than treating existing green belt boundaries as untouchable holy writ, we need transparent, locally led, green belt reviews that lead to sustainable, well-designed homes close to transport, while preserving truly accessible green spaces. Some green belt could also be 'moved', recognising that our big cities have become far more populous since some of these areas were first designated in the 1950s. Land now close to built-out towns and transport links could be released in return for similar acreages being preserved elsewhere.

For every acre of green belt released, local authorities could use part of their LVC gains to help organise and pay for industrial wastelands to be prepared for housing. 'Brownfield' sites are typically built on only when land prices rise enough to cover the high cost of development. Urban development corporations, such as the one established in the 1980s to regenerate east London's docklands, could assemble such plots of land more effectively than private developers – on a one-for-one basis as green belt is cleared for development. This would discourage the use of green belt becoming an 'easy option' – as its use would be contingent on developing 'brownfield' land too.

The need to re-classify green belt is particularly acute in locations close to public transport, particularly in Manchester, Birmingham and Greater London, adjacent to Crossrail – the new east–west line across London, linking Reading in Berkshire with Shenfield in Essex and Abbey Wood in Kent. Professor Paul Cheshire of the London School of Economics points out that, thanks to Crossrail, small towns like Taplow and Iver in Buckinghamshire are now within half an hour of the capital's central business district.

'It is close to insane to spend £18 billion on Crossrail and not take advantage of the tracts of land that will suddenly be within a short commute of central London,' says Professor Cheshire, 'because in 1955 – before Crossrail was dreamt of, when London was staggering back to its feet after WWII and car ownership was less than a tenth as common as now – all the land around the outlying stations was declared off limits.'[48]

When David Cameron was Prime Minister, he oversaw the 2011 NPPF and then, in 2013, encouraged local authorities to consider building on part of the green belt.[49] Soon after, though, he changed his tune, arguing precisely the reverse.[50] Strong leadership and green belt reviews are now required, certainly within two miles of railway and bus stations – allowing passengers to walk or cycle. Releasing just 0.3 per cent of the green belt would provide space for almost 200,000 new homes. Utilising a mere 5 per cent of designated green belt would release the space required to clear the UK's vast backlog shortage of homes entirely, while providing space for several decades of further expansion – all of it, by definition, close to towns and cities where people want to work and live. Those protesting should be firmly reminded that, even if England's green belt became 5 per cent smaller than today, it would still be 115 per cent bigger than it was in 1979.

The formation of LDCs outlined above would generate much honest discussion about shifting local green belt boundaries – which, in many cases, were set over sixty years ago. The prospect of large planning gains feeding into local schools, hospitals and other public amenities could transform such debates, with property values being enhanced rather than harmed by development and entrenched local opposition giving way to compromise and progress.

VI) NEW-BUILD HOMES

Since 2013, Help to Buy has handed all-powerful housing developers huge profits by channelling first-time buyers into often sub-standard new-build homes. Such homes are now even more over-priced than they were prior to HTB, given that the housebuilding giants have seen thousands of desperate young homebuyers coming, laden with sack-loads of taxpayers' cash. George Osborne was repeatedly warned that introducing HTB would simply stoke up new-build prices, but the then Chancellor just ploughed on.

The problem is that the traditional 'feel-good factor' associated with rising house prices has now been eclipsed by a broader discontent driven by the sharp increase in the number of 'priced-out' young adults, the vast majority of whom have not benefited from HTB. Theresa May, of course, maintained the misguided approach of her political nemesis, pumping yet more billions into HTB in a desperate bid to win easy headlines.

HTB was sold by ministers as a way to encourage UK housebuilders to build more homes as the residential construction industry recovered from the 2007/08 global financial crisis. The evidence is it has turbocharged the profits of a handful of powerful housebuilders instead, without leading to a significant increase in the number of homes actually built compared to the pre-crisis average. And, above all, HTB has resulted in a spate of shockingly sub-standard new-build homes, with all the human misery that entails.

It is outrageous housing developers are not required by law to allow buyers of new-build homes to conduct their own independent survey before completion. It makes no sense that, as is currently the case, those purchasing such homes – often the biggest and most important transaction of their lives – enjoy less consumer protection than someone buying a toaster, as demonstrated in Chapter VII. The severe lack of legal safeguards to protect new-build homebuyers is a sad indictment of the market power of the UK's housebuilders, and their ability to resist the most basic legislation regulating their product.

By presenting such developers with thousands of young potential buyers who, having been lent money by the state, are then limited to buying only new-build, HTB has served to increase that market power – with an obvious negative impact on the level of true competition and related customer service. By boosting demand in the face of ongoing supply constraints, the HTB scheme has been deeply counterproductive – and should be immediately withdrawn.

VII) GREAT BRITISH SELL-OFF

A 2016 survey by the estate agents Savills found that the public sector owns around 6 per cent of all freehold land – almost a million hectares – rising to 15 per cent in urban areas, including countless prime sites for redevelopment.[51] Over two-fifths of freehold land in Brighton and Hove, Barking and Dagenham and six other local authority 'hotspots' is held by the state, this study shows. While some of the UK's public sector land is controlled by ministries – including MHCLG, the Ministry of Defence and the Department of Health – over two-thirds is held by local authorities.

The state holds enormous amounts of land, in very developable places. Transport for London, for instance, owns around 6,000 acres in the capital and Network Rail has substantial landholdings, often close to stations. The NHS also has large holdings. In a recent report, NHS Digital identified 1,332 hectares of surplus land across 550 sites, just ninety-one hectares of which had previously been sold.[52]

If the state released just one twentieth of its land for development, that would be enough, at the current UK average density of forty-five homes per hectare, to build well over two million homes – far more if state-owned land in urban areas was used, where building densities are much higher. Yet, as outlined in Chapter V, sales of public land for residential development have been hopelessly low.

From 1997 to 2010, the public land sold for new homes was enough to build an average of only around one thousand units each year.

Between 2011 and 2015, this improved, with public land released adequate to build an projected 109,500 homes, an annual average of over 27,000 a year.[53] Yet Whitehall appears entirely unaware of how many homes have actually been built on land sold during this period. The Commons Public Accounts was told in 2016 that, despite the 100,000-plus capacity, the number of new homes actually built on this land could be as low as 200.[54] Since 2015, public land disposals for home building have sunk once again, to an average capacity of just 9,600 units per year – a major missed opportunity.

The government must cut through Whitehall torpor, urgently and significantly ramping up sales from its own land holdings for residential development. Large, listed housebuilders should be excluded from most such sales. Non-building land agents must always be excluded. Sales of the most attractive small plots, particularly in city centres, should be restricted to local SME builders – who, in need of cash flow, generally build very quickly.

With certain buyers not permitted to bid, state land – whether sold via competitive tender or open auction – may sometimes fetch 'sub-market' prices. Treasury dogma that this is unacceptable must be fiercely resisted. Getting local housing supply moving makes eminent fiscal sense. If more homes are built and growth is stimulated, the state will reap much higher revenues than if land is left idle. The current unaffordability of housing, due to an acute lack of available land, is driving an ever-rising housing benefit bill. If there were more affordable homes to buy and rent, that bill would drastically fall.

State land sold to all builders, large or small, should come with 'permission in principle' status.[55] The implementation after two years of an LVT on unfinished plots, as recommended here, would anyway mean delays are kept to a minimum. But once subsequent 'technical details consent' is granted, a condition of sale on some plots where housing need is particularly acute could be that if homes are not completed within two years, land ownership reverts to the state. An alternative, in other locations where rapid development is required, would be to sell state land with 'pink zone' status in place – as outlined above.

Each year, then, enough state land should be sold to developers to enable the construction of at least 50,000 homes. In addition, surplus state land could form the basis of a government land bank – to be used by local authorities to meet local need, primarily affordable and social housing. The freehold for public land should remain in the public sector, with long leases extended to local authorities, housing associations and community land trusts, providing a long-term income stream for the public sector. Questions on what state plots to sell, with what planning status and to which size of builder should, to a significant extent, be devolved to local authorities and city mayors. This entire sales process must be absolutely open and transparent – not only to ensure fairness, but to guard against corruption. Any housebuilder who tries to invoke 'commercial in confidence' requirements while buying state-held land would be immediately excluded from future sales.

VIII) LAND OWNERSHIP TRANSPARENCY

'The greatest problem facing a researcher seeking to examine land supply in any detail is the absence of any aggregate database regarding land ownership,' concluded the Office of Fair Trading (OFT) in 2008. 'The UK's land databases present only a part of the overall picture of land ownership.'[56]

The UK has a remarkably opaque system of land ownership. There is much scope to increase the transparency of the land supply system through the compulsory release of detailed data on land market activity – and also stalled sites. Better data would create a more level playing field and enable SMEs to find sites more easily. The 2014 Lyons Review recommended the Land Registry should open up land ownership information to the public and that it should be a legal requirement to register land option agreements, prices and transactions. This would enhance the operation of the land market. It would also enable local authorities to play a more active role in land assembly, while properly assessing the record of landowners, agents and developers in bringing forward and building out sites.[57]

In its 2017 White Paper, the government set targets to achieve comprehensive land registration by 2030 with all publicly held land in areas of high housing need registered by 2020, with the rest to follow by 2025.[58] This timetable is far too slow. Homes England should quickly designate priority 'high-demand' localities where 'build-out' incentives are targeted, while publishing regular 'build-out' gaps for each large developer. The agency should also initiate a wholesale upgrade of the Land Registry – which is opaque, incomplete and unfit for purpose.

In addition, all options agreements should be centrally registered, even agreements currently enforceable only in offshore jurisdictions. While private land ownership is an entirely legitimate and proper concept, who owns and controls the land is a matter of legitimate public interest – and amounts to knowledge that is vital for effective public policymaking.

A government that is serious about ensuring the market for land works properly would require all options agreements to be brought onshore and into the open, subject to UK law and enforceable in British courts. A one-year cut-off should be announced, stating that such agreements will only be recognised in the UK after a future date if they are registered centrally and subject to UK jurisdiction.

IX) END THE FOUR-YEAR LAW

The lack of affordable accommodation in London, Oxford, Manchester and elsewhere has led to the 'beds-in-sheds' epidemic, as discussed in the Introduction. The housing shortage combined with high rents has seen a sharp rise in the number of local authorities launching heat-seeking drones in a bid to monitor the use of out-buildings in residential areas to provide sub-standard, and often unsafe and unsanitary, rented accommodation. Official figures on over-crowding are patchy and inadequate, but a London-wide survey undertaken as long ago as 2012 found that 40 per cent of London boroughs, mostly in outer London, felt that 'beds in sheds' was a 'significant and growing issue'.[59]

National planning law currently imposes a four-year limit on planning enforcement. Any action against the unauthorised use of a building must be undertaken within that period, or the activity becomes legal in terms of planning. If a 'beds-in-sheds' property remains undetected for over four years, then the landlord can apply to regularise the use of the property through a 'certificate of lawful existing use'. This four-year limit should be scrapped in situations where the use of outbuildings for sleeping accomodation has been deliberately concealed and rental income not declared for tax pur-poses. A thorough audit must also be conducted to identify the full extent of the 'beds-in-sheds' phenomenon. As well as sub-standard housing, it also involves significant tax evasion by rogue landlords and the non-payment of council tax by tenants – so there is a fiscal motivation to tackle this issue too.

X) INDUSTRY STRUCTURE

Alongside measures to discourage large developers from delaying build-out, more specific assistance should be given to the smallest builders – those building under 100 units a year. They need help not only with accessing finance but also dealing with the planning system – which still presents SMEs with big difficulties in terms of time, expense and unpredictability.

The government has made progress, working with clearing banks to encourage the extension of credit to SME builders. But given that faster build-out rates are of enormous importance to broader society, more action is required – in the form of limited Treasury guarantees for approved SME builders, particularly those undertaking schemes involving considerable affordable housing. Rather than Help to Buy, the benefits of which were largely felt by large volume developers, we need a multibillion-pound, sustained 'Help to Build' scheme for the smallest SMEs – with the government standing behind a share of selected small builders' credit arrangements, for a limited amount of time, as it currently does for homebuyers under Help to Buy.

For SMEs producing fewer than 100 units a year, Section 106 obligations should be removed, with such firms paying only the flat-rate Community Infrastructure Levy (CIL) instead. This will lessen lengthy negotiations, significantly speeding up build-out on smaller sites. And, for an initial ten-year period, as the housebuilding industry is restructured, individual developments of fewer than ten units built by SMEs not benefiting from Help to Build finance outlined above should be free of all affordable housing requirements. If the government reverses the 1961 Land Compensation Act, and landowners and developers are required to share planning uplift fifty–fifty with local authorities, as recommended here, the use of S-106 and CIL would anyway be curtailed.

The rapid consolidation of the UK housebuilding industry since the global financial crisis and the sharp increase in build-out delays since 2010 amounts to circumstantial evidence of restrictive practices – certainly enough to warrant open and detailed investigation. Given the public interest issues at stake, the 2017/18 Letwin Review – a behind-closed-doors examination of this vital industry, conducted by a small secretariat – was not nearly enough.

A House of Lords Committee in 2016 described the UK housebuilding sector as having 'all the characteristics of an oligopoly'. Large developers, operating in a sector that should be extremely competitive, involving long-standing and widely available technologies and methods, are chalking up enormous profit growth, with top executives being paid bonuses amounting to hundreds of millions of pounds. An affordability crisis is preventing more than half of an entire generation of young adults from buying a home. That crisis is getting worse. The increasingly dominant volume developers, in response to a taxpayer-funded scheme to help young adults buy a home, returned to archaic and abusive market practices such as selling sub-standard new-build properties on cynically punitive leaseholds.

As such, an immediate Competition and Markets Authority (CMA) inquiry is needed into the structure of the UK's housebuilding market. The last such investigation took place in 2008, conducted by the OFT. Since then, the housebuilding industry has become far more concentrated, with the share of the market accounted for by large 'volume' builders almost doubling, from 31 per cent to 59 per cent. The share built by SMEs producing fewer than 100 units a year fell over the same period – from 28 per cent to just 12 per cent.[60]

Since 2008, many SMEs have folded into insolvency or been taken over, their land holdings consolidated by larger developers. The patchy nature of the UK's public records in relation to land ownership and control makes it almost impossible to assess the extent to which the concentration of landbanking and options agreements is actually restricting competition. It strikes the author as entirely reasonable, then, that amid growing public outrage at the unaffordability and low quality of new-build homes, the OFT's successor, the CMA, should now launch a full and immediate investigation into the structure of the UK's housebuilding industry. Such an inquiry, in fact, is long overdue – and that it hasn't yet happened is itself a sign of the unhealthy and entirely disproportionate influence that this powerful lobby exerts over our elected representatives.

CONCLUSION

It is possible to solve our housing problem ... but it requires confrontation with vested interests, and an awful lot of those vested interests are, it has to be said, connected to the Conservative Party.[1]

ROGER SCRUTON, 2019

Housing provision is often controversial and provokes strong re-actions – not least when an increasing share of the population feels it is getting a raw deal. This is hardly surprising given that a home, whether owner-occupied or rented from a private landlord or the state, is a basic human need, fundamental to our physical, social and mental wellbeing.

It is generally accepted that the UK needs around 250,000–300,000 new homes each year to meet population growth and household formation. Our chronic shortage of homes has been years in the making, with successive governments failing to ensure enough houses and flats were built – both commercial properties for sale or rent and social housing too.

This fundamental lack of supply, coupled with the Bank of England's ultra-loose monetary policies since 2009, has seen house prices spiral, resulting in the emergence of 'generation rent'. Back in 1991, 67 per cent of 25–34-year-olds owned their own property. Twenty-five years later, in 2016, that figure had fallen to just 38 per cent.

The average house price across the UK is now eight times the average wage – having doubled since 1998. This is a historically high multiple, impossible to finance with a regular mortgage. Even youngsters holding down professional jobs are increasingly priced out. That's why half of FTBs are now dependent on 'the bank of Mum and Dad', rising to two-thirds in London and the south-east – an option obviously available only to some. The UK's housing market, then, once a source of social mobility and security for those willing to work and save, now generates widespread discontent and anger – as, for so many, the instinctive and entirely reasonable ambition of home ownership is thwarted. High rents and a chronic social housing shortage have meanwhile driven a shocking rise in homelessness and over-crowding.

Since taking office in 2010, the Conservatives have allowed the UK's increasingly oligopolistic housebuilding industry to delay the conversion of rising numbers of planning permissions granted into actual homes, boosting prices and profits by imposing a deliberate housebuilding go-slow. The campaign group Shelter estimates that no less than one in three homes granted planning permission between 2012 and 2016 has not been built – amounting to 320,000 units. In London, the share of such 'phantom homes' is one in two.[2] Over the same period, the profits of the UK's five largest housebuilders soared by 388 per cent, reaching £3.3 billion in 2016. These facts are clear evidence that the UK's housing market isn't working.

Rather than taking measures to rein in prices by ensuring more homes are built, the Tories have instead stoked up the demand side of the market via 'Help to Buy' – a massive taxpayer subsidy to raise the purchasing power of those buying new-build homes. As a result, new-build prices surged 25 per cent ahead of the price of second-hand homes, making them unaffordable for no less than 83 per cent of all working families in commercially rented accommodation across England, rising to 89 per cent in the south-west and 93 per cent in the West Midlands.[3]

David Cameron said he wanted 'the dream of home ownership to be achievable for everyone' – yet an average of just 123,560 homes were built in each year of his premiership, the lowest of any Prime Minister since the early 1920s.[4] As the crisis intensified, Theresa May's government talked tough about 'fixing the housing market'. Yet her main housing policy was simply to twice extend the HTB scheme launched by Cameron's Chancellor George Osborne – significantly boosting the market power and profits of large developers, a group that has historically contributed generously to the Conservative Party's coffers.

Over the last twenty years, the proportion of people living in the private rented sector has doubled.[5] Many young professionals who live in cities are spending over half their disposable income on rent. Almost 2.5 million working households with below-average incomes need to allocate a third or more of their disposable income towards housing costs. Both groups are unlikely to be able to save for a deposit on a property, let alone put anything aside to help with starting a family or for later life. And, meanwhile, many older homeowners are deeply concerned that their children and grand-children will be unable to afford their own home.

The roots of this UK housing shortage stretch back a long way. Over the last twenty years, around 2.3 million too few homes have been built, according to Professor Paul Cheshire at the London School of Economics. Tackling what is now an acute crisis is going to require much determination and political courage. But the alternative is a di-vided nation, with an ever-widening gap between the property haves and have-nots. This 'property owning democracy' – where the rate of home ownership is now below the EU average – is heading for a situation where only those with wealthy parents can get a foot on the property ladder and elderly people are forced to keep working long after retirement age to pay rent or keeping making mortgage payments.

While the bulk of the solution to the UK's housing shortage lies with the private sector, building homes for commercial sale and rent, Britain is always going to need a significant and regularly replenished stock of subsidised social housing – another area where successive governments have failed. In response to the Grenfell Tower tragedy, Theresa May announced funding for just 5,000 social units a year for five years. Set against a 1.2 million-strong council house waiting list, this was risible.

A wide range of policy reforms is required to raise significantly the rate of housebuilding, to start to address our huge backlog shortage and, over a period, gradually bring prices back more in line with earnings – making homes affordable for would-be owner-occupiers, while providing enough decent social housing, too. But it is a central argument of this book that one particular and rather bold policy shift is a *sine qua non* – an essential, necessary condition finally to 'fix' the UK's broken housing market.

1961 AND ALL THAT

It is vital the government creates an environment in which housebuilders can obtain land at reasonable prices, and planning permission to build in a timely and relatively predictable manner. It is, after all, high and rising land costs which are the main reason why average house prices across the UK have spiralled to eight times average wages. This means reversing the 1961 Land Compensation Act so landowners are no longer legally entitled to full 'hope value' – the value of the land following any conceivable development.

The massive 'planning uplift' gains when residential permission to build is granted – which, in some high-demand areas, can currently make agricultural land up to 200 or 300 times more valuable – should be shared fifty–fifty between landowners and local authorities. This land value capture (LVC) by the state will dampen speculative demand for land, gradually lower prices and make it easier for SME builders to finance land purchases at a reasonable cost. Lowering this major barrier to entry will help break the stranglehold of the over-mighty 'volume' builders that dominate UK housebuilding.

In addition, a targeted land value tax (LVT) should be used to encourage the building out of plots where permission has been granted. After two years, developers should become liable to pay full council tax on any unfinished property – with planning permission viewed as nothing less than a contract to build, between developers and the community. Local authorities should also be empowered to form Local Development Corporations (LDCs) with legal authority to use the threat of compulsory purchase orders (CPOs) to buy land. Having granted outline planning permission, LDCs should sell building plots at a profit to a variety of developers – reserving at least half for SME builders, who have strong cashflow incentives to build quickly.

Local authorities currently use S106 agreements and the CIL to try to claw back some planning uplift from developers, in the form of affordable housing and other community-related benefits. This system is expensive, time-consuming, routinely 'gamed' by large housebuilders reneging on such agreements – and results in far too little of the planning uplift accruing to the broader community. The introduction of a systemic, transparent and uniformly implemented LVC mechanism – with a clear fifty–fifty split – will mean local authorities have funds to help provide new and upgraded schools, hospitals and other local 'place-making' infrastructure when new housing developments are built. This principle – used in the UK during the 1950s prior to the 1961 Act, and still widely employed across continental Europe, the US, Asia and beyond – could transform local attitudes towards housing development, tackling engrained Nimbyism.

There is growing political support to reverse the 1961 legislation.

Reintroducing genuine LVC would enable the state to buy land at a reasonable cost and raise money towards the construction of a fresh wave of New Towns, while replenishing the UK's badly depleted stock of social housing. These reforms will be fiercely resisted by big developers, land agents and large landowners – the same lobby which reversed the original 1947 planning settlement, pushing for the 1961 legislation, and which continues to benefit handsomely from the status quo.

Repealing the 1961 Land Compensation Act will no doubt be characterised by opponents of the move as 'extreme', 'spiteful' and 'left-wing'. Yet it is by no means anti-free market to use LVC, or for the state to be more actively involved in buying and preparing land for residential development. It is the UK that is the exception among advanced societies, in leaving such vital activities solely to an over-mighty commercial housebuilding sector.

Those who instantly reject the premise of *Home Truths* should consider that a major advocate of the state buying and parcelling land, while using significant LVC, was Keith Joseph, Housing Minister in the mid-1960s. Joseph argued against the 1961 legislation – as highlighted in Chapter X, but was unable to convince Macmillan and the rest of the Cabinet. He then went on, of course, to become a trailblazer for the free-market reforms of Margaret Thatcher.

The UK housing market, as it currently operates, with the 1961 legislation in place, is deeply dysfunctional. It is causing widespread societal damage – in the form not just of thwarted home ownership and rising wealth inequality, but also sky-high rents, insufficient social housing, a spiralling housing benefit bill and often deeply inadequate social infrastructure. On top of that, we can include rising household indebtedness and lower pension saving, as buyers struggle to secure over-priced homes with huge mortgages, and increasingly long commutes, as parents move further away from work to afford enough space to raise a family.

Under the 1947 legislation, introduced in a different age, the state took 100 per cent of the 'planning uplift' – which was unsustainable and, in any case, discouraged landowners from selling. What's needed instead is a more moderate fifty–fifty split. What's also needed are honest, transparent reviews of the green belt – which now covers 13 per cent of England's entire land mass, having more than doubled since 1979. Big parts of the green belt are urban scrub, offering no environmental benefit whatsoever. Much of the rest is high-intensity arable farmland, off-limits to the public and doused with chemicals – it is anything but 'green'. Releasing a mere 5 per cent of our massively expanded green belt would create space to clear the UK's vast backlog shortage of homes, while providing for several decades of further expansion.

The state needs to become a lot more serious about bringing forward existing government-owned land for development – which amounts to 15 per cent of all freehold acreage in urban areas. Ministers also need to grasp the nettle and instigate a full CMA inquiry into the UK's housebuilding sector. In 1960, the ten biggest UK housebuilders accounted for just 9 per cent of all new homes built.[6] When we last consistently built over 250,000 homes a year, during the early and mid-1980s, SMEs accounted for two-thirds of such completions. The UK housebuilding sector today is very different – [with the three largest developers accounting for a quarter of homes built each year and over half provided by the biggest eight firms.[7]

The spate of sub-standard homes, ghastly customer service and spiralling profits points to clear restrictive practices at the top of this industry – one which is now characterised by little genuine competition, too often resulting in appalling consumer outcomes. Our Land Registry and register of options agreements used to control land coming to market are both opaque, laughably incomplete and chronically unfit for purpose. Deliberate and concerted action is required to make the land market more transparent and to inject genuine competition into this sector – beginning with a full CMA inquiry.

While the emphasis should be on the supply side – reversing the 1961 legislation, reintroducing meaningful LVC and moving towards a more 'rules-based' planning system – some demand-side reforms would also be useful. Help to Buy has become the antithesis of a useful demand-side measure – and should be immediately scrapped. There is scope, though, significantly to reduce and ultimately abolish stamp duty on property purchases. This would spark more housing transactions, thereby boosting turnover in the secondary market and encouraging the more efficient use of the UK's housing stock.

During the late 1980s, well over two million properties were bought and sold each year, twice as many as today. Levied on homebuyers, stamp duty is a steep tax on moving home, which discourages homeowners from selling – particularly older people in larger, under-occupied but desperately needed family homes. 'Stamp duty is among the most inefficient and damaging of all taxes,' according to the highly respected Mirrlees Review on tax reform.[8]

The merits of removing stamp duty are significant, given that it currently stops many mutually beneficial transactions from happening between those downsizing and those moving up the housing ladder. Care is required, of course – if stamp duty were removed in one go, house prices could rise sharply, with sellers sensing that buyers suddenly had 'more scope' to pay. That said, the balance of property taxation should steadily shift away from transactions and towards LVC. Also needed is a proper realignment of council tax thresholds, which have barely moved since the early 1990s. But shared planning uplift could help local authorities keep council tax rises lower over time – once again, making housing development more popular.

Another area where demand-side measures may be necessary relates to the heavy purchase of new homes for investment purposes by overseas buyers. This has spread beyond prime areas of central London to the suburbs of the capital, and also to Manchester, Oxford, Cambridge, Leeds, Liverpool and beyond. Investors from China, India, Singapore and the Gulf are now buying thousands of units each year, reflecting not only their confidence in the UK economy and legal system, but the assessment of international observers that the UK's property shortage is so endemic, and the vested interest ranged against change so entrenched, that prices will continue to spiral.

While we should be cautious about too much market intervention, and personal homes bought by overseas buyers should clearly be exempt, home ownership for UK citizens is so economically and socially advantageous – and so keenly desired – that democratically elected governments should do all they can to support it. Countries attractive to foreign investors – including Australia, Switzerland, Denmark and New Zealand – have taken steps to favour domestic buyers of new-build homes. The UK, with our well-deserved reputation for competition and liberal economic policymaking, can afford to be part of that group, taking measures to prevent countless British families becoming the long-term tenants of landlords based and paying tax overseas. As such, UK non-residents and non-domiciled residents should be restricted to 10 per cent of any new-build development over twenty units.

These demand-side measures, though, while challenging, are far easier, and matter far less, than making the fundamental supply-side change – which is to tackle the rampant speculation characterising the UK's dysfunctional market for land, which is at the heart of our broader 'broken' housing market. The 1961 legislation was introduced at the behest of powerful vested interests, determined to unravel the post-war settlement. Reversing that change will, once again, involve a sizeable political battle.

DELIVERING THE GOODS

Capitalism works, and is sustainable, when it distributes wealth broadly – not evenly, but broadly. That spreading of wealth ensures, in turn, that the market economy generates and is further bolstered by widespread popular consent. Yet, across Britain, with young adults struggling to attain living standards enjoyed by their parents – and, above all, failing to secure reasonably priced accommodation to buy or even rent – capitalism is becoming less popular. A lack of decent social housing, which is aggravating the UK's growing epidemic of over-crowding and homelessness, is also generating calls for far more interventionist – and ultimately entirely counter-productive – policies.

'Capitalism needs neither propaganda nor apostles,' wrote the iconic economist Ludwig von Mises in 1947. 'Its achievements speak for themselves – capitalism delivers the goods'.[9] For far too many, though, capitalism is singularly failing to 'deliver the goods'. Swathes of voters now view the UK economy not so much as capitalist, but corporatist or even cronyist – and not without justification.

Throughout history, the rough edges of capitalism have needed to be smoothed. That will always be true – and it can be done with a humane, properly resourced welfare state. While the UK's bene-fit system is patchy, and notoriously tough to reform, for the most part it does a reasonable job. But capitalism is also about ensuring a degree of fairness and the spreading of opportunities, not least among the aspirational classes – those working hard and striving to improve the lot of themselves and their families. Britain's broken housing market is the principal cause of discontent among those who feel 'the system' is against them – not least priced-out young adults who, despite gaining qualifications and holding down good jobs, are unable to buy.

Discontent with 'the system' goes beyond housing. More and more consumers are feeling that businesses in general are ripping them off. Perceived corporate excesses, such as high profits and prices, are fuelling a growing belief that capitalism is rigged, with the benefits accruing to a small elite at the expense of the ordinary UK households. Research conducted in 2017 found that eight out of ten UK consumer markets – including telecoms, banking and gas and electricity – were 'concentrated', that is to say dominated by a small number of large companies.[10] The concentration of the telecoms market has increased over the past decade with respect to broadband and mobile telephony. Banking is now dominated by the big players to an even greater extent than before 2008, not least the market for current accounts. The household utility market is similarly in the grip of a handful of energy companies. These corporate structures result in a range of negative outcomes for UK consumers – including a lack of choice, poorer customer service, low trust levels, 'super-normal' profits, under-investment and high prices.

All these concerns apply, in particular, to the UK housebuilding industry – not just in terms of the provision of sub-standard new-build homes, but the operation of the market for land which, in turn, has driven prices of existing homes, which form the vast bulk of all transactions, to historically high levels compared to earnings. If markets fail to work well, and capitalism doesn't 'deliver', lack of confidence in 'the system' could become endemic – particularly when the failure relates to an issue as visceral as the roof over our heads. If this isn't addressed, we could easily end up with far more extreme politics and draconian state interventions, driven by a loss of faith among mainstream voters.

All this helps explain why Jeremy Corbyn enjoyed such a strong showing in the June 2017 election, coming within a few thousand votes of Downing Street – off the back of a wave of support from discontented thirty- and forty-somethings who were sick and tired of spiralling housing costs, and particularly those priced out of buying their own home.

It is now imperative that the Britain tackles its chronic homes shortage. Unless this happens, UK politics, and capitalism, could take a seriously wrong turn. We need far more homes to be built, for both sale and rent, available on both a commercial basis and for social rent too. Ministers need to prevent large, foot-dragging developers from controlling local property markets, imposing punitive LVT levies on acreage with planning permission that remains undeveloped. Above all, LVC needs to be used to tame land prices, launch a fresh wave of New Towns and social housing and – most importantly – shift local political debate about housing development towards far more positive outcomes.

Free markets are political and cultural constructs. Every now and then, the rules need to be overhauled to tip the balance of power away from the overbearing, all-powerful corporate lobbies and back towards consumers. Instead of empty rhetoric about how 'the market knows best', what we really need is genuine competition, and recognition that rising profitability and mark-ups reflect the reality that some businesses have become too powerful.

We should take our cue, if not from von Mises, then from the US economist Mancur Olson – who put his finger on the problem we now face in his 1982 masterpiece *The Rise and Decline of Nations*. Olson's thesis is that the longer a society enjoys political stability, the more likely it is to develop powerful special-interest lobbies that in turn make it less efficient economically. He argued that mature industrial economies, as they develop, become hobbled by 'vested interests, unwilling and uninterested in change'.[11] That's the greatest long-term danger to capitalism, what Olson referred to as 'the silting up of the channels of economic progress' by established industry players, who are able to lobby governments, and defend and extend their market dominance by preventing meaningful regulation and reform that maintains broad political consent for 'the system'.[12]

Western capitalism in the twenty-first century, in the UK and elsewhere, is functioning less well than it should. Too-big-to-fail banks that extort government bailouts are anathema to free markets. Monopoly corporations that restrict competition and exploit consumers are anathema to free markets. An oligopolistic house-building sector, deliberately restricting the supply of new homes to keep prices and profits high, is anathema to free markets. And spiralling wealth inequality and plummeting social mobility are now undermining the very social contract upon which capitalism itself is built. All these trends are increasingly apparent in modern Britain.

Capitalism need not lead to an increasingly polarised society, providing the right checks and balances are in place. But governments of all shades must constantly face down corporate behaviour that causes systemic instability, and/or involves excessive commercial greed. That's something which UK politicians from all parties, for some time now, have largely failed to do. Being pro market does not always mean being pro big business. Sometimes it means precisely the opposite.

A major programme of housebuilding will bring significant benefits in terms of future labour market flexibility and rising productivity, but also a more general economic boost. Every UK recovery from recession over the past century has been associated with a sharp rise in housebuilding – with the exception of the post-2008 recovery. It is no coincidence, given the absence of anything approaching a building boom over the last decade, that Britain has just chalked up the longest and slowest economic recovery in our history.

The 'iron triangle of vested interests' opposing fundamental reform – outlined in Chapter IV – is bad news for young priced-out adults struggling to buy their own home or even rent somewhere at a reasonable price. Powerful developers and landowners, one side of the triangle, exert massive political influence, using party donations and the threat of even less housebuilding to prevent change. The second side of the triangle, the banking sector, will also rail against meaningful reform – claiming, if only behind closed doors, that introducing LVC will lead to a house prices collapse and, in turn, another financial crisis, given the wide exposure of UK banks to residential property. The same scaremongering view has thwarted countless attempts over the years, via a variety of measures, to end the chronic under-supply of UK homes.

As concern at the UK's property divide grows, the political geometry is starting to shift – not least among existing homeowners, the third side of the iron triangle. Young adults who can't buy a home are angry, of course. But increasing numbers of older voters, who do own property, are becoming alarmed their children can't do the same. As such, the electoral arithmetic is changing – as shown by survey data showing opposition to 'more housebuilding in my local area' is now starting to fall.

The coalition pushing for the specific change advocated here – a reversal of the 1961 Land Compensation Act – now stretches from campaign groups including Shelter, to a broad range of thinktanks across the political spectrum. More recently, we've seen support from influential centre-right politicians including Sajid Javid and Nick Boles and leading developers such as Tony Pidgley, the founder and chairman of Berkeley Homes.

When it comes to supporting specific housing developments, the truth is that local communities, whatever the polling data says, continue to fiercely resist. Across England, local political parties founded on the basis of opposition to development have been winning local council seats.[13] While planning permissions have been granted at a faster pace in recent years, the process remains enormously fraught, politicised and uncertain – all of which locks out SME builders, allowing the large developers to maintain their grip on the market. It is vital not only that we reform our land market, then, but also our planning system – shifting to the more 'rules-based' system used in most other advanced industrial economies. And, above all, we need significant LVC receipts, retained at the local level, to build the schools, hospitals and other local infrastructure that will help tip the political balance, making new housing developments less unpopular.

If the UK is to thrive during the decade after Brexit, with a buoyant economy, it is imperative that the government now puts housebuilding, and the need to shake up the regulatory structures within which this vital industry operates, at the heart of its economic strategy. This will seriously upset the large developers and other powerful vested interests – but so be it. For if we fail to build more homes, ordinary working people will find it ever harder to keep a roof over their heads, and the damage to the wider economy, society and our broader politics will only get worse.

ROSES BLOOM IN METRO-LAND

The term 'Metro-Land' is barely used these days. Some people know it as the title of the 1980 Julian Barnes novel – adapted into a film in 1997. Indeed, Barnes grew up a few miles from my childhood home of Kingsbury, in the Metro-Land suburb of Northwood – which inspired his first novel, about two boyhood friends with differing views of adulthood. While I loved my childhood home, I was well aware, particularly once I became a teenager and read widely, that suburbia was often derided by the UK's cultural critics. George Orwell famously described suburban living as 'a prison with the cells all in a row ... semi-detached torture chambers'.[14] The sociologist Michael Young claimed that 'one suburb is much like another in an atomised society. Rarely does community flourish.'[15] Both observations, in my experience, could not be more mistaken.

The rapidly built Metro-Land suburbs on the edge of London were castigated by architectural experts of the time. They viewed the mocking of Tudor and Georgian period houses as an affront to style. Yet, these Metro-Land homes – replicated on the outskirts of cities across the UK – were wildly popular with the emerging lower-middle classes who wanted to own their own homes. While the wealthy hated the new developments, and looked down on them, for millions of ordinary people, these properties allowed them to break from often generations of servitude to exploitative landlords, offering an escape from the insecurity of renting, with the chance eventually to own, outright, a valuable asset. Those who scoffed at such progress generally did so from the position of privilege and financial security – hence their lack of understanding.

Growing up in a house of first-generation home ownership, I was acutely aware of its importance. Most of my childhood friends were from similar families or were living in low-rise, decent-quality social housing. What I experienced, far from the 'lack of community' and 'drudgery', was a place characterised by enterprise and, above all, ambition. The Kingsbury of my childhood may have been anonymous and unfashionable, but from its rows of 'semi-detached torture chambers' sprang some astonishing people – including England football and cricket captains, Stuart Pearce and Mike Gatting, along with countless musicians such as Rolling Stones drummer Charlie Watts, jazz virtuoso Courtney Pine and song-writing legend George Michael. In 'Round Here', Michael pays explicit tribute to Kingsbury, in both his lyrics and the official video of the song, using old still pictures and footage of houses and shops from the neighbourhood of his youth.

This neighbourhood – where I also grew up – was a melting pot, part of what was then the UK's most ethnically diverse borough. There was an amalgam of Irish, Jewish and Hindu households, all first- or second-generation immigrants, as well as indigenous British families too. It was very 'ordinary' and yet people worked hard and strove to do well. And, crucially, the security afforded by home ownership and good social housing meant that, while it was by no means an affluent area, there was a vibrant, well-integrated community, despite a huge range of ethnic and social backgrounds, and crime was relatively low. All of that was achieved, I am convinced, because we lived in low-density housing, with plenty of green space – stemming from the fact that our homes were built back in the 1930s, on relatively cheap land by developers operating in a highly competitive environment.

My parents' generation benefited from housing that was affordable, allowing them to become part of a huge leap forward in terms of home ownership. The year I was born, 1969, marked the turning point – when the majority of UK households owned their own home. My generation had the same opportunity, with most of my peers buying their first property in their late twenties or early thirties. Today's young adults don't have that – and many people struggle even to rent a place of their own. We are rapidly approaching the point where that 1969 watershed is reversed, with the UK turning into a nation of renters and rentiers. That would by no means represent progress.

Housing is the most pressing domestic challenge facing the UK today. Far too few houses and flats have been built over the last thirty years – to both rent and buy, on a commercial basis and for social housing too. Relentless demand, in the face of inadequate supply, has seen prices spiral upward, while over-crowding, homelessness and rough-sleeping have grown to the extent that they've become nothing less than a modern-day epidemic.

A new Cabinet post should be created, with the appointment of a Housing Secretary whose sole responsibility is relentlessly to focus on addressing the UK's chronic homes shortage. Once Brexit is resolved, this issue should become the stuff of front-line, daily politics – as it was back in the 1920s and 1950s, times of similar national emergency.

The manifest lack of housing in this country is now so serious and causing such economic and social damage, and the causes behind it so entrenched, that it can only be tackled with a series of bold, disruptive reforms. Unless such reforms are brought forward and implemented, then the British public's dwindling respect for our political leaders, capitalism and democracy itself will continue to ebb away.

ACKNOWLEDGEMENTS

Home Truths covers contemporary, fast-moving and in many cases rather complex ideas and aspects of public policy. Writing such a book while producing regular newspaper columns and television documentaries would be testing at the best of times. But the Brexit-related turmoil of recent months, and resulting Parliamentary high-drama, has been incredibly time-consuming – as it has been for all journalists closely involved in politics. Producing *Home Truths* – a book about a subject other than Brexit – has only been possible during this astonishing period with the generous support of professional colleagues, friends and family.

In November 2016, I made a *Dispatches* programme for Channel 4 – *Britain's Homebuilding Scandal* – exploring the slow build-out of homes by large developers already granted planning permission. Over the summer of 2019, I presented another housing-related *Dispatches – Britain's New Build Scandal* – examining the shoddy quality of homes sold under the government's flagship Help to Buy scheme. The research conducted for both films fed into this book – and I'd like to thank Vicki Cooper and Jane Drinkwater, the respective producer-directors, for their skill and camaraderie. My sincere thanks also, for continued opportunities to explore important economic issues on primetime television, to executive producer Eamonn Matthews,

Dispatches editor Louisa Compton, and Dorothy Byrne, head of news and current affairs at Channel Four.

During the spring of 2018, I wrote a series of essays on housing policy for the website Unherd.com – which, again, helped to inform this book. I'm grateful to Tim Montgomerie, Charlotte Pickles, Sally Chatterton and Peter Franklin for their help and encouragement in bringing that series to fruition – and also to the investment manager Paul Marshall for providing the launch funding for Unherd.

I have been lucky to have benefited, over many years, from conversations with countless housing policy experts and practitioners, including: Grieg Adams, Jack Airey, Kate Barker, Liam Booth-Smith, Nick Boys Smith, Paul Cheshire, Rose Grayston, Nick King, Sean Hannaby, Paula Higgins, Toby Lloyd, Alex Morton, John Muellbauer, John Myers, James Sommerville, Ed Turner and Christine Whitehead. These specialists have forgotten more about housing than I will ever know – and I'm grateful for their time and generosity. I've also learnt from related conversations with Professor Jagjit Chadha, Scott Corfe, Robert Colvile, Michael Jacobs, Graham Robb and Merryn Somerset Webb. I am grateful to them all.

At Westminster, the MPs with whom I've shared my housing policy obsession include Richard Bacon, Clive Betts, Frank Field, Siobhan McDonagh, Vince Cable, Kemi Badenoch, Nick Boles and Neil O'Brien – all of whom have taught me a great deal through their writing and conversation. From the Upper House, I've also learnt from Lord (Michael) Forsyth, Lord (Richard) Layard and Lord (John) Shipley – and I'm particularly grateful to Richard for writing the Foreword to this book.

Along with these parliamentarians and other experts, I must also thank the countless ministers, shadow ministers, civil servants, local government officials and developers with whom I discussed the politics and economics of UK housing policy while writing this book. They are too numerous to name and many have, anyway, asked not to be named.

I'd like to thank Olivia Beattie, Editorial Director of Biteback Publishing, who has been a staunch supporter of *Home Truths*. As domestic politics became ever more uncertain, and the timing of this book wavered in the stiff breeze of 'events', Olivia remained positive throughout – offering exactly the right combination of discipline and encouragement. I am immensely grateful to her. My copyeditor at Biteback, Stephanie Carey, has been cool, calm and extremely effective. I'm also grateful to Suzanne Sangster, Vicky Jessop and, of course, James Stephens at Biteback.

Writing a book is a big commitment – and I have benefited from the patience and kindness of professional colleagues. I'd like to thank, in particular, Ben Marlow, Christopher Williams and Tom Welsh at the *Telegraph* and Colin Robertson and James Clothier at *The Sun* – as well as my literary agent Toby Mundy of TMA and Sue Ayton of Knight Ayton Management. Thank you, also, to the brilliant people on the *Telegraph* graphics desk for creating the graphs contained in *Home Truths*.

I'd also like to thank friends and family who put up with prolonged absences from regular domestic life and holidays – above all Lucy, Ailis, Maeve and Ned, who have, as ever, shown great tolerance and understanding as I struggled to finish this book. Thank you, guys, I won't do it again – at least not for a while (!) – and I love you all very much.

Liam Halligan
September 2019

ABOUT THE AUTHOR

Liam Halligan has written his weekly 'Economic Agenda' column in the *Sunday Telegraph* since 2003 – which enjoys a wide international following and has been recognised with a British Press Award. He also writes regularly for *The Spectator* and *The Sun*.

He is the co-author (with Gerard Lyons) of *Clean Brexit: Why Leaving the EU Still Makes Sense – Building a Post-Brexit Economy for All* (Biteback Publishing, 2017).

Halligan has reported from Moscow for *The Economist*, was political correspondent at the *Financial Times* and spent eight years as economics correspondent at *Channel 4 News*. He continues to present hard-hitting *Dispatches* documentaries on economics and business themes for Channel 4 – and has won the Wincott Business Broadcasting Award an unprecedented four times.

With economics degrees from Warwick University and St Antony's College, Oxford, Halligan has held numerous economic research posts, including at the Social Market Foundation, the International Monetary Fund and the London School of Economics. He also has extensive business experience, in both the media and asset management.

Halligan is a governor of the John Lyon School, Harrow (which he attended on a scholarship), and sits on the advisory board of the Centre for Competitive Advantage in the Global Economy, an

ESRC-funded research body based at Warwick University. Raised in Kingsbury, London NW9, he now lives in Saffron Walden with Lucy and their three children, and tweets from @LiamHalligan.

BIBLIOGRAPHY

Adam, Stuart, Daniel Chandler, Andrew Hood and Robert Joyce (2015), 'Social housing in England: a survey', IFS Briefing Note BN178, Institute for Fiscal Studies

Addison, Christopher (1922), *The Betrayal of the Slums*, H. Jenkins

Afolami, Bim (2018), 'How Can We Make Planning Popular?' in *New Blue: Ideas for a New Generation*, Centre for Policy Studies, May 2018

Airey, Jack (2017), 'Disrupting the Housing Market: A policy programme to save the home-owning democracy', Localis, October 2017

Airey, Jack, Roger Scruton and Robin Wales (2018), 'Building More and Building Beautiful', Policy Exchange

Airey, Jack and Richard Blakeway (2019), 'Tomorrow's Places: A plan for building a generation of new millennial towns on the edge of London', Policy Exchange

Aubrey, Thomas (2017), 'Estimating land value capture for England – updated analysis', Centre for Progressive Capitalism, March 2017

Aubrey, Thomas (2018), 'Gathering the windfall: How changing land law can unlock England's housing supply potential', Centre for Progressive Policy, Working Paper, September 2018

Barker, Kate (2004), 'Review of Housing Supply – Delivering Stability: Securing our Future Housing Needs', HM Treasury

Barker, Kate (2014), *Where's the plan?*, Publishing Partnership

Barlow, Anderson (1940), 'Report of the Royal Commission on the Distribution of the Industrial Population', Cmd 6153, HMSO

Battiston, Diego, Richard Dickens, Alan Manning and Jonathan Wadsworth (2014), 'Immigration and Access to Social Housing in the UK', Centre for Economic Performance Discussion Paper No. 1264, London School of Economics, April 2014

Bentley, Daniel (2016), 'Housing Supply and Household Growth, National and Local', Civitas Briefing

Bentley, Daniel (2017), 'The Land Question: Fixing the dysfunction at the root of the Housing Crisis', Civitas

Bentley, Daniel (2018), 'Reform of the land compensation rules: How much could it save on the cost of a public-sector house-building programme?', Civitas, March 2018

Bentley, Daniel and Thomas Aubrey (2018), 'Written evidence to the Housing, Communities and Local Government Select Committee', House of Commons, LVC 096

Betjeman, John (1954), *A Few Late Chrysanthemums*, John Murray

Bogdanor, Vernon and Robert Skidelsky (1970), *The Age of Affluence, 1952–1964*, Macmillan

Bogdanor, Vernon (2013), 'Sir Keith Joseph and the market economy', Gresham Lecture, 21 May 2013

Boles, Nick (2017), 'Square Deal for Housing', nickboles.co.uk, November 2017

Bottazzi, Renata, Thomas Crossley and Matthew Wakefield (2012), 'Late starters or excluded generations? A cohort analysis of catch-up in home ownership in England', IFS Working Paper W12/10

Boughton, John (2018), *Municipal Dreams: The Rise and Fall of Council Housing*, Verso Books

Boyfield, Keith and Robert Wickham (2019), 'Delivering More Homes: Radical action to unblock the system', IEA Current Controversies No. 66, Institute for Economics Affairs, February 2019

Boys Smith, Nicholas (2018), 'More good homes – Making planning more proportionate, predictable and equitable', Create Streets/ Legatum Institute, November 2018

Bunn, Philip, Alice Pugh and Chris Yeates (2018), 'The distributional impact of monetary policy easing in the UK between 2008 and 2014', Bank of England Staff Working Paper No. 720

Cable, Vince (2019), 'Beyond Brexit – Liberal politics for the age of identity', Liberal Democrats

Callcutt, John (2007), 'The Callcutt Review of House-building Delivery', Department for Communities and Local Government

Centre for Policy Studies (2018), *New Blue: Ideas for a New Generation*, May 2018

Chadha, Jagjit (2018), 'The Housing Market and the Macroeconomy', National Institute Economic Review No. 243, NIESR, February 2018

Chaloner, Justin, Alexandra Dreisin and Mark Pragnell (2015), 'Building New Social Rent Homes', Capital Economics, June 2015

Cheshire, Paul (2014), 'Turning houses into gold: the failure of British planning', LSE Centre Piece, Spring

Cheshire, Paul (2016), 'Where should we build on the Greenbelt?', LSE blog, 25 March 2016

Cheshire, Paul (2018), 'Empty homes, longer commutes: one of the many unintended consequences of more restrictive local planning', Presentation to the Adam Smith Institute, March 2018

Cheshire, Paul, Christian Hilber and Hans Koster (2018), 'Empty homes, longer commutes: the unintended consequences of more restrictive local planning', *Journal of Public Economics*, Vol. 158, pp. 126–51

Chesterton, G. K. (1920), *The Superstition of Divorce*, New Witness

Childs, Peter and Michael Storry (eds) (1999), *Encyclopaedia of Contemporary British Culture*, Routledge

Clifford, Ben (2018), 'Extended Permitted Development Rights in England', University College London Bartlett School of Planning

Conservative Party (2017), 'Forward Together: Our Plan for a stronger Britain and a prosperous future', Conservative Party manifesto

Corfe, Scott and Nicole Gicheva (2017), 'Concentration not competition: the state of UK consumer markets', Social Market Foundation, October 2017

Corlett, Adam, Stephen Clarke and Dan Tomlinson (2017), 'The Living Standards Audit 2017', Resolution Foundation

Corlett, Adam and Lindsay Judge (2017), 'Home Affront – Housing across the generations', Resolution Foundation, September 2017

Cox, Andrew W. (1984), *Adversary politics and land: The Conflict Over Land and Property Policy in Post-War Britain*, Cambridge University Press

Cribb, Jonathan, Andrew Hood and Jack Hoyle (2018), 'The decline of homeownership among young adults', IFS Briefing Note BN224, Institute for Fiscal Studies

Cribb, Jonathan, Andrew Hood and Jack Hoyle (2016), 'The Economic Circumstances of Different Generations: The Latest Picture', IFS Briefing Note BN187, Institute for Fiscal Studies

Cullingworth, Barry and Vincent Nadin (2006), *Town and country planning in the UK*, Routledge

Department of Communities and Local Government (2006), 'Transferable Lessons from the New Towns', DCLG/Oxford Brookes University, July 2006

Disraeli, Benjamin (1883), *Wit and Wisdom of Benjamin Disraeli: Collected from his Writings and Speeches*, Longmans Green

Dustmann, Christian, Maria Casanova, Michael Fertig, Ian Preston and Christoph Schmidt (2003), 'The impact of EU enlargement on migration flows', Home Office Online Report 25/03

Eurostat (2018), 'Distribution of population by tenure status – Type of household and income group', EU-SILC survey, ILC_lvho02

Fraser, Derek (1973), *The Evolution of the British Welfare State*, Palgrave Macmillan

Gardiner, Juliet (2010), *The Thirties: An Intimate History*, Harper Collins

George, Henry (1879), *Progress and Poverty*, D. Appleton & Co.

Gibbons, Stephen, Susana Mourato and Guilherme Mendes Resende (2011), 'The Amenity Value of English Nature: A Hedonic Price Approach', SERC Discussion Paper No. 74

Gilbert, E. W. (1947), 'The Industrialization of Oxford', *Geographical Journal*, January–March 1947

Glaeser, Edward and Joseph Gyourko (2002), 'The Impact of Zoning on Housing Affordability', National Bureau of Economic Research Working Paper No. 8835

Gosling, George Campbell (2018), 'Lloyd George's Ministry Men: World War One Centenary', University of Oxford

Green Party (2017), 'A Confident and Caring Britain', Green Party manifesto

Griffith, Matt (2011), 'We must fix it: Delivering reform of the building sector to meet the UK's housing and economic challenges', Institute for Public Policy Research

Hall, Peter and Colin Ward (2014), *Sociable Cities: The 21st-Century Reinvention of the Garden City*, Routledge

Halligan, Liam and Gerard Lyons (2017), *Clean Brexit – How to make a success of leaving the European Union*, Biteback Publishing

Halligan, Liam (2018), 'UK Housing – a manifesto for change', National Institute for Economic and Social Research Housing Conference, 1 June 2018

Hilber, Christian and Wouter Vermeulen (2014), 'The Impact of Supply Constraints on House Prices in England', *Economic Journal*, Vol. 126, No. 591, pp. 358–405

Hilbers, Paul, Alexander Hoffmaister, Angana Banerji and Haiyan Shi (2008), 'House Price Developments in Europe: A Comparison', IMF Working Paper WP/08/211

Hills, John (2007), 'Ends and Means: The Future Roles of Social

Housing in England', Centre for the Analysis of Social Exclusion, Report 34, CASE/DCLG, February 2017

HM Government (2011), 'Laying the Foundations: A Housing Strategy for England', Ministry of Housing Communities and Local Government

HM Government (2012), 'National Planning Policy Framework', Ministry of Housing Communities and Local Government

HM Government (2017), 'Fixing Our Broken Housing Market', Ministry for Housing, Communities and Local Government, Cm 9352

HM Government (2018), 'Government Response to the Housing, Communities and Local Government Select Committee inquiry on land value capture', Ministry for Housing, Communities and Local Government, CM 9734, November 2018

HM Government (2018), 'Independent review of build out: final report – Sir Oliver Letwin', Ministry of Housing, Communities and Local Government, CM 9720, October 2018

Holmans, A. E. (1987), *Housing Policy in Britain*, Croom Helm

Home Builders Federation (2014), 'Permissions to Land: Busting the Myths about House Builders and "Land Banking"', May 2014

Home Builders Federation (2017), 'Reversing the Decline of Small Housebuilders: Reinvigorating entrepreneurialism and building more homes', HBF, January 2017

Home Builders Federation (2019), 'National New Homes Customer Satisfaction Survey (CSS)', HBF/NHBC, March 2019

Hood, Andrew and Laura Oakley (2014), 'The social security system: long-term trends and recent changes', IFS Briefing Note BN156, Institute for Fiscal Studies

House of Commons (2017), 'Public Accounts Committee Oral Evidence: Housing: State of the Nation', HC 958, 22 February 2017

House of Lords (2016), 'Select Committee on Economic Affairs: Building More Homes', First Report of Session 2016/17, HL Paper 20

House of Lords (2016a) Oral and Written Evidence, 'Select Committee on Economic Affairs: The Economics of the UK Housing Market'

Housing, Communities and Local Government Select Committee (2018), 'Land Value Capture', Tenth Report of Session 2017–19, House of Commons, HC 766, September 2018

Housing, Communities and Local Government Select Committee (2019), 'Building regulations and fire safety: consultation response and connected issues, Seventeenth Report of the Session 2017–19', House of Commons, HC 2546, July 2019

Howard, Ebenezer (1898, 2010), *A Peaceful Path to Real Reform*, Cambridge University Press

Institute for Fiscal Studies (2011), 'Mirrlees Review: Reforming the Tax System for the 21st Century', September 2011

Jackson, Alan (1991), *Semi-Detached London: Suburban Development, Life and Transport, 1900–39*, Wild Swan Publications

Jefferys, Pete and Toby Lloyd (2017), 'New Civic House-Building: Rediscovering our tradition of building beautiful and affordable homes', Shelter Policy Briefing

Judge, Lindsay (2019), 'Moving Matters: Housing costs and labour market mobility', Resolution Foundation, June 2019

Judge, Lindsay (2019), 'The one million missing homes?' Resolution Foundation blog, 12 January 2019

Knoll, Katharina, Moritz Schularick and Thomas Steger (2017), 'No price like home: Global house prices, 1870–2012', *American Economic Review*, Vol. 107, No. 2, pp. 331–53

Kynaston, David (2009), *Family Britain, 1951–59*, Bloomsbury

Labour Party (2017), 'For the Many, Not the Few', Labour Party manifesto

Labour Party (2018), 'Housing for the Many – a Labour Party Green Paper'

Larson, William (2015), 'New Estimates of Value of Land of the United States', Bureau of Economic Analysis, April 2015

Leunig, Tim (2011), 'Community land auctions: working towards implementation', Centre Forum, November 2011

Liberal Democrats (2017), 'Change Britain's Future', Liberal Democrat manifesto

Linklater, Andro (2014) *Owning the Earth*, Bloomsbury

Local Government Association (2013), 'An analysis of unimplemented planning permission for residential dwellings'

London First (2015), 'Redefining Density: making the best use of London's land to build more and better homes'

Lund, Brian (2016), *Housing politics in the United Kingdom*, Policy Press

Lyons, Michael (2014), 'The Lyons Review: Mobilising across the nation to build the homes our children need', Labour Party

Malpass, Peter and Alan Murie (1999), *Housing Policy and Practice* (5th edition), Palgrave

Marshall, J. L. (1969), 'The Pattern of House-Building in the Inter-War period in England and Wales', *Scottish Journal of Political Economy*, Vol. 16, No. 1

McPhillips, Marcus (2017), 'Phantom Homes – Planning Permissions, Completions and Profits', Shelter Research Briefing, July 2017

Merrett, Stephen (1979), *State housing in Britain*, Routledge & Kegan Paul

Metcalfe, David (2016), 'Work, Immigration and the Labour Market: Incorporating the role of the Migration Advisory Committee', Migration Advisory Council Report and London School of Economics, June 2016

Ministry of Housing, Communities and Local Government (2018), 'Analysis of the determinants of house price changes', April 2018

Ministry of Housing, Communities and Local Government (2018), 'Public attitudes to house building: findings from the British Social Attitudes survey 2017', June 2018

Ministry of Housing, Communities and Local Government (2018),

'Social housing lettings: April 2017 to March 2018, England', November 2018

Moe, Edwin (2007), *Governance, Growth and Global Leadership: The Role of the State in Technological Progress, 1750–2000*, Ashgate Publishing

Moretti, Enrico and Chang-Tai Hsieh (2015), 'Why Do Cities Matter? Local Growth and Aggregate Growth', Kreisman working paper on Housing Law and Policy No. 30, University of Chicago Law School

Morgan, Kenneth (1986), *Consensus and Disunity: The Lloyd George Coalition Government, 1918–1922*, Clarendon Press

Morgan, Malcolm and Heather Cruikshank (2014), 'Quantifying the extent of space shortages: English dwellings', *Journal of Building Research and Information*, Vol. 42, No. 6

Morton, Alex (2018), 'From Rent to Own – How to restore home ownership by turning private tenants into owners', Policy Exchange, October 2018

Muellbauer, John (2015), 'Proposals for unblocking housing supply and funding infrastructure', 30 October 2015 (mimeo)

Muellbauer, John (2015), 'Six fiscal reforms for the UK's "lost generation"', Local Tax Commission

Muellbauer, John (2018), 'What Germany can teach us about repairing our broken housing market', National Institute for Economic and Social Research, 2 August 2018

Mulheirn, Ian and Nishaal Gooroochurn (2018), 'Modelling house prices and home ownership', NIESR Housing Conference, 1 June 2018

Myers, John (2017), 'Yes In My Back Yard: How To End The Housing Crisis, Boost The Economy And Win More Votes', London Yimby/Adam Smith Institute

National Association of Estate Agents (2018), 'Leasehold: A Life Sentence?', NAEA/Property Mark, September 2018

National Audit Office (2016), 'Disposal of Public Land for New Homes', HMSO, July 2016

National Audit Office (2019), 'Help to Buy: Equity Loan scheme – progress review', HC 2216 Session 2017–2019, June 2019

National Ecosystem Assessment (2011), 'The UK National Ecosystem Assessment Technical Report', UNEP-WCMC

New Economics Foundation (2018), 'What lies beneath: how to fix the broken land system at the heart of our housing crisis', July 2018

O'Brien, Neil (2018), 'Green, pleasant and affordable: Why we need a new approach to supply and demand to solve Britain's housing problem', Onward, June 2018

Office for National Statistics (2017), 'Housing Affordability in England and Wales: 1997 to 2016', March 2017

Office for National Statistics (2017), 'Response to the ONS consultation on the household projections for England', 30 June 2017

Office for National Statistics, 'Overview of the UK population', July 2017

Office for National Statistics (2018), 'Household projections in England: 2016-based', 20 September 2018

Office of Fair Trading (2008), 'Homebuilding in the UK: A market study', September 2018

Olson, Mancur (1982), *The Rise and Decline of Nations*, Yale University Press

Organisation for Economic Co-operation and Development (2017), 'Housing Stock and Construction', Social Policy Division – Directorate of Employment, Labour and Social Affairs, August 2017

Orwell, George (1939), *Coming up for Air*, Victor Gollancz

Oxley, Michael and Jacqueline Smith (1996), *Housing Policy and Rented Housing in Europe*, Routledge

Park, Alison, Elizabeth Clery, John Curtice, Miranda Phillips and David Utting (2012), 'British Social Attitudes Survey 28', National Centre for Social Research

Perry, John and Mark Stephens (2018), *How the purpose of social housing has changed and is changing*, Section 1, Chapter 3, UK Housing Review, Chartered Institute of Housing

Persimmon Plc (2019), 'Delivering on our Long-Term Strategy', 2018

Phillips, Ben and Cukkoo Joseph (2017), 'Regional housing supply and demand in Australia', Australian National University Centre for Social Research & Methods, Working Paper No. 1/2017

Philp, Chris (2017), 'Homes for Everyone – How to get Britain building and restore the home ownership dream', Centre for Policy Studies, December 2017

Powell, Christopher (1996), *The British building industry since 1800: An Economic History*, Taylor & Francis

Ravetz, Alison (1982), *Remaking Cities*, Croom Helm

Renard, Vincent (2009), 'Property Rights Protection and Spatial Planning in European Countries' in Gregory Ingram and Yu-Hung Hong (eds) *Property Rights and Land Policies: Proceedings of the 2008 Land Policy Conference*

Resolution Foundation (2019), 'Home Ownership in the UK'

Resolution Foundation (2019), 'Old Answers to New Questions – The Future of Social Housing in the UK'

Rohe, William and Mark Lindblad (2013), 'Re-examining the Social Benefits of Home-Ownership after the Housing Crisis', Joint Centre for Housing Studies, Harvard University

Rose, John (2017), 'The Housing Supply Myth', Kwantlen Polytechnic University, British Columbia Working Paper

Rowthorn, Robert (2015), 'The Costs and Benefits of Large-scale Immigration', Civitas

Royal Borough of Kensington and Chelsea (2012), 'Grenfell Tower Regeneration Project: Engagement Statement', Kensington and Chelsea TMO, October 2012

Rudlin, David and Nicholas Falk (2014), 'Uxcester: Garden City – submission for the Wolfson Economics Prize', Urbed Consultancy

Ryan-Collins, Josh, Toby Lloyd and Laurie Macfarlane (2017), *Rethinking the Economics of Land and Housing*, Zed Publishing

Ryan-Collins, Josh (2018), *Why can't you afford a home?* Polity Press

Sá, Filipa (2011), 'Immigration and House Prices in the UK', IZA DP No. 5893, July 2011

Sabisky, Andrew (2017), 'Children of when: why housing is the solution to Britain's fertility crisis', Adam Smith Institute

Savills (2016), 'New Homes and Accelerating Delivery on Public Sector Land, Savills-Telereal Trillium', April 2016

Schwab, Klaus (2017), 'The Global Competitiveness Report 2016–2017', World Economic Forum, September 2016

Scott, Leslie (1941), 'Report of the Committee on Land Utilisation in Rural Areas', Cmd 6378, HMSO

Shelter (2007), 'Rights and wrongs: The homelessness safety net 30 years on'

Shelter (2012), 'Bricks or Benefits: Rebalancing housing investment'

Shelter/KPMG (2015), 'Building the Homes We Need – a programme for the 2015 government'

Shelter (2017), 'Phantom Homes – Planning Permissions, Completions and Profits', July 2017

Shelter (2019), 'Building for our future: a vision for social housing', January 2019

Shelter (2019), 'Grounds for Change: The case for land reform in modern England', June 2019

Shorrocks, Anthony, Jim Davies and Rodrigo Lluberas (2017), 'Global Wealth Report', Credit Suisse

Smith, Louise (2016), 'Green Belt Briefing Paper', House of Commons Library No. 00934

Social Mobility Commission (2019), 'State of the Nation 2018–19: Social Mobility in Great Britain', HMSO

Standing, Guy (2016), *The Corruption of Capitalism: Why Rentiers Thrive and Work Does Not Pay*, Biteback Publishing

Stephens, Mark, Christine Whitehead and Moira Munro (2005), 'Lessons from the Past, Challenges for the Future for Housing Policy', DCLG

Stephens, Mark, John Perry, Steve Wilcox, Peter Williams and Gillian Young (2018), 'UK Housing Review – Autumn Briefing Paper', Chartered Institute of Housing and Heriot-Watt University, October 2018

Stillwell, Martin (2017), 'Homes Fit for Heroes': http://www.social-housinghistory.uk/

Strauss, William and Neil Howe (1991), *Generations: The History of America's Future, 1584 to 2069*, Harper Perennial

Swenarton, Mark (1981), *Homes fit for Heroes: the politics and architecture of early state housing in Britain*, Heinemann

Thomas, Ray (1997), 'The new towns – taking a long-term view', *Town and Country Planning*, Vol. 66, No. 5, pp. 138–9

Turner, Clive (2015), 'Homes Through the Decades: The Making of Modern Housing', NHBC Foundation

Uthwatt, Augustus (1942), 'The Final report of the Expert Committee on Compensation and Betterment', Cmd 6368, HMSO

Vargas-Silva, Carlos and Cinzia Rienzo (2018), 'Migrants in the UK: An Overview', The Migration Observatory, Oxford University, October 2018

Von Mises, Ludwig (1947), *Money, Method and the Market Process*, Kluwer Academic Publishers

Warman, Matt (2018), 'Who Governs Britain – Democracy and Local Government in the Digital Age', Centre for Policy Studies, July 2018

Wellings, Fred (2006), *British House-builders: History and Analysis*, Blackwell

Whitehead, Christine, Ann Edge, Ian Gordon, Kath Scanlon and Tony Travers (2011), 'The impact of migration on access to housing and the housing market', LSE/Migration Advisory Committee, December 2011

Williams, Michael (2016), *Sixteen Excursions into the Lost Delights of Britain's Railways*, Random House

Wilson, Wendy and Cassie Barton (2018), 'Tackling the undersupply of housing in England', House of Commons Briefing Paper No. 07671, December 2018

Winch, Donald and Patrick Karl O'Brien (2002), *The Political Economy of British Historical Experience, 1688–1914*, British Academy

ENDNOTES

INTRODUCTION

1   This phrase was used in *The Wonderful Wizard of Oz*, the celebrated children's novel by L. Frank Baum, published in the United States at the turn of the previous century. Baum's work formed the basis of the 1939 Hollywood classic *The Wizard of Oz*, starring Judy Garland as Dorothy. At the end of the film, having travelled to the magical land of Oz, Dorothy takes her dog Toto in her arms, knocks the heels of her sparkly red shoes together three times and intones, 'There's no place like home, there's no place like home, there's no place like home.' She then whirls through the air, travels back to where she came from and is soon rolling on the grass of the Kansas prairie. Seeing the farmhouse where she lives, Dorothy runs up to her Aunt Em, saying, 'I'm so glad to be home again!'

2   See, for instance, A. E. Holmans, *Housing Policy in Britain: A History* (Croom Helm, 1987) or Christopher Powell, *The British Building Industry since 1800: An Economic History* (Taylor & Francis, 1996). For a concise overview of UK housing policy since the Industrial Revolution, see Chapter 4 of Josh Ryan-Collins, Toby Lloyd and Laurie Macfarlane, *Rethinking the Economics of Land and Housing* (Zed Publishing, 2017). An authoritative summary of recent housing legislation is provided by 'Building More Homes', House of Lords Select Committee on Economic Affairs, July 2016, First paper of Session 2016/17, HL 20: https://publications. parliament.uk/pa/ld201617/ldselect/ldeconaf/20/20.pdf

I: THE BRITISH DREAM

1   Taken from the commentary of *Metro-Land*, a BBC television documentary written and presented by John Betjeman and directed by Edward Mirzoeff, first broadcast on 26 February 1973. See *Metro-Land* (1973), British Film Institute: http://www.screenonline.org. uk/tv/id/1259604/index.html

2   When Kingsbury Station opened in 1932, it was on the Stanmore branch of the Metropolitan Railway, which became the Metropolitan Line on the London Underground network after London Transport was formed in 1933. In 1939, Kingsbury Station was switched to the Bakerloo Line, until it became part of the new Jubilee Line forty years later in 1979. My childhood home was also close to Preston Road Station – added to the original Metropolitan Railway in 1908, and which remains a Metropolitan Line station to this day.

3   These terms, originally used by the advertising and marketing industry, have become ubiquitous. 'Millennials, also known as Generation Y, are the demographic cohort born between the early 1980s and the early 2000s. Those born since then are 'Generation Z'. Millennials are sometimes referred to as 'echo boomers' due to a major surge in birth rates across the Western world in the 1980s and 1990s, and because they are often the children of the 'baby boomers' – those born between the mid-1940s and mid-1960s. See William

Strauss and Neil Howe, *Generations: The History of America's Future, 1584 to 2069* (Harper Perennial, 1991), p. 335.

4   Data from Labour Force Survey conducted by the Office for National Statistics. Quoted in 'Home Ownership in the UK', Resolution Foundation, 16 January 2019: https://www.resolutionfoundation.org/data/housing/

5   Andrew Sabisky, 'Children of when: why housing is the solution to Britain's fertility crisis', Adam Smith Institute, 16 July 2017: https://www.adamsmith.org/research/children-of-when-why-housing-is-the-solution-to-britains-fertility-crisis

6   Mark Swenarton, *Homes fit for Heroes: the politics and architecture of early state housing in Britain* (Heinemann, 1981), p. 216.

7   Quoted in George Campbell Gosling, 'Lloyd George's Ministry Men: World War One Centenary', University of Oxford, 4 November 2015.

8   This conversation took place in 1919. Quoted in Derek Fraser, *The Evolution of the British Welfare State* (Palgrave, 1973), p. 181.

9   Clive Turner, 'Homes Through the Decades: The Making of Modern Housing', NHBC Foundation, March 2015: http://www.nhbc.co.uk/cms/publish/consumer/NewsandComment/HomesThroughTheDecades.pdf

10   For a fuller discussion of Lloyd George's legacy see Kenneth Morgan, *Consensus and Disunity: The Lloyd George Coalition Government, 1918–1922* (Clarendon Press, 1986).

11   Martin Stillwell, 'Homes Fit for Heroes', April 2017, p. 7: http://www.socialhousinghistory.uk/wp/wp-content/uploads/2017/04/Homes_Fit_For_Heroes.pdf#zoom=100

12   J. L. Marshall, 'The Pattern of House-Building in the Inter-War period in England and Wales', *Scottish Journal of Political Economy*, Vol. 16, No. 1 (1969).

13   My home was part of the Lindsay Park Estate. See Philip Grant, 'The Metroland Dream – Your Comben & Wakeling home in Wembley', Wembley Matters blog, 27 January 2019: https://wembleymatters.blogspot.com/2019/01/guest-post-by-philip-grant-i-dont-often.html. The fate of Comben and Wakeling is illustrative of the huge consolidation that's taken place in the UK housebuilding industry. The company was founded by James White Comben and William Henry in 1907, who sold their Fulham grocery business to venture into construction, incorporating as a private company in 1924. See Alan Jackson, *Semi-Detached London: Suburban Development, Life and Transport, 1900–39* (Wild Swan Publications, 1991). Almost fifty years later, in 1972, Comben and Wakeling bought Ryedale Homes, with the combined group subsequently trading as Comben Homes. In 1984, Comben was acquired by Trafalgar House – at the time, the UK's fifth largest housebuilder. In 1996, Trafalgar itself was then bought by today's housebuilding giant Persimmon. The implications of the UK's highly consolidated housebuilding industry are explored in Chapter IV.

14   See Juliet Gardiner, *The Thirties: An Intimate History* (Harper Collins, 2009).

15   See A. E. Holmans, *Housing Policy in Britain* (Croom Helm, 1987), p. 91.

16   'Let Us Face the Future: A Declaration of Labour Policy for the Consideration of the Nation', 1945: http://www.labour-party.org.uk/manifestos/1945/1945-labour-manifesto.shtml

17   This was a phrase coined, of course, by Churchill to describe the period of the Second World War when the UK stood alone – between the fall of France in June 1940 and the Axis invasion of the Soviet Union in June 1941. The phrase applies particularly to the months from June to October 1940, between the evacuation from Dunkirk and the successful end of the Battle of Britain, when there was perceived to be a direct threat of invasion.

18   This now ubiquitous term, used across the world, came into use soon after the Second World War. The earliest use of 'urban sprawl' that the author can find is by E. W. Gilbert in 'The Industrialization of Oxford', *Geographical Journal* (1947), p. 21. The author writes: 'Oxford's recent history is an example of what occurred in many other towns in this country between the wars. Urban sprawl, ribbon development, overcrowded streets, danger on the roads, destruction of beauty are the price paid in Oxford and in many places in England for lack of planning.'

19 Daniel Bentley, 'The Land Question: Fixing the dysfunction at the root of the Housing Crisis', Civitas, 2017, p. 40.

20 Anderson Barlow, 'Report of the Royal Commission on the Distribution of the Industrial Population', Cmd 6153 (HMSO, 1940); Leslie Scott, 'Report of the Committee on Land Utilisation in Rural Areas', Cmd 6378 (HMSO, 1941); Augustus Uthwatt, 'The Final report of the Expert Committee on Compensation and Betterment', Cmd 6368 (HMSO, 1942).

21 House of Commons, Hansard, 29 January 1947, Vol. 432, cc. 981–5: https://api.parliament.uk/historic-hansard/commons/1947/jan/29/town-and-country-planning-bill

22 Vernon Bogdanor and Robert Skidelsky, *The Age of Affluence, 1952–1964* (Macmillan, 1970).

23 See Andrew Cox, *Adversary Politics and Land: The Conflict Over Land and Property Policy in Post-War Britain* (Cambridge University Press, 1984), p. 94.

24 Ebenezer Howard's book *Tomorrow: A Peaceful Path to Real Reform* was published in 1898, then reprinted as *Garden Cities of Tomorrow* in 1902. He envisaged self-contained suburban towns of around 30,000 people, close to major cities, enjoying both urban and rural benefits and with citizens enjoying an economic interest in them. Although Howard's precise Garden City proposals were never widely adopted, his ideas are recognised to have been hugely influential around the world. Howard's ideas, and their contemporary relevance, are explored more fully in Chapters VIII and IX.

25 See Alison Ravetz, *Remaking Cities* (Croom Helm, 1982), p. 67.

26 Daniel Bentley, 'The Land Question', op. cit., pp. 47–8.

27 Clive Turner, 'Homes Through the Decades', op. cit., p. 19.

28 C. A. L. Hilber and W. Vermeulen, 'The Impact of Supply Constraints on House Prices in England', *Economic Journal*, Vol. 126, No. 591 (2016), pp. 358–405. Tom Archer and Ian Cole, 'Profits Before Volume? Major House Builders and the Crisis of Housing Supply', Sheffield Hallam University Centre for Regional Economic and Social Research, October 2016: https://www4.shu.ac.uk/research/cresr/sites/shu.ac.uk/files/profits-before-volume-housebuilders-crisis-housing-supply.pdf

29 'UK House Prices since 1952', Nationwide Building Society: https://www.nationwide.co.uk/about/house-price-index/download-data – xtab:uk-series

30 Ministry for Housing, Communities and Local Government (MHCLG), 'Fixing Our Broken Housing Market', February 2017, Cm 9352: https://www.gov.uk/government/uploads/system/uploads/attachment_data/file/590464/Fixing_our_broken_housing_market_-_print_ready_version.pdf

31 Anna Minton, 'Why Britain's "broken" planning system means local people miss out', *Financial Times*, 23 January 2015: https://www.ft.com/content/0f72b534-9ccb-11e4-971b-00144feabdc0

32 Clive Turner, 'Homes Through the Decades', op. cit., p. 20.

33 This line was from a verse composed by the journalist and songwriter George R. Sims: 'I know a land where the wild flowers grow, Near, near at hand if by train you go, Metro-land, Metro-land'. Another music publisher popularised a 'Vocal One-Step' called 'My Little Metro-land Home', with words by Boyle Lawrence and music by Henry Thrale. The chorus is, perhaps, a marketing man's dream: 'It's happiness found, it's paradise crowned, My Little Metro-land Home'. See Michael Williams, *Sixteen Excursions into the Lost Delights of Britain's Railways* (Random House, 2016), p. 59.

34 See John Betjeman, *A Few Late Chrysanthemums* (John Murray, 1954).

35 Christopher Howse, 'Preserve us from Betjeman Country', *Telegraph*, 15 July 2009: https://www.telegraph.co.uk/comment/columnists/christopherhowse/5827492/Preserve-us-from-Betjeman-Country.html

36 Clive Turner, 'Homes Through the Decades', op. cit., p. 20.

37 Greater London Association Conservatives, 'Secret Sleepers: London's problem with "Beds in Sheds"', December 2017: https://www.glaconservatives.co.uk/uploads/1/1/7/8/117899427/beds_in_sheds_report_.pdf

38 Jacob Jarvis, 'Police find 26 beds in "slum-like" three-bedroom semi-detached house in London', *Evening Standard*, 27 September 2018: https://www.standard.co.uk/news/london/police-find-26-beds-in-slumlike-threebed-kingsbury-property-in-latest-beds-in-sheds-raid-a3947811.html

39 Ealing Council, 'Southall landlord fined for "beds in sheds" offences', 9 November 2018: https://www.ealing.gov.uk/news/article/1838/southall_landlord_fined_for_beds_in_sheds_offences

40 Ealing Council, 'Huge fine for "beds in sheds"', 22 November 2018: https://www.ealing.gov.uk/news/article/1841/huge_fine_for_beds_in_sheds_southall_landlord

41 Helen Catt, 'Oxford has hundreds of "beds in sheds"', 24 June 2014: https://www.bbc.co.uk/news/av/uk-england-oxfordshire-28010717/oxford-has-hundreds-of-beds-in-sheds. Nigel Barlow, 'Beds in sheds crackdown in Salford', About Manchester, 6 February 2017: https://aboutmanchester.co.uk/beds-in-sheds-crackdown-in-salford/

42 Shelter based its analysis on official figures of those rough sleeping plus others placed in 'emergency' accommodation by social services, such as a hostel, refuge or bed and breakfast accommodation. See Shelter, 'Far from Alone, Homelessness in Britain 2017', 8 November 2017: http://england.shelter.org.uk/__data/assets/pdf_file/0017/1440053/8112017_Far_From_Alone.pdf

43 'The Homelessness Monitor: England 2019', Crisis, 15 May 2019: https://www.crisis.org.uk/ending-homelessness/homelessness-knowledge-hub/homelessness-monitor/england/the-homelessness-monitor-england-2019/

II: THE UK HOUSING CRISIS IN TWELVE GRAPHS

1   'Housing Anguish', *The Times*, 22 December 1969.

2   Office for National Statistics, 'Social Trends', No. 39 (2009), Chapter 2: Households and Families: http://news.bbc.co.uk/1/shared/bsp/hi/pdfs/15_04_09_socialtrends.pdf

3   See MHCLG, 'Permanent Dwellings Completed, by Tenure and Country', Live Table 209: https://www.gov.uk/government/statistical-data-sets/live-tables-on-house-building

4   Wendy Wilson and Cassie Barton, 'Tackling the under-supply of housing in England', House of Commons Briefing Paper No. 07671, 12 December 2018: https://researchbriefings.parliament.uk/ResearchBriefing/Summary/CBP-7671

5   Building Societies Association, 'Laying the foundations for Modern Methods of Con-struction', November 2017: https://www.bsa.org.uk/BSA/files/20/20cee386-9dc6-4e0e-9ae9-504e3bbe4171.pdf

6   See Liam Halligan, 'Home to Roost', *The Spectator*, 5 November 2016: https://www.spectator.co.uk/2016/11/britains-lack-of-house-building-has-come-home-to-roost/

7   See C. A. L. Hilber and W. Vermeulen, 'The Impact of Supply Constraints on House Prices in England', op. cit.

8   UK House Price Index, Land Registry: http://landregistry.data.gov.uk/app/ukhpi

9   See Economic Research Council, 'Chart of the Week, Week 40 2015: Historical Real Average Salary', 2015: http://ercouncil.org/2015/chart-of-the-weekweek-41-2015-historical-real-average-salary/

10 'The "monster" mortgage is back – is it a risk?', *The Guardian*, 21 July 2018: https://www/theguardian.com/money/2018/jul/21/mortgage-clydesdale-bank-first-time-buyers

11 MHCLG, 'Fixing Our Broken Housing Market', op. cit., p. 15

12 At the time, the Ministry for Housing, Communities and Local Government was known as the Department for Communities and Local Government, but it is referred to as MHCLG throughout.

13 House of Commons, 'Public Accounts Committee oral evidence: Housing: State of the Nation', HC 958, Q. 132, 22 February 2017, p. 43: http://data.parliament.uk/writtenevidence/committeeevidence.svc/evidencedocument/public-accounts-committee/housing-state-of-the-nation/oral/47584.pdf

14 See Kate Barker, 'Review of Housing Supply – Delivering Stability: Securing our Future

Housing Needs', HM Treasury, March 2004: http://webarchive.nationalarchives.gov.uk/20120704150618/http://www.hm-treasury.gov.uk/d/barker_review_execsum_91.pdf

15 See MHCLG, 'Laying the Foundations: A Housing Strategy for England', HM Government, 2011: https://www.gov.uk/government/uploads/system/uploads/attachment_data/file/7532/2033676.pdf

16 Housing completion numbers in this section are author calculations based on raw data drawn from MHCLG, Live Table 209: https://www.gov.uk/government/statistical-data-sets/live-tables-on-house-building

17 House of Lords, 'Building More Homes', op. cit., p. 31.

18 Figures cited in Chris Philp, 'Homes for Everyone', Centre for Policy Studies, December 2017: http://www.cps.org.uk/files/reports/original/171212092648-HomesforEveryoneChrisPhilpMP.pdf

19 See Jagjit Chadha, 'The Housing Market and the Macroeconomy', National Institute Economic Review, No. 243 (February 2018): http://journals.sagepub.com/doi/full/10.1177/002795011824300103

20 'The good that governments can do', Theresa May's speech to Conservative Party conference, 5 October 2016: https://press.conservatives.com/post/151378268295/prime-minister-the-good-that-government-can-do

21 Conservative Party, 'Forward Together: Our Plan for a Stronger Britain and a Prosperous Future', 2017, p. 72: https://s3-eu-west-1.amazonaws.com/2017-manifestos/Conservative+Manifesto+2017.pdf

22 MHCLG, 'James Brokenshire welcomes rise in number of new homes', 15 November 2018: https://www.gov.uk/government/news/james-brokenshire-welcomes-rise-in-number-of-new-homes

23 See MHCLG, 'Net Additional Dwellings', Live Table 120. These numbers refer to England only: https://www.gov.uk/government/statistical-data-sets/live-tables-on-net-supply-of-housing

24 Office for National Statistics, 'Household projections for England – household type projections: 2016-based', 4 December 2018: https://www.ons.gov.uk/peoplepopulationandcommunity/populationandmigration/populationprojections/bulletins/2016basedhouseholdprojectionsinengland/2016based

25 Office for National Statistics, 'Overview of the UK population', July 2017: https://www.ons.gov.uk/peoplepopulationandcommunity/populationandmigration/populationestimates/articles/overviewoftheukpopulation/july2017

26 See Robert Colvile, 'This has been the worst decade for house-building since World War Two, and it's all our fault', Telegraph, 1 January 2018: https://www.telegraph.co.uk/news/2019/01/01/has-worst-decade-house-building-since-world-war-two-fault/

27 'UK House Prices since 1952', Nationwide Building Society: https://www.nationwide.co.uk/about/house-price-index/download-data – xtab:uk-series

28 Organisation for Economic Co-operation and Development, 'Analytical House Prices Indicators', 2018: https://stats.oecd.org/Index.aspx?DataSetCode=HOUSE_PRICES

29 Philip Bunn, Alice Pugh and Chris Yeates, 'The distributional impact of monetary policy easing in the UK between 2008 and 2014', Bank of England Staff Working Paper No. 720, 2018, p. 33.

30 Figures for the EU, including the UK, are from Eurostat, 'Distribution of population by tenure status, type of household and income group' (EU-SILC survey [ilc_lvho02], May 2018): http://appsso.eurostat.ec.europa.eu/nui/submitViewTableAction.do

31 Statistics Canada, 'Housing in Canada – Key Results, from the 2016 Census', October 2017: https://www150.statcan.gc.ca/n1/daily-quotidien/171025/dq171025c-eng.htm.
Australian Bureau of Statistics, 'Housing Occupancy and Costs, 2015–16', October 2017: https://www.abs.gov.au/ausstats/abs@.nsf/mf/4130.0.
US Census Bureau, 'Quarterly Residential Vacancies and Home Ownership, Second Quarter 2018', July 2018, Table 4: https://www.census.gov/housing/hvs/index.html

32 This data is derived from the Family Resources Survey 1995/96 and 2015/16, using calculations by the Institute for Fiscal Studies. The sample is restricted to Great Britain as data on Northern Ireland are not available for earlier years. See Jonathan Cribb, Andrew Hood and Jack Hoyle, 'The decline of home-ownership among young adults', IFS Briefing Note BN224, Institute for Fiscal Studies, 2018: https://www.ifs.org.uk/uploads/publications/bns/BN224.pdf

33 See data from UK Finance, formerly the Council of Mortgage Lenders: https://www.ukfinance.org.uk/remortgaging-boost-continued-in-october/

34 See Nationwide, 'First time buyer house price to earnings ratios', April 2018: https://www.nationwide.co.uk/-/media/MainSite/documents/about/house-price-index/downloads/ftb-hper.xls

35 Adam Corlett and Lindsay Judge, 'Home Affront – Housing across the generations', Resolution Foundation, September 2017: https://www.resolutionfoundation.org/app/uploads/2017/09/Home-Affront.pdf

36 This calculation includes only the cost of mortgage interest payments by homeowners, with capital repayment considered a form of saving. According to the property consultant Savills, renters paid private landlords £54 billion during the twelve months to the end of June 2017, more than double total mortgage interest paid by homeowners, as rising prices pushed more and more people into the rental sector. The interest paid by owner-occupier borrowers fell by £6.4 billion to £26.5 billion between 2012 and 2016, Savills calculate, while the amount paid to landlords rose £14 billion over the same five-year period. See 'Renters pay £54 billion to private landlords', Financial Times, 1 October 2017: https://www.ft.com/content/58bb3090-a53d-11e7-9e4f-7f5e6a7c98a2

37 Cribb, Jonathan, Andrew Hood and Jack Hoyle, 'The Economic Circumstances of Different Generations: The Latest Picture', IFS Briefing Note BN187, Institute for Fiscal Studies, 2016: https://www.ifs.org.uk/uploads/publications/bns/bn187.pdf

38 See, for instance, Adam Corlett and Lindsay Judge, 'Home Affront', op. cit., and Renata Bottazzi, Thomas Crossley and Matthew Wakefield, 'Late starters or excluded generations? A cohort analysis of catch-up in home ownership in England', IFS Working Paper W12/10, April 2012: https://www.ifs.org.uk/wps/wp1210.pdf

39 In 1996, the average age for women to have their first child was twenty-eight years and two months. By 2016, that age had risen to thirty years and three months. See 'Births by parents' characteristics in England and Wales, 2016', Office for National Statistics, Bulletin, 27 November 2017: https://www.ons.gov.uk/peoplepopulationandcommunity/birthsdeathsandmarriages/livebirths/bulletins/birthsbyparentscharacteristicsinenglandandwales/2016

40 MHCLG, Live Table 209.

41 National Ecosystem Assessment, 'The UK National Ecosystem Assessment Technical Report', UNEP-WCMC (Cambridge Studies, 2011): http://uknea.unep-wcmc.org/Resources/tabid/82/Default.aspx

42 The history of the UK's green belt, and proposed reforms, are discussed extensively in Chapter IV.

43 Michael Lyons, 'The Lyons Review: Mobilizing across the nation to build the homes our children need', Labour Party, 2014, p. 20: https://www.policyforum.labour.org.uk/uploads/editor/files/The_Lyons_Housing_Review_2.pdf

44 See Carlo Lavalle and Jean-Philippe Aurambout, 'Population weighted density (LUISA Platform)', European Commission, Joint Research Centre (JRC), 2014: http://data.europa.eu/89h/jrc-luisa-ui-population-weighted-density-ref-2014

45 See Nick Boles, 'Square Deal for Housing', November 2017: http://www.squaredeal.org.uk/square-deal-for-housing/

46 London First, 'Redefining Density: making the best use of London's land to build more and better homes', 2015: https://www.londonfirst.co.uk/sites/default/files/documents/2018-05/Redefining-Density.pdf

III: A PLACE OF OUR OWN

1   Sir Edward Lister, chairman of the Homes and Communities Agency. Foreword to Jack Airey, 'Disrupting the Housing Market: A policy programme to save the home-owning democracy', Localis, October 2017. The author was a member of the advisory panel which informed the preparation of this report: http://www.localis.org.uk/research/disrupting-housing-market/. The Homes and Communities Agency, formed in 2008, is a public body that funds new affordable homes in England. In January 2018, it was renamed Homes England. At the time of writing, Sir Edward Lister is chief strategic advisor to Prime Minister Boris Johnson.

2   'The British Dream', Theresa May's speech to Conservative Party conference, 4 October 2017: https://www.conservatives.com/sharethefacts/2017/10/theresa-mays-conference-speech

3   See, for example, Prime Minister's Questions, 1 March 2017: http://jeremycorbyn.org.uk/articles/jeremy-corbyn-prime-ministers-questions-housing-crisis-bedroom-tax/

4   These figures, for England only, are derived from successive editions of the English Housing Survey. See, for example, 'English Housing Survey 2017 to 2018: Headline Report': https://www.gov.uk/government/statistics/english-housing-survey-2017-to-2018-headline-report

5   See 'CML Research shows 80 per cent of people aspire to own their own home', Council of Mortgage Lenders press release, 20 October 2016: https://www.cml.org.uk/news/press-releases/cml-research-shows-80-of-people-aspire-to-own-home-in-ten-years/. Also Alison Park et al., 'British Social Attitudes Survey 28', National Centre for Social Research, 2012, p. 123: http://www.bsa.natcen.ac.uk/media/38952/bsa28_8housing.pdf

6   English Housing Survey, 2015/16. This figure includes housing benefit. Excluding those receiving housing benefit, privately renting households spend no less than 41 per cent of household income on rent.

7   See Adam Corlett, Stephen Clarke and Dan Tomlinson, 'The Living Standards Audit 2017', Resolution Foundation, 2017: https://www.resolutionfoundation.org/app/uploads/2017/07/The-Living-Standards-Audit-2017-FINAL.pdf

8   Data from the English Housing Survey quoted in Jack Airey, 'Disrupting the Housing Market', op.cit., p. 18.

9   For a summary of such research in an international context, see William Rohe and Mark Lindblad, 'Re-examining the Social Benefits of Home-Ownership after the Housing Crisis', Joint Centre for Housing Studies, Harvard University, 2017.

10   Internal MHCLG memo obtained by author. These estimates are based on Labour Force Survey data.

11   Evan John, 'Calling time on long commutes', Trades Union Congress, November 2017: https://www.tuc.org.uk/blogs/calling-time-long-commutes

12   'The Bank of Mum and Dad Report', Legal and General, August 2017: http://www.legalandgeneralgroup.com/media/1077/bomad_report_2017_aug.pdf

13   MHCLG, English Housing Survey Headline Report, 2016/17, Annex Table 1.1.

14   Calculations based on MHCLG data in Alex Morton, 'From Rent to Own – How to restore home ownership by turning private tenants into owners', Policy Exchange, October 2018, p. 8.

15   See polling by YouGov for Localis, reported in Jack Airey, 'Disrupting the Housing Market', op. cit., p. 3.

16   See 'UK Housing Market outlook – the continuing rise of Generation Rent', PriceWaterhouse-Coopers, 2015, p. 5.

17   Paul Hilbers, Alexander Hoffmaister, Angana Banerji and Haiyan Shi, 'House Price Developments in Europe: a comparison', IMF Working Paper WP/08/211, 2008: http://www.imf.org/external/pubs/ft/wp/2008/wp08211.pdf

18   See Eurostat, 'House Prices Statistics', 2019: https://ec.europa.eu/eurostat/webhousing-price-statistics/data/database

19 'London dominates UK jobs growth over past decade', BBC News, 27 November 2018: https://www.bbc.co.uk/news/uk-england-46288515

20 'Oxbridge blues: tech hubs bursting at the seams', *The Times*, 3 September 2017: https://www.thetimes.co.uk/article/cambridge-oxbridge-blues-tech-hubs-housing-shortage-pm7m9tddh

21 Lindsay Judge, 'Moving Matters: Housing costs and labour market mobility', Resolution Foundation, July 2019: https://www.resolutionfoundation.org/publications/moving-matters-housing-costs-and-labour-market-mobility/

22 Enrico Moretti and Chang-Tai Hsieh, 'Why Do Cities Matter? Local Growth and Aggregate Growth', Kreisman working paper on Housing Law and Policy No. 30, University of Chicago Law School, 2015. The argument developed here owes much to John Myers, 'The Housing crisis: an act of devastating economic self-harm', CapX, 11 August 2017: https://capx.co/the-housing-crisis-an-act-of-devastating-economic-self-harm/

23 See William Larson, 'New Estimates of Value of Land of the United States', Bureau of Economic Analysis, April 2015: https://www.bea.gov/research/papers/2015/new-estimates-value-land-united-states
Figures on the total stock of wealth in each country can be found in Anthony Shorrocks, Jim Davies and Rodrigo Lluberas, 'Global Wealth Report', Credit Suisse, 2017, Table 2.4, p. 102: https://www.credit-suisse.com/corporate/en/research/research-institute/global-wealth-report.html

24 Office for National Statistics, 'The UK national balance sheet estimate 2018', 29 August 2018, p. 5: file:///Users/user/Downloads/The UK national balance sheet estimates 2018.pdf

25 Sir Jon Cunliffe, 'House prices "biggest risk" to UK economy', BBC News, 3 July 2014: https://www.bbc.co.uk/news/business-28140588

26 'IMF warns UK government over housing bubble risk', BBC News, 6 June 2014: https://www.bbc.co.uk/news/business-27731567

27 See 'UK House Prices since 1952', Nationwide Building Society: https://www.nationwide.co.uk/about/house-price-index/download-data – xtab:uk-series

28 'The Monster-Mortgage is back – is it a risk?' *The Guardian*, 21 July 2018: https://www.theguardian.com/money/2018/jul/21/mortgage-clydesdale-bank-first-time-buyers

29 Office for National Statistics, 'Making ends meet: are households living beyond their means?', 26 July 2018: https://www.ons.gov.uk/economy/nationalaccounts/uksectoraccounts/articles/makingendsmeetarehouseholdslivingbeyondtheirmeans/2018-07-26

30 'Bank of England says it is watching mortgage price war "like a hawk"', *The Guardian*, 24 May 2019: https://www.theguardian.com/business/2019/may/24/bank-of-england-warns-risky-lending-mortgage-market

31 Resolution Foundation, 'Britain's increasingly unevenly shared property wealth is driving up inequality after a decade-long fall', June 2017: http://www.resolutionfoundation.org/media/press-releases/britains-increasingly-unevenly-shared-property-wealth-is-driving-up-inequality-after-a-decade-long-fall/

32 *New Blue: Ideas for a New Generation* (Centre for Policy Studies, May 2018), p. 16: https://www.cps.org.uk/files/reports/original/181015101703-FromRentToOwn.pdf

33 See, for instance, Liam Halligan, 'Our housing shortage leaves door open for Premier Corbyn', *The Sun*, 4 November 2016: https://www.thesun.co.uk/news/2114589/as-government-ponders-return-for-prefabs-our-shortage-of-homes-leaves-door-open-for-premier-corbyn/

34 'Making Housing Fairer', Theresa May speech, 5 March 2018: https://www.gov.uk/government/speeches/pm-speech-on-making-housing-fairer-5-march

35 See ComRes for the Centre for Policy Studies, 'Housing Poll', September 2018: https://www.comresglobal.com/wp-content/uploads/2018/10/CPS-Housing-Past-Vote-28092018-1.pdf

36 'Society is indeed a contract ... a partnership not only between those who are living, but between those who are living, those who are dead and those who are to be born.' See Robert Burke, *Reflections on the Revolution in France* (Yale University Press, 2003), p. 82. Burke's original work was published in 1790.

IV: A BROKEN MARKET

1   Speech at the opening of Shaftesbury Park Estate, 18 July 1874. Cited in Benjamin Disraeli, *Wit and Wisdom of Benjamin Disraeli – Collected from his Writings and Speeches* (Longmans, Green, 1883), p. 38.

2   MHCLG, 'Fixing Our Broken Housing Market', op. cit.

3   See Pete Jefferys and Toby Lloyd, 'New Civic House-Building: Rediscovering our tradition of building beautiful and affordable homes', Shelter Policy Briefing, 2017, p. 16: https://england. shelter.org.uk/__data/assets/pdf_file/0005/1348223/2017_03_02_New_Civic_ Housebuilding_Policy_Report.pdf

4   See MHCLG, Table 244: House building: Permanent Dwellings started and completed, by tenure.

5   'UK House Prices since 1952', Nationwide Building Society: https://www.nationwide.co.uk/ about/house-price-index/download-data – xtab:uk-series

6   See National Planning Policy Framework (MHCLG, 2012): https://www.gov.uk/guidance/ national-planning-policy-framework. A revised NPPF was completed in February 2019.

7   Glenigan and Barbour ABI planning pipeline data obtained by the author from MHCLG. These numbers are fourth-quarter annual rolling totals for each respective year and apply to England only.

8   This paragraph is based on internal MHCLG estimates, obtained by the author, based on Glenigan and Barbour ABI planning pipeline data.

9   Local Government Association, 'An analysis of unimplemented planning permission for residential dwellings', 2013: https://unidoc.wiltshire.gov.uk/UniDoc/Document/File/ MTMvMDQ2NzYvRlVMLDU1NDczMA==

10 See Chamberlain Walker, 'The role of land pipelines in the UK house-building process', September 2017: https://cweconomics.co.uk/wp-content/uploads/2017/10/CWEconomics Report_Land_Banking.pdf

11 Internal MHCLG memo, based on Glenigan data, obtained by the author.

12 See 'Reversing the Decline of Small Housebuilders: Reinvigorating entrepreneurialism and building more homes', Home Builders Federation, 2017: https://www.hbf.co.uk/ documents/6879/HBF_SME_Report_2017_Web.pdf

13 Fred Wellings, *British House-builders: History and Analysis* (Blackwell, 2006).

14 Michael Lyons, 'The Lyons Review', op. cit.

15 MGCLG, 'Fixing Our Broken Housing Market', op. cit.

16 See Matt Griffith, 'We must fix it: Delivering reform of the building sector to meet the UK's housing and economic challenges', Institute for Public Policy Research, 2011: https://www. ippr.org/publications/we-must-fix-it-delivering-reform-of-the-building-sector-to-meet- the-uks-housing-and-economic-challenges. See also Tom Archer and Ian Cole, 'Profits Before Volume?', op. cit.

17 I owe this phrase to Guy Standing, *The Corruption of Capitalism: Why Rentiers Thrive and Work Does Not Pay* (Biteback Publishing, 2016). 'Scarcity may be natural, as in the case of the truffle, because demand outstrips nature's bounty, or because there are physical constraints on production or exploitation. But in modern capitalism, scarcity is more often contrived, because a minority possesses all or most of an asset, because rules make it hard to produce or sell, or demand is deliberately stoked to outstrip supply.'

18 House of Lords, 'Building More Homes', op. cit., p. 24: https://publications.parliament.uk/ pa/ld201617/ldselect/ldeconaf/20/20.pdf

19 The Metropolitan green belt around London was first proposed by the Greater London Regional Planning Committee in 1935. The Town and Country Planning Act of 1947 then allowed local authorities to include green belt proposals in their development plans. In 1955, Minister of Housing Duncan Sandys encouraged local authorities across the country to consider protecting land around their towns and cities by formally designating clearly defined green belts.

20 National Ecosystem Assessment, 'The UK National Ecosystem Assessment Technical Report', op. cit.

21 See Louise Smith, Green Belt Briefing Paper, House of Commons Library, 2016, No. 00934.

22 Paul Cheshire, 'Turning houses into gold: the failure of British planning', LSE Centre Piece, Spring 2014: http://cep.lse.ac.uk/pubs/download/cp421.pdf

23 Michael Lyons, 'The Lyons Review', op. cit.

24 Kate Barker, *Where's the plan?* (Publishing Partnership, 2014).

25 'Slaying dragons: the stifling British green belt', Unherd, 24 April 2018: https://unherd.com/2018/04/slaying-dragons-green-belt/?=refinnar

26 See National Planning Policy Framework (MHCLG, 2014), paras 136 and 137: https://www.gov.uk/guidance/national-planning-policy-framework

27 'Theresa May to renew "personal mission" to fix broken housing market', *The Guardian*, 15 November 2017: https://www.theguardian.com/politics/2017/nov/15/theresa-may-conservatives-broken-housing-market-housebuilding-budget

28 'Theresa May joins campaign to save Poundfield in Cookham', *Maidenhead Advertiser*, 4 May 2016: https://www.maidenhead-advertiser.co.uk/news/cookhams/70008/Theresa-May-joins-campaign-to-save.html

29 Conservative Party, 'Forward Together', op. cit., p. 71: https://www.conservatives.com/manifesto

30 National Ecosystem Assessment, 'The UK National Ecosystem Assessment Technical Report', op. cit.

31 See Stephen Gibbons, Susana Mourato and Guilherme Mendes Resende, 'The Amenity Value of English Nature: A Hedonic Price Approach', SERC Discussion Paper No. 74, 2011.

32 Paul Cheshire, 'Turning houses into gold', op. cit., pp. 17–18.

33 See Paul Cheshire, 'Empty homes, longer commutes: one of the many unintended consequences of more restrictive local planning', Presentation to the Adam Smith Institute, 28 March 2018, slide 2: https://static1.squarespace.com/static/56eddde762cd9413e151ac92/t/5abd0887758d46f7ea637201/1522337942910/ PER CENTC+28+03+2018+v01.pdf

34 Under Section 106 of the Town and Country Planning Act 1990, a landowner or developer seeking planning permission can make a bilateral agreement under which the applicant agrees to pay a financial contribution to the council and/or meet other obligations. Section 106 payments are based on the impacts of a specific development and, as well as including the provision of affordable housing, may also be used to cover site-specific issues such as drainage or access. Section 106 is often confused with the Community Infrastructure Levy – which is a tariff-based payment calculated on the total floor space of a development, with councils setting their own rate per square metre. CIL payments are designed to cover the costs of all local infrastructure needs – such as schools, transport and flood defences – deemed to occur as a result of any new development.

35 See MHCLG, 'Definitions of general housing terms', November 2012: https://www.gov.uk/guidance/definitions-of-general-housing-terms – social-and-affordable-housing

36 'The high cost of viability assessments: 2,500 affordable homes lost in just one year', Shelter blog, 1 November 2017: https://blog.shelter.org.uk/2017/11/the-high-cost-of-viability-assessments-2500-affordable-homes-lost-in-just-one-year/

37 The Housing Delivery Test is Whitehall's assessment of whether councils and other planning authorities are overseeing development of enough homes for their area. It is presented as a percentage of homes delivered against the number required over the past three years – with 95 per cent constituting a 'pass'. The initial 2018 assessment concluded that 109 English planning authorities missed the pass rate – around a third of the total. Councils falling short but meeting 85 per cent of their housing requirement are compelled to put an action plan in place to boost housing delivery. Those with less than 85 per cent fulfilment must rewrite their local housing plan and identify 20 per cent more land for development than currently allocated in their five-year pipeline. If, after 2020, any council drops below

75 per cent delivery, then its locally agreed housing plan is then overridden by national planning rules, which enforce 'the presumption in favour of sustained development' in a more blanket fashion. See MHCLG, 'Housing Delivery Test: 2018 Measurement', 2019: https://www.gov.uk/government/publications/housing-delivery-test-2018-measurement

38   See Kate Barker, 'Review of Housing Supply', op. cit., and Matt Griffith, 'We must fix it', op. cit.

39   John Callcutt, 'The Callcutt Review of House-building Delivery', Department for Communities and Local Government, November 2007. At the time of writing, John Callcutt is CEO of the housebuilder Crest Nicholson: http://webarchive.nationalarchives. gov.uk/20101208170101/http://www.callcuttreview.co.uk/downloads/callcuttreview_221107. pdf. The Callcutt Review was the second of four major officially commissioned studies into slow housebuilding and declining home ownership during the fifteen years prior to the publication of this book. The Barker Report appeared in 2004, then the Callcutt Report in 2007. This was followed by the Lyons Housing Review of 2014, written by a former BBC chairman, and the 2016 Redfern Review, compiled by Pete Redfern, CEO of Taylor Wimpey.

40   Office of Fair Trading, 'Homebuilding in the UK: A market study', September 2008: http:// webarchive.nationalarchives.gov.uk/20140402181400/http://www.oft.gov.uk/shared_oft/ reports/comp_policy/oft1020.pdf

41   See House of Lords, 'Building More Homes', op. cit., p. 22, Table 3.

42   Home Builders Federation, 'Permissions to Land: Busting the Myths about House Builders and "Land Banking"', May 2014.

43   Tom Archer and Ian Cole, 'Profits Before Volume?', op. cit., p. 13.

44   Greater London Authority, 'Barriers to Housing Delivery: What Are the Market-Perceived Barriers to Residential Development in London?', 21 October 2012: https://www.london.gov. uk/sites/default/files/gla_migrate_files_destination/Barriers to Housing Delivery 2012.pdf

45   See Chamberlain Walker, 'The role of land pipelines in the UK house-building process', op. cit.

46   Sajid Javid, speech to Conservative Party conference, 3 October 2016: http://press. conservatives.com/post/151284016515/javid-speech-to-conservative-party-conference

47   'Sajid Javid goes to war with Nimbys and land bankers', *The Times*, 31 January 2018: https:// www.thetimes.co.uk/article/sajid-javid-goes-to-war-with-nimbys-and-land-bankers- kt6bbwz85

48   *Property Week*, 'Property provides 37% of Tory corporate donations', 2 June 2017: https://www.propertyweek.com/news/property-provides-37-of-tory-corporate-donations/ 5089611.article

49   Construction Index, 'Tories boosted by construction donations', 25 August 2017: https:// www.theconstructionindex.co.uk/news/view/tories-buouyed-by-construction-donations

50   'David Cameron warns lobbying is next political scandal', *Telegraph*, 8 February 2010: https://www.telegraph.co.uk/news/election-2010/7189466/David-Cameron-warns- lobbying-is-next-political-scandal.html

51   For more on this vital subject see Anna Minton, '"Scaring the living daylights out of people": the local lobby and the failure of democracy', Spinwatch, 2013: http://spinwatch.org/images /Reports/Scaring_the_living_daylight_final_27_March_13.pdf

V: HOW MINISTERS MADE THE HOUSING CRISIS WORSE

1   Sir Ernest Benn was a civil servant turned writer and publisher. He was an uncle of Labour Cabinet minister Tony Benn MP. Ernest Benn wrote this remark in a chapter he contributed to Henry Spring, *What is Truth?* (Orange Press, 1944), p. 31. It is often wrongly attributed to Groucho Marx.

2   See 'Inside Westminster: George Osborne's housing boom will echo into the future', *The Independent*, 9 October 2013. Conversation verified with other sources by author: https://

www.independent.co.uk/incoming/inside-westminster-george-osborne-s-housing-boom-will-echo-into-the-future-8869835.html

3   'First-time buyers face scramble for FirstBuy loans', *The Guardian*, 26 March 2011: https://www.theguardian.com/money/2011/mar/26/first-time-buyer-firstbuy
FirstBuy was itself modelled on HomeBuy Direct – a scheme launched by Labour in September 2008. This was slightly more generous, allowing would-be homeowners to take out a mortgage for just 70 per cent of the cost of a property, with the remaining 30 per cent funded via an 'equity loan'.

4   'Budget 2013: Chancellor extends home-buying schemes', BBC News, 20 March 2013: https://www.bbc.co.uk/news/business-21849974

5   In Wales, the price cap was £300,000 and in Scotland the maximum has varied depending on when an application was made. A 'mortgage guarantee' was also introduced, with the government (i.e. taxpayers) acting as partial guarantor on a limited number of home loans. That guarantee scheme was discontinued in 2016.

6   'Bank of England has no veto on Help to Buy, says governor', BBC News, 28 November 2013: https://www.bbc.co.uk/news/business-25124058

7   'Former U.K. Chancellor Lawson Calls For Help-To-Buy Program Curb', Bloomberg News: https://www.bloomberg.com/news/2014-05-01/former-u-k-chancellor-lawson-calls-for-help-to-buy-program-curb.html

8   Internal unpublished Whitehall memo, obtained by author.

9   'Financial experts question Help to buy claims', *Inside Housing*, 27 March 2013: https://www.insidehousing.co.uk/news/news/financial-experts-question-help-to-buy-claims-35119. A former member of the Bank of England's Monetary Policy Committee, Nickell was also the first chair of the government's National Housing and Planning Authority Advice Unit, set up in June 2007 in response to the Barker Review.

10   Stephen Finlay, P. Williams and C. Whitehead, 'Evaluation of the Help to Buy Equity Loan Scheme', DCLG, 2016: https://www.gov.uk/government/uploads/system/uploads/attachment_data/file/499701/Evaluation_of_Help_to_Buy_Equity_Loan_FINAL.pdf

11   'Help to buy won't build the young any houses', Adam Smith Institute, 1 October 2017: https://www.adamsmith.org/news/no-help-to-buy

12   Shelter Chief Executive Polly Neate, quoted in *The Independent*, 13 January 2018: https://www.independent.co.uk/news/uk/politics/help-to-buy-property-millions-pounds-government-housing-home-ownership-shelter-a8156631.html

13   Tom Archer and Ian Cole, 'Profits Before Volume?', op. cit.

14   Taylor Wimpey PLC, 'Creating Sustainable Value', 2014: https://www.taylorwimpey.co.uk/~/media/Head Office/IR Comms images/ARA 2014/Annual Report and Accounts 2014.pdf

15   Shelter, 'How much help is Help to Buy: Help to Buy and the impact on house prices', September 2015: https://england.shelter.org.uk/__data/assets/pdf_file/0010/1188073/2015_09_how_much_help_is_Help_to_Buy.pdf

16   See 'Wealthy homeowners received millions in public money under Government scheme to help first-time buyers', *The Independent*, 13 January 2018: https://www.independent.co.uk/news/uk/politics/help-to-buy-property-millions-pounds-government-housing-home-ownership-shelter-a8156631.html

17   This figure comes from the Leasehold Knowledge Partnership, part of the House of Commons All-Party Parliamentary Group on Leasehold Reform. The LKP reports homebuyers being charged up to £100 to have a letter answered by the freeholder, with others being billed for thousands of pounds for permission to build a simple extension. Seven out of ten buyers of recently built leasehold homes, many of whom are young with little or no business experience, say they used conveyance solicitors recommended by the developer and the risks were not drawn to their attention. The sale of HTB leasehold homes is now the subject of multiple legal actions.

18 'Help to Buy adds £1 billion to house-builder valuations', *Financial Times*, 2 October 2017: https://www.ft.com/content/5a2171aa-a778-11e7-93c5-648314d2c72c

19 'Eye-catching stamp duty cut will do nothing to solve our housing crisis', *Telegraph*, 23 November 2017. The OBR was similarly unimpressed with an earlier demand-side attempt to help FTBs. In 2016, Osborne introduced a 'lifetime ISA', enabling under-forties to save for a home deposit alongside a pension, with the government offering a 25 per cent top-up, to a £4,000 annual limit, on savings used to buy a home. 'We think [the lifetime ISA] is more likely than not to lead to higher demand for the relatively fixed supply of UK housing, and so to higher prices', said the OBR's budget-day fine print. A year later, the OBR reported a much poorer take-up than the Treasury had anticipated for Osborne's 'lifetime ISA', and also for his earlier 'Help to Buy' ISA, with the schemes marred in part by regulatory delays and a lack of willing providers.

20 'The decline of homeownership among young adults', IFS Briefing Note BN224, February 2018: https://www.ifs.org.uk/uploads/publications/bns/BN224.pdf

21 Profit figures are before tax and financing costs. See Tom Archer and Ian Cole, 'Profits Before Volume?', op. cit.

22 'House builders charge premium for Help to Buy properties', *Financial Times*, 8 August 2017: https://www.ft.com/content/d763c9fa-7c31-11e7-9108-edda0bcbc928

23 MHCLG, 'Fixing Our Broken Housing Market', op. cit.

24 See RTPI, 'Planning Risk and Development,' April 2018: http://www.rtpi.org.uk/media/2792494/Planning-risk-and-development.pdf

25 'The Councils that grant consent without being asked', *Planning Resource*, 6 June 2019: https://www.planningresource.co.uk/article/1586067/councils-grant-consent-without-asked

26 There was also an administrative reorganisation, with Homes and Communities Agency expanding to become Homes England, which Hammond said would 'bring together money, expertise and planning and compulsory purchase powers' to deliver new homes.

27 House of Lords, 'Building More Homes', op. cit., p. 5.

VI: 'NO SHORTAGE' NONSENSE

1 English dramatist and writer, 3 January 1803–8 June 1857. See Blanchard Jerrold, *Specimens of Douglas Jerrold's Wit* (Ticknor and Fields, 1859), p. 168.

2 See 'Most public sector workers can only afford to own home in 8 per cent of UK towns, report finds', *The Independent*, 17 June 2019: https://www.independent.co.uk/news/uk/home-news/public-sector-property-house-prices-nurses-teachers-police-housing-towns-affordability-a8960821.html

3 'Jeremy Corbyn was just 2,227 votes away from a chance to be Prime Minister', *The Independent*, 9 June 2017: https://www.independent.co.uk/news/uk/politics/corbyn-election-results-votes-away-prime-minister-theresa-may-hung-parliament-a7782581.html

4 'The Redfern Review into the decline of home ownership', November 2016: http://britainthinks.com/pdfs/TW082_RR_online_PDF.pdf

5 Ian Mulheirn, 'Building more homes won't solve the housing crisis', CapX, 6 February 2018: https://capx.co/building-more-homes-wont-solve-the-housing-crisis/. Mulheirn has since left Oxford Economics and, at the time of writing, is executive director for Renewing the Centre at the Tony Blair Institute.

6 'Britain does not have a housing shortage,' wrote Matthew Parris in *The Spectator* in February 2018, just days after Mulheirn's CapX article appeared. 'We have a problem with the cost not the availability of homes. This can't be solved by building more houses, because it is not caused by an insufficiency of houses.' See Matthew Parris, 'There is no housing crisis – it would be easier if there were', *The Spectator*, 10 February 2018: https://www.spectator.co.uk/2018/02/there-is-no-housing-crisis-it-would-be-easier-if-there-were/

7   MHCLG, 'Fixing our Broken Housing Market', op. cit., p. 9. In support of this conclusion, the White Paper cited Kate Barker, 'Review of Housing Supply', op. cit.; House of Lords, 'Building More Homes', op. cit.; and KPMG/Shelter, 'Building the Homes We Need – a programme for the 2015 government': http://www.shelter.org.uk/__data/assets/pdf_file/0019 /802270/Building_the_homes_we_need_-_a_programme_for_the_2015_government.pdf

8   Ian Mulheirn, 'Mission: Unnecessary', Medium blog, 30 January 2018: https://medium.com/@ian.mulheirn/mission-unnecessary-66feebd5b469

9   The raw numbers can be accessed at ONS Table 'Young adults living with their parents': https://www.ons.gov.uk/peoplepopulationandcommunity/birthsdeathsandmarriages/families/datasets/youngadultslivingwiththeirparents

10   These numbers, also 2006–2016, are based on the Labour Force Survey and quoted in an unpublished MHCLG memo obtained by the author.

11   See House of Lords (2016a), Oral and Written Evidence, 'Select Committee on Economic Affairs: The Economics of the UK Housing Market', p. 1433: https://www.parliament.uk/documents/lords-committees/economic-affairs/Economics-of-the-UK-Housing-Market/The-Economics-of-the-UK-Housing-Market-FINAL.pdf

12   See House of Lords (2016a), p. 564.

13   Daniel Bentley, 'Housing Supply and Household Growth, National and Local', Civitas briefing, 2016, p. 2: http://www.civitas.org.uk/man/content/files/housingsupplyandhouseholdgrowth.pdf

14   Boys Smith is best known for setting up Create Streets, a research institute that supports 'community-led regeneration' and prioritises high-density, low-rise buildings over tower blocks. He was appointed as interim chair of the Building Better, Building Beautiful Commission in May 2019, after Roger Scruton was removed from the role due to comments about Muslim, Chinese and Hungarian people he made in a *New Statesman* interview which Housing Secretary James Brokenshire found 'unacceptable' – a charge Scruton vigorously denied. After the *New Statesman* was found to have misrepresented Scruton, he was reinstated as co-chair, alongside Boys Smith.

15   Lindsay Judge, 'The one million missing homes?', Resolution Foundation blog, 12 January 2019: https://www.resolutionfoundation.org/media/blog/the-one-million-missing-homes/

16   Office for National Statistics, 'Housing Affordability in England and Wales: 1997 to 2016', March 2017, p. 2: https://www.ons.gov.uk/peoplepopulationandcommunity/housing/bulletins/housingaffordabilityinenglandandwales/1997to2016

17   See MHCLG, 'Permanent Dwellings Completed', Live Table 209. https://www.gov.uk/government/statistical-data-sets/live-tables-on-house-building and 'Net Additional Dwellings', Live Table 120. These numbers refer to England only: https://www.gov.uk/government/statistical-data-sets/live-tables-on-net-supply-of-housing

18   Ian Mulheirn, 'Building more homes won't solve the housing crisis' op. cit.

19   'Is this the answer to the UK's housing problem?', Nationwide blog, 6 December 2017: https://www.nationwide.co.uk/guides/news/all-news/2017/12/robert-gardners-hpi-blog

20   Other signatories included the Royal Institute of British Architects, the National Housing Federation, the Campaign to Protect Rural England, the Metro Mayor of Liverpool city region and the Chartered Institute of Housing. See 'Call for rethink on UK planning rules for housing', *Financial Times*, 28 January 2019: https://www.ft.com/content/3ce36f32-20b0-11e9-b126-46fc3ad87c65

21   See '"Slums of the future"? UK office-to-homes policy sparks fears', *Financial Times*, 26 December 2018: https://www.ft.com/content/48fbe55c-ffb2-11e8-ac00-57a2a826423e

22   Ben Clifford, 'Extended Permitted Development Rights in England', University College London Bartlett School of Planning, 2018: https://www.ucl.ac.uk/news/2018/may/office-residential-developments-providing-poor-quality-housing

23   'MP and Councillors trade blame over creation of Newbury Park block labelled among "worst new flats in Britain"', *Ilford Recorder*, 28 August 2018: https://www.ilfordrecorder.co.uk/news/newbury-house-councillors-trade-blame-1-5670450

24 'Inside Harlow's office block "human warehouse" housing', BBC News, 3 April 2019: https://www.bbc.co.uk/news/uk-england-essex-47720887

25 'Labour pledges to end "slum" office housing', BBC News, 24 April 2019: https://www.bbc.co.uk/news/business-48031661

26 Ian Mulheirn and Nishaal Gooroochurn, 'Modelling house prices and home ownership', NIESR Housing Conference, 1 June 2018, p. 17: https://www.niesr.ac.uk/sites/default/files/files/MulheirnNIESR Housing Conference.pdf.

27 Edward Glaeser and Joseph Gyourko, 'The Impact of Zoning on Housing Affordability', National Bureau of Economic Research, Working Paper No. 8835, 2002: https://www.nber.org/papers/w8835

28 C. A. L. Hilber and W. Vermeulen, 'The Impact of Supply Constraints on House Prices in England', op. cit.

29 Philip Bunn, Alice Pugh and Chris Yeates, 'The distributional impact of monetary policy easing in the UK between 2008 and 2014', op. cit., p. 33.

30 Office for National Statistics, 'Transfer of household projections to ONS', 23 January 2017: https://www.ons.gov.uk/news/news/transferofhouseholdprojectionstoons.

31 'Slower household growth in England raises policy questions', Financial Times, 20 September 2018: https://www.ft.com/content/e718d348-bcce-11e8-8274-55b72926558f

32 Office for National Statistics, 'Household projections in England: 2016-based', 20 September 2018: https://www.ons.gov.uk/peoplepopulationandcommunity/populationand migration/populationprojections/bulletins/2016basedhouseholdprojectionsinengland/2016basedhouseholdprojectionsinengland

33 Office for National Statistics, 'Response to the ONS consultation on the household projections for England', 30 June 2017, p. 8: https://consultations.ons.gov.uk/communication-division/changes-to-household-projections-for-england/

34 John Rose, 'The Housing Supply Myth', Kwantlen Polytechnic University, British Columbia, Working Paper No. 1, 24 November 2017: https://www.kpu.ca/sites/default/files/The Housing Supply Myth Report John Rose.pdf

35 Ben Phillips and Cukkoo Joseph, 'Regional housing supply and demand in Australia', Australian National University Centre for Social Research & Methods, Working Paper No. 1/2017, November 2017: http://csrm.cass.anu.edu.au/sites/default/files/docs/2018/12/CSRM_WP1_2017_HOUSING_SUPPLY.pdf

36 Mark Stephens, John Perry, Steve Wilcox, Peter Williams and Gillian Young, 'UK Housing Review – Autumn Briefing Paper', Chartered Institute of Housing and Heriot-Watt University, October 2018, p. 7: http://www.cih.org/resources/PDF/Policy free download pdfs/UK Housing Review 2018 Autumn briefing paper final.pdf

37 Private conversation with author.

38 Pew Research Global Attitudes Survey 2019, Question 54a: https://www.pewresearch.org/global/2019/03/04/u-s-german-relations-methodology-spring-2018-global-attitudes-survey/

39 For a useful discussion of this impact, see Robert Rowthorn, 'The Costs and Benefits of Large-scale Immigration', Civitas, December 2015: http://www.civitas.org.uk/content/files/largescaleimmigration.pdf
    Rowthorn notes that 'unskilled workers have suffered some reduction in their wages due to competition from immigrants' and highlights pressure placed on public services.

40 David Metcalfe, 'Work, Immigration and the Labour Market: Incorporating the role of the Migration Advisory Committee', Migration Advisory Council Report and London School of Economics, June 2016: https://assets.publishing.service.gov.uk/government/uploads/system/uploads/attachment_data/file/547697/MAC-_report_immigration_and_the_labour_market.pdf

41 For more details see 'Long Term International Net Migration' tables: https://www.ons.gov.uk/employmentandlabourmarket/peopleinwork/employmentandemployeetypes/bulletins/uklabourmarket/dec2016

This 2015 UK net immigration total doubles again if you include those granted a national insurance number during that same year who stayed in the UK for less than twelve months. Even if such workers make lengthy visits to Britain for many successive years, but stay for less than a year each time, they are not counted in the headline immigration numbers. Including new national insurance numbers granted to non-UK nationals, annual net UK migration in 2015 was close to the population of Leeds. See Liam Halligan and Gerard Lyons, *Clean Brexit: How to make a success of leaving the European Union* (Biteback Publishing, 2017), pp. 231–2.

42   MHCLG, 'Analysis of the determinants of house price changes', April 2018: https://assets. publishing.service.gov.uk/government/uploads/system/uploads/attachment_data/ file/699846/OFF_SEN_Ad_Hoc_SFR_House_prices_v_PDF.pdf

43   'Minister Dominic Raab told to publish proof that immigration raises house prices', *The Times*, 9 April 2018: https://www.thetimes.co.uk/article/51b08b32-3b75-11e8-b8eb-a2b1e54e4e88

44   'An immigration system that works in the national interest', Theresa May speech, 12 December 2012: https://www.gov.uk/government/speeches/home-secretary-speech-on-an-immigration-system-that-works-in-the-national-interest

45   Christine Whitehead, Ann Edge, Ian Gordon, Kath Scanlon and Tony Travers, 'The impact of migration on access to housing and the housing market', London School of Economics and Migration Advisory Committee, December 2011: https://assets.publishing.service.gov. uk/government/uploads/system/uploads/attachment_data/file/257238/lse-housing.pdf

46   Filipa Sá, 'Immigration and House Prices in the UK', IZA DP No. 5893, July 2011, p. 3: http:// ftp.iza.org/dp5893.pdf

47   See Houses of Parliament, 'Migrants and Housing', Parliamentary Office of Science and Technology, Postnote No. 560, August 2017, p. 3: https://researchbriefings.parliament.uk/ ResearchBriefing/Summary/POST-PN-0560

48   Opinium Research interviewed a sample of 1,004 UK adults aged eighteen and over. See 'UK housing crisis: poll reveals city V country split on who to blame', *The Guardian*, 30 April 2016: https://www.theguardian.com/cities/2016/apr/30/housing-crisis-poll-city-country-split-blame

49   Office for National Statistics, 'Overview of the UK population: July 2017': https://www.ons. gov.uk/peoplepopulationandcommunity/populationandmigration/populationestimates/ articles/overviewoftheukpopulation/july2017

50   The A8 nations are the Czech Republic, Estonia, Hungary, Latvia, Lithuania, Poland, Slovakia and Slovenia.

51   Christian Dustmann, Maria Casanova, Michael Fertig, Ian Preston and Christoph Schmidt, 'The impact of EU enlargement on migration flows', Home Office Online Report 25/03: https://www.ucl.ac.uk/~uctpb21/reports/HomeOffice25_03.pdf

52   Organisation for Economic Co-operation and Development, 'Housing Stock and Construction', Social Policy Division – Directorate of Employment, Labour and Social Affairs, August 2017, p. 6: http://www.oecd.org/els/family/HM1-1-Housing-stock-and-construction.pdf

53   House of Lords, 'The Economics of the UK Housing Market', Oral and written evidence, Select Committee on Economic Affairs, 15 December 2015, Q45, p. 402: https://www. parliament.uk/documents/lords-committees/economic-affairs/Economics-of-the-UK-Housing-Market/The-Economics-of-the-UK-Housing-Market-FINAL.pdf

54   The case of the Netherlands illustrates the same point. The Dutch population increased 0.6 per cent a year between 1970 and 2015 and annual GDP growth was 2.4 per cent on average – both similar figures to the UK. Yet the Dutch housing stock expanded by 100 per cent over this period, more than double the UK rate. During the forty-five years from 1970, real house prices in the Netherlands grew 240 per cent, compared to 480 per cent in the UK.

55   For the statistics behind these statements see Organisation for Economic Co-Operation and Development, 'Housing Stock and Construction', op. cit., Table HM1.1.1b; Michael Oxley and Jacqueline Smith, *Housing Policy and Rented Housing in Europe* (Routledge, 1996); and

Eurostat, 'Housing cost overburden rate by tenure status', EU-SILC survey, 2015: https://data.europa.eu/euodp/en/data/dataset/Hmvp07X4Wawh4QrCR5vfLQ
This analysis owes much to Neil O'Brien, 'Green, pleasant and affordable: Why we need a new approach to supply and demand to solve Britain's housing problem', Onward, June 2018.

56   Diego Battiston, Richard Dickens, Alan Manning and Jonathan Wadsworth, 'Immigration and Access to Social Housing in the UK', Centre for Economic Performance Discussion Paper No. 1264, London School of Economics, April 2014: http://cep.lse.ac.uk/pubs/download/dp1264.pdf

57   Figures relate to England only. Office for National Statistics, 'International Migration and the changing nature of housing in England', ONS dataset, 2017: https://www.ons.gov.uk/peoplepopulationandcommunity/populationandmigration/internationalmigration/articles/internationalmigrationandthechangingnatureofhousinginenglandwhatdoestheavailableevidenceshow/2017-05-25

58   MHCLG, 'Social Housing Lettings: April 2017 to March 2018, England', November 2018: https://assets.publishing.service.gov.uk/government/uploads/system/uploads/attachment_data/file/759738/Social_Housing_Lettings_April2017_to_March2018_England.pdf

59   Carlos Vargas-Silva and Cinzia Rienzo, 'Migrants in the UK: An Overview', The Migration Observatory, Oxford University, October 2018: https://migrationobservatory.ox.ac.uk/resources/briefings/migrants-in-the-uk-an-overview/

60   'Construction industry in plea to retain migrant workers', The Guardian, 3 March 2015: https://www.theguardian.com/business/economics-blog/2015/mar/03/construction-industry-plea-retain-migrant-workers

61   'Construction slows as Brexit fog thickens', Investors Chronicle, 26 September 2019: https://www.investorschronicle.co.uk/sector-focus/2019/09/26/construction-slows-as-brexit-fog-thickens/

62   'David Cameron: net immigration will be capped at tens of thousands', Telegraph, 10 January 2010: https://www.telegraph.co.uk/news/politics/6961675/David-Cameron-net-immigration-will-be-capped-at-tens-of-thousands.html

63   Figures from the House of Commons Library cited in Neil O'Brien, 'Green, pleasant and affordable', op. cit.

VII: NEW-BUILD NIGHTMARES

1   Churchill made this remark in the House of Commons on 28 October 1943. See Hansard, HC Deb, 28 October 1943, Vol. 393, cc. 403–73: https://api.parliament.uk/historic-hansard/commons/1943/oct/28/house-of-commons-rebuilding

2   The York-based group includes subsidiary brands Charles Church and Westbury among others.

3   Interview with the author, Wakefield, Yorkshire, June 2019.

4   Interview with the author, Pembroke, Wales, June 2019.

5   See 'The Persimmon Pledge': https://www.persimmonhomes.com/persimmon-pledge.

6   National Audit Office, 'Help to Buy: Equity Loan Scheme – Progress Review', HC 2216, Session 2017–19, June 2019, Figure 12, p. 35. The data derives from each developer's annual reports – and includes all activity, including construction in both Wales and Scotland for most of the top five developers: https://www.nao.org.uk/wp-content/uploads/2019/06/Help-to-Buy-Equity-Loan-scheme-progress-review.pdf. See also: Britain's top developers are still building fewer homes than before the financial crisis, Daily Mail, 22 September 2019: https://www.dailymail.co.uk/news/article-6195229/Britains-developers-building-fewer-homes-financial-crisis.html

7   Pre-tax profit. Figures taken from company annual reports. See also 'Help-To-Buy: Scheme has helped biggest developers to double profits', The Times, 8 September 2018: https://www.thetimes.co.uk/article/help-to-buy-scheme-has-helped-biggest-developers-to-double-profits-759qq3h7m

8   The UK population in 2007 was 61.46 million, rising to 67.55 million in 2018: http://worldpopulationreview.com/countries/united-kingdom-population/

9   Persimmon Plc, 'Delivering on our Long-Term Strategy', 2018: https://www.persimmonhomes.com/corporate/media/370173/persimmon_ar18.pdf

10   'Persimmon boss Jeff Fairburn asked to leave over £75 million bonus backlash', *The Independent*, 7 November 2018: https://www.independent.co.uk/news/business/news/jeff-fairburn-persimmon-bonus-ceo-controversy-bbc-interview-a8621351.html

11   'Outrage as help-to-buy boosts Persimmon profits to £1 billion', *The Guardian*, 26 February 2019: https://www.theguardian.com/business/2019/feb/26/persimmon-profits-help-to-buy-scheme

12   'Persimmon investors approve £39m pay package for Jeff Fairburn', *Building*, 2 May 2019: https://www.building.co.uk/news/persimmon-investors-approve-39m-pay-package-for-jeff-fairburn-/5099264.article

13   'Construction companies suspended from Prompt Payment Code', *PBC Today*, 30 April 2019: https://www.pbctoday.co.uk/news/planning-construction-news/construction-suspended-prompt-payment/56187/. Other construction companies suspended from PPC at the same time as Persimmon included Balfour Beatty, Costain and Laing O'Rourke. Thousands of firms who sign up to the code, administered by the Chartered Institute of Credit Management on behalf of the government, pledge to uphold best practice for payment standards in order to help end the culture of late payment, particularly for small businesses. This includes a commitment to pay 95 per cent of all supplier invoices within sixty days.

14   Home Builders Federation, 'National New Homes Customer Satisfaction Survey (CSS)', HBF/NHBC, March 2019: https://www.hbf.co.uk/documents/8389/CSS_HBF_Brochure_2019_with_table.pdf. Persimmon is one of the bottom five builders, all with three-star ratings. The other, much smaller, firms in this category are, as of March 2019, Keepmoat, Galliford Try, Keir Living and Lovell.

15   Pride in the Job Awards, National House Building Council, 2018: http://www.nhbc.co.uk/AwardsandEvents/Pride-in-the-job/Award-Archive-2018/

16   See https://forum.snagging.org/index.php

17   See 'Angry homeowners hang giant sign outside new build warning off other buyers', *Metro*, 29 April 2019: https://metro.co.uk/2019/04/29/angry-homeowners-hang-giant-sign-outside-new-build-warning-off-buyers-9336903/

18   Fire barriers are used to form a complete seal between different areas of a home, and without them, experts say, fire and smoke can spread five to ten times faster. Revelations related to both Persimmon and Bellway homes were contained in a BBC documentary. See 'New-build homes not fire safe', *BBC Watchdog Live*, 1 May 2019: https://www.bbc.co.uk/news/business-48113301

19   Greig Adams, interview with the author, June 2019. Adams is both a chartered building surveyor and a chartered building engineer: https://www.surveyorexpert.co.uk/about-me

20   https://www.facebook.com/groups/DoNotBuyPersimmon/
     https://uk.trustpilot.com/review/www.persimmonhomes.com
     https://www.reviews.co.uk/company-reviews/store/persimmonhomes
     https://forums.moneysavingexpert.com/showthread.php?t=5843646

21   See Department of Communities and Local Government, 'Tackling unfair practices in the leasehold market, Summary of consultation responses and Government response', DCLG, 2017.

22   National Association of Estate Agents, 'Leasehold: A Life Sentence?', NAEA/Property Mark, September 2018.
     https://www.propertymark.co.uk/media/1047279/propertymark-leasehold-report.pdf

23   'House owners rue leasehold purchases', BBC News, 7 September 2018: https://www.bbc.co.uk/news/business-45431914

24   National Association of Estate Agents, 'Leasehold: A Life Sentence?', op. cit., p. 9.

25   Monthly PPI refunds and compensation, Financial Conduct Authority, July 2019: https://www.fca.org.uk/data/monthly-ppi-refunds-and-compensation – header

26 'Help-To-Buy cheat Persimmon racks up £1 billion profits – and spread the plague of leasehold houses around the country', *Leasehold Knowledge Partnership*, 23 February 2019: https://www.leaseholdknowledge.com/help-to-buy-cheat-persimmon-racks-up-1bn-profits-and-spread-the-plague-of-leasehold-houses-around-the-country. The Leasehold Knowledge Partnership is a registered charity and the secretariat of the All-Party Parliamentary Group on leasehold and commonhold reform chaired by MPs Sir Peter Bottomley (Conservative), Jim Fitzpatrick (Labour) and Sir Ed Davey (Liberal Democrat). They are also the patrons of LKP. The deputy chairs are Justin Madders (Labour), Marie Rimmer (Labour) and Baroness Gardner (Conservative). The Leasehold Knowledge Partnership, in its own words, 'exists to protect ordinary leaseholders who get caught up in the leasehold game. Most don't know the rules, and yet they are up against professionals for whom this form of tenure can be highly profitable.'

27 MHCLG, 'Public pledge for leaseholders', 29 June 2019: https://www.gov.uk/government/publications/leaseholder-pledge/public-pledge-for-leaseholders

28 'Taxpayers continue to fund purchase of toxic leasehold homes through Help to Buy', ministers admit, *Daily Mail*, 13 February 2019: https://www.thisismoney.co.uk/money/markets/article-6701889/Taxpayers-continue-fund-purchase-toxic-leasehold-homes-Help-Buy-ministers-admit.html

29 'Government bans leasehold for Help-to-Buy houses', *Telegraph*, 27 June 2019: https://www.telegraph.co.uk/money/consumer-affairs/government-bans-leasehold-help-buy-houses/

30 Finishing Touches, Persimmon Brochure, edition 7.S2: https://www.persimmonhomes.com/admin/libraries/assetitems/xassethandler.axd?aii=52333

31 Greig Adams, interview with the author, June 2019.

32 Paula Higgins, founder and CEO, HomeOwners Alliance, interview with the author: https://hoa.org.uk/about-us/people/

33 'New homes warranty firm pays millions to leading homebuilders', *The Guardian*, 5 February 2017: https://www.theguardian.com/business/2017/feb/05/new-homes-warranty-firm-pays-millions-to-leading-homebuilders

34 See, for instance, the NHBC's statement in the following article: '£150 for two years of house problems: Owner hits out at "insult" over new-build defects', *Eastern Daily Press*, 13 July 2019: https://www.edp24.co.uk/edp-property/new-build-snagging-issues-in-norfolk-1-6157617

35 'Directors of new homes warranty firm criticised for lack of independence', *The Guardian*, 6 February 2017: https://www.theguardian.com/business/2017/feb/06/new-homes-warranty-nhbc-uk

36 Kate Barker, 'Review of Housing Supply', op. cit., p. 11.

37 MHCLG, 'Fixing Our Broken Housing Market', op. cit., p. 47

38 '9 in 10 favour of "snagging retention" on new builds', *Property Reporter*, 8 April 2019: https://www.propertyreporter.co.uk/property/9-in-10-in-favour-of-snagging-retention-on-new-builds.html

39 'Persimmon launches retention policy after quality concerns', *FT Advisor*, 21 March 2019: https://www.ftadviser.com/mortgages/2019/03/21/persimmon-launches-retention-policy-after-quality-concerns/. 'Persimmon's new homebuyers' "retention" at least shows willing', *The Guardian*, 21 March 2019: https://www.theguardian.com/business/nils-pratley-on-finance/2019/mar/21/persimmons-new-homebuyers-retention-at-least-shows-willing

40 Persimmon PLC, 'Announcement of Independent Review', 5 April 2019, p. 2: file:///Users/user/Downloads/persimmon-independent-review_website (1).pdf

41 'Persimmon launches retention scheme for homebuyers', *Construction Enquirer*, March 2019: https://www.constructionenquirer.com/2019/03/21/persimmon-launches-retention-scheme-for-home-buyers/

42 'Persimmon extends customer retention period to a week', *Housing Today*, 4 July 2019: https://www.housingtoday.co.uk/news/persimmon-extends-customer-retention-period-to-a-week/5100438.article

43 These figures are based on an analysis of 10,000 floorplans of homes built since the 1930s. 'What is the average house size in the UK?', *LABC Warranty*, 16 May 2019: https://www. labcwarranty.co.uk/blog/are-britain-s-houses-getting-smaller-new-data/

44 Malcolm Morgan and Heather Cruikshank, 'Quantifying the extent of space shortages: English dwellings', *Journal of Building Research and Information*, Vol. 42, No. 6 (2014): https://www.tandfonline.com/doi/full/10.1080/09613218.2014.922271

45 'Creating space for beauty – Interim Report', Building Better, Building Beautiful Commission, July 2019: https://assets.publishing.service.gov.uk/government/uploads/system/uploads/ attachment_data/file/815493/BBBBC_Commission_Interim_Report.pdf

46 As reported by the author: 'Theresa May missed her opportunity to show Britain she's got a grip on the housing crisis', *The Sun*, 6 October 2017: https://www.thesun.co.uk/ news/4621733/theresa-may-housing-crisis-speech/

47 'Help-to-buy: Scheme has helped biggest developers to double profits', *The Times*, 8 September 2018: https://www.thetimes.co.uk/article/help-to-buy-scheme-has-helped-biggest-developers-to-double-profits-759qq3h7m

48 Interview with the author, Glasgow Caledonian University, July 2016.

49 'Persimmon: House-building giant faces loss of contract amid government concerns over Help to Buy scheme', *The Independent*, 23 February 2019: https://www.independent. co.uk/news/business/persimmon-house-building-contract-help-to-buy-james-brokenshire-a8793181.html

50 Persimmon PLC, 'Announcement of Independent Review', op. cit.

51 'Persimmon investors approve £39m pay package for Jeff Fairburn', op. cit.

52 'Britain's New Build Scandal', *Dispatches*, 15 July 2019: https://www.channel4.com/ programmes/dispatches/on-demand/70109-001

53 'Tory MP slams "con-artist" Persimmon over Help to Buy faults', *City AM*, 17 July 2019: https://www.cityam.com/tory-mp-slams-con-artist-persimmon-over-help-to-buy-faults/

54 Interview with the author, House of Commons, May 2019.

55 See 'The Persimmon Pledge', op. cit.

VIII: FAT OF THE LAND

1 Land Tenure Reform Association, 'Report of the Inaugural Public Meeting', 1871, pp. 9–10. Quoted in Donald Winch and Patrick Karl O'Brien, *The Political Economy of British Historical Experience, 1688–1914* (British Academy, 2002).

2 'The UK Tops Forbes' Best Countries for Business 2018', *Forbes*, 19 December 2017: https:// www.forbes.com/sites/kurtbadenhausen/2017/12/19/the-u-k-tops-forbes-best-countries-for-business-2018/ – 63fdb02c26de

3 'A skilled, talented, diverse workforce is essential to economic success. However, at this critical time for the future of Great Britain, social mobility is stagnant and people from professional and managerial backgrounds continue to enjoy profound advantages in the labour market, compared to those from working-class backgrounds.' See Social Mobility Commission, 'State of the Nation 2018–19: Social Mobility in Great Britain', HMSO, 2019, p. 2. 'Social mobility in UK "virtually stagnant" since 2014', *The Guardian*, 30 April 2019: https://www. theguardian.com/society/2019/apr/30/social-mobility-in-uk-virtually-stagnant-since-2014

4 As of 2019/20, the tax-free inheritance tax allowance was £325,000 – which, at the time of writing, is lower than the average house price across the south-east. This nil-band allowance has remained the same since 2010/11, despite the average UK-wide house price rising by some 30 per cent during that period. Standard inheritance tax rate is levied at 40 per cent above that £325,000 threshold.

5 Basic-rate taxpayers pay capital gains tax of 10 per cent on assets and 18 per cent on residential property that isn't their principal residence. Higher- and additional-rate taxpayers pay rates of 20 per cent and 28 per cent. For the share of tax revenues gained from CGT and other property

taxation see 'Tax revenues: where does the money come from and what are the next government's challenges?', Institute for Fiscal Studies, 1 May 2017: https://www.ifs.org.uk/publications/9178

6   Milton Friedman (1912–2006) was an American economist who received the 1976 Nobel Memorial Prize in Economic Sciences for his research on consumption analysis, monetary theory and stabilisation policy. Friedman's political philosophy extolled the virtues of free markets with minimal intervention. From the early 1960s, Friedman promoted a macroeconomic viewpoint known as 'monetarism' – which stressed low taxation, carefully controlled growth of the money supply and limited government spending, a contrast to post-war Keynesian policies. Friedman was an advisor to Republican President Ronald Reagan and Conservative British Prime Minister Margaret Thatcher.

7   Adam Smith (1723–1790) is often referred to as 'The Father of Economics' or 'The Father of Capitalism'. His magnum opus – *The Nature and Causes of the Wealth of Nations* (1776) – laid the foundations of classical free market economic theory.

8   Henry George (1839–1897) was an American journalist, politician and political economist whose writings have been celebrated by figures as diverse as Franklin Delano Roosevelt, George Bernard Shaw and Albert Einstein. 'It would require less than the fingers of the two hands to enumerate those who, from Plato down, rank with Henry George among the world's social philosophers,' wrote Professor John Dewey of Columbia University in a preface to the fiftieth anniversary edition of *Progress and Poverty*. 'No man, no graduate of a higher educational institution, has a right to regard himself as an educated man in social thought unless he has some first-hand acquaintance with the theoretical contribution of this great American thinker.'

9   Labour Party, 'For the Many, Not the Few', 2017, p. 86: https://labour.org.uk/wp-content/uploads/2017/10/labour-manifesto-2017.pdf

10   'Change Britain's Future', Liberal Democrat manifesto, 2017, p. 40: https://d3n8a8pro7vhmx.cloudfront.net/themes/5909d4366ad575794c000000/attachments/original/1495020157/Manifesto-Final.pdf?1495020157
'A Confident and Caring Britain', Green Party manifesto, 2017, p. 17: https://www.greenparty.org.uk/assets/files/gp2017/greenguaranteepdf.pdf

11   Across 151 local authorities and other charging authorities which levied CIL in 2017/18, some £348 million was raised and the Mayor of London raised an additional £109 million through CIL. See Community Infrastructure Levy: Written question – HL15404, Hansard, 14 May 2019: https://www.parliament.uk/business/publications/written-questions-answers-statements/written-question/Lords/2019-04-29/HL15404/

12   Clive Turner, 'Homes Through the Decades', op. cit.

13   Brian Lund, *Housing Politics in the United Kingdom* (Policy Press, 2016), p. 33.

14   Daniel Bentley, 'The Land Question', op. cit., p. 48.

15   Office for National Statistics, 'The UK national balance sheet estimates: 2018', 2019: https://www.ons.gov.uk/economy/nationalaccounts/uksectoraccounts/bulletins/nationalbalancesheet/2018

16   Stephen Merrett, *State Housing in Britain* (Routledge & Kegan Paul, 1979), p. 73.

17   Andrew Cox, *Adversary Politics and Land: The Conflict Over Land and Property Policy in Post-War Britain* (Cambridge University Press, 1984), p. 114.

18   Federation of Master Builders, 'FMB Survey 2018', p. 10: https://www.fmb.org.uk/media/41090/18-09-05-house-builders-27-survey-2018-final.pdf?utm_source=Report&utm_medium=pdf&utm_campaign=Housebuilderssurvey

19   Bill Tanner, 'Land reform foundation for a new generation of social housing', 24 *Housing*, 17 June 2019: https://www.24housing.co.uk/news/land-reform-foundation-for-a-new-generation-of-social-housing/

20   Savills Real Estate Services, 'The Savills Housing Sector Survey 2019', June 2019: http://pdf.euro.savills.co.uk/uk/residential---other/savills-housing-sector-survey-2019.pdf

21 Thomas Aubrey, 'Gathering the Windfall: How Changing Land Law Can Unlock England's Housing Supply Potential', Centre for Progressive Policy, Working Paper 03/2018, September 2018, p. 5: https://www.progressive-policy.net/downloads/files/LVC-Report-Sep-2018.pdf

22 Klaus Schwab, 'The Global Competitiveness Report 2016–2017', World Economic Forum, 28 September2016:https://www.weforum.org/reports/the-global-competitiveness-report-2016-2017-1

23 Thomas Aubrey, 'Estimating land value capture for England – updated analysis', 13 March 2017: https://centreforprogressivecapitalism-archive.net/2017/03/estimating-land-value-capture-england-updated-analysis/

24 Peter Hall and Colin Ward, *Sociable Cities: The 21st-Century Reinvention of the Garden City* (Routledge, 2014).

25 Genesis 45:17–18 (King James Version).

26 Thomas Aubrey, 'Gathering the windfall: How changing land law can unlock England's housing supply potential', op. cit., p. 3.

27 Kate Barker, 'Review of Housing Supply', op. cit., p. 7.

28 Michael Lyons, 'The Lyons Review', op. cit., p. 21.

29 National Ecosystem Assessment, 'The UK National Ecosystem Assessment Technical Report', op. cit., p. 23.

30 KPMG/Shelter, 'Building the homes we need: a programme for the 2015 Government', op. cit., p. 39.

31 New Economics Foundation, 'What lies beneath: how to fix the broken land system at the heart of our housing crisis', July 2018, p. 2.

32 Daniel Bentley, 'Reform of the land compensation rules: How much could it save on the cost of a public-sector housebuilding programme?', Civitas, March 2018: http://www.civitas.org.uk/content/files/reformofthelandcompensationrules.pdf

33 National Housing Federation, 'Submission: Budget 2018', 28 September 18: http://s3-eu-west-1.amazonaws.com/pub.housing.org.uk/Autumn_Budget_2018_submission.pdf

34 Nick Boles, 'Square Deal for Housing', op. cit.

35 Neil O'Brien, 'Green, pleasant and affordable', op. cit.

36 In December 2017, Chris Philp MP proposed a new system of CPOs that share planning uplift fifty-fifty between landowners and local authorities. In May 2018, Bim Afolami MP suggested an extra levy on land once it is earmarked in a local council development plans, ahead of specific permission to build. And in July 2018, Matt Warman MP argued for a levy based on the final sale of the land. See Chris Philp, 'Homes for Everyone – How to get Britain building and restore the home ownership dream', Centre for Policy Studies, December 2017: https://www.cps.org.uk/files/reports/original/171212092648-HomesforEveryoneChrisPhilpMP.pdf Bim Afolami, 'How Can We Make Planning Popular?' in *New Blue: Ideas for a New Generation* (Centre for Policy Studies, 2018): https://www.cps.org.uk/files/reports/original/180509164435-CPSNewBlue.pdf Matt Warman, 'Who Governs Britain – Democracy and Local Government in the Digital Age', Centre for Policy Studies, July 2018: https://www.cps.org.uk/files/reports/original/180720173103-WhoGovernsBritain.pdf

37 John Muellbauer, 'What Germany can teach us about repairing our broken housing market', National Institute for Economic and Social Research, 2 August 2018: https://www.niesr.ac.uk/blog/what-germany-can-teach-us-about-repairing-our-broken-housing-market

38 John Muellbauer, 'Six fiscal reforms for the UK's "lost generation"', Local Tax Commission, 2015: http://localtaxcommission.scot/wp-content/uploads/Six-fiscal-reforms-for-the-UK-John-Muellbauer.pdf

39 Tim Leunig, 'Community land auctions: working towards implementation', Centre Forum, November 2011: https://www.centreforum.org/assets/pubs/community-land-auctions.pdf

40 Richard Layard, 'Economics of the Housing Market – a note', 11 April 2016 (mimeo).

41 Onward et al., 'Sharing land value with communities: An open letter', 20 August 2018: https://www.ukonward.com/landreform/ First published in August 2018, the letter has since been 're-published' online as additional signatories have been added.

42   For more information about Yimby, and the organisation's ideas, see John Myers, 'Yes In My Back Yard – How To End The Housing Crisis, Boost The Economy And Win More Votes', London Yimby/Adam Smith Institute, 2017: https://static1.squarespace. com/static/56eddde762cd9413e151ac92/t/598c8b62be42d6f7f8e30ebe/1502382968482/ John+Myers+-+YIMBY+-+Final.pdf

43   Housing, Communities and Local Government Committee, 'Land Value Capture', Tenth Report of Session 2017–19, House of Commons, HC 766, September 2018, p. 3: https:// publications.parliament.uk/pa/cm201719/cmselect/cmcomloc/766/766.pdf

44   Housing, Communities and Local Government Committee, 'Land Value Capture', ibid. para. 111, p. 41.

45   MHCLG, 'Government Response to the Housing, Communities and Local Government Select Committee inquiry on land value capture', Cm 9734, November 2018, para. 11, p. 8: https://assets.publishing.service.gov.uk/government/uploads/system/uploads/attachment_ data/file/760031/Cm9734_land_value.pdf

46   Winston Churchill, 'The Mother of all Monopolies', speech delivered at King's Theatre, Edinburgh, 17 July 1909. The 1909 People's Budget was introduced by a Liberal government and placed unprecedented taxes on the lands and incomes of Britain's wealthy to fund new social welfare programmes. It passed the House of Commons in 1909 but was blocked by the House of Lords for a year, before becoming law in 1910. It was championed by Chancellor of the Exchequer David Lloyd George and his young ally Winston Churchill, then President of the Board of Trade.

47   'Rooff wins challenge in Olympics compensation battle', Estates Gazette, 18 April 2011: https://www.egi.co.uk/news/rooff-wins-challenge-in-olympics-compensation-battle/?eg_ tr_frm_cmpt=true

48   Housing, Communities and Local Government Committee 'Land Value Capture', op. cit., para. 97, p. 36.

49   Housing, Communities and Local Government Committee 'Land Value Capture', op. cit., p. 36.

50   See Vincent Renard, 'Property Rights Protection and Spatial Planning in European Countries' in Gregory Ingram and Yu-Hung Hong (eds) Property Rights and Land Policies: proceedings of the 2008 Land Policy Conference (Lincoln Institute of Land Policy, 2009).

51   Thomas Aubrey, 'Gathering the windfall: How changing land law can unlock England's housing supply potential', op. cit., p. 12.

52   MHCLG, 'Public attitudes to house building: findings from the British Social Attitudes survey 2017', June 2018 https://www.gov.uk/government/publications/ public-attitudes-to-house-building-findings-from-the-british-social-attitudes-survey-2017

53   Labour Party, 'Housing for the Many – a Labour Party Green Paper', April 2018: http:// labour.org.uk/wp-content/uploads/2018/04/Housing-for-the-Many-final.pdf

54   Cable said this in a speech given at the Royal Institute of British Architects on 26 June 2018. The speech is reprinted in Vince Cable, 'Beyond Brexit: Liberal politics for the age of identity', Liberal Democrats, 2019, p. 62.

55   Sajid Javid, speech to Conservative Party conference, 3 October 2016: http://press. conservatives.com/post/151284016515/javid-speech-to-conservative-party-conference

56   'Sajid Javid goes to war with nimbys and land bankers', The Times, 31 January 2018: https://www.thetimes.co.uk/article/sajid-javid-goes-to-war-with-nimbys-and-land- bankers-kt6bbwz85

57   MHCLG, 'Independent review of build out: final report – Sir Oliver Letwin', Cm 9720, October 2018: https://assets.publishing.service.gov.uk/government/uploads/system/ uploads/attachment_data/file/752124/Letwin_review_web_version.pdf

58   'Budget 2018: Government confirms new Help to Buy scheme from 2021', Home Builders Federation press release, 29 October 2018: https://www.hbf.co.uk/newsletter/ view/824?pk_campaign=newsletter_824

59 'Planning update: Written statement – HCWS1408', Secretary of State James Brokenshire, 13 March 2019: https://www.parliament.uk/business/publications/written-questions-answers-statements/written-statement/Commons/2019-03-13/HCWS1408/

60 'The flaw that will torpedo the government's housebuilding ambitions', Joint statement by Shelter, Civitas and the Centre for Progressive Policy, 17 March 2019: https://www.progressive-policy.net/publications/the-flaw-that-will-torpedo-the-governments-housebuilding-ambitions

61 Response to questions put by Liam Halligan to Oliver Letwin, Policy Exchange Housing Seminar, Westminster, 26 April 2019.

IX: BEYOND GRENFELL

1 Song performed by the rap artist Stormzy at the Brit Awards, 21 February 2018.

2 'Victims of Grenfell Tower inferno who bought their homes say authorities have abandoned them', Telegraph, 10 July 2019: https://www.telegraph.co.uk/news/2017/07/10/victims-grenfell-tower-inferno-bought-homes-say-authorities/

3 Royal Borough of Kensington and Chelsea, 'Grenfell Tower Regeneration Project: Engagement Statement', Kensington and Chelsea TMO, November 2012: https://www.rbkc.gov.uk/idoxWAM/doc/Other-960662.pdf?extension=.pdf&id=960662&location=VOLUME2&contentType=application/pdf&pageCount=1

4 'Hats off to the London Fire Brigade: Praise for heroic firefighters who dashed into burning Grenfell Tower to save lives', Evening Standard, 14 June 2017: https://www.standard.co.uk/news/london/grenfell-tower-praise-for-heroic-london-firefighters-who-dashed-into-burning-building-to-save-lives-a3565161.html

5 'Grenfell Tower inquiry: LFB "failed residents and firefighters"', BBC News, 10 December 2018: https://www.bbc.co.uk/news/uk-46508545

6 'Fire brigade raised fears about cladding with councils', BBC News, 28 June 2017: https://www.bbc.co.uk/news/uk-40422922

7 'Isle of Man "shame" over Summerland fire disaster', BBC News, 2 August 2013: https://www.bbc.co.uk/news/world-europe-isle-of-man-23449990

8 'Should Knowsley Heights blaze have been a warning from history for Grenfell?', Liverpool Echo, 3 July 2017: https://www.liverpoolecho.co.uk/news/liverpool-news/should-knowsley-heights-blaze-been-13271446

9 'Southwark council pleads guilty over worst ever tower block fire', The Guardian, 24 February 2017: https://www.theguardian.com/uk-news/2017/feb/24/southwark-council-admits-safety-failings-tower-block-lakanal-house-blaze

10 'Peter Apps, Special investigation – The lost lessons of Lakanal: how politicians missed the chance to stop Grenfell', Inside Housing, 3 July 2019: https://www.insidehousing.co.uk/insight/insight/special-investigation--the-lost-lessons-of-lakanal-how-politicians-missed-the-chance-to-stop-grenfell-61834

11 Peter Childs and Michael Storry (eds), Encyclopedia of Contemporary British Culture (Routledge, 1999), p. 159.

12 Cathy Come Home, BBC One, broadcast 16 November 1966, BFI Film Online: http://www.screenonline.org.uk/tv/id/438481/

13 'Television that changed our world', The Scotsman, 22 July 2005: https://www.scotsman.com/news/uk-news/television-that-changed-our-world-1-720880

14 Shelter, 'Our History': http://england.shelter.org.uk/what_we_do/history

15 'Witness History: Cathy Come Home 45 Years On', BBC World Service, 16 November 2011: https://www.bbc.co.uk/programmes/poolf1d3

16 Shelter, 'Rights and wrongs: The homelessness safety net 30 years on', November 2007: https://england.shelter.org.uk/__data/assets/pdf_file/0015/48012/Briefing_Rights_and_Wrongs_Nov_2007.pdf

17 See Municipal Dreams blog: https://municipaldreams.wordpress.com/2017/06/
Also, John Boughton, Municipal Dreams: The Rise and Fall of Council Housing (Verso, 2018).

18   Housing, Communities and Local Government Select Committee, 'Building regulations and fire safety: consultation response and connected issues', Seventeenth Report of the Session 2017–19, House of Commons, HC 2546.

19   'Delays to safety reforms "risk a repeat of Grenfell disaster"', *The Guardian*, 18 July 2019: https://www.theguardian.com/uk-news/2019/jul/17/delays-to-safety-reforms-risk-a-repeat-of-grenfell-disaster

20   'Theresa May announces £2 billion for council homes expansion', BBC News, 4 October 2017: https://www.bbc.co.uk/news/uk-politics-41502601

21   'May pledges £2 billion for affordable housing development', *Building*, 19 September 2018: https://www.building.co.uk/news/may-pledges-2bn-for-affordable-housing-development/5095619.article

22   MHCLG, Table 120: components of housing supply; net additional dwellings, England 2006/07 to 2017/18: https://www.gov.uk/government/statistical-data-sets/live-tables-on-net-supply-of-housing

23   '"Shocking": Secretary of State doesn't know number of council houses built last year', *Iain Dale Show*, LBC, 30 April 2019: https://www.lbc.co.uk/radio/presenters/iain-dale/shocking-housing-secretary-council-houses/

24   'Bristol chooses Labour's Marvin Rees as new Mayor', *The Guardian*, 7 May 2016: https://www.theguardian.com/uk-news/2016/may/07/bristol-chooses-labours-marvin-rees-as-new-mayor-over-george-ferguson

25   'Old answers to new questions? The future of social housing in the UK', Resolution Foundation, 8 April 2019.

26   'History of Council Housing', University of the West of England, 2008: http://fet.uwe.ac.uk/conweb/house_ages/council_housing/print.htm

27   Saltaire is a Victorian model village in Shipley, West Yorkshire. It was built in 1851 by Sir Titus Salt, a leading industrialist in the Yorkshire woollen industry. Work commenced on Port Sunlight in 1888 – a village and suburb on the Wirral, Merseyside, developed by Lever Brothers to accommodate workers in its soap factory (now part of Unilever). Bournville is a village built on the south side of Birmingham from the mid-1890s onwards by the Cadbury family.

28   'The World's Oldest Council Estate: Then and Now', The Londonist, 6 October 2016: https://londonist.com/2015/02/worlds-oldest-council-estate-at-125-then-and-now
      From the 1860s onwards, the Old Nichol was perhaps London's most feared slum. Its notoriety was enhanced by Arthur Morrison's fictionalised account of it, *A Child of the Jago* (1896). A contemporary newspaper account describes life in the Old Nichol: 'There is nothing picturesque in such misery; it is but one painful and monotonous round of vice, filth and poverty, huddled in dark cellars, ruined garrets, bare and blackened rooms, teeming with disease and death, and without the means, even if there were the inclination, for the most ordinary observations of decency or cleanliness.' From 'Dwellings of the Poor in Bethnal Green', *Illustrated London News*, 24 October 1863: http://www.mernick.org.uk/thhol/dwelpoor.html

29   Housing and Town Planning Bill, Hansard, HC Deb, 8 April 2019, Vol. 114, cc. 1962–3: https://api.parliament.uk/historic-hansard/commons/1919/apr/08/housing-and-town-planning-bill
      Major Waldorf Astor, 2nd Viscount Astor (1879–1952) was an American-born newspaper proprietor turned MP. As the 1919 legislation was clearing Parliament, Astor was Addison's Parliamentary Private Secretary. His wife was Nancy Astor, another US-born British politician, who became the first female MP to take her Commons seat after she held Plymouth, her husband's former seat, for the Conservatives in a by-election in November 1919.

30   Christopher Addison, *The Betrayal of the Slums* (H. Jenkins, 1922), p. 128: https://archive.org/details/betrayalofslums00addirich/page/128

31   MHCLG, 'House building: permanent dwellings started and completed, by tenure', Table 244: https://www.gov.uk/government/statistical-data-sets/live-tables-on-house-building

32   Stuart Adam, Daniel Chandler, Andrew Hood and Robert Joyce, 'Social housing in England: a survey', IFS Briefing Note BN178, Institute for Fiscal Studies, November 2015, p. 8, Fig. 1: https://www.ifs.org.uk/uploads/publications/bns/BN178.pdf

33 Peter Malpass and Alan Murie, *Housing Policy and Practice*, 5th edition (Palgrave, 1999), p. 58.

34 Mark Stephens, Christine Whitehead and Moira Munro, 'Lessons from the Past, Challenges for the Future for Housing Policy', DCLG, 2005.

35 Andro Linklater, *Owning the Earth* (Bloomsbury, 2014), p. 366.

36 MHCLG, Live Table 209. All figures in this section refer to England.

37 See MHCLG, 'Additional affordable homes provided by tenure, England', Live Table 1000: https://assets.publishing.service.gov.uk/government/uploads/system/uploads/attachment_data/file/809386/Live_Table_1000.xlsx

38 'Affordable housebuilding up 12 per cent', *Inside Housing*, 18 November 2018: https://www.insidehousing.co.uk/news/news/affordable-housebuilding-up-12-59219
See also MHCLG, 'Affordable Housing Supply: April 2017 to March 2018 England, Statistical Release', 22 November 2018: https://assets.publishing.service.gov.uk/government/uploads/system/uploads/attachment_data/file/758389/Affordable_Housing_Supply_2017-18.pdf

39 See MHCLG, 'Affordable Housing Starts and Completions funded by Homes England and the Greater London Authority', Live Table 1012.

40 Wendy Wilson and Cassie Barton, 'Tackling the under-supply of housing in England', House of Commons Briefing Paper No. 07671, December 2018. p. 22.

41 John Hills, 'Ends and Means: The Future Roles of Social Housing in England, Centre for the Analysis of Social Exclusion', Report 34, CASE/DCLG, February 2017, p. 56, Table 6.1: http://eprints.lse.ac.uk/5568/1/Ends_and_Means_The_future_roles_of_social_housing_in_England_1.pdf

42 HM Treasury, 'Public Expenditure Statistical Analyses 2018', Table 5.2: https://www.gov.uk/government/statistics/public-expenditure-statistical-analyses-2018

43 DWP, 'Benefit Expenditure Caseload Table 2017', Table 1b: https://www.gov.uk/government/publications/benefit-expenditure-and-caseload-tables-2017

44 Shelter, 'Bricks or Benefits: Rebalancing housing investment', 2012: https://england.shelter.org.uk/__data/assets/pdf_file/0009/436275/Bricksorbenefitsfullreport.pdf

45 John Perry and Mark Stephens, 'How the purpose of social housing has changed and is changing', UK Housing Review, Chartered Institute of Housing, Section 1, Chapter 3, Fig. 1.3.2, p. 36: https://www.ukhousingreview.org.uk/ukhr18/docs/UKHR-2018-Contemporary-Issues-Ch3.pdf

46 National Housing Federation, 'How public money is spent on housing', 2018: https://www.housing.org.uk/how-public-money-is-spent-on-housing/

47 See Resolution Foundation, 'Old Answers to New Questions: The future of social housing in the UK', 2019: https://www.resolutionfoundation.org/events/old-answers-to-new-questions-the-future-of-social-housing-in-the-uk/

48 English Housing Survey, 'Headline Report, 2017–18', p. 3: https://assets.publishing.service.gov.uk/government/uploads/system/uploads/attachment_data/file/774820/2017-18_EHS_Headline_Report.pdf]

49 Justin Chaloner, Alexandra Dreisin and Mark Pragnell, 'Building New Social Rent Homes', Capital Economics, 2015: http://www.almos.org.uk/include/getDoc.php?did=7124&fid=8238

50 See Liam Halligan: 'We're on the fast track to a £100 billion white elephant', *Telegraph*, 10 February 2019: https://www.telegraph.co.uk/politics/2019/02/10/fast-track-100-billion-white-elephant/

51 The Shelter report contained detailed economic modelling work carried out by the commercial consultancy Capital Economics. See Shelter, 'Building for our future: a vision for social housing', January 2019: file:///Users/user/Downloads/Shelter UK – A vision for social housing – Executive summary.pdf

52 'Call for rethink on UK planning rules for housing', *Financial Times*, 28 January 2019: https://www.ft.com/content/3ce36f32-20b0-11e9-b126-46fc3ad87c65

53 'John Boughton: Council housing is the bedrock of the future, not a relic of the past', Shelter guest blog, 31 July 2019: https://blog.shelter.org.uk/2019/07/council-housing-is-the-bedrock-of-the-future-not-a-relic-of-the-past/

54 Office for National Statistics, 'The UK national balance sheet: 2017 estimates', Figure 3

55 Katharina Knoll, Moritz Schularick and Thomas Steger, 'No price like home: global house

prices, 1870–2012', *American Economic Review*, Vol. 107, No. 2 (2017), pp. 331–53: https://www.aeaweb.org/articles?id=10.1257/aer.20150501

56 Peter Foynes, 'The Rise of High-Rise: Post-War Housing in Hackney', *Hackney History*, Vol. 1 (1995), p. 31.

57 Savills Research, 'The Savills Housing Sector Survey 2018', p. 9.

58 J. Morphet and B. Clifford, 'Local authority direct provision of housing', National Planning Forum and Royal Town and Country Planning Institute, 2017, p. 52.

59 National Housing Federation, 'Landowners make £13bn profit in one year, as high land prices stifle affordable housing', September 2018.

X: A MANIFESTO FOR CHANGE

1 G. K. Chesterton, *The Superstition of Divorce* (New Witness, 1920), Chapter III.

2 See endnotes 54 and 55 in Chapter IX.

3 Thomas Aubrey, 'Gathering the windfall: How changing land law can unlock England's housing supply potential', op. cit., p. 3.

4 Interview with the author, 12 May 2019.

5 'Berkeley Group chairman Tony Pidgley on Brexit, buildings and bonus backlashes', *City AM*, 16 January 2019: https://www.cityam.com/berkeley-group-chairman-tony-pidgley-brexit-buildings-and/

6 Conversation with the author, 31 May 2019, Berkeley Homes Headquarters, Cobham, Surrey.

7 'Mixed views as Berkeley Homes and The Howard win planning appeal for new school and 295 homes in Effingham', *Guildford Dragon*, 21 March 2018: http://www.guildford-dragon.com/2018/03/21/mixed-views-as-berkeley-homes-and-the-howard-win-planning-appeal-for-new-school-and-295-homes-in-effingham/

8 'Howard of Effingham development: What the rebuilt school will look like', *Surrey Live*, 22 March 2018: https://www.getsurrey.co.uk/news/surrey-news/howard-effingham-development-what-rebuilt-14444632

9 Pidgley was appointed to Lord Heseltine's Estate Regeneration advisory panel in 2016 and is also a member of the Thames Estuary 2050 Growth Commission. He has advised successive London Mayors on housing policy, advised central government on the disposal of public sector land and is a former president of the London Chamber of Commerce and Industry.

10 Hansard, 18 November 1963, Vol. 684, cc. 656: https://api.parliament.uk/historic-hansard/commons/1963/nov/18/housing-and-land-prices

11 Hansard, 18 November 1963, Vol. 684, cc. 658: https://api.parliament.uk/historic-hansard/commons/1963/nov/18/housing-and-land-prices

12 The Cabinet Papers, 'Housing and the Land Commission: Dual Property Market', National Archive: http://www.nationalarchives.gov.uk/cabinetpapers/themes/housing-land-commission.htm

13 Vernon Bogdanor, 'Sir Keith Joseph and the market economy', Gresham Lecture, 21 May 2013: https://www.gresham.ac.uk/lectures-and-events/sir-keith-joseph-and-the-market-economy

14 See Daniel Bentley, 'The Land Question', op. cit., p. 50.

15 Housing, Communities and Local Government Select Committee, 'Land Value Capture', op. cit., p. 16.

16 Kate Barker, 'Review of Housing Supply', op. cit., p. 87, Recommendation 26.

17 The National Infrastructure Commission points to the potential of 'increased land values' along the Oxford–Milton Keynes–Cambridge corridor 'to allow local authorities and government to capture a share of uplifts to support infrastructure investment'. See National Infrastructure Commission, 'Cambridge–Milton Keynes–Oxford Corridor: Interim report', November 2016, p. 9: https://www.nic.org.uk/wp-content/uploads/Cambridge-Milton-Keynes-Oxford-interim-report.pdf

18 Housing, Communities and Local Government Select Committee, 'Land Value Capture', op. cit., p. 41, para. 113.

19 David Rudlin argues for the near doubling of existing large towns in line with garden city principles, to provide 86,000 new homes for 150,000 people built over thirty to thirty-five years. Rudlin argues that there may be as many as forty cities in England that could be doubled in size in this way, such as York, Norwich, Stafford and Cheltenham, with 20 per cent of the new homes classified as affordable housing. See David Rudlin and Nicholas Falk, 'Uxcester: Garden City – submission for the Wolfson Economics Prize', Urbed Consultancy, 2014: http://urbed.coop/sites/default/files/20140815 URBED Wolfson Stage 2_low res3.pdf

20 'New Town Development Corporation powers for councils announced', *Royal Institute of British Architects*, 21 June 2018: https://www.architecture.com/knowledge-and-resources/knowledge-landing-page/new-town-development-corporation-powers-for-councils-announced

21 Department of Communities and Local Government , 'Transferable Lessons from the New Towns', DCLG/Oxford Brookes University, July 2006, p. 30: https://www.westminster.ac.uk/sites/default/public-files/general-documents/Transferable-Lessons-from-the-New-Towns.pdf

22 Some argue that because the Milton Keynes Development Corporation (MKDC) acquired the bulk of its land in 1970, and was still a successful New Town, no change to the 1961 legislation is required. At the time of purchase, though, most of the land designated by MKDC did not have – or was not thought to have – 'hope value'. The development corporation bought around 300 hectares from local landowner Bernard Myers, offering just over twice agricultural values. Myers subsequently challenged the compensation award, and in 1974 his claim was upheld by the Court of Appeal. In the end, Myers got around three times his original compensation – but that was still just a fraction of what turned out to be the full residential value, so Milton Keynes remained an economically viable New Town. Yet the Myers case, and subsequent others, cemented landowners' entitlement to 'hope value' when land is sold. In addition, as Daniel Bentley and Thomas Aubrey pointed out in a 2018 submission made to the Housing, Communities and Local Government Select Committee, 'the ratio between agricultural and residential values has widened considerably from 35 in 1969 to over 100 today'. As such, 'potential compensation awards – even if landowners are paid only a proportion rather than the full residential value – have moved much further apart', say Bentley and Aubrey. 'Hence, the potential liabilities for a local authority or a development corporation are of a different magnitude today'.
See Daniel Bentley and Thomas Aubrey, 'Written evidence to the Housing, Communities and Local Government Select Committee', House of Commons, June 2018, LVC 096: http://data.parliament.uk/WrittenEvidence/CommitteeEvidence.svc/EvidenceDocument/Housing, Communities and Local Government/Land Value Capture/written/85910.html

23 'Look to Milton Keynes for the solution to the housing crisis', *City AM*, 16 October 2017, p. 20: https://www.bemk.co.uk/news/look-to-milton-keynes-for-the-solution-to-the-housing-crisis-city-am-reports

24 'The massive 15,000 home Ebbsfleet Garden City set to transform north Kent', *Kent Live*, 18 May 2019: https://www.kentlive.news/news/property/indepth-look-ebbsfleet-garden-city-2626336

25 MHCLG, 'House building: permanent dwellings started and completed, by tenure', Table 244: https://www.gov.uk/government/statistical-data-sets/live-tables-on-house-building

26 'England needs 340,000 new homes a year, says NHF', *Inside Housing*, 18 May 2018: https://www.insidehousing.co.uk/home/home/england-needs-340000-new-homes-a-year-says-nhf-56355

27 See Shelter, 'Building for our future', op. cit.

28 Conservative Party, 'Forward Together', op. cit.

29 Labour Party, 'For the Many, Not the Few', op. cit.

30 Jack Airey, 'Disrupting the Housing Market', op. cit., p. 40.

31 Shelter, 'Grounds for Change: The case for land reform in modern England', June 2019: https://england.shelter.org.uk/__data/assets/pdf_file/0010/1779418/Grounds_For_Change.pdf

32 Shelter, 'Grounds for Change: The case for land reform in modern England', ibid., p. 18.

33 Daniel Bentley, 'Reform of the land compensation rules', op. cit.

34 'Most councils to make use of HRA borrowing cap lift, finds LGA', *Public Finance*, 15

March 2019: https://www.publicfinance.co.uk/news/2019/03/most-councils-make-use-hra-borrowing-cap-lift-finds-lga

35 'Housing chiefs paid more than PM "have lost trust of tenants"', *The Times*, 17 July 2018: https://www.thetimes.co.uk/article/housing-chiefs-paid-more-than-pm-have-lost-trust-of-tenants-hfflfkj9c

36 'Five housing associations get credit downgrades from S&P', *Inside Housing*, 31 July 2019: https://www.insidehousing.co.uk/news/news/five-housing-associations-get-credit-downgrades-from-sp-62503

37 'UK housing associations use lure of luxury in social mission', *Financial Times*, 6 September 2017: https://www.ft.com/content/809abb7c-85cf-11e7-bf50-e1c239b45787

38 'Council Housing is coming back with a vengeance: interview with Housing Minister Kit Malthouse', *Inside Housing*, 9 July 2019: https://www.insidehousing.co.uk/insight/insight/kit-malthouse-council-housing-is-coming-back-with-a-vengeance-62153

39 Glenigan and Barbour ABI planning pipeline data obtained by the author from MHCLG. These numbers are fourth-quarter annual rolling totals for each respective year and apply to England only.

40 Local Government Association, 'An analysis of unimplemented planning permission for residential dwellings', 2013: https://unidoc.wiltshire.gov.uk/UniDoc/Document/File/MTMvMDQ2NzYvRlVMLDU1NDczMA==

41 See Chamberlain Walker, 'The role of land pipelines in the UK house-building process', op. cit.

42 Local Government Association press release, 16 February 2018: https://www.local.gov.uk/about/news/more-423000-homes-planning-permission-waiting-be-built

43 Nick Boles, 'Square Deal for Housing', op. cit.

44 Nicholas Boys Smith, 'More good homes – Making planning more proportionate, predictable and equitable', Create Streets/Legatum Institute, November 2018: http://www.createstreets.com/wp-content/uploads/2018/11/MoreGoodHomes-Nov-2018.pdf

45 See Chris Philp, 'Homes for everybody – How to get Britain building and restore the home ownership dream', Centre for Policy Studies, October 2017: http://www.cps.org.uk/files/reports/original/171212092648-HomesforEveryoneChrisPhilpMP.pdf

46 See MHCLG, National Planning Policy Framework, 2012, paras 136 and 137: https://www.gov.uk/guidance/national-planning-policy-framework

47 Vince Cable, 'Beyond Brexit', op. cit., p. 63.

48 Paul Cheshire, 'Where should we build on the Greenbelt?', LSE blog, 25 March 2016: http://eprints.lse.ac.uk/74471/1/blogs.lse.ac.uk-Where should we build on the Greenbelt.pdf

49 'Cameron: We must build on Greenbelt land', *The Times*, 19 November 2013: https://www.thetimes.co.uk/article/cameron-wemust-build-on-green-belt-land-n63d99qvhp0

50 'Cameron: I'm a countryman and will protect the Greenbelt', *Telegraph*, 2 March 2015: http://www.telegraph.co.uk/news/earth/hands-off-our-land/11444802/David-Cameron-I-am-a-countryman-and-I-will-protectthe-Green-Belt.html

51 Savills, 'New Homes and Accelerating Delivery on Public Sector Land', Savills-Telereal Trillium, April 2016: http://pdf.euro.savills.co.uk/uk/residential---other/new-homes-on-public-sector-land.pdf
The UK housing stock is currently around 25 million homes and housebuilding density over the last three decades has averaged thirty-two homes per hectare. With one million hectares, then, the government alone owns enough land, in theory, to increase the number of British homes by around 130 per cent.

52 NHS Surplus Land 2016/17 England, NHS Digital, June 2017

53 National Audit Office, 'Disposal of Public land for New Homes', HMSO, July 2016: https://www.nao.org.uk/wp-content/uploads/2016/07/Disposal-of-public-land-for-new-homes.pdf

54 'Only 200 houses built on public land that could have held 100,000', *Financial Times*, 25 January 2016: https://www.ft.com/content/a0a85c84-c38a-11e5-b3b1-7b2481276e45

55 As outlined in Chapter V, the concept of permission in principle was introduced by the Housing and Planning Act 2016. More detail was contained in the Town and Country Planning (Brownfield Land Register) Regulations 2017 and the Town and Country Planning (Permission in Principle) Order 2017.

56 Office of Fair Trading, 'Homebuilding in the UK', op. cit., p. 106: https://webarchive.nationalarchives.gov.uk/20140402181400/http://www.oft.gov.uk/shared_oft/reports/comp_policy/oft1020.pdf

57 Michael Lyons, 'The Lyons Review', op. cit., p. 63

58 MHCLG, 'Fixing Our Broken Housing Market', op. cit., paras 1.17–21.

59 'Rogue Landlords and "Beds in Sheds"', A London Councils Member Briefing, November 2012: http://www.londoncouncils.gov.uk/node/1380

60 MHCLG, 'Fixing Our Broken Housing Market', op. cit., p. 47.

CONCLUSION

1 Roger Scruton, 'The Future of Conservatism – in conversation with Douglas Murray', Spectator podcast, 7 May 2019: https://blogs.spectator.co.uk/2019/05/full-transcript-douglas-murray-in-conversation-with-roger-scruton/

2 Shelter, 'Phantom Homes – Planning Permissions, Completions and Profits', Research Briefing, July 2017: https://england.shelter.org.uk/__data/assets/pdf_file/0005/1396778/2017_07_07_Phantom_Homes_-_Profits,_Planning_Permissions_and_Completions.pdf

3 Shelter based these calculations on ONS HPSSA median new-build prices, average regional first-time buyer deposits (or 5 per cent for Help to Buy), loan-to-income ratios from CML and household incomes (excluding income-related benefits) from the Family Resources Survey. Quoted in Pete Jefferys and Toby Lloyd, 'New Civic Housebuilding: Rediscovering our tradition of building beautiful and affordable homes', Shelter Policy Briefing, 2017, p. 7.

4 'David Cameron: housing investment is about hopes and dreams', Telegraph, 21 November 2011: https://www.telegraph.co.uk/news/politics/david-cameron/8904021/David-Cameron-housing-investment-is-about-hopes-and-dreams.html

5 MHCLG, 'Fixing Our Broken Housing Market', op. cit., p. 5.

6 Fred Wellings, British Housebuilders: History and Analysis (Blackwell, 2006).

7 MHCLG, 'Fixing Our Broken Housing Market', op. cit.

8 Institute for Fiscal Studies, 'Mirrlees Review: Reforming the Tax System for the 21st Century', September 2011): https://www.ifs.org.uk/publications/mirrleesreview.
An authoritative study suggests that removing stamp duty would have led to an extra 146,000 residential property transactions over the five years to June 2017. See Centre for Economic and Business Research, November 2017: http://www.propertyindustryeye.com/almost-150000-extra-transactions-may-have-taken-place-if-stamp-duty-were-abolished-economists/

9 Ludwig Von Mises, Money, Method and the Market Process (Kluwer Academic Publishers, 1947), p. 242.

10 Scott Corfe and Nicole Gicheva, 'Concentration not competition: the state of UK consumer markets', Social Market Foundation, October 2017: http://www.smf.co.uk/wp-content/uploads/2017/10/Concentration-not-competition.pdf

11 See Edwin Moe, Governance, Growth and Global Leadership: The Role of the State in Technological Progress, 1750–2000 (Ashgate Publishing, 2007), p. 17.

12 Mancur Olson, The Rise and Decline of Nations (Yale University Press, 1982), p. 4.

13 Examples include Residents for Guildford and Villages (R4GV) in Surrey and Residents for Uttlesford (R4U) in Essex.

14 George Orwell, Coming up for Air (Victor Gollancz, 1939), Chapter 2.

15 Quoted in David Kynaston, Family Britain, 1951–59 (Bloomsbury, 2009), p. 86.

INDEX